Media Communication
An Introduction to Theory and Process

James Watson

Third Edition

palgrave
macmillan

First Edition published 1998
Second Edition published 2003
Third Edition published 2008 by
PALGRAVE MACMILLAN
Houndmills, Basingstoke, Hampshire RG21 6XS and
175 Fifth Avenue, New York, N.Y. 10010
Companies and representatives throughout the world

PALGRAVE MACMILLAN is the global academic imprint of the Palgrave Macmillan division of St. Martin's Press, LLC and of Palgrave Macmillan Ltd. Macmillan® is a registered trademark in the United States, United Kingdom and other countries. Palgrave is a registered trademark in the European Union and other countries.

ISBN-13: 978–0–230–53549–7
ISBN-10: 0–230–53549–6

This book is printed on paper suitable for recycling and made from fully managed and sustained forest sources. Logging, pulping and manufacturing processes are expected to conform to the environmental regulations of the country of origin.

A catalogue record for this book is available from the British Library.

A catalog record for this book is available from the Library of Congress.

10   9   8   7   6   5   4   3   2   1
17   16   15   14   13   12   11   10   09   08

Printed and bound in China

577473

Media Communication

For Kitty
our daughters Rosalind, Miranda and Francesca
and our granddaughters Alexandra and Bethany

Contents

List of Figures   xi
Preface to the Third Edition   xii
Acknowledgements   xix

Introduction: Studying Media   1

1 Setting the Scene: Media in Context   13
  Communication, culture, power   14
  Hegemony: an overview   22
  Technology and the march of time   29
  Public Service Broadcasting: sailing in choppy waters   32
  New world 'dysorder'   34
  Context and study   35
  Summary   36

2 The Language of Study   41
  The language of transmission   42
  Signs, codes, texts   49
  Orders of signification   59
  Audience: the language of reception   62
  Summary   64

**3 The Audience for Media: Perspectives on Use
    and Response**   70
  Identifying the complexities of audience response to media   71
  Uses and gratifications theory   73
  Issues of dependency   77
  The emancipatory use of media   78
  Cultivation theory   80
  The resistive audience   81
  Significant others   86

	Ethnographic perspectives	90
	Corporate intrusions	92
	Resistance through appropriation	94
	The fragmented audience and problems of measurement	98
	Summary	100
4	**Media in Society: Purpose and Performance**	**107**
	Propaganda, profit, power	108
	The public service model: technology and competition	113
	Six normative functions of media	116
	Functioning according to roles	121
	Principles of media performance: possibilities and problems	126
	Media performance and human rights	132
	Summary	137
5	**The News: Gates, Agendas and Values**	**142**
	The cultural orientation of news	143
	Selecting the news: gatekeeping	145
	Setting the agendas of news	150
	News values	158
	Ideology and the news	167
	Tabloid news values	171
	Summary	174
6	**Narrative: The Media as Storytellers**	**179**
	Homo narrens: the storytelling animal	180
	Narrative frames	184
	Genre, codes and character	187
	Newsworthiness, fictionworthiness	193
	News as narrative	199
	Summary	203
7	**The Practice of Media: Pressures and Constraints**	**208**
	Media communication and the 'project of self'	209
	A framework for analysis	210
	The dilemmas of professionalism	221
	News management and the hazards of source	227
	Uneven playing fields 1: gender imbalance	232
	Uneven playing fields 2: ethnic imbalance	237
	Summary	242

8   The Global Arena: Issues of Dominance and Control   248
      Information, disinformation, 'mythinformation'   249
      Power games, public relations   255
      Struggles for dominance: private sector v. public sector   259
      The narrowing base of media ownership   261
      Corporate power and the media   262
      Limiting plurality: 'democratic deficits'   267
      Global imbalances in informational and cultural exchange   270
      Summary   274

9   Network Communication: Visions and Realities   280
      Cybervisions 1: dreams of freedom   281
      Cybervisions 2: the Net as agent of change   285
      Realities 1: the corporate embrace   287
      Realities 2: shadow of the Panopticon – the Net is
         watching you   293
      Self, other and 'reality' in cyberspace   299
      Summary   307

10   Research as Exploration and Development   313
      Engaging the truth: research perspectives   314
      Approaches to research 1: content analysis   317
      Approaches to research 2: ethnography   319
      Approaches to research 3: focus groups   326
      The recognition of pleasure   333
      Researching audience use of media technology   334
      The Internet as a research tool   337
      Researching network communication   341
      Segmentation: the marketplace approach   344
      Convergence of research approaches   347
      Research as authentication: the picture that didn't lie   349
      Summary   351

11   21st Century Perspectives   359
      Power: pacts, profits, patriotism   360
      The retreat from regulation   366
      Audience: deconvergence   369
      The media environment: global warnings   372
      De-Westernizing media studies   376
      Practitioners and public: resistance through coalition   378
      The global responsibilities of media communication   381
      Summary   383

Concluding Remarks 390

Appendix 1: A Brief ABC of Perceived Media Effects 392
Appendix 2: Screen Violence as Influence and Commodity:
  An Ongoing Debate 395
Bibliography 409
Glossary 420
Index 438

List of Figures

i.1 The media prism   4
1.1 Socio-cultural pyramid   20
1.2 Features of hegemony   23
2.1 Shannon and Weaver's model (1949)   43
2.2 Two of Wilbur Schramm's models (1954)   46
2.3 Gerbner's model of communication (1956)   48
2.4 Signifier–signified   50
2.5 A semiological model   66
3.1 One-step, two-step, multi-step flow models
       of communication   87
4.1 'KNOWLEDGE IS POWER'   108
4.2 Speaking with forked tongue?   112
4.3 Criteria of public service communication   130
5.1 White's simple gatekeeping model (1950)   146
5.2 McNelly's model of news flow (1959)   147
5.3 Bass's 'double action' model of international news
       flow (1969)   149
5.4 McCombs and Shaw's agenda-setting model of media
       effects (1976)   151
5.5 Rogers and Dearing's model of the agenda-setting
       process (1988)   153
5.6 Tripolar model of agendas: policy, corporate and media   154
5.7 Galtung and Ruge's model of selective gatekeeping (1965)   158
5.8 Westerståhl and Johansson's model of news factors in
       foreign news (1994)   168
7.1 The 'communicator arm' of Maletzke's model of the
       mass communication process (1963)   210
7.2 Maletzke's full model of the mass communication
       process (1963)   214
7.3 Another example of police prejudice   238
8.1 A 'tripolar' model: the dynamics of public agenda-setting   263
10.1 Research as co-orientation   347
10.2 'Spain's Falling Soldier': piecing together the evidence   349
11.1 Four stages of audience fragmentation   369

Preface to the Third Edition

For an author whose subject-matter is essentially contemporary, it was immensely frustrating to be submitting the 2nd edition of this book in 2003 just as the invasion of Iraq by American and British forces was taking place. There had been ample time to include references to the events of 9/11 and reflect on the responses of the media worldwide to what many described as an atrocity that would impact on the lives of all of us.

The deadline for *Media Communication* drew the curtain on a scrutiny of what happened later – the overthrow of Saddam Hussein, the increasingly unpopular occupation of Iraq and the controversial scenarios of war coverage in the press and on TV that followed.

This edition attempts to catch up with those events and target media performance in relation to what has been described by politicians as a global war on terrorism. We probably can't wait for historians to coolly appraise just what has been happening in the opening decade of the new millennium. Is it religion or racism that has provoked some commentators to talk of a global 'clash of cultures' or are we simply witnessing power struggles in relation to the imminent scarcity of resources?

Deep and worrying schisms have occurred between and within nations, prompting alarmist responses – repressive new legislation, for example, restricting traditional freedoms in the name of preserving security. *The Rules of the Game: Terrorism, Community and Human Rights*, a report commissioned by the Rowntree Research Trust and written by Stuart Weir, Andrew Blick and Tufyal Choudhury,[1] argues that government was driving a 'tabloid' agenda in the war on terrorism; that is, sensational, exaggerated and, in the view of the report, ultimately self-defeating.

Attitudes to what can or cannot be said in public, or even private, have, in relation to religion for instance, become hot-wired. People's faith, whether it be Christian, Muslim or Sikh, has been granted a very special privilege at every level of society and in every form of communication: the right not to be challenged on the most fundamental aspect of all, the existence of their gods.

Thus in the UK a major development in education has been the rapid increase in faith schools. Fundamentalism seems to have advanced from the periphery of public life to somewhere near its centre. Creationism verges on the fashionable, nudging its way into science curricula in some schools both in the USA and the UK; indeed in rural Kentucky the world's first Creationist Museum opened in 2007, with the motto 'Prepare to Believe!'

A decade or less ago such trends might have been unthinkable. Yet the clash of ideologies – Capitalist and Communist – which dominated the world stage since the Second World War would seem to have been replaced in combat terms by Christian and Muslim; at least on the face of it. One of the tasks of communication, of rational discourse (if that is a possibility these days) is to divine whether this is a real or a phoney conflict; whether what is reported in the press or seen on television is a simplistic picture of what is really happening in the world. There could be no more important task for the media to address and coolly analyze what appear to be such volatile and unpredictable socio-political contexts.

Director of research at IslamExpo, Soumaya Ghannoushi, in a UK *Guardian* article, 'Religious hatred is no more than a variety of racism',[2] had this to say about the cauldron mix of religion, race and terrorism:

> We are witnessing the emergence of a new type of hatred, where religion and culture overlap with race and ethnicity. The climate generated by the war on terror…has allowed the far-right to redirect its poison of exclusionism from specific racial minorities to specific religio-racial monorities; from the black and Asian to the Muslim black and Asian.

She talks of the emergence of a 'dangerous language…one that moves smoothly from race to religion, from terrorism to Islam, from al-Qaida to Muslims'. With not a little help from some of the media, (she refers to the 'war-craving *Sun*'), 'a society of fear and suspicion' is in the making.

Serving public interest

Such has been the threat, and the perceived threat, to what politicians have glibly termed 'our way of life', 'the way we do things here' that a recurring theme in public discourse has been the definition, and thereby defence, of national identity. Those media voices with the power to contribute to such a debate bear a heavy responsibility if they are to serve public as differentiated from private or sectarian interest.

It is regrettable that, in the UK at least, the key voice of reason – public service broadcasting, in particular the BBC – has itself suffered a crisis of purpose and identity; not necessarily because of its own shortcomings, but because its predicament is to owe service to masters whose objectives are often in conflict.

In the best of all possible worlds, a government's first concern is the welfare and interest of the public. In the best of all possible worlds, public service broadcasting has an identical concern. However, a government goes to war: is that necessarily in the public interest? What then, is the duty of the public service broadcaster?

The decision by the BBC to transmit news and views which challenged the decision by Britain to join the United States in the invasion of Iraq resulted in head-on collision. The outcome was the resignation of the corporation's chairman and director general, not to mention the reporter whose news item had caused the furore (see the box entitled 'Dodgy dossier' in Chapter 7, The Practice of Media: Pressures and Constraints (p. 226)).

That damaged the BBC, arguably undermining its confidence, tarnishing its public image and making it vulnerable to snipings from all quarters – this at a time when the corporation's public service role is as vital as it is at risk from commercial competition. Evidence revealed in the summer of 2007 of elements in both the BBC and independent television, as it were economizing with the rules concerning prize competitions, might on the face of it be classified as small beer in the grand order of things. But an accumulation of these, amplified by press reports and comment, is liable to diminish public confidence and trust.

Net revolution

Running concurrently with the above issues has been the exponential growth of network communication. In the West at least, we are plunged into what has varyingly been termed the era of *mobilization*, of

participatory media or *socializing communication*, not new in its essence, of course, but in its scale and reach.

What once upon a time was merely a telephone freed of wires and of a convenient size to slip in a pocket, has now become a multimedia station. We take photos with it; we film with it; we key in to the world wide web; we watch TV on it. People are interacting electronically as never before; and that interaction is two-way: social shaping emanates from the possibilities of new media, but the users have the power to reciprocate, largely free from the influences of hierarchy so characteristic of traditional mass media.

Today we talk of blogging, texting, spoofing and mobbing; we recognize the rise of citizen journalism and its incursion into the normal practices of the press, radio and TV. There is scarcely a newspaper that does not review the spectrum of blogs for comments on events of the day; while suddenly thousands are tuning in to video home-mades that have made YouTube, Facebook and Myspace among the hottest properties on the market.

New media do not, nor are likely to, displace the 'old' media; but they build on them, extend them, personalize them, re-shape them. We can talk now of New Media Studies, itself an extension of traditional studies of mass communication. This sphere of research and analysis offers exciting prospects for a subject that inevitably has to change with the times.

A key focus of new media study is the social dimension of interactive electronic communication, exploring people's use of technology for the purposes of cultural and social exchange. It examines the nature of the hybridity of new media usage. In the words of Leah A. Lievrouw and Sonia Livingstone in their Introduction to the *Handbook of New Media*,[3] it scrutinizes '[m]oves from mass media, singular, towards network societies and relations, plural,' and these 'have entailed corresponding shifts in people's engagement with media technologies and each other…'.

Questions for investigation abound: how far is mobilization changing practices at all levels? What are the consequences of the increased use of new media? In the era of the open encyclopaedia such as Wikipedia (seemingly liberated from editorial control, its texts open to correction, addition and inevitably distortion by the minute), is knowledge itself liberated or put at risk; and if it is both, what can be done to seek verification beyond mere assertion, to balance truth with freedom?

If, as seems to be generally the case in the West, access to the airwaves allows each one of us to be reporter, commentator, analyst, video or DVD producer, what will be the long-term effect of this seismic change on traditional practices of mass communication? Current overviews of media process need to do two things, acknowledge the potential for change brought about by digital technology and its availability to the mass as never before, and recognize that hegemonic structures are unlikely to lie down before the onslaught; rather, it is my view, those structures will do what the music industry has long had a habit of doing with 'rebel' bands: incorporate them into the mainstream.

There will inevitably be more liberty of expression, for the flow often seems to be so overwhelming that it is impervious to traditional control mechanisms. However, freedoms are not always complementary or mutually supporting. We may delight in the intoxicating possibilities of online life and lifestyle exchange, but we do well to remind ourselves of the degree to which contemporary societies, particularly in Britain and America, are locked into the Age of Surveillance.

Panopticon gaze

Terrorism has given the green light to politicians to bring in laws purporting to protect us but in circumstances all too easy for governments to hold on record every aspect of our lives. Privacy may already, for most of us, be sleepwalking into the past. As this edition goes to press, we may be seeing the introduction of ID cards, the ultimate panopticon (see Chapter 9, Network Communication: Visions and Realities).

Life, in the face of terrorism, we are told, leaves us all on the edge. Things are different now, goes the message, so governments have to react quickly. To ensure our security, we must surrender a little of our liberty, until the process becomes a formula: the greater the danger we are in, the more rigorous must be the laws of control.

Of interest to us is how the media greet such measures. Is their role to be that of the guard-dog or the watchdog (see Chapter 4, Media in Society: Purpose and Performance and Chapter 8, The Global Arena: Issues of Dominance and Control)? These and so many other questions linking media with the exercise of power are the meat and drink of the study of media.

They are critically important not just for students but for citizens everywhere; and I make no apology for repeating here how vitally important all this makes the study of media communication in the 21st century. Such are the powers to lead or mislead still in possession of mass media that study – the chance to examine, scrutinize, analyze and research media – is and should always be a citizen's right.

The pace of life

We seem these days to be in thrall to immediacy, so stopping to think, to probe as well as to savour, is an imperative. Equally we are subject to so much instantly available information that many of us wilt under the weight of it. Confusion is as likely an outcome as clarity. We lose our way in what resembles a blizzard. As John Keane points out in *The Media and Democracy*,[4] 'The world seems so full of information that what is scarce is citizens' capacity to make sense of it'.

The pace of contemporary life fuses present and future, the one arriving before we have become accommodated to the other. We do well then to pace ourselves by maintaining a perspective on the past that has brought us here. It would of course be comforting to think that humans, especially our leaders, learnt lessons from the past. Faced with the evidence of Napoleon's disastrous invasion of Russia, what was Hitler doing repeating history; and was it ignorance, defiance arising out of arrogance that took Bush and Blair into a war in Iraq in full knowledge of the precedent of Vietnam?

What part did the media play in these events – supportive allies or critical friends and, come the next war, how then will they react, alerted by past experience or impervious to it? We need to dig and delve, to question and to challenge. Perhaps most of all we need to focus on where all these things start, in the very language itself. Truth may turn out to be the first casualty of war, as Phillip Knightley argues in his classic book on war reporting,[5] but the first weapon is the word.

Language defines; and it largely owes definition to those with the power to communicate beyond the confines of the interpersonal. When words such as 'choice' and 'freedom' appear in public discourse the b??? for definition commences. They are used, indeed often appro- ?, to suit the ends of those wielding power and authority. Study ? questioning activity and, as journalists themselves often find, ask- ing questions can be dangerous.

That so many journalists lose their lives every year in pursuing their trade is testimony to the risks they take in first asking questions then speaking out. Theirs is the choice we as students of media communi- cation should both respect and, as far as is feasible, emulate.

Modifications and additions

Readers familiar with the 2nd edition of *Media Communication* will find that it has not only been updated but substantially re-written. The chapter themes remain the same, and follow the same order, only some titles have been adjusted in line with new shaping. For ease of use, Notes are now placed at the end of each chapter or section. A Bibliography arranged under topic headings (Audience, Broadcasting, News, for example) has been added; otherwise, the chapter format of Aims, Summary, Key Terms, Suggested Activities and Now Read On remains the same, subject to revision and addition.

Notes

1. Stuart Weir, Andrew Blick and Tufyal Choudhury, *The Rules of the Game: Terrorism, Community and Human Rights.* Commissioned by the Joseph Rowntree Trust, 2006.
2. Soumaya Ghannoushi, 'Religious hatred is no more than a variety of racism', UK *Guardian*, 13 November 2006.
3. Leah A. Lievrouw and Sonia Livingstone (eds), *Handbook of New Media* (UK/US: Sage, Updated Student Edition, 2006).
4. John Keane, *The Media and Democracy* (UK: Polity Press, 1991).
5. Phillip Knightley, *The First Casualty: The War Correspondent as Hero and Myth-maker from the Crimea to Kosovo* (UK: Prion Books, 2000), with an introduction by John Pilger.

Acknowledgements

I am indebted to scores of authors, present and past, whose work has helped immensely in my own teaching and writing; to hundreds of students over the years who have shared their uncertainties with me but have also been a source of inspiration and support; to my colleagues whose friendship and good humour have kept me human (though I have no evidence they would agree with this) and to my family whose forbearance, like the imagination, has (to date) known no limits.

The author and publishers wish to thank the following for permission to use copyright material:

Association for Education in Journalism and Mass Communication for Figure 5.1 from D.M. White, 'The gatekeepers: a case study in the selection of news', *Journalism Quarterly*, 27 (1950); and Figure 5.3 from A.Z. Bass in *Journalism Quarterly*, 46 (1969)

Board of Trustees of the University of Illinois Press for Figure 2.1 from Shannon and Weaver, *The Mathematical Theory of Communication*, University of Illinois Press (1949, 1998)

Magnum Photos for the photograph reproduced in Figure 10.2

Oxford University Press for Figure 5.2 from J.T. McNelly, '"Intermediary" communicators in the international news', *Journal of Communication*, Spring (1976)

Pearson Education Limited for Figure 3.1 from Windahl and McQuail, *Communication Models for the Study of Mass Communications*, 2nd edition, Longman (1992)

Sage Publications Limited for Figure 5.7 from Galtung and Ruge in *Journal of International Peace Research*, 1 (1965)

Springer Science and Business Media for Figure 2.3 from Gerbner, 'Towards a general model of communication' in *Audio Visual Review*, 4 (1956)

The Guardian for the article reproduced in Figure 4.2, 8 January 2002 edition, written by Ian Black

The University of Chicago Press for Figure 5.4 from McCombs and Shaw, 'Agenda setting model of media effects', *Public Opinion Quarterly*, 36 (1972)

Every effort has been made to trace all the copyright-holders, but if any have been inadvertently overlooked the publishers will be pleased to make the necessary arrangement at the first opportunity.

Introduction: Studying Media

Rule One: avoid getting depressed by the critics of Media Studies. However they put their case, the argument seems to be that studying and practising media are 'neither use nor ornament'. We know that such opinions arise from ignorance of what exactly the study of the subject involves. So be patient; where possible, explain what you do. After all, it is a universal maxim that there is never enough communication; and Media Studies is all about communication – practising it and analyzing it – in all its forms. It is also a subject that *challenges*, one that questions seemingly established truths and truisms. Indeed that might be the key reason why Media Studies is treated with suspicion: it encourages students to *think*.

This book sets out to provide an overview of the 'study' part of courses in media communication. Throughout my teaching over many years I have urged a first principle in the study of communication, that it can only be meaningfully explored and understood if the *contexts* in which it is practised are taken into account. In Chapter 1, Setting the Scene: Media in Context, I have attempted to map, albeit briefly, the terrain where media operate.

Increasingly the media have found themselves positioned at the heart of cultural, social, political and economic contexts; and these contexts both influence media performance and are influenced by it. The media are part of trends, responsive to them and often instrumental in publicizing, and therefore influencing, the direction and extent of such trends.

It is vital to recognize that events have antecedents: they have a history as does the manner in which the media cover those events. Although it has not been within the scope of this volume to investigate historical developments in the media, the importance of these – for further research on the part of the student – is frequently stressed; and this presupposes a view that students of media count competence in research methods among their communication skills.

Terminology: friend not foe

Study is itself situated in contexts, one of which, focused on in Chapter 2, The Language of Study, is that part of the linguistic map which shows signs and symbols; in our case, the terminology (some say jargon) of the subject. Unless you are familiar with the special terms that have evolved in the study of communication, and then become common scholarly practice in discussing, describing and analyzing, access to anything more than a superficial 'reading' of media texts, media processes and audience responses to those texts and processes will be limited.

At first sight the terminology – in any specialist subject – can appear off-putting. Yet familiarity and practice soon prove its usefulness. I have already used one term basic to our studies – *reading*. For the student of communication this means more than a simple exercise in reading words. Images of all kinds are the subject matter of study, calling on and developing powers of observation and analysis – of meaning-making – worthy of Sherlock Holmes. Indeed it might be argued that Holmes is not a bad role model for the study of communication (so long, I suppose, as his cocaine habit is overlooked).

The terminology of communication study is catholic and has been imported from a number of disciplines – cultural studies, economics, ethnography, film studies, linguistics, philosophy, political science, the study of organizations, psychology and sociology. It permits users to refer to concepts, theories and practices without having to explain them repeatedly.

We may, in discussing the news, refer to *gatekeeping* and *agenda-setting*, terms employed to describe complex media processes (see Chapter 5, The News: Gates, Agendas and Values). Their use is as unavoidable and as necessary as labelling your possessions, knowing people's names or having a number on your door. Hikers lost on the moors in a fog are more likely to progress to safety if they understand the symbols (the terminology) on the map of the terrain.

The special language of communication offers more than mere signposting. It serves, also, as a framework for investigation and interpretation. It helps, for instance, to separate out, at least initially, the *denotational* (descriptive) aspects of any text from the *connotational* (interpretative). It prompts us to recognize the difference, that one is a prelude to the other, at the same time suggesting that in any analysis it is advisable to set the scene (by working at the denotational level) before plunging into the more subjective realms of interpretation and conjecture (the connotational level). As in all the best academic practices, theory works hand in hand with skills.

In brief, then, the language of study enables us to operate with confidence by reminding us what to look out for, whether we are studying the front pages of the tabloids, advertisements, TV soaps, movies, party political broadcasts, rap music or the latest fashions. It enables us to probe behind the surfaces of things, to 'unmask' appearances; to spot what isn't said as well as what is – the hidden agendas of mass communication.

Starting with audience

Because the subject of media communication is so vast it is inevitable that media courses will vary in their structure and content. I have tried to take this into account, though most courses will deal with the five basic elements of media:

- Texts
- Production: the processes of message-making; of narratives and representation
- Contexts: cultural, social, political, economic; and involving institutions
- Reception
- Technology: trends and developments.

Ideally these ought not to be studied separately because they are obviously interactive and interdependent, but there is no getting away from the fact that study is inevitably *sequenced* and so is a book on study.

In a sense the study of media communication can be said to resemble a circular building with a number of entrances. Perhaps a more apt metaphor is the prism. Figure I.1 illustrates different approaches to study while at the same time emphasizing the connectedness of each perspective; as with the prism, viewing one side nevertheless permits illumination of all sides.

You can start with the nature of the medium itself, which would include a focus upon media technology and its impact. Alternatively, after presenting a contextual and terminological framework, I have elected to explore Response Theory, beginning with the nature of audience for media (Chapter 3, The Audience for Media: Perspectives on Use and Response).

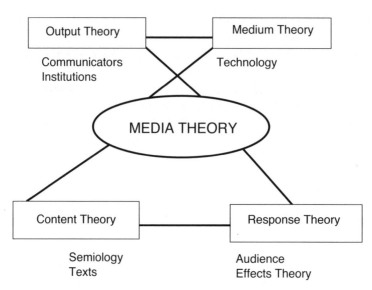

Figure i.1 The media prism

This allows us to begin where 'the student is at', for everyone is a consumer of media and has been since childhood. Students do not come to the subject, as they might if they were to take a course in nuclear physics, with little previous knowledge. You arrive with a history of media experience which is part of your own history and that of your family and friends; and in the age of network commununication you are also essentially a *participator*, an encoder as well as decoder of messages.

It would seem productive to build on this knowledge, experience and awareness; and if motivation were needed, then the pleasure of consumption is likely to stir the necessary interest (after all, there aren't many subjects where homework might comprise a visit to the cinema or watching your favourite sit-com on TV).

Another reason for beginning with audience is the shift in emphasis that has taken place over the years in the study of media. At one time the focus was exclusively on the production side of media – Output Theory. Then attention switched to the examination of texts. Interest then moved on to the ways in which audiences deal with media texts.

Audiences have gone from being seen as a 'mass', generally consuming messages as they were intended to be consumed – that is, acceptingly – to being credited with a degree of independence of thought and judgement. The mass became a composite of individuals with individual needs and responses; and those individuals were members of families, peer groups, work groups, communities; not dupes of media but capable of using media for their own ends; in short, the *active audience*.

Nothing in media, or its study, stands still: reception by audience has to be analyzed in relationship to the rapidity of new technological developments and the increased role institutions play in mass communication – their reach, and their power to influence (a topic to which I return in Chapter 8, The Global Arena: Issues of Dominance and Control).

The communicators and their world

If students are first and foremost consumers of media, many may also eventually become producers of media, and Chapter 4, Media in Society: Purpose and Performance, seeks to identify the functions of media in the community – to inform, educate, entertain, and what else? The media are so prominent in any modern state, their influence extending far beyond local and national boundaries, that everyone, from presidents and prime ministers to pressure groups concerned about the impact of media on human attitudes and behaviour, insists on having a say in defining the purpose of media.

Essentially the media operate in what is defined as *public space* or the *public sphere*. In fact, in modern times, they arguably embody that space by being 'the voice of the people'. Chapter 4 seeks to examine functions through the public roles in which the media cast themselves, and those which society affirms or questions.

Expectations about these roles are regularly, unavoidably, in conflict, and this conflict is best examined by focusing on how media actually perform: do the tabloids keep us fully informed? Of course in some things they keep us more than fully informed; but in other matters they are curiously silent. The task of the student of media communication is to ask why.

The importance of the news

Up to this point in the book the media scene will have been looked at through a wide-angle lens. We are at the point when we need to switch to the operational level of media production. In Chapter 5, The News: Gates, Agendas and Values, I have set out to examine, in close-up, the processes through which the raw material of news passes on its way to the public, via the press and broadcasting.

The news is important to us because it purports to represent 'the world out there'; its realities. We need only pause for a moment to assess just how much of our knowledge of the world is *mediated* by newspapers, radio and TV. The pictures in our heads are pictures for the most part put there by the media; and our attitudes towards those pictures, our definition of their meaning – our recognition of their reality – owes much to what the media have selected, omitted, shaped and interpreted.

Perhaps more than any other media format, the news claims to represent reality, the way things are; and in that representation there is the underpinning assumption that some of those things represented are the way they should be. That underpinning we call *ideology*, a term defined in Chapter 1 and revisited in Chapter 2.

In our studies we will readily come to recognize the complexity of realities and that the media impose *frames* or grids upon those realities. They offer 'versions' of reality. In some cases, an active audience response may reject the media's definition of reality or at least question it. The student of media soon appreciates that while news may look 'natural' that naturalness is 'constructed'; and such constructs require careful examination.

Telling stories

It is not merely a quaint habit that journalists refer to 'writing stories'. One might say that the world we recognize is made up of stories of one kind or another. It follows that, central to the study of communication at any level, is exploration of *narrative*. In everything we do or say, in everything we wear, we are narrating a story about ourselves.

From morn till night we are addressed by messages in story form. Stories attempt to sell us washing powder or perfume, cars or holidays. By telling us what we ought to wear or what car we ought to be seen driving, the tales spun by commercials also hint at what we are or what we might become. They remind us that life has style, that people can pursue identity through lifestyle; and that lifestyle is just a purchase away. Commercials often constitute the parables of our time.

Chapter 6, Narrative: the Media as Storytellers, looks at how narrative formats and devices are employed in order to attract and sustain the attention of audience and evoke responses in terms of attitude and behaviour. We react to stories in many ways: they touch us rationally and emotionally. Often they come with sermons built in. They position us culturally, morally and politically.

When we watch TV soaps we may get a strong feeling that we are being preached at: we may be cynical about this, or we may be grateful for the message being conveyed. What we can be certain about is that the message is there. Chapter 6 sets out to assist the process of unpicking narrative. It may also provide you with handy hints to guide your own storytelling – news reporting, script writing, storyboarding and the creation of advertisements. *De*construction should, in any media course, be balanced by *con*struction.

Not shooting the messenger

In olden days bringers of bad news often got punished as though they were somehow personally responsible for it. Today we blame the media for many things, in some cases justifiably. Damning the messenger, however, gets us nowhere; attempting to understand the predicament of the journalist, photographer, film maker and broadcaster is, however, necessary – not only for study, but also for those ambitious to work in the media.

Chapter 7, The Practice of Media: Pressures and Constraints, discusses the social, cultural, political, legal and institutional constraints that are part of the day-to-day experience of the media practitioner. Many hazards lie in the path of best practice (assuming, of course, that best practice can be satisfactorily defined). For example, the pursuit of truth may be obstructed by the red light of laws such as, in Britain, the Official Secrets Act; or a politically sensitive investigation may be halted by those in high places who own or control the means of communication.

Striving after objectivity, balance or impartiality (assuming that these too can be convincingly defined) may also hit institutionally erected buffers. A newspaper whose owner is committed to supporting political Party X is unlikely to encourage journalists wishing to write, without bias (assuming that too can be defined!), about the policies of rival Party Y.

Media, corporations, controversy

The functions and roles of media, the specifics of news production, the pressures and constraints met with by media practitioners sooner rather than later have to be examined in the light of ownership and control. Increasingly the nature of control, and the issues arising from the exercise of control, has become global. Chapter 8, The Global

Arena: Issues of Dominance and Control, surveys trends and focuses on concerns, in particular about the interlinking of two convergences – of media technology and media ownership by transnational corporations – both of which have far-reaching implications for the future of public service media.

Cyberspace Calling?

This heading was the title of a chapter in the first edition of *Media Communication*. It was written in the heady, pioneering days when all sorts of romantic claims were being made for the Internet. Cyberspace did call and millions upon millions have answered that call. The new title of this chapter, substantially re-written for the second edition and again for the third, is rather more down-to-earth – Network Communication: Visions and Realities

The shift acknowledges that what was once a seemingly open prairie has been subject to a degree of fencing in, partly as a result of corporate ambitions to extend their worldly empires into cyberspace and partly resulting from governments' concern about worlds of communicative exchange over which they have so little control.

The sheer speed at which Internet use has developed is a challenge for any analysis in book form: one blinks, and either the technology or variations on its reach and its use have shot ahead of even the most ardent scrutineer, leaving behind a clean pair of digital heels. As these words are written, network communication seems to be less about soaring and surfing, more about socializing, experimenting with identity, sampling communicative experiences usually unavailable in the 'real' world and crimes and misdemeanours sanctioned by anonymity.

While change might be swift and unpredictable, key issues of freedom and control have ongoing significance. Here I continue to examine widespread anxieties concerning the vulnerability of the Internet to surveillance, as well as the vulnerability of data itself in a rootless context where identity can be concealed, shed and reinvented, where He may become She; and where the virtual has the potential – as some enthusiasts declare – to be more meaningful than reality itself.

Study as exploration

The point is made in Chapter 2 that the language of the study of communication is also its history. Equally we can trace the evolution of the subject through the work of researchers in the field. Chapter 10, Research as Exploration and Development, takes up this theme, briefly tracing the progress of our knowledge and understanding of media by highlighting the research findings and observations of some of the subject's most notable pioneers.

The varying approaches to research of these pioneers is as interesting as their results, and should provide useful prompts to your own research tasks; after all, the nature of the development of the study of media communication will eventually take its lead and its direction from current generations of students.

For those planning to be media practitioners, knowledge of the theories of media supported by evidence will have lasting value, being either confirmed or challenged by media experience. At the very least, it will provide you with a useful frame of reference, a set of indicators to present and future performance.

Cultural concerns

Chapter 11, 21st Century Perspectives, returns to the issue of the relationship of the media to the exercise of power, in particular focusing on the global convergence in media ownership and the impact this is seen to have on media practices and the public. Controversies abound concerning a number of interconecting *'izations'* – consumerization, McDonaldization, Disneyization, all manifestations of the corporate dominance of media production worldwide.

The clashes and the alliances of agendas – Policy, Public, Media and Corporate – are briefly revisited in the light of the *deconvergence* or fragmentation of the audience brought about by new technology and deregulation. Additionally, as pointed out in the Preface, it has been necessary to add to the fissile mix the impact of terrorism, the reaction across the world to the presence of (mainly) American and British troops in Afghanistan and Iraq, to the Israeli invasion of Lebanon in 2006 and to what many have viewed as the widespread demonization of Muslim communities that has taken place since 9/11 and the London bombings in July 2005.

In conclusion, Chapter 11 re-emphasizes a point made throughout *Media Communication*: the importance of study *in context* – and as never before the media context is both global and local. Our studies need to keep these connecting and often competing scenarios in clear focus, examining the one in relation to the other. We need to acknowledge that while the overview identifies the contours and general patterns of the media landscape it may also overlook salient features which can only be perceived and understood by locating study among particular people in particular places, in particular circumstances.

Using this book

As a general introduction to the subject, *Media Communication* antici-pates broader and deeper study, using many references that are in-tended to send you out on further explorations. The **Notes** at the end of each chapter, while basically documenting references, also extend points made in the text and can be used to trail more specialist aspects of the field.

In addition to an introduction, summary and set of notes, three fea-tures round off each chapter:

- For recap purposes, there is a list of **Key terms** used in the chapter. These you can quickly check again by looking up the **Glossary** which follows the Bibliography.
- **Suggested activities** are modest tasks in research and analysis are proposed here offering you a chance to practise a range of commu-nicative skills appropriate to the study of media.
- **Now read on** gives a brief selection of notable texts that reach out beyond the limits of what has been covered in each chapter and which may prove of use in your researches for essays, seminar presentations and dissertations. An addition to this edition is a Bib-liography, subdivided under topic headings.

The occasional use of **boxes** in the main text serves a number of pur-poses – to insert supplementary information, explanations or view-points; to give prominence to notable quotations and to highlight im-portant definitions. Boxes also help to break up the text, thus making it more manageable. They assist in signposting places in the book which you may wish to return to.

There are two Appendices, the first a listing of a few of the many perceived effects the media are claimed to have on audiences. The second focuses on a regularly expressed concern about screen violence and audiences. It outlines conflicting viewpoints, emphasizing that, before effects can be properly assessed, it is imperative to identify the manifold forms of violence and the texts in which they operate.

Postscript

One of the world's best-known scholars of media, Umberto Eco, writes in the Preface to *Travels in Hyperreality* (translated from the Italian by William Weaver and published in Britain by Picador, 1986):

> I believe it is my job as a scholar and a citizen to show how we are surrounded by 'messages', products of political power, of economic power, of the entertainment industry and...to say that we must know how to analyze and criticize them.

Eco admits that while he is capable of writing learned volumes, 'work that demands time, peace of mind, patience' he also feels compelled in journalism and in teaching to communicate his ideas now rather than later:

> That is why I like to teach, to expound still-imperfect ideas and hear the students' reaction. That is why I like to write for the newspapers, to retread myself the next day, and to read the reaction of others.

Eco is declaring that nothing is for sure but that whatever the theory, wholly or only partially formed, it must be subject to regular questioning and that the ideas and opinions of others are critical in the ongoing exploration of meaning. He confesses that this is a difficult game, 'because it does not always consist of being reassured when you meet with agreement and having doubts when you are faced with dissent'.

For Eco, '[t]here is no rule; there is only the risk of contradiction'. Such a point of view may strike you as compounding uncertainty with uncertainty, but it helps define the nature of the study of communication, which is as much about feelings as the working of the intellect, as much about values as knowledge.

Sometimes, Eco argues, 'you have to speak because you feel the moral obligation to say something, not because you have the "scientific" certainty that you are saying it in an unassailable way'. I would venture to suggest that Eco might have added that sooner or later everything boils down to how we *perceive* the world. To this end I shall round off with the comments of a very cynical canary, which I shall place in a box for want of a cage.

In a short story by the 19th century Brazilian writer Machado de Assis called *A Canary's Ideas*, a man finds a canary in a junk shop and is astonished to discover that the bird can not only talk but speaks with philosophical eloquence. When the man asks, 'Has your master always been the man sitting over there?' the bird answers reprovingly, 'What master? The man over there is my servant...' Amazed at the nature of the bird's perception of its existence, the man says, 'But pardon me, what do you think of this world? What is the world to you?'

'The world,' retorts the canary with a certain professional air, 'is a second-hand shop with a small rectangular bamboo cage hanging from a nail. The canary is lord of the cage it lives in and the shop that surrounds it. Beyond that, everything is illusion and deception.'

Setting the Scene: Media in Context

1

AIMS

➤ To make the case that the study of media communication cannot be isolated from an understanding of wider social, cultural, political and economic contexts.

➤ Briefly to describe and explain some of the most significant of these contexts.

➤ To explore the idea that social realities are determined by language and those with dominant influence over its public use; and to link communication with notions of power and the ordering of socio-cultural activities.

➤ To introduce the concepts of ideology and hegemony and to relate these to interacting trends in the modern world – rapid advances in media technology, the convergence of ownership and control, the globalization of media operations and the decline of the public sphere; all against a background overshadowed by the so-called 'war on terror'.

This chapter presents an overview of the contexts – cultural and social – in which the media operate. Without a grasp of the influences which have shaped media, study of it at the micro-level – newspapers, films, TV programmes, advertising – is to risk falling in a trap which the media often do themselves, of portraying realities as though they exist only in the present, disconnected from the past. To see the wood as a whole, we must step back from the trees a little. The media as we know them are only the latest in a long line of message systems, beginning with marks on cave walls, the evolution of non-verbal and spoken language and eventually becoming the core activity of communities, societies and nations. Here the role of language as a definer of reality is examined.

Notions of ideology, hegemony and consumerization are introduced and related to communicative practices and the increasingly dominant part played in modern society by the great corporations; in particular concerning the rivalry between public and private spheres of communication.

Also seen as contextual factors are time and space, each subject to transformations by new technologies. Global competition between forces of centralization and decentralization, of progress and reaction to progress, are identified as significant trends. Finally, it has to be acknowledged that western practices, Western discourses, having achieved a degree of world dominance in recent decades are now in trouble. The military occupation of Afghanistan and Iraq created for the United States and Britain enemies at home and abroad; bred anger, outrage, hatred and terrorism; in short making the world a more fissile and dangerous place. This is not a history of the events following 9/11, but any account of roles, functions and performance of media must take the cultural and political 'climate' into consideration.

Communication, culture, power

Sometimes we have words for things that continue, regardless, to evade total definition. One of these is 'culture'. Just as the Eskimo has a number of words for 'snow' to fulfil instrumental necessity within a physical context of eternal ice, so we have a number of words and phrases in which 'culture' features. We 'cultivate' the earth and we 'cultivate' relationships.

Societies are said to 'enculturalize', that is cultivate people by various means such as education and persuasion through art and public address to enter, be part of, contributory to, existing cultures. Occasionally when I have asked students to define *socialization* their answer has been, 'It's going out with your friends and enjoying yourself'. This is, of course, 'socializing'; but it is certainly a feature of most cultures. It is a useful mistake, helping us to mark the difference: socialization is generally what other people do to us – shaping us to fit into society; while socializing is what we do for ourselves.

Such behaviour is acceptable and encouraged, so long as it is not considered *antisocial*. In this case, society may take action to bring us 'back into line'. As we shall see, the media are prominent among the public arbiters of our behaviour. They, as it were, 'speak society's lines', claiming for themselves the role of a community's conscience as well as performing as its ever-vigilant guard dog. At this early stage, we may view them as an agency of order.

To varying degrees, all societies enculturalize those who belong in them with social *values* out of which have sprung, perhaps over centuries, *norms* or rules, some written and clear-cut, others inferred rather than being explicit, all pointing in the direction of expected patterns of behaviour. Language is the primary means by which the values, norms and acceptable/not acceptable patterns of society are formed, expressed and reinforced. Also, it is the primary means of defining our realities.

Krishan Kumar in his chapter on sociology in *Exploring Reality*[1] writes that 'in using language, or other kinds of signs such as gestures, we impose a sort of grid on reality. Since language and other symbolic systems are social products, this is a socially constructed grid. So our reality is a social reality'.

Kumar states:

A physical gesture such as a raised hand can be a threat or a greeting. We have no way of knowing which, unless we have learned to understand the place such a 'sign' has in the culture of the person or people concerned. Until we know that – and it could be fairly important that we know it fast – the gesture remains literally empty, devoid of all meaning or significance. Language places it and gives it meaning. Without a word to describe a thing, it remains unintelligible – to all intents and purposes, non-existent.

It follows that those whose words – and therefore definitions – can effectively reach the largest number of people have the greatest potential to define what is what; to say *this* is reality, to declare *this* is how things are or how they must be. The media, of course, along with other social agencies such as the family and education, are at the centre of this process, influenced by, and influencing, the others.

When former British Prime Minister Margaret Thatcher made her historic remark that there 'is no such thing as society, only individuals and their families' she was, some critics argued, using language in an Orwellian sense: Winston Smith, George Orwell's hero in the novel *Nineteen Eighty Four* (1949), is employed in the Ministry of Truth. His job is to slim down the language so that meaningful words, once removed from the nation's vocabulary, would also remove that which was meant. Thus the word 'free' was only retained – in what Orwell appropriately terms Newspeak – in the sense of 'This dog is free from lice'.

Commonality and difference

For the moment let us put our trust in the existence of society, however difficult it might be to define. Society speaks of itself, acquires a sense of *commonality* (of things shared) through its culture – its language, laws and customs, geography, history, arts, technology and even the weather. Without commonality, and the means to sustain that commonality, a society may fall apart.

What holds together the many disparate and often conflicting parts of a society is communication. It has the power to unite, to forge the spirit of union, of belonging in community and nation. Equally communication can serve as an instrument of demarcation between individuals and communities. National anthems exist to remind us that their purpose is to unite 'us' in the face of 'them', whether this is on the field of battle or on the field of sport.

Students of media communication will be well aware that in wartime the media generally urge national cohesion and speak with a united voice (against the enemy). They are responsible for the 'feel-good factor'. In peacetime, however, conflict 'within' – between rival political parties, between employers and workers, between majorities and minorities – rules the headlines.

All too often language is used as a weapon that widens divisions, nurtures alienation, provokes social, ethnic or racial hatreds. While communication may be a path to the truth it can also be used to obscure it. What is beyond debate is that communication has 'power value': it has long been classified as a *form* of power which those who possess power seek to control and those who do not possess power seek to acquire.

Communication has the power to define, persuade, inform and to disinform. An analysis of communication at the level of community and nation is obliged to recognize that truth is not necessarily separated from falsehood; rather, the process of *propaganda* blurs the elements in order to be persuasive.

The capacity of words and images to be distorted, bent to purposes that have little or no connection with the truth, is seemingly limitless. We are aware of this. 'Economizing with the truth' (that is, using language to conceal rather than reveal) is such a common practice in everyday life that plain honest speaking often comes as a shock. It is advisable, therefore, in our response to the use of language, for us to assess the 'truthworthiness' of the *source* as well as the content and form of the message.

In *Munitions of the Mind: A History of Propaganda From the Ancient World to the Present Day*,[2] Philip M. Taylor puts the matter succinctly:

> Communication with a view to persuasion is an inherent human quality. It can take place in a private conversation or a mass rally, in

a church or cinema, as well as on a battlefield. It can manifest itself in the form of a statue or a building, a coin or a painting, a flag or a postage stamp.

To the above list Taylor adds '[s]peech, sermons, songs, art, radio waves, television pictures'. Whether they operate between individuals or people in millions, the task of the analyst remains the same – to investigate the *intent* of the act of communication and the ways in which members of the intended audience respond to that communication.

It is arguable that most mass communication, whether it is a party political broadcast, the TV news, a pop song, a soap opera or sit-com is in some way or another, to a greater or lesser extent, an exercise in propaganda (of preaching, if you like). Taylor writes:

> Propaganda uses communication to convey a message, an idea, an ideology [see later in the chapter for definitions of ideology] that is designed primarily to serve the self-interests of the person or people doing the communicating.

As we shall see in Chapter 3, this does not necessarily mean that those who receive messages, propaganda or otherwise, actually welcome the communication, believe it or accept it: they have their own self-interests, their own values. No enculturalization is irresistible.

Power forms in society

Whatever aspects of culture we explore we invariably return to questions concerning the nature and exercise of power, for power makes things change, or prevents things changing. Whether defined as the ability to make decisions and to have those decisions carried out, to influence hearts and minds, to alter states of being or simply to hire and fire workers, power is the key factor in the dynamics of any culture.

In *The Media and Modernity: A Social Theory of the Media*,[3] John B. Thompson identifies four forms of power exercised in society – economic, political, coercive and symbolic. Economic power emanates from the possession of wealth or the means by which wealth is generated; political power rests in decision-making arising from being in a position of elected, appointed or inherited authority; coercive power springs from the use of, or potential use of, superior strength. Invasion of one country by another is an example of coercive power. Symbolic power works through images (linguistic, pictorial, aural) to create and mobilize support for a cause and it is integral to the operation of the other power forms.

Other classifications include *position*, *resource* and *charismatic* (or personality) power, each overlapping with Thompson's categories and each one somehow connected with communication processes. A case can be made for recognizing *technological* power, what Karl Marx referred to as the *means of production*, as a category in its own right. John of Gutenberg's invention of the mechanical printing press around 1450 was not substantially the result of either economic or political imperatives, but it soon proved to be a winner economically. Politically and culturally it brought about profound and far-reaching changes.

By symbolizing knowledge as something potentially accessible to all and rendering the act of reading an exercise in individualism and a possible source of subversion, printing transformed the known world by becoming 'a power in the land'. In easily reproducible and permanent form, it spread knowledge and ideas beyond the traditional boundary-fence of the privileged to the 'common people'. In doing so, it offered them glimpses (and sometimes visions) of their own potential power.

The apparatuses of power

Yet the media have never been either separate from or independent of the forces which create them and which in turn they shape and influence. They work, as Thompson points out, within institutional frameworks. As such they operate as forms of *cultural apparatus*, part of the machinery of state or of powerful interest groups within the state.

Historically the media have more often served as the voice of the powerful than of the people. They have been classified by the French philosopher Louis Althusser[4] as one of the prime ISAs, *Ideological State Apparatuses*, along with religion, family structures and education: that is, they are crucially important channels for the transmission of 'rules of conduct' in society; the guardians of a culture's dominant norms and values. They play a part in all power-forms, including, in terms of giving it support and encouragement, coercive power.

Coercion, the exercise of power by force, manifests itself through what Althusser terms RSAs, *Repressive State Apparatuses* – army, police, prisons. It is never physically absent but it is in the main, in peacetime, culturally concealed. Its visible and tangible presence depends on whether the other power forms are considered to be under threat. In wartime, of course, coercive power moves from the back region to the front region of our lives; and at no other time is symbolic power exercised by the media so graphically, so blatantly or so persuasively.

In times of war, the media traditionally become the trumpeters of conflict with the enemy. They do not fire the guns but their clamour for the guns to be fired is an essential part of the process of gathering the people's support for the war effort. ISAs and RSAs conflate, become one and the media speak, for the most part, with a single voice; their task, to create consensus and unity at home, to identify and target the enemy; their role, that of mobilizers of opinion, boosters of national morale.

Assertion, desertion

Several British newspapers objected to the military invasion of Iraq by the United States and Britain in 2003, in particular the *Daily Mirror*. The paper's headline of Tuesday 18 March declared the war UNLAWFUL, UNETHICAL, UNSTOPPABLE. On 8 July the paper featured three cabinet ministers including the then Prime Minister Tony Blair below three-inch high lettering: GUILTY! And below, OF TAKING US INTO WAR ON THE FALSE GROUNDS THAT IRAQ HAD WMD [weapons of mass destruction] AND WAS ABOUT TO USE THEM ON US.

However, the *Mirror* soon hurried to announce that 'we back our forces'. Once British troops were involved, their lives at risk, the media objectors to the war generally fell quiet or fell into line. A supplementary explanation of the *Mirror's* switch of allegiance was the drop in the paper's circulation, seemingly as a result of the paper's anti-war stance.

Cultures have the capacity to nurture social equality but their most familiar structural pattern is hierarchical. Figure 1.1 portrays a pyramid structure divided according to social class. Traditionally those at the top of the socio-cultural pyramid have more money, more property and in theory more (or better) education than those classes below them. Resultantly, they have privileged access to information and knowledge; and to the means by which that information and knowledge is transmitted.

Those at the pinnacle of hierarchy possess what has been termed *cultural capital* by the French philospher Pierre Bourdieu in *Distinction: A Social Critique of the Judgement of Taste*.[5] This, like cash in the bank or property, is a means of obtaining credit. Cultural capital can take the form of education, knowledge of history and the arts, awareness of conduct and tastes that can be of socio-cultural benefit. Bourdieu talks

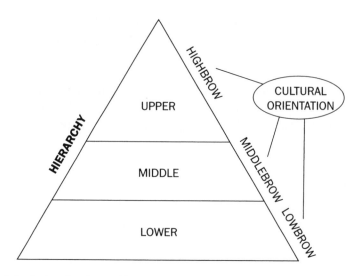

Figure 1.1 Socio-cultural pyramid

of 'an economy of social goods' governed by a hierarchy of taste. Cultural capital is a form of property. It serves to differentiate between those who possess it and those who do not.

Put quite simply, a child whose home is full of books, the walls hung with pictures of the great masters of art, possesses cultural capital. This may in future 'open doors' which may be shut to others less fortunate. In this sense, culture is an agent of selection, of demarcation, an instrument of inequality. Wealthy (and sometimes not-so-wealthy) parents 'purchase' the cultural capital of a fee-charging education because it is perceived to constitute an *investment* that will eventually accrue *profit*.

Hierarchies of taste

A nation's internal conflicts largely arise from differences of class, race and religion, each in one way or another prompted or reinforced by unequal distribution of rights and resources. Such conflicts can be viewed as clashes over *value*, between commonality and hierarchy, the one emphasizing that which binds – the sharing, the other that which distinguishes by division. In the language of marketing and advertising, this process is called *segmentation*, dividing people according to their actual or potential purchasing habits.

Hierarchy is a dominant feature of most societies not only in terms of the power to command others but in matters of taste and conduct as the notion of cultural capital indicates. For example, the expressions *highbrow, middlebrow* and *lowbrow* shown in Figure 1.1 imply, and appear to replicate, social and educational division. Culture is commandeered by structure.

Traditionally, for those privileged people near the top of the hierarchy, culture has been embodied in fine paintings or classical music. For those at the base of the hierarchy there is the kind of TV programme which the Pilkington Committee Report on Broadcasting[6] in the UK so deplored, characterized, in Pilkington's judgement, by triviality; or what George Orwell termed 'prolefeed'.

Culture can be seen to have been re-defined – appropriated – in order to serve the perceptions of a dominant order. The 1962 Pilkington Report is of interest to us now not because of the reliability of its judgement but because of the way it reveals the *stratification* of culture along lines of class difference. It interests the student of media because of the assumptions underlying the Committee's mind-set: popular meant trivial; trivial meant 'bad' or inferior.

Today things are much more fluid: academics in universities across the globe now dedicate their working lives to the study of this 'trivia'. There must be almost as many academic studies analyzing the significance of soaps, sit-coms, comics and other manifestations of 'popular culture' as there are volumes on the highbrow culture represented by Proust or Mozart.

History: the propaganda of the privileged?

History automatically discarded everything that smelled of the people. History books told us about how the rich dressed, what they ate, their taste in music, and how they organized their homes. All they told us about the poor was their stupidity, uprisings, exploitations and revolts.

Jèsus Martin-Barbero, *Communication, Culture and Hegemony: From the Media to Mediations* (US/UK: Sage, 1993).

Social class continues to be an important component of hierarchy, but if the opinions of today's most avid scrutineers of those things which are common to us and which also differentiate us – the advertisers – are a useful indicator, our 'class' is more flexibly defined by our lifestyle, or the lifestyle we aspire to, and of course the occupation which provides us with our spending power.

Hegemony: an overview

Discussion of cultural apparatuses, the shaping of norms and values and the forging of consensus brings us to one of the most important concepts in the theory of culture and the exercise of power. For most people, life can be lived quite happily and fulfillingly without their ever having the slightest idea what *hegemony* might mean. Yet the word, and what the word stands for, what it attempts to explain, is critical to the study of culture, communication, history, anthropology, sociology, politics and economics.

In its simplest sense, hegemony means 'control over'; yet in referring to 'hegemonic control' we are not repeating the same thing using another phrase, but describing a special *form* of control, one based not upon coercion or force, but resulting from successful persuasion or enculturalization. Hegemony is working when there is general consensus, that is when the mass of the population (or most of it) accepts the controlling influence and decision-making of that part of society termed, by the American writer C. Wright Mills,[7] the *Power Elite* – those members of a community who hold or influence the holding of the reins of power.

Hegemony is rule by won consent. Of all the agencies of hegemonic control the media are generally perceived to be the most powerful, hence the requirement for the Power Elite to exert pressure if not control over the media: better still, to own it.

Hegemony works through ideological state apparatuses (education, religion, the arts, media) and operates best when those apparatuses are speaking in harmony with one another.

We attribute the theory of hegemony to the Italian philosopher Antonio Gramsci (1899–1937) who argued that a state of hegemony is achieved when a provisional alliance of certain groups exerts a consensus which makes the power of the dominant group appear natural and legitimate.[8] It can only be sustained by the won consent of the dominated.

Hegemony works most smoothly when there is a substantial degree of social, economic, political and cultural security in a society. When security is undermined, social division rampant, hegemony is at risk and Althusser's repressive state apparatuses are brought into action. Hegemony serves to provide the Power Elite with the consent of the ruled. A conjectural model of hegemony is illustrated in Figure 1.2.

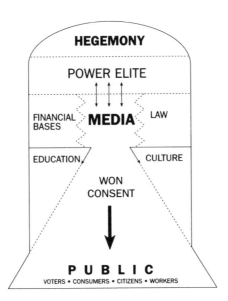

Figure 1.2 Features of hegemony

Hegemonies differ at different times and in different circumstances, but what is common to all of them is the governing influence of *ideology*, the public expression of what in personal terms we describe as values. Ideology is ever present; and every power form is suffused by it. From a position of dominance it is impatient of competitors. It provides the conceptual 'cement' that upholds the structures of the powerful, defends their interests and is instrumental in helping to preserve the *status quo* – the way things are; the way they are ordered.

The 20th century, following the Second World War (1939–45), witnessed two giant hegemonic systems eyeballing one another – Capitalism versus Communism. Compared to our own, it was an age when there were degrees of certainty. The clash of ideologies meant, perhaps to oversimplify things to the point of being defamatory, that we knew our friends and our enemies. For governments and people in the West (the Good Guys of Western mythology) we gazed beyond iron curtains and bristling nuclear arsenals towards the Bad Guys (the 'Evil Empire', President Reagan's description of Russia).

From this stand-to, this ideological confrontation, emanated the stories of our time. We heard about Reds under the bed, shook our heads over the totalitarianism of Russia and its satellites, in contrast congratulating ourselves on the freedoms our own hegemonic structures permitted.

Shifting alliances

Ideology may often be literally inscribed in stone, recording the hegemonic certainties of the past (though these tend to be certainties only in hindsight). In the living world nothing is for certain and for hegemony to be sustained it has to be light on its feet, essentially opportunist. Our enemies of yesteryear may swiftly become our friends and allies; and alliances are a key feature in the creation and sustenance of hegemony.

Governments commit to alliances of shared interest, externally and internally. On home territory they work in loose partnerships with other powerful institutions, commercial and industrial, whose aims are similar if not identical; institutions that often include in their business portfolios extensive ownership of media.

The nature of the alliances that operate between the major players in politics and economics is rarely made publicly explicit and features modestly if at all in media reporting. That is part of its strength. Yet what *is* made explicit is the 'good' such institutions do in and for society. Commercial institutions support – sponsor – those features of the cultural scene such as sport, the arts and entertainment which attract media coverage, simultaneously conferring prestige by association and nurturing public approval. Thus sport, the arts and entertainment can be ranked among ISAs, instrumental in sustaining the hegemonic process.

Major world sporting events such as the Olympics become showcases for the interlinking hegemonies of nation and commerce, the celebration of patriotism neatly framed within, and framing, the logos of Coca-Cola, McDonald's, Nike and Reebok.

Goodbye to all that?

The collapse of the Communist state in the 'Eastern bloc' seemed for a while to be an opportunity for mankind to resolve the problems caused by rival ideologies. Indeed some Western commentators argued that with one major ideology out of the way, and none to challenge the other, history (as a record of conflict) was at an end.[9] Alas, eyes had over the decades been trained too concentratedly upon so-termed Cold War politics. As the Millennium dawned, new crises began to flood in to fill the gaps left by the old.

This is not the place to offer explanations and analysis of the new 'global ballgame', featuring such players as American imperialism,

Al-Qaida (the new 'red menace'), or the play of scenarios, some old, like the ongoing tragedy of Palestine, some new, like the militancy of Islam in the face of provocation. The events of 9/11 and their aftermath resulted in a vicious polarization between cultures which has brought about tensions across national boundaries and, perhaps more frighteningly, within them.

At this point the student of media is obliged to ask, and to seek confirmatory evidence, whether the media fulfilled the role of honest broker, insisting on discovering the facts and conveying these in a balanced way; or whether they chose to conform to hegemonic pressures.

A cursory view of media responses to the 'war on terrorism' suggests that these demonstrated an all-too-eager willingness to opt for partisanship over impartiality, readily following the government line on events, and replicating for public consumption explanations of those events. At the same time the American media bought in to such cultural predictions as those made by Samuel P. Huntington in his best-selling book, *The Clash of Civilizations: Remaking World Order*.[10] Huntington saw future world schisms as occurring along the fault-lines between Western, predominantly Christian, cultures and the culture of Islam.

In the view of much of the media, Huntington's predictions were materializing with every passing event. Plenty of academics and others challenged Huntington, considering his reading of cultural shifts as simplistic and misleading, but their comments were inadequate to stem the tide of prejudice.

Government and media occupied the same ground in the defence of *Us* against the new *Them*, subscribing to the same or similar scenarios: we and what we stand for are in mortal jeopardy. It is, therefore, justifiable and perfectly proper to take offensive and defensive action to protect ourselves. It is a narrative as old as the hills. Governments become impatient with the traditional means of hegemonic control; ISAs (like, for instance, a Bill of Rights or a Freedom of Information Act) suddenly appear to be an obstacle to ensuring the protection of the people. Those in power readily see grounds for mobilizing Althusser's RSAs, bringing in legislation that curtails freedoms won by generations if not centuries of struggle.

The 'enemy within' may be the terrorist, but equally opportunist are the agencies of control in any country charged with ensuring that country's survival. In such circumstances, the role which the media take up is critical: is it their responsibility to back up authority in the face of crisis, to affirm and legitimize measures that diminish the liberties of individuals, groups and communities; or to exercise scrupulous vigilance, as watchdogs of the people's liberties rather than guard dogs of the powerful?

In the face of acts of terror, whatever their reason or justification, the question is not an easy one to answer; yet in the study of media it has to remain at the forefront of our minds. Consistency of response, holding to old certainties, is, in the current global turmoil, going to be frustratingly elusive. It may also be worth querying whether the seeming 'clash of civilizations' is actually about ideologies at all. Rather it could be about the earth's finite resources; in short, the scarcity of oil and water, as well as their location and distribution.

Flexibility of hegemony

Todd Gitlin in his chapter 'Prime time ideology: the hegemonic process in television entertainment' in *Television: The Critical View*, edited by Horace Newcomb,[11] argues that in liberal capitalism 'hegemonic ideology develops by domesticating opposition, absorbing it into forms compatible with the core ideological structure. Consent is managed by absorption as well as exclusion'.

He adds, crucially, that hegemony survives because its ideology is flexible: 'The hegemonic ideology changes in order to remain hegemonic; that is the particular nature of the dominant ideology of liberal capitalism.' Having stressed that the hegemonic system is 'not cut-and-dried, not definitive', Gitlin, referring to the closing decade of the 20th century, offers us the following portrait of hegemony as practised in Western, capitalist states:

> ... the dominant ideology has shifted toward sanctifying consumer satisfaction as the premium definition of 'the pursuit of happiness', in this way justifying corporate domination of the economy. What is hegemonic in consumer capitalist ideology is precisely the notion that happiness, or liberty, or equality, or fraternity can be affirmed through the existing private commodity forms, under the benign, protective eye of the national security state.

Before moving on, let us be clear what Gitlin is saying here. First, he is defining hegemonic practice within the framework of capitalism. Happiness is defined as pleasure through spending (as contrasted, say, with *saving*). Because the great corporations are so central to the provision of this happiness what has become an indisputable fact – their dominance of national and international economies – has come to be presented as, and largely accepted as, the natural order of things. Their propaganda dwells centrally in consumer satisfaction, aided and abetted by the magic wand of advertising.

The latest commercials from Renault, Castlemaine XXXX, British Airways or Pepsi-Cola are as familiar to us – to the entire population and beyond – as the symbols of religion. Indeed some might even claim that they are its substitute, a creed of pleasure through spending. Yet Gitlin sees rather more than pleasure on the supermarket shelf of the corporations: liberty, equality and fraternity, features of human existence not traditionally associated with getting and spending, are also for sale.

Gitlin considers, rather, that such qualities are *commodified*; presented in symbolic forms and promoted in commercial terms. By ensuring consumer choice, capitalism has made possible the *liberty* to choose. By bringing down prices in the marketplace, the corporations facilitate *equality* of opportunity. By abolishing the deprivations that split society, the corporations hasten if not entirely achieve *fraternity* among individuals and nations. This is not to say that there are no exclusions. Indeed as will be noted later, the rosy picture painted by the commercials is only seriously intended for a minority of the world's population.

Culture incorporated

As Gitlin makes clear, in the modern world hegemony's greatest institutional exponents and its staunchest defenders are the national and transnational corporations. At the same time they are the most powerful modifiers of hegemony, shaping it to their own needs – their own *intents* – to the point of having state governments, as it were, in their pockets.

It is difficult to avoid corporate involvement in our lives. We study in organizations and we work for them. Potentially they control the water we drink, the food we eat, the clothes we wear, the music we listen to, the sports we watch and the information we rely on.

Corporations dominate the visual landscape of our cities: their skyscraper office blocks remind us, symbolically, of the awesome presence of powers which can be exerted beyond the ballot box and beyond national boundaries. And sometimes, as in New York on 11 September 2001, such symbols of power are subject to terrorist attack that is both devastatingly real and chillingly symbolic. As for the leaders of corporations, we refer to them as Captains of Industry and sometimes Princes, just as we talk about Press Barons and Media Moguls.

Unlike individuals, a corporation does not require a passport to travel the world. It does not require permission to transfer manufacture from one part of the globe to another, bringing fresh employment opportunities to the new, leaving unemployment in the old. At least, we might say, corporations still do not have the vote; but they do have what Herbert Schiller in *Culture Inc. The Corporate Takeover of Public Expression*[12] calls a 'para-electoral' power; a 'factor which has accounted for the essential features and direction of the times' – far more, in fact, than the styles of the American political parties.

Schiller writes:

> This deep and underlying element, long predating the Second World War but becoming more pronounced after it, has been the phenomenal growth and expanding influence of the private business corporation. Through all the political and social changes of the last fifty years, the private corporate sector in the American economy has widened its economic, political, and cultural role in domestic and international activities.

Schiller argues that the rise and rise of corporations has been matched by the decline in the power of – in the case of America – independent farmers, organized labour and a strong urban consciousness.

From our point of view as observers of the media scene, we note the dramatic extent to which transnational corporations have gathered under their control newspapers, film companies, advertising agencies, radio and TV stations, music publishers, telecommunication systems, news agencies, websites – you name it, they've got it!

In addition, through sponsorship, the great corporations promote their name through 'good works', helping to finance libraries, universities, museums, art galleries, orchestras, festivals (on the condition that nothing damages the corporate image of the sponsor). Schiller and other commentators see this as the wholesale *appropriation* of culture and therefore dominance over it.

Schiller's bleak vision is challenged by John B. Thompson (*The Media and Modernity*[3]) who lends more weight to the notion of audience resistance to the cultural dominance exerted by the great corporations. Thompson questions Schiller's assertion about American cultural triumphalism. In the 'sphere of information and communication as well as in the domain of economic activity,' argues Thompson, 'the global patterns and relations of power do not fit neatly into the framework of unrivalled American dominance'.

New power orientations?

The bases of economic and industrial power, Thompson states, have shifted eastwards to the nations of the Pacific basin, the so-called Tiger Economies. As if to symbolize this challenge to traditional American dominance, Malaysia in 1996, not content with boasting the tallest building in the world, Petronas Towers, commissioned the longest: standing on stilts over the Klang river, the £1.3 billion Giga World constitutes a mile-and-a-half of offices, theatres and malls complete with mono-rail.

Thompson's case faltered somewhat when, in the closing years of the 20th century, the Tigers' own aspirations to share more of the global 'hegemonic pie' were dimmed by recession. However, the deficit has been more than made up by the growing might, industrially and commercially, of China; and symbolically with the 101-storey Shanghai World Financial Centre, the new record holder, completed in 2008.

Thompson queries Schiller's view that American culture 'colonizes' the cultures of other countries, thus tending to pollute and displace indigenous cultures. The assumption is that such cultures were pure and unadulterated at some recent point in history. Thompson describes this as 'a somewhat romantic view which, in many cases, does not stand up to careful scrutiny'.

With the events mentioned earlier in this chapter following 9/11 – the invasion of Iraq, the mayhem provoked by occupation, the bristling stand-off between the USA and Iraq's neighbour, Iran, worldwide unease about where terrorism will strike next – what constitutes cultural dominance, American hegemony, indeed the 'Western way of life' has been terrain undergoing seismic changes. The key descriptors are doubt, uncertainty, division, distrust and latterly a degree of rare self-questioning among the dominators.

Technology and the march of time

If there is one word that can summarize both Western life and the process of media, it is *speed*. Time not only flies it seems to be perpetually driven to fly faster. In many industrialized societies people work longer hours than they did twenty years ago. Curious this, when that magnificent piece of work-saving technology, the computer, releases us from so much repetitive and time-consuming drudgery.

Or does it? The computer processes information so rapidly that it 'makes' time and having made it, stands idle unless given more work to do – by humans. The desktop was soon supplemented by the laptop, the laptop by the handset, the handset by the mobile. What convenience, but also what control! Working life, through electronic means, commandeers what historically was private and protectable. Once upon a time people on trains read books or chatted to companions or even strangers. Some still do, operating the off-button, but they are fast becoming eccentrics. The primal fear these days, is to be out of touch, out of contact.

Between Gutenberg in the 15th century and the advent of the Industrial Revolution towards the end of the 18th, the publishing of texts remained only as fast as the working of human hands. With the coming of steam-power, hands gave way to machines. Frederick Koenig's steam press was installed at the London *Times* in 1814. It was followed by a host of new inventions to accelerate the manufacture of paper for printing, the composition of type and to multiply the number of newspaper copies that could be printed per hour. Print, swiftly available and, thanks to rail transport, accessible to the greater part of the population, shaped the social, cultural, political and economic contexts of the 19th century. Information, along with cotton, coal, steel and ship-building, became big business. The information age was born.

Time, of course, did not speed up, but what could be done within a span of time did, particularly with the coming of telegraphy in the 1840s and 1850s. This all seems old-hat now for we tend to think of telegraphy as one of those technological curios to be located in the boot sale of history along with gas lamps and clattery typewriters. But pause for a moment: telegraphy changed the world; it both altered time and conquered space and we are still living through the legacy of that achievement.

Prior to telegraphy, communication, unless it was between people in direct contact with one another, was reliant on transportation. Telegraphy (and later telephony in the 1870s) demolished distance as a 'barrier' to communication. As far as the passing on of information was concerned it no longer mattered how far away London was from New York or Sydney. Telegraphy made it possible to ignore time zones.

This had far-reaching effects upon the world of commerce, colonialism and a whole array of ways of doing things. Further, as James W. Carey argues in *Communication as Culture: Essays on Media and Society*,[13] the telegraphic facility became 'an agency for the alteration of ideas'.

Cultural impact

Paradoxically, while re-defining time and distance, telegraphy also placed distance between people. In the past, business had been conducted face to face. Carey writes in his chapter on technology and ideology that with the coming of telegraphy 'the volume and speed of transactions demanded a new form of organization of essentially impersonal relations – that is, relations not among known persons but among buyers and sellers whose only relation was mediated through an organization and a structure of management'.

A second ideological feature given emphasis by telegraphy and the miracle of electricity concerns the notion of unity, of communities being brought closer by instant transmission and receipt of information, a concept turned into the headline phrase 'global village', yet even earlier summarized in verse by Martin F. Typper in 1875:[14]

Yes, this electric chain from East to West
More than mere metal, more than mammon can
Binds us together – kinsmen, in the best,
As most affectionate and frankest bond;
Brethren as one; and looking far beyond
The world in an Electric Union blest!

Also arising out of this electronic union were implications for the control of time which in turn was to serve as social and linguistic control. Telegraphy facilitated control by making it possible to impose a technology-made grid on time. Admittedly this was a grid which could not switch day into night, could not prevent people Down Under being abed when people on the other side of the globe were up and ready for business, but it made systems of global communication possible. It turned time into a commodity that could be measured and dispensed according to socio-economic requirements. As Carey says, 'The control of time allows for the coordination of activity and, therefore, effective social control'.

Convergences

I began this chapter by sketching in the crucial role of language as a delineator of context. Technology in the form of telegraphy had a profound impact on the use of language and the knowledge which that language transmitted. James Carey writes that the wire services demanded 'a form of language stripped of the local, the regional, and colloquial... something closer to a "scientific" language' and under 'rigid control'.

Suddenly words were time and time was money. The telegraph created modern journalism and indeed influenced other forms of writing. The novelist Ernest Hemingway confessed to the influence of *telegraphese* on his own style, calling it 'the lingo of the cable'. Today we have another lingo – *texting*, as abbreviated as telegraphy but essentially personal and idiosyncratic. On the face of it this newish form of discoursing seems independent of control, if, that is, we forget the lurking possibility of digital surveillance capable of tracing what's being said, where and when.

Parallel with technological convergence, and not unconnected with it, is the convergence of agencies of control. Governments encircle and probe networking with legislation and surveillance, while big business scoops up the expanding real estate of network communication. At vast expense, Rupert Murdoch adds MySpace to his imperial portfolio, while Google gathers YouTube in an £800m embrace.

Public Service Broadcasting: sailing in choppy waters

In the Introduction I stressed the importance, in mass communication, of the principle of public service and the vital role played in society by public service broadcasting (PSB). Both are perpetually in danger of either being overlooked or their significance undermined, either by default or intent. Throughout the 1980s and 1990s in the Western world PSB faced not only rapidly growing competition from private sector services but doubts on the part of governments as to its future viability. The PSB rationale – that it is available to the whole community, that public interest takes precedence over commercial interest and that these principles be enshrined in regulation – has been consistently challenged by private commercial interests.

In Britain since the 1920s PSB has been a central feature of public life, first wholly represented by the BBC and later taking the form of a duopoly with the Independent Broadcasting Authority. The key to both these public services has been *service*. Even when commercial TV was launched in Britain in 1955 (in America commercial stations had been running since 1941), the goal of profit was balanced by principles of public service empowered by charter.

The British have been used to sharing, via radio or TV, the great cultural and sporting events which – however tenuously, however patchily

– have contributed to the nation's sense of cohesiveness, of unity. Similar patterns of PSB developed elsewhere in Europe, in France, Germany, Italy, the Netherlands, the Nordic countries, Spain and elsewhere.

In fulfilling this function, public service broadcasting has provided many gifts to the community, informational and cultural, striving to achieve balance, breadth and innovation. The private sector has also to please audiences, and often does so without the sacrifice of quality. Nevertheless the prime objective of private sector mass communication is profit. If service is profitable then the private sector will provide it; if it is not, the imperatives of the marketplace must be responded to.

As with reporting on the accusations by some authors of corporate enculturalization, a cautionary word needs to be added here that PSB is far from one-and-the-same thing as the *public sphere* in which the public are participants in the regulation of their lives. Indeed Hans Verstraeten in a *European Journal of Communication* article, 'The media and the transformation of the public sphere',[15] warns that:

> the concept of the 'public sphere'... should on no account be confused with the statute of public broadcasting... On the contrary, the brief history of Western European public broadcasting supplies us with numerous examples of how public broadcasting companies in political reality contributed to the control of the public sphere rather than its dynamic expansion.

True; and if we identify features of the public sphere as being full public access to the means of communication, as providing meaningful forums of debate, of rational discussion; of a plurality of ideas and stand-points, and perhaps most importantly the systematic opportunity to scrutinize and criticize government policies, then PSB has often fallen short of the ideal. But supporters of PSB argue that it is all we have got; and its demise would leave the public sphere entirely at the mercy of private enterprise.

The debate about public versus private is prominent and ongoing and highlights serious differences of opinion – of ideology – about the functions, role and performance of mass communication. Throughout the Thatcher and Major years in Britain, and in the United States during the presidencies of Ronald Reagan, George Bush Senior and even Democrat president Bill Clinton, the private was esteemed and privileged over the public, the one triumphal, the other in retreat: Private good, Public bad; hence the dominant trends of deregulation and privatization.

Threats to the future of the BBC receded with the election victories of New Labour in 1997, 2001 and 2005. The Corporation has been granted security till 2012, but its performance is subject to rigorous financial scrutiny, with the expectation that the institution swims or sinks in the maelstrom of competing television channels. The key question concerning the future of PSB is whether it can justify what makes it special, its emphasis on service and quality; in turn whether, with 900 or so alternatives to chose from, Joe Public will effectively remonstrate that the annual licence fee has become a costly anachronism.

A retreat from support for the public sphere in whatever form it manifests itself is always a possibility in circumstances where cost and price are allowed to take precedence over *value*. It is important, then, for students of media to attend to the difference, for the demise or radical downsizing of PSB would have implications for employment in the media and for media education and training.

New world 'dysorder'

In his chapter 'Ethnic discourse and the new world dysorder', in *Communication and Culture in War and Peace*, edited by Colleen Roach,[16] Majid Tehranian uses the term 'dysorder' to describe the contemporary world as he sees it. He conflates 'disorder' with 'dysfunction', or breakdown. He perceives this condition to be the result both of the ending of the Cold War, 'which has unleased centrifugal [tending away from the centre], ethnic and tribal forces within nation-states', and modern, centralizing trends in global culture and communication.

The term, employed before 9/11 and the invasion of Iraq in 2003, has gained in prescience. It usefully encapsulates the immediate with the longer-term. On the one hand corporations and the communication systems which they largely control work towards global centralization; on the other groups of people within broader communities struggle to exert identity, difference and independence, demanding demarcation rather than unification. Tehranian conjectures that '[m]odernization as a process of universal levelling of societies into relatively homogenous entities' has prompted diverse, powerful and combustible reactions.

By 'homogenous' we mean 'sameness', uniformity. In global terms this homogeneity relates to the cultural forms disseminated by transnational corporations employing new communications technology. This levelling out, Tehranian argues, is more apparent than real. In fact the 'levelling' has camouflaged 'a hegemonic project by a new modern, technocratic, internationalist elite' speaking 'the language of a new international, a new world order': that is, one dominated by the West and Western capitalism.

Tehranian sees the 'periphery' reacting against the 'core' in a range of destabilizing ways. This scenario was most dramatically played out in the terrorist attacks on the US Pentagon and New York's World Trade Centre in 2001, the whole event being captured live on TV and transmitted via satellite to all corners of the earth. Never before had the dominant order been so devastatingly subverted both in horrific fact and symbolically for all to witness.

Invasion of Iraq confirmed the military superiority of America, supported by Britain; but occupation was to be characterized by the dysfunctionality of internal divisions between rival religious factions that the occupying forces could scarcely begin to understand, and daily slaughter over which they had little control.

The ramifications of the 'war on terror' which many preferred to see as a crusade against Islam, or an attack on Arab peoples as a whole, now affect the lives of all of us, culturally, socially and politically. Religions assert their conflicting 'certainties' in every walk of life, in education, the arts, in what is permissible to say or publish, to broadcast or to film. At the level of personal conduct, issues such as what is acceptable to wear or not to wear prompt headline debate concerning the affirmation of faith or the need to avoid giving offence. Freedom, in all its aspects, has become a house undergoing a makeover.

Context and study

Obviously it is beyond the scope of an introductory chapter to attempt more than a cursory view of the cultural web of which the media are such an integral part. The ways in which the media address matters such as gender, sex, ethnicity, religion, law and order; the way they respond to key issues such as women's rights and racial equality; their disposition towards dissidents, foreigners, the socially disadvantaged and minorities of all kinds are likely to be the bread-and-butter of media study. Above all we are interested in the ways in which audiences 'make sense' of media and that is the theme of Chapter 3.

The study of media communication is itself not free of ideological frameworks; and every approach to study has its ideological angle, its shaping motive. For me, study of communication is both a scrutiny of the ways in which humans interact communicatively within socio-cultural contexts and an examination of the role of communication in relation to human rights and responsibilities; hence the recurring link made in this book between communication and democracy, and communication's key function as an agency of change.

In this sense, the study of media should be considered a democratic right and a democratic duty. It ought to be a central part of a nation's educational curriculum and if it is not, a useful early essay question might be to ask why not. James Carey's case for the subject's breadth and depth is equally ambitious in its aims. In *Communication as Culture*[13] he writes:

> The analysis of mass communication will have to examine the several cultural worlds in which people simultaneously exist – the tensions, often radical tension, between them, the patterns of mood and motivation distinctive to each, and the interpenetration among them...

He goes on:

> The task now for students of mass communication or contemporary culture is to turn... advances in the science of culture towards the characteristic products of contemporary life: news stories, bureaucratic language, love songs, political rhetoric, daytime serials, scientific reports, television drama, talk shows, and the wider world of contemporary leisure, ritual, and information.

A tall order but a compelling one.

Summary

This chapter gives emphasis to, and expands on, the point that communication can only be meaningfully studied in relation to its cultural contexts. We need to pay due attention to the power of language to define our world, to encapsulate commonality and difference. The role of organizations in communities, nationally and internationally is linked to the workings of hegemony of which ideology is an integral component.

While technology has not altered time and space it has had a profound impact on how we view and use them; in particular the nature of our communication. Contextual trends are identified as convergence, both technological and in terms of media control, and between cultures and ideologies, yet also of divergence in terms of the conflict over public and private. While communications are becoming more global in character, world societies seem to be shifting in the opposite direction, towards fragmentation from the centre and the demand by localite peoples to have more control over their lives.

If world events since 9/11 can be described in terms of climate, the first decade has been turbulent, planet earth subject to man-made tremors that have divided peoples along lines of religion, race, ethnicity and region. Terrorism has proved its effectiveness as a grabber of world headlines, aided and abetted by the unforgettable images of reprisal in the 'war on terror' – video and still pictures of the beatings of civilians in Baghdad's Abu Ghraib prison or the affront to justice and humanity of the American prison camps at Guantanamo Bay.

In such a climate, the media walk a tightrope between responsibly informing the public about events, and striving to interpret them, while at the same time catering for the public's appetite for diversion and escape. If, as a result of media coverage, we as audience gain the impression that the world is 'too much with us', if we experience fatigue at the sight of others' suffering, the temptation is to turn away, switch off. This is the one thing the media must avoid at any cost, hence their often unremitting search for novelty and sensation and an approach to events driven by the criteria of speed and immediacy.

KEY TERMS

socialization enculturalization commonality intent
power (economic, political, coercive; position, source, charismatic)
ideological state apparatus (ISA) repressive state apparatus (RSA)
hierarchy cultural capital hegemony power elite ideology alliances
appropriation convergences public service broadcasting (PSB)
public sphere deregulation privatization 'dysorder'

Suggested activities

1. Discussion points:

    (a) Culture is communication;

    (b) Ideology is inescapable;

    (c) The study of media is also the study of politics.

2. Follow up the theme that 'language defines our world'. How far do you agree with this in an age when pictures compete with words for attention and influence? You might wish to jot down notes for

an article arguing that in contemporary society words are losing out to images.

3. Draw up a list of sources from which information on the ownership of media might be compiled. It will be important to know not only which corporations own which media but what other industrial and commercial interests those corporations have. Focus on possible conflicts of interest, for example a newspaper's right to publish in the face of the mother-company's desire for commercial confidentiality.

4. You have been asked to take part in a debate on the privatization of broadcasting. Your brief is to make a case for the protection of public service broadcasting. Compose a 5-minute speech on the merits of PSB.

5. Prepare a one-page treatment for a documentary film company on the theme of Terrorism as Publicity.

Now read on

James Carey's *Communication as Culture: Essays on Media and Society* (UK: Routledge, 1992), quoted in this chapter (see Note 13) is strongly recommended and is generally considered a prime text in the study of culture and media. Three more recently published volumes deserve attention though they will require extra concentration – Peter Dahlgren's *Television and the Public Sphere: Citizenship, Democracy and the Media*, Nick Stevenson's *Understanding Media Cultures*, both published in the UK by Sage in 1995, and, also from Sage, James W. Neulliep's *Intercultural Communication: A Contextual Approach* (3rd edition, 2006).

An earlier classic is Raymond Williams' *Television, Technology and Cultural Form* (UK: Fontana, 1974), while key elements of European media history are given contextual illumination in Brian Winston's *Messages: Free Expression, Media and the West from Gutenberg to Overload* (UK: Routledge, 2005). Also recommended from Routledge in 2005 is *Media and Cultural Theory* by James Curran and David Morley and *Media/Theory* by Shaun Moore. With reference to media, politics and citizenship try *Citizens or Consumers: What the Media Tell Us About Political Participation* (UK/US: Open University Press, 2005) by Justin Lewis, Sanna Inthorn and Karin Wahl-Jorgensen.

On ideology, see Tuen A. van Dijk's *Ideology: A Multidisciplinary Approach* (UK: Sage, 1998). For global perspectives, Terni Rantanen's *The Media and Globalization* (UK/US: Sage, 2005) is recommended. For the analysis of gender issues, see *Women and Media: International Perspectives*

(UK: Blackwell, 2004), edited by Karen Ross and Carolyn M. Byerly, and Michelle Elizabeth Tusan's *Women Making News: Gender and Journalism in Modern Britain* (US: University of Illinois Press, 2005).

Notes

1. Krishan Kumar, 'Sociology' in *Exploring Reality* edited by Dan Cohn-Sherbok and Michael Irwin (UK: Allen & Unwin, 1987).
2. Philip M. Taylor, *Munitions of the Mind: A History of Propaganda from the Ancient World to the Present Day* (UK: Manchester University Press, 1995).
3. John B. Thompson, *The Media and Modernity: A Social Theory of the Media* (UK: Polity, 1995).
4. Louis Althusser, 'Ideology and ideological state apparatuses' in *Lenin and Philosophy and Other Essays* (UK: New Left Books, 1971).
5. Pierre Bourdieu, *Distinction: A Social Critique of the Judgement of Taste* (US: Harvard University Press, 1984).
6. The Pilkington Committee Report on Broadcasting (1962) came down hard on the sort of programmes broadcast by commercial TV: 'Our conclusion is that triviality is a natural vice of television, and that where it prevails it operates to lower standards of enjoyment and understanding'. 'Prolefeed' was the rubbishy entertainment brought to the mass of the people, the proletariat, by the ruling party of Oceania in Orwell's *1984*.
7. Power Elite: term employed by C. Wright Mills in *Power, Politics and People* (UK: Oxford University Press, 1963) to describe those members of society who possess power and influence, and who do so either on the public stage, like politicians, or behind the scenes, like leaders of industry or commerce; or simply people at the top of social hierarchies with influence through wealth or personal contacts. In short, the Establishment; specifically that part of it which influences decision-making at all levels of society.
8. Antonio Gramsci, *Selections from the Prison Notebooks* (UK: Lawrence & Wishart, 1971).
9. In 1989 Frances Fukuyama wrote an essay, 'The end of history?' published in *The National Interest*, a US current affairs journal. Such was the widespread attention paid to it that the author expanded his thesis. *The End of History and the Last Man* was published by Free Press in 1992 (Late Modern paperback, 2005). Fukuyama's theory was that capitalism had no competition, hence the end of ideological conflict.
10. Samuel P. Huntington, *The Clash of Civilizations: Remaking World Order* (US: Simon & Schuster, 1996).
11. Todd Gitlin, 'Prime time television: the hegemonic process in television entertainment' in Horace Newcomb (ed.), *Television: The Critical View* (US: Oxford University Press, 1994).

12. Herbert I. Schiller, *Culture Inc. The Corporate Takeover of Public Expression* (US: Oxford University Press, 1989).

13. James W. Carey, *Communication as Culture: Essays on Media and Society* (UK: Routledge, 1992); his chapter on technology and ideology.

14. Martin F. Typper, *Prime* (1875), quoted in Carey (Note 13).

15. Hans Verstraeten, 'The media and the transformation of the public sphere: a contribution for a critical political economy of the public sphere', *European Journal of Communication*, September 1996.

16. Majid Tehranian, 'Ethnic discourse and the new world dysorder' in Colleen Roach (ed.), *Communication and Culture in War and Peace* (UK: Sage, 1993).

The Language of Study

AIMS

➤ To provide an overview, with explanations and illustrations, of the core terms used in the study of media communication.
➤ To locate terminology under three related headings – transmission, text and reception and in doing so note a number of landmarks of study that have generated specialist terms.
➤ At the same time to assist recognition that terminology reflects different 'points of entry' into the study of the subject, differences of approach, emphasis and interpretation.

The study of communication is an amalgam of many disciplines and this is reflected in its diverse terminology. In some ways it resembles the contents of a magpie's nest. It could hardly be otherwise in what is still often referred to as a latecomer in academic studies whose content is drawn from fields as diverse as telecommunications, anthropology, psychology, sociology, linguistics, cultural studies and political science.

Here I focus on terms that, at least in a general way, reflect the evolution of the subject. In the early days the emphasis of study was on mass communication as propaganda, then as mainly one-way transmission. The terminology was essentially of an instrumental, mechanistic nature – identifying the 'parts' that constitute the workings of mass communication.

From a long tradition of linguistic analysis emerged study focusing on the language of signs and codes, and a concentration on the content or text of communication. In turn, and inevitably, attention widened to take in the 'reading' of these texts by audience, and response theory became a dominant mode of communication study.

It is all too easy to over-simplify the evolutionary map of studies. Scholars in different countries work to different timescales and have differing preoccupations. Here then I confess to certain generalizations which specialists in the field might question. However, just as some commentators query the existence of *meaning* as a meaningful term in the study of communication, I would suggest that the meaning of terms undergoes endless modification.

If it suits the purpose of achieving clarity of understanding, if it aids exchanges of 'meaning' then terminology must lend itself to flexible use; and sometimes we may wish to 'borrow' a term from its academic field of origin and employ it in a new and interesting way. I would make the case that different approaches to analysis often interact, overlap and work to mutual benefit: inevitably so does the terminology which we should regard as the servant of our studies, not the master. Its usefulness diminishes if it locks us into hard-and-fast ways of approaching the subject.

The language of transmission

The terminology of study is most readily located in *models* of communication, usually diagrams attempting to illustrate the interconnections and interactions of elements in the process of communicating. Such models reflect the preoccupations of those who design and define them. The term 'model' is also used to describe aspects of communication as a whole; and there are rival models – or *paradigms* – springing from differing interpretations of process.

We refer, for example, to a *propagandist* or *mass manipulative model*, originating with scholarly interest in the mass persuasion techniques employed by the Nazi propaganda machine in Germany before and during the Second World War. Introducing a symposium on the historical tributaries of media research in the *Journal of Communication*,[1] John Durham Peters writes, 'Hitler, in a curious way, presided over the birth of mass communications research, and not only by chasing so much scholarly talent to the United States and elsewhere'.

During the post-war period when relations between the West and Soviet Russia cooled into Cold War and conflicting ideologies drew upon mass communication to urge their case, the propagandist model remained a focus of study, particularly in the United States. It was giving ground, however, to two rival perspectives: the model of *transmission* and that of *ritual* or *symbol* which we associate with cultural studies.

The transmission model emphasizes the process of communicating information from A to B, from sender to receiver; the ritual/symbolic model stresses the process of *exchange*. The one is in the main, instrumental; it is linear in direction and technological in orientation; the other is circular or spiral in nature and is couched in the interactive practices of people in cultural situations. One might also term it a socio-cultural model.

The men from Bell Telephones

In 1949 two engineers, Claude Shannon and Warren Weaver, researching for the Bell Telephone Laboratories, produced what they termed the *Mathematical Theory of Communication*. Their findings were published by the University of Illinois Press[2] and gave to the world some of the first specialist terminology of the study of communications.

Shannon and Weaver set in progress lines of investigation and theorizing that focused on the production, or supply-side, of mass communication. Their remit from Bell Telephones was to find out just how much interference could be tolerated on the telephone line before the message became difficult or impossible to understand (see Figure 2.1). In the model, the sender of the telephone message is termed the Information Source, the receiver is the Destination: it is very much a 'depersonalized' approach. In this case the Transmitter and Receiver are telephones and telephone lines.

What interested Shannon and Weaver, and for us it is the most useful part of the model, is the Noise Source; and the part *noise* plays in

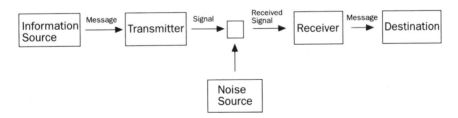

Figure 2.1 Shannon and Weaver's model (1949)
Essentially the authors of this, the first classic model of communication, were studying the nature of communication by telephone, here denoted as *Transmitter* and *Receiver*. The term *Noise Source* has come to describe a whole range of factors which 'get in the way' of the clarity of the message. Just the same, Shannon and Weaver found that despite as much as 50 per cent information loss through interference, the basics of a message could still be understood. This capacity they put down to the habit humans have of building into their exchanges *redundancy* (see the main text).

the communicative process remains of key interest to study, whether we are approaching it from a tranmissional or a socio-cultural direction. The authors of the *Mathematical Theory of Communication* identified three modes of noise, or message-interference.

Level A concerns *technical* or *mechanical* noise. Later users of the term have broadened this definition to include many other aspects of message impedance, such as hot (or cold) days in the classroom or office, distractions such as late-afternoon lectures, things of interest happening outside the window; and they can be *literally* noise – neighbours blasting out the latest chart-buster while you are trying to complete an essay for tomorrow's deadline.

Level B, *semantic* noise, concerns the meaning of an exchange: was it understood? Once again, Shannon and Weaver's term has become common currency and by regular use widened in terminological scope. If we acknowledge 'semantic problems' we are talking of ways in which meaning is not clear or is varyingly interpreted. Perhaps we do not understand the language through which a message is expressed. Even when the encoder and decoder share a common language the use of particular expressions, or of specialist terminology, may prove a barrier to effective communication. We may of course use the same words – 'freedom' for instance – but, as a result of our different political standpoints, differ semantically, that is in our definition of the word.

Level C concerns the effectiveness of the communication in terms of its reception. Later scholars have chosen to define Level C as *psychological* noise: you are worried, preoccupied, you have received bad news; you dislike or distrust the communicator – these factors can cause noise at the psychological level.

Shannon and Weaver were able to report to Bell on a key feature of message-sending and reception in relation to noise, which they referred to as *redundancy*. They gauged that even with substantial interference on the telephone line a person could reliably pick up the gist of the sender's message; and this was because redundancy – that which is strictly inessential to the core message – was built in to the exchange.

In its relation to work situations, to be redundant is to be out of a job, surplus to requirements. In communication that which is surplus to the requirements of the message remains essential to message-reception while also serving a vital role in terms of the quality of the interactive exchange. It may comprise greetings, references to the weather, repetition, re-phrasing, checking, digressions or simply pauses.

Indeed the absence of the use of customary greetings and exchange (what have been termed 'idiot salutations') can not only result in information-loss, perhaps because essential data has been delivered too swiftly, but could also create psychological noise. An abrupt manner – on or off the telephone – may signal to the receiver an impression of unfriendliness, even of dismissiveness, which may not be the sender's intention.

The steersman

Today we refer to the Shannon and Weaver model chiefly to identify what it omits. Transmission works best when it is two-way and therefore no model should exclude reference to *feedback*, the most critical feature of any model of transmission, and a field of study in its own right. The Greek word for steersman was adopted in 1947 by Norbert Wiener, an American mathematician, and Arturo Rosenbleuth, a physician, to coin a term to describe the science of cybernetics, the study of feedback systems in humans, animals and machines.

The steersman metaphor is an apt one for examining the nature of communicative interactions. The success of the steersman's voyage depends on the keen observation of wind and tide, on adjusting sails and steering as weather conditions change. Wiener's work[3] became famous and cybernetics developed into an essentially interdisciplinary study, ranging in its interest from the control systems of the body, the information flow in business and industrial organizations to the monitoring of space missions and the ultimate world of feedback, computer science.

All models of process include, or imply, feedback. Just as it may be said that, without recall, nothing has been learnt, so we might claim that without feedback communication cannot progress. This is truer of interpersonal than mass media communication, of course, but over the long term feedback from audience, gained through market research, is a crucial element of the survival or success of every form of media. In any event, our study of feedback should explore its different manifestations – positive, negative, instant, delayed and intermittent, short-term and long-term.

Wilbur Schramm: steps towards the interactive

Another pioneer, Wilbur Schramm,[4] in 1954 posed the two models reproduced in Figure 2.2. In the first of these Shannon and Weaver's

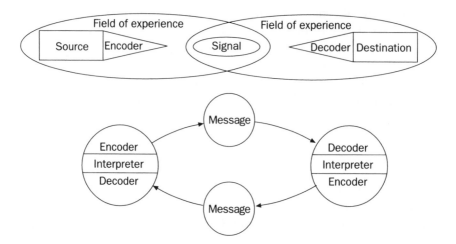

Figure 2.2 Two of Wilbur Schramm's models (1954)

Source and Destination are replicated, but transmitter and receiver become Encoder and Decoder. In the second model a significant transformation takes places: *people* have become the encoders and decoders of messages.

The first model is still mechanistic but it includes an important personal dimension, what Schramm calls *fields of experience*. Where the encoder's field of experience overlaps with that of the decoder communication is likely to be at its most effective. In the second model linearity is abandoned in recognition of the *interactive* nature of the communicative act.

The message has first to be assembled, encoded, and then interpreted or decoded; and the process of interpretation is constant and endless. True, both Schramm's models concern essentially interpersonal communication but it does not require a great stretch of the imagination to extend their use to include media as encoder-interpreters and audience as decoder-interpreters.

Where fields of experience do not overlap we are likely to locate, as cause or effect, semantic and psychological noise, for that experience may be deeply embedded in cultural norms and values. The narrowing or widening of socio-cultural divisions, territorial or ideological conflicts, will to a considerable extent depend upon the attitudes and performance of the voices of community and nation, the mass media.

Key questions: Lasswell's Five, Gerbner's Ten

Not all the early models of communication are diagrammatic in form. Indeed perhaps the best-known model (and arguably one of the most useful) simply comprises five key questions. Harold Lasswell, in a 1948 publication, *The Communication of Ideas*,[5] suggests we might interrogate the mass communication process as follows, asking:

Who
Says *what*
In which *channel*
To *whom*
And with what *effect*?

While not extending the vocabulary of study, the Lasswell model offers us a simple structure of analysis. *Who* are the communicators; *What* is the content, the message of the communicators. The *channel* comprises the means of communication, the technology and the mode or *medium* into which the message is encoded and transmitted. *Whom* is audience and one aim of analysis is to gauge the nature of reception. New terminology has tended to cluster and evolve around those five features of process.

Lasswell was a leading light of the propagandist phase of scholarly interest in media yet in the 1950s he called for more research into whether propaganda had the effect on the public that had been claimed for it. In 1956 another American, George Gerbner, whose influence as a commentator on mass communication spanned several generations, extended Lasswell's five questions to ten essentials of the communicative process:[6]

1. Someone
2. perceives an event
3. and reacts
4. in a situation
5. through some means
6. to make available materials
7. in some form
8. and context
9. conveying content
10. with some consequence.

We can welcome here simple but essential additions to our reper-
toire of terms. An *event*, something perhaps which may eventually be
turned into news, has to be *perceived* as such, as something worth reporting. This suggests the familiar and unavoidable process of *selection*.
Events only get reported, it can be said, if someone somewhere perceives them to be 'worthy', or to be specific, *newsworthy* – a term which
will be examined in Chapter 5.

Gerbner recognizes a difference between *situation*, that is, the situation the reporters or photographers might find themselves in and the
context in which the processing of the content-message takes place. He
then presents us with a more complex model of mass communication
(Figure 2.3). At first sight the model is forbidding but it rewards close
attention.

M is the responder to an event, the Mediator, and once that event
traverses the horizontal axis, it has become a *percept*, an event perceived. It is the perception of the event which conditions its processing into message form. In turn the message undergoes modification as
it progresses through the *means* of production which itself is subject to
the institutional nature and workings of the newspaper or broadcasting
company responsible for transmission.

The difference between the content of a message (E) and its style (S)
or form is importantly made clear. The lower horizontal axis concerns

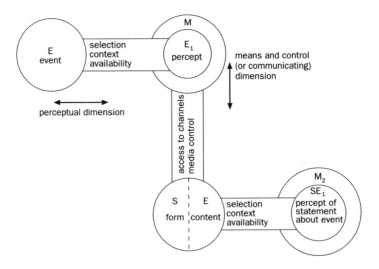

Figure 2.3 Gerbner's model of communication (1956)
Described by Denis McQuail in *Communication* (UK: Longman, 1975) as perhaps 'the most
comprehensive attempt yet to specify the component stages and activities of communication'.

the nature of reception. Just as communicators select, and in selecting are influenced by context and limited by *availability* (of information, for example), similar criteria operate as far as audience is concerned. The percept of the mediator meets with the percept (SE1) of audience (M2) and becomes ground for interpretation; of confirming, disconfirming, neutrality or indifference.

Gerbner's model identifies the processing of an event from origin to reception. What it does not do is elaborate on the complexity of the message itself; an omission scholars coming to the subject from different directions have attempted to redress.

Signs, codes, texts

What Gerbner has called style-content, semiology (or semiotics), the scientific study of signs and sign systems, describes as *text* and it is the text, and its meaning, that becomes the focus of interest. The theories of the pioneers of semiology/semiotics such as the Swiss linguist Ferdinand de Saussure (1857–1913), the American philosopher and logician, Charles Peirce (1834–1914) and the French cultural critic Roland Barthes (1915–1980), have become deeply embedded in the percepts, practices and language of cultural and communication studies.

De Saussure[7] spoke of language as a 'profusion of signs'. This was not just a picturesque way of describing things. It proposed that we see the whole of communication and behaviour as assemblies of signs, governed by *codes*, or sets of rules, which by careful observation and analysis furnish clues to the decipherment of meaning. The relationship of signs, the interaction between them, which de Saussure called, *valeur*, was the determinant of meaning.

Where the study of the process of mass communication has generally taken a sweeping, *macroscopic* view, semiology prefers a more *microscopic* approach, often dissecting (or *deconstructing*) texts, and the language they are expressed in, with surgical precision. At the same time semiology opens up possibilities for employing the same analytical tools for examining all forms of communication, and at all levels – interpersonal, group, organizational or in relation to mass communication.

Signs: signifiers and signified

Some years ago on a visit to the Greek island of Crete I was walking a remote path that seemed to lead to nowhere when I came upon a sign – a small wooden board nailed to a post stuck in the ground. It bore

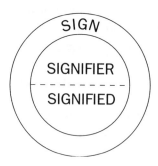

Figure 2.4 Signifier–signified
Each communicative sign comprises what we see or hear (the signifier) and what it stands for (that which is signified).

an advertisement for General Accident Assurance. The sign and its message seemed so out of place – so out of context – that I could not help seeing it as *surreal* rather than real; a message entirely altered in its meaning by the context in which the sign appeared.

The example is cited in order to suggest the importance of the differentiation made in Figure 2.4. The sign is made up of two components, the *signifier* (de Saussure's term) and the *signified*. The second is the 'idea' (Gerbner's *percept* if you like) of the first. Charles Peirce[8] called the signifier *object* and British scholars C.K. Ogden and I.A. Richards, the *referent*.[9]

As far as the General Accident advertisement was concerned, the notice itself was the signifier. That which was signified, however, is open to interpretation. Quite clearly General Accident's intention was that signifier and signified should be one and the same, a promotional device for General Accident assurance services. However for me, as 'reader' of the sign, that which was signified was conditioned by when, where and how I saw the sign.

John Fiske puts the matter neatly in his *Introduction to Communication Studies*:[10]

> The signifier is the sign's image as we perceive it – the marks on the paper or the sounds in the air, the signified is the mental concept to which it refers. This mental concept is broadly common to all members of the same culture who share the same language.

At first sight this may seem to be splitting hairs, until we recognize how easily that which is meant can be separated from the signs, or sign system to which it may have initially belonged. Take a sign, like the General Accident advertisement, out of its familiar context, release it from its conventional use, and it may undergo a transformation of meaning. Everything depends on the situation and on a range of contextual factors; and everything stresses what has been termed the *multi-accentuality* of the sign.

All this implies that meaning is something which does not reside in the sign, or assemblage of signs, but is *negotiable*; that is, meaning may be *assigned* by consumers of the sign. This position represents a substantial shift from the transmissional model of communicative interaction: the message emanating from the sender/encoder is no longer a 'property' like a parcel mailed in the post and simply received and responded to; rather, the receiver/decoder is *empowered* more forthrightly in this alternative model of communication.

Iconic, indexical, symbolic

Charles Peirce assembled signs into three categories. The *iconic* resembles that which it describes. Photographs and maps are iconic. *Indexical* signs work by association: smoke, for example, is an index of fire; a jacket over a chair may be an index of someone's presence or absence; the close-up of a revolver in a film usually has the indexical purpose of hinting that the gun is about to be used.

The *symbol* may have no resemblance to what it purports to signify. The letters of the alphabet are symbols. Their meaningfulness as signs exists through common consent and their use is governed by codes such as grammatical rules. As Edmund Leach points out in *Culture and Communication*,[11] 'a sign is always a member of a set of contrasting signs which function within a specific cultural context'. We may feel inclined to mix, for example, letters, numbers and musical notes in random order. The signs are all genuine but in combination they are meaningless (unless, of course, they have been assembled according to a secret code).

A sign can be simultaneously iconic, indexical and symbolic. The colour red resembles blood, indicates danger, symbolizes dominance, strength, the warlike. Equally a sign can pass from one category to another according to time and circumstance. The swastika is an example: it has been a sign of good luck, a decorative sign employed in Greek and Roman mosaic pavements, the emblem of Nazi Germany and, consequently, the symbol of racial genocide.

> ### Saying it with roses
>
> Gillian Dyer in *Advertising as Communication*[12] writes: 'A rose is a symbol of love or passion not because a rose looks like love or passion or even because the flower causes it. It is just that members of some cultures have over the years used the rose in certain circumstances to mean love.' In most cases, says Dyer, 'there are the rudiments of a "natural" bond between signifiers and signified in many symbols'.
>
> 'An example of a pure symbol, with no such bond, would be that of the white horse used by White Horse Whisky, where the horse standing in a bar or on top of a mountain or at a building site stands for the bottle of whisky itself, although there is no "logical" connection between the bottle and the sign horse.'

This capacity of the signified to alter in meaning according to the situation in which the signifier is encountered keys in with a basic premise of cultural studies, that reality is a social construct brought about by the uses of language (that is, symbols). In short, symbols not objects govern our world; hence the power of signs within a process of symbolic exchange.

Arbitrary and permissive

Signs rarely work singly. For the most part they are assembled into texts according to codes, or sets of observances, rules or guidelines; and these codes range between those which are arbitrary, or fixed, and those of a more flexible nature. For example, the Morse Code is arbitrary. The use of the dots and dashes representing letters of the alphabet is governed by strict rules and if the signs are not employed according to the rules the 'transmission' becomes meaningless.

Presentational codes – 'rules' of dress and appearance – can themselves range between the strict and the permissive. When Michael Foot, a former leader of the British Labour party, appeared at the Cenotaph in London on Armistice Day wearing a donkey jacket (it was a bitterly cold day) he was taken to task in the media. He was perceived to have breached a code of presentation demanding that public figures signify by their clothing their respect for the dead of two world wars. The signifier here was an item of clothing worn to keep out the cold: the signified, however, according to the media (particularly those papers antipathetic to Labour Party policies), was disrespect.

In Michael Foot's case the signs being given off as a result of his choice of representation were probably unintentional. Of more contemporary interest has been the fuss arising from the wearing by Muslim women of traditional dress such as the veil and the burka. In 'normal' times this had rarely been a matter for comment. In 'abnormal' times following the London bombings of July 2005, the prevailing tensions between Muslims and non-Muslims manifested themselves in many ways, including issues of presentation. Traditional dress was now deemed in some quarters to be symbolic of separation, as demonstrating allegiance to faith above all else.

Suddenly the symbols of religious and other allegiances were in the headlines, resulting in banning decisions that could only be described as ludicrous if they had not had such serious implications. It became politically incorrect in some quarters to wear even a crucifix if a person's work involved dealing with the public. Signs once decoded as symbols of difference became widely accepted as such, nurtured by contextual anxieties, aided and abetted by often-prejudicial readings by the media.

Operational codes

In the media there are numerous codes of an ethical and legal nature relating to professional practice, but in particular we are interested in *operational* codes. These govern the norms and practices – the *conventions* – of production, and will be examined in Chapter 5 on the news. In Chapter 6 on narrative, we will explore codes at work in both fictional and news stories.

With specific reference to television, John Fiske in *Television Culture*[13] identifies the following operational codes: *natural* codes that relate to our lived, socio-cultural world (these could also be termed codes of realism); *technical* codes that are concerned with the modes of operation of the medium; and *ideological* codes which work towards the shaping of collective perceptions.

We refer also to *aesthetic* codes that apply to the *appreciation* of artefacts – literature, music, art, architecture, design. What is considered aesthetic – of 'quality' – is arbitrated by conventions that generally reflect the dominance of those 'opinion leaders of taste' in any given society at a given time. Such conventions provoke innovators to breach them; and in turn the innovative becomes convention.

Today, it could be argued, we make our own aesthetic judgements from the vast plurality of signifiers available to us; and what matters is not the 'aesthetic', or pleasure-giving property of that which is 'encoded' but how we make use of it in our lives, whether it is a painting or a pair of Armani shoes; and we might remind ourselves here that our response is rarely just an individual one: it is affected by those around us, Significant Others who importantly influence our tastes, choices and judgement or, like the advertising fraternity, by transforming goods and services into symbols of desire and identity, motivate us to buy.

Paradigms and syntagms

De Saussure made a distinction between *la langue* and *parole*, the one describing language as a complete system of forms and structures existing in the brains of communicators – their *potential* for speech – the other by language in action, as it is specifically assembled and employed.

In the analysis of language and language-use we discriminate between the *paradigm* and the *syntagm*. An example of a paradigm is the alphabet, the available 26 individual letters from which the syntagm – words and sentences – are constructed. Each message, then, is selected from a paradigm and assembled into a syntagm. In culinary terms, the ingredients are paradigmatic, the meal itself is the syntagm. Coherence, if not meaning, depends upon 'meaningful' juxtaposition when the symbols are placed together.

Artists of the Surrealist movement in the first half of the 20th century delighted in breaking paradigmatic rules in order to create syntagms which either eluded meaning-making or somehow strove for new possibilities of meaning. So long as chefs remain within the rules of edibility (that is, avoid poisoning us), they too may wish to break with convention, to dabble with paradigms by, for example, alternating sweets and savouries or serving them up together.

Paradigms are sets of possibilities from which choices are made. In film making, for example, we might describe close-ups, panning shots, the zoom or rapid cutting as visual paradigms, and sound effects, atmospheric music and silence as aural paradigms. The putting together of those devices in a 'meaningful' order or narrative is the syntagm. We work towards meaning through a process of making choices; and just as important are the choices we have not made. Meaning is about omission as well as commission.

We can see this paradigmatic–syntagmatic process going on every day in mass communication. We wonder why this piece of news footage is used to make a point rather than possible alternatives. We wonder why some news items have been selected and others rejected and why those chosen are placed in the order in which they are reported. A different paradigmatic selection might have produced a different syntagmatic combination, or 'story', and therefore an altogether different meaning.

All the world's a text

Codes govern signs which, assembled, become texts. Roland Barthes[14] makes a useful distinction between what he calls the *work*, that which the encoder or encoders have produced, and the *text* which is what the decoders experience and interpret: you take a photograph (the work). You show it to me and what I 'read' is the text.

The distinction echoes one posed by Erving Goffman[15] in his work on self-presentation in everyday life. He talks of signs – impressions – which are *given*, that is intended, and those which are *given off*, over which the individual has little or no control and may even be completely unaware of, but which are interpreted by others. In mass communication there is acute awareness that the message transmitted is not guaranteed to be either interpreted as intended or interpreted at all. As we shall see later, audiences may be watching TV but they may not be paying attention despite the encoder's efforts to command it.

Just as there are fixed and flexible codes there are *closed* and *open* texts. A party political broadcast is an example of a closed text. Every effort is made in production and presentation to close down alternative readings of the programme. To this end, facts which do not fit in to the propagandist message are omitted; and facts which fit are given emphasis.

News presentation comes under the closed text heading. Its intention is to sufficiently impress us by the professionalism of production – and the 'closure' which the use of newsreaders and the voice-overs of reporters helps determine – into believing that what The News tells us *is* the news. No one ever appears before the introductory music and the headlines waving a red flag and warning us that The News is a highly selective *version* of what has happened.

A work of art such as a painting, piece of sculpture or a photograph may constitute a more open text, allowing us room for free analysis and interpretation. Visiting the National Museum of Photography, Film and Television one of my students complained there was no literature to explain the photographs in an exhibition of scenes from family life. The student decided that the show was therefore meaningless.

What was missing was *anchorage*, the kind of closure we are so familiar with, and often dependent upon, in media practice – the picture in the context of a page, beneath a headline and with an explanatory caption. Open texts can be sources of anxiety, it would seem, as well as potentially liberating.

Metonym and metaphor

Linguistics have contributed much to the ways in which we analyze texts, cultures and media practices; not the least we have been made watchfully aware of the use in media of *metonym* and *metaphor*. The first is indexical in nature. A metonym is a figure of speech in which the thing really meant is represented by something synonymous or closely associated with it.

The word 'Press' is a metonym standing for all newspapers; the word 'stage' is a metonym for all aspects of the theatre. A photograph of starving African children may be read as *standing for* the general African situation. The news, whether in newspapers or on TV, is metonymic because it conveys the real while at the same suggesting that the specifics of what is being reported are typical of the wider picture.

Metonymy can be seen as an agent of propaganda and of *stereotyping*: protesting crowds are all the same; striking workers? street beggars? social security 'scroungers'? asylum seekers? – typical! In contrast, metaphors work by expressing something belonging to one paradigm, or plane, in terms of another plane. The English *Times* during the 19th century was nicknamed 'The Thunderer'. The metaphor had great resonance. In our mind's ear we imagine the thunder-clap that commands attention, shakes the earth and politicians in their shoes. The metaphor might distance us from reality, but it creates pictures in our head that carry their own conviction.

Once activated, metaphors are difficult to control: plain truth often shrinks before them. After all, we might ask, did the *Times* really earn its resounding title? If metonyms have the semblance of reality then metaphors glory in symbols. Thunder symbolizes outspokenness, power to command attention. The effectiveness of the metaphor lies in its vivid impact and also its imprecision. What, for instance, occurs after thunder; and what does the lightning symbolize? Arguably it could stand for retribution by an angry government.

Metaphors can be deeply enriching, allowing us to see things in new and unexpected ways. Without them, poetry would scarcely exist; and without them newspaper headline writers would live a duller working life. Metaphors can inspire us, entertain us, unite us and, of course, serve to divide us because of their emotive potential. For example, framing the conflicts of interest that inevitably arise in society according to the metaphor of war and using language appropriate to that metaphor ('attack', 'victory', 'retreat', 'defeat', 'the enemy') has the potential to arouse in the public powerful emotional responses.

The interactivity of texts

From the point of view of reception, media texts rarely come singly. They comprise what Madan Sarup describes in his *Introductory Guide to Post-Structuralism and Postmodernism*[16] as an 'intersecting and infinitely expandable web called intertextuality'. Texts interconnect and interact with each other, serving to modify, alter or reinforce textual meaning.

Images from films and TV are endlessly recycled in commercials, posters, magazine advertisements to the point where we are not sure where those images came from originally or what their primary purpose was. And when we do encounter the images in their primary setting we carry with us mental traces of their secondary, tertiary or millennial activation.

For the French cultural critic Jean Baudrillard[17] the sheer volume of signifiers in the contemporary world of mass communication is less a web than a blizzard. In fact so confusing is the situation, so detached from their original signification are the myriad signifiers we are bombarded with throughout our waking day, Baudrillard pessimistically conjectures that meaning is too lost in the blizzard to be worth the trouble of attempting to define it.

The metaphor of the blizzard suggests a condition, blinding and confusing, which is not obviously the result of any deliberate shaping or structuring. Yet we should not, as students of media, underestimate the capacity of the agencies of mass communication for, as it were, blizzard control or conclude in the confusion of the storm that ideology is absent.

In 1996 BBC Television screened an interesting commercial (one of a series using its most popular programmes and artistes) to publicize itself as a worldwide broadcasting service. It used the cast of the long-running TV soap, *Eastenders*. At first sight all the familiar signifiers were present – the characters, their chief venue (the Queen Vic) and a typical pub quiz. However, as soon as the quiz began, the signifiers took wing.

We usually associate what goes on at the bar and around the tables of the Vic with problems, with personal and family conflicts, open or suppressed. However, the *intent* of the commercial was to stress togetherness. Everyone in the Vic, physically, and in terms of purpose, was facing in the same direction, not squabbling but, as it were, singing in unison. That *signifies* something different from what we are accustomed to, but the shock, and the entertainment value, took hold when the cast broke out into foreign languages, extolling the virtues of the BBC and *Eastenders* as the Corporation's most popular export.

The nature of *Eastenders* had been imaginatively subverted, turned on its head, for the 'real' soap, if I might put it that way, derives its strength and fascination from its convincing portrayal of a localized sub-culture and community. It is a slice-of-life drama characterized by its closed, or semi-closed cultural context. The commercial, however, converted the cast of cockneys into multi-linguists and by doing so transformed *Eastenders* from a tale about Walford, London, into a story about TV texts as *commodity*.

Indeed this is largely what intertextuality does, even if that is not always evident either to producers or consumers: it sells itself by replication and in turn it sells the idea of itself and those things, cultural and consumerist, with which it comes into contact. If the Egyptian pharaoh Tutankhamen could have profited from his exploitation by generations of publicity-minded archeologists, museum curators, fine-art publishers, magazine editors, poster-makers, directors of resurrected Mummy movies and TV documentarists, he would have had wealth enough to build himself a pyramid higher than the Empire State Building.

Discourse: the macro-text

We have seen that signs are assembled according to codes (fixed or flexible) into texts (open or closed). In turn, texts contribute to, are part of, broader 'canvases' of communication called *discourses*. The News is a discourse; that is, a way of telling us things and in the telling it also explains them. In terms of public awareness and esteem, The News has the status of a *dominant* discourse.

In *Social Semiotics*[18] Robert Hodge and Gunther Kress define discourse as 'the site where social forms of organization engage with systems of signs in the production of texts, thus reproducing the sets of meanings and values which make up a text'. Kress, in an earlier book, *Linguistic Processes in Sociocultural Practices*,[19] refers to the institutional nature of discourse which gives expression to institutional meanings and values. In this sense discourse is the 'talk' of the powerful – the power elite – in the community; the means by which they impose, or seek to impose, their definitions:

> Beyond that, they [discourses] define, describe, delimit what is possible to say (and by extension what is possible to do or not to do) with respect to the area of concern of that institution, whether marginally or centrally.

Discourse, then, is not only a means of communicative exchange, it implies a set of rules concerning the nature of that exchange. If the institution is a media corporation, like the BBC, public and private discourses will be framed not only by institutional rules but also by rules governing the institution as a whole. The Corporation's Charter constitutes one aspect of the BBC's permitted discourse but so do external pressures such as the part played in broadcasting legislation by government.

Texts are the 'micro-data' of 'macro-exchanges' called discourses; and just as the text is embedded in the discourse, so the discourse is embedded in the system. That system is an arena of debate and conflict. Some discourses dominate, others are subordinate but in a pluralist society no discourse has a natural monopoly.

We have arrived at a confluence, a meeting, of theoretical perspectives, for the nature of discourse as a terrain of struggle brings us back to the notions of *hegemony* and *ideology* discussed in Chapter 1.

Orders of signification

In the interpretation of signs, Roland Barthes[14] posed three orders of signification – *denotation*, *connotation* and *myth*. The first order of meaning, denotation, is the level at which identification and recognition take place. It is essentially the descriptive stage: all the prime characters of *Eastenders* are sitting in the Vic. They are taking part in a pub quiz and they are answering in foreign languages. At the level of connotation, or the second order of meaning, we begin to ask the question Why? – why are they assembled in such a way; why are they speaking in tongues? At one level we read what is going on; at the other, we read *in* to it, interpret it.

It is at this, the level of connotation, that value judgements are made and where what we value may clash with the value expressed in the text. For Barthes the same orders apply whether a text is being read or created: we take a photograph; denotation is the basic process, the mechanical reproduction of the image that the camera has been pointed at. The connotational component involves the decisions made by the person taking the photograph, the selection he or she has made from available paradigmatic choices.

Contrary pereceptions, competing values

The clue to how we operate at the connotational level may be found in the language we use, the terms we select to describe things or situations. We might refer to 'freedom fighters' who 'risk their lives for a cause'. Others might describe the same persons doing the same things as 'terrorists' who 'wreak mindless violence upon the public'. At the connotational level we are saying as much about ourselves, our perceptions, our mind-set, our mental script, as the subject we are analyzing.

Yet this is not to mark out the denotational as the terrain of objectivity in comparison with connotation as the terrain of subjectivity. The denotational is not value-free, untinged by ideology. The apparent objectivity of fact-prior-to-analysis may disguise a degree of selectivity that is ideologically motivated. In a sense the denotational may be more ideology-prone because that ideology is disguised as fact.

Barthes sees in public communication a number of features working towards meaning, or signification, at the level of connotation. There are our feelings, emotions and values; the cultural contexts which influence our perceptions and expectations; and these include our place in society, high, low, prestigious, ignored or neutral. At the same time we are influenced by an intertextual carousel of signifiers – flags, fashions, uniforms, brand names, logos; each, Barthes believes, supporting and reinforcing dominant discourses.

The level of myth

Barthes would have rejected Baudrillard's metaphor of the blizzard of signifiers. His descriptor – operating within and influencing the frames of discourse – was 'myth'. In *Introducing Communication Studies*[10] John Fiske wishes Barthes 'had not used this term because normally it refers to ideas that are false'. We use the expression 'It is a myth that ...', meaning there is little or no truth in an assertion.

'Myth' used in its general sense refers to the distant past when ancient peoples invented stories to illustrate truths, about the origins of life, for instance. Barthes' definition of myth is not entirely different from this because he sees society constantly 'inventing' stories that seek to explain socio-cultural-political truths. In perhaps his best-known book, *Mythologies*, Barthes begins by defining myth as 'a type of speech', 'a system of communication', but also 'a type of speech chosen by history'. Myths have power but they are characterized, like metaphors (which in a sense they are) by imprecision:

> Myth does not deny things, on the contrary, its function is to talk about them; simply it purifies them, it makes them innocent, it gives them a natural and eternal justification, it gives them a clarity which is not that of an explanation but that of statement of fact.

Barthes links myth with the ideology of the bourgeois society that reflects a social ordering which myth renders 'natural', a 'statement of fact', seemingly incontrovertible:

> In passing from history to nature, myth acts economically: it abolishes the complexity of human acts, it gives them the simplicity of essences ... it organises a world which is without contradictions because it is without depth, a world wide open and wallowing in the evident, it establishes a blissful clarity: things appear to mean something by themselves.

The Nazi party in 1930s Germany promoted the myth of Arian superiority. In the hands of the state propaganda machine, the myth helped forge the unity of the German nation: it restored national pride following Germany's defeat in the First World War (1914–18) and subsequent economic recession. Myths need only to be believed in, and acted upon, to become real. It took another world war to resist that myth and force it into retreat.

To carry conviction myth requires to be constantly *expressed* through public means of communication – the press, broadcasting, cinema, literature, art and architecture. Like everlasting life, myth is short on proof but not the power to win converts. Much has been made since the 1970s of Barthes' myth-theme. For our purposes here we need to acknowledge the role in myth-making of mass communication while at the same time noting that myths change, and are challenged by counter-myths.

Audience: the language of reception

At the beginning of this chapter I argued that the terminology of study has been fed by a number of tributaries. The 'semiological tributary' has been outlined here, joining the mainstream via a different route from transmission models attempting to explain communicative processes. With Roland Barthes we sense a transition. He works the territory of signs and codes but he relates the texts assembled out of signs to cultural and political contexts. If de Saussure was essentially a linguistic animal, Barthes is a cultural creature; and, as his interest in myth as a dominant mode of explaining contemporary society exemplifies, very much a *political* being.

The convergence of these streams of terminology is largely the result of the impact of cultural studies scholarship and its interest in the relationship between mass communication, audience and the exercise of power. Professor Stuart Hall, then working from the University of Birmingham Centre for Contemporary Culture Studies, assisted by a number of scholars whose research has contributed to our knowledge of media–audience exchange, has been prominent among those who have championed a multiple focus on media production, texts and reception.

In his article 'The determination of news photographs' in an important book of the 1970s, *The Manufacture of News*, edited by Stanley Cohen and Jock Young,[20] Hall introduces us to the term *preferred reading*. This duly acknowledges that a text is *read*, scrutinized, rather than merely glanced at. It also reminds us that a text may be visual (and aural) as well as verbal, and that many texts are combinations of what is seen and heard. In the case of photographs, captions add to the clues which direct our understanding.

The preferred reading springs from the intent of the transmitter of the work. In the case of a news photograph, the preferred reading is how the paper would like its audience to accept, or interpret its message; and the meaning of that reading, Hall believes, will rest largely with the traditional social and political values of the time. They will signal a degree of hegemonic influence if not of control; and that preferred reading will directly or indirectly connect with the interests of the power elite, prominent among whom are the media institutions.

Responses classified

Hall defines three modes of response to texts that audiences can take up – *dominant, negotiated* and *oppositional*. In the first, audiences respond to the discourse approvingly. They take on board the preferred reading more or less in its entirety. The negotiated response suggests a more questioning attitude. Perhaps the main parameters of the discourse are accepted but parts of it are greeted with queries and doubts. The oppositional response rejects the message altogether.

We can see the various responses at work in relation to a party political broadcast on TV. Supporters of Party X are likely to nod with approval; floating voters may be partly persuaded, but are tempted to say, 'Yes, but...' while supporters of Party Y may switch off, shout at the screen or go and put the kettle on.

Later commentators have been of the opinion that this and similar categorizations oversimplify the complex responses of audience. What has been termed a *popular* response describes inattention on the part of audience, where the preferred reading is not even glanced at, never mind read.

A useful term to link with preferred reading is that originating with the Italian scholar Umberto Eco. In 'Towards a semiotic inquiry into the television message' published in *Working Papers in Cultural Studies*, No. 3,[21] Eco refers to *aberrant decoding*. This means a 'wrong' or aberrant reading of the *work*, that is according to the preferred reading of the communicator or communicators. Deliberately, out of principle, partiality or cussedness; or by misperception, misunderstanding or accident, the work has been misread.

Yet it is only an aberrant decoding in that it runs counter to the communicator's purpose (unless, of course, the encoder, an artist, for instance, seeks deliberately to prompt multiple readings). When we as audience read texts we approach them with our life history in tow – what we agree with, what we disagree with, what we find acceptable and what we don't, and what we are used to. Accompanying us are our own values, our own stories.

This is what makes meaning so elusive and so volatile. The student of communication must cope with such uncertainty while at the same time sharpening the skills of analysis. There are plenty of answers, but no *right* answers, only some which carry more conviction than others (at a given time, among certain people in specific circumstances).

Our reading of texts confirms that meanings are not only elusive and volatile, they are multi-layered. Surface meanings may undergo modifications as we dig beyond the surface to deeper ones, while manifest meanings – those made clear and prominent – may conceal the latent meanings that are either hidden or have not yet taken shape. As we shall see in the next chapter, reception has been of central interest to those scholars we associate with investigating the *uses* to which audience put media products, and the *gratifications* audiences gain from those products. Their research findings are referred to as Uses and Gratifications Theory.

The response codes suggested by Hall are really only ratings of approval/disapproval, acceptance/rejection. Our responses as audience are more complex than that. They are *cognitive*, *affective* and *connative* in nature. In the cognitive mode we operate rationally, intellectually. We seek information, we analyze, we search for understanding. In our affective mode our feelings are at work, our senses, emotions and imaginations stimulated.

In the connative mode we are stimulated into behavioural responses, even if it is only feeling an echo in our limbs of the athletes' actions as we watch them on TV in the comfort of our armchair. Our responses are subconscious as well as conscious, are interactive, sometimes instant, sometimes delayed, indicating that research into audience response must be as interested in long-term as short-term media 'effects'.

The terminology of production and consumption is employed and examined in detail throughout the rest of this book. The identity and nature of audience is explored in Chapter 3, and in Chapter 5 the ever-expanding language of news theory is explained and discussed. In Chapter 10 we encounter the language of audience research and discover that the advertising industry has assembled a virtual dictionary of names for us, the consuming public.

Summary

This chapter provides an overview of the core language of communication and media study. It acknowledges the debt the 'subject' owes to other disciplines and recognizes that the terminology has been, as communication studies have evolved, fed by different 'tributaries' that have flowed into a common estuary.

The propagandist or mass manipulative model dominant during the period immediately prior to and during the Second World War became, in the 1950s and 1960s, matched and to a degree subsumed by the transmission model of message sending–receiving. This contributed terms stressing the instrumental nature of communication and indicating an essentially *linear* process.

Linguistics contributed a *structuralist* approach to analysis in which the structures and systems of language became a critical focus of attention. In a cultural studies sense these structures were viewed and examined within socio-cultural contexts. Semiology/Semiotics, an amalgam of theoretical perspectives, brought to the study of communication a vision of the nature of communication as an expression of culture and devices of analysis, encouraging us to penetrate the levels of meaning; warning us to note its complex and mercurial nature, constantly subject to contextual influences.

Terminology has followed scholarly preoccupations. Once meaning had been deemed the product of *negotiation*, between the creator of the text, the text itself and the consumer of the text, interest in the nature of that consumption process – what audience does with messages – became a prime interest of study.

Mass communication carries the dominant discourses of our time. Consequently there has been vigorous scrutiny of the operation of the mass media in relation to the exercise of power, by the powerful, over culture; and the actual or potential counterpower of audiences, nationally and globally, to negotiate meaning in the face of what Jean Baudrillard has termed a blizzard of signifiers.

We are at the point when we need to ask what 'sense' the audience makes of the 'blizzard' of information, of signs loaded with preferred readings which daily greet the public. How aberrantly do we decode the messages of mass communication; how aberrantly *can* we decode them? Chapter 3 sets out to address such questions.

KEY TERMS

transmission, transaction, negotiated   source, sender, transmitter, receiver, destination   message   channel   medium   feedback/cybernetics
semantic, psychological, fields of experience
encoder/decoder   sign   code   text   iconic, indexical, symbolic
paradigm/syntagm   metonym, metaphor   orders of signification:
denotation, connotation, myth   intertextuality   discourse
codes of reception: dominant, negotiated, oppositional, popular,
cognitive/affective/connative

Suggested activities

1. There are many variables that influence the nature of encoding and decoding – the education of the participants, for example. Make a list of IVs – intervening variables – which may modify the individual's reading of a newspaper, magazine or advertisement.

2. Collect a number of images featuring teenagers, past and present. Try a textual analysis of the way such young people present themselves to each other and to the world, and how in turn they are represented – in a favourable light or in an unfavourable light. Structure the analysis according to Barthes' orders of signification. Note the signifiers – those intended to be significant by the youths themselves, but also the way the photograph wishes us to 'read' the images. They say every picture tells a story: what kind of stories might such pictures illustrate?

3. Magazine or TV advertisements provide fertile ground for the analysis of signs. Take two contrasting ads and examine how the elements, the signifiers, are encoded to elicit the desired response. Note the use of words to reinforce the message.

   Do the ads make references to other sets of signs, or imply a knowledge on the part of the decoder of such signs? Do the ads appropriate aspects of culture (like using a famous painting or evocative situation)? What do you consider are the reasons for using such points of reference?

4. To remind you of how some of the major terms mentioned in this chapter interlink and interact, see Figure 2.5.

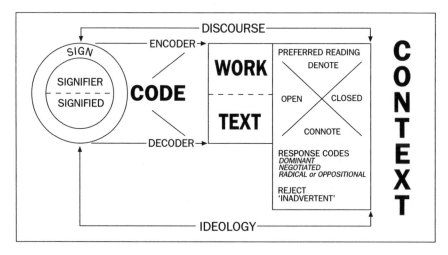

Figure 2.5 A semiological model

Without looking back at the chapter, ask yourself the following questions:

What is the difference between the signifier and the signified?
What is a code?

What does the term 'work' refer to?

What is meant by preferred reading?

What are denotation and connotation?

What are open/closed texts?

What do we mean by dominant, negotiated and oppositional reading?

If you had to insert the term 'myth' into the diagram, where would you put it?

Now read on

A useful starter, linking language and analytical concepts, is Judy Delin's *The Language of Everyday Life: An Introduction* (UK: Sage, 2000). Diane Macdonell examines in depth the nature and nurture of discourse in *Theories of Discourse* (UK: Blackwood, 1986). Further exploration in this area would benefit from a reading of *Feminism and Discourse: Psychological Perspectives*, edited by Sue Wilkinson and Celia Kitzinger (UK: Sage, 1995).

Also from Sage, published in 1996, is a two-volume work edited by Tuen A. van Dijk, *Discourse Studies: A Multidisciplinary Introduction* (volume 1 entitled *Discourse as Structure and Process*; volume 2, *Discourse as Social Interaction*). See also *Media Discourses* (UK/US, Open University Press, 2005) by Donald Matheson. Explanations of key concepts in cultural studies can be found in *The Media Communications Book* (UK: Arnold, 2001), edited by Oliver Boyd-Barrett, Chris Newbold and Hilde van den Buulck and in *Introducing Cultural Studies: Learning Through Practice* (US/UK: Sage, 2007) by David Walton. For a close focus on the deconstruction of texts, see Alan McKee's *Textual Analysis: A Beginner's Guide* (US/UK: Sage, 2003).

Notes

1. John Durham Peters, 'Tangled Legacies', an introduction to a symposium tracing the evolution of mass communication research published in the *Journal of Communication*, Summer 1996. The 'scholarly talent' chased out of Nazi Germany included academics of the Social Institute for Research, later called the Frankfurt School of Theorists, such as Theodor Adorno and Herbert Marcuse. The philosopher Hannah Arendt was another scholar who crossed the Atlantic and established a world reputation with her writings.

2. Claude Shannon and Warren Weaver, *Mathematical Theory of Communication* (US: University of Illinois Press, 1949).

3. Norbert Wiener, *Cybernetics: Or Control and Communication in the Animal and the Machine* (US: Wiley, 1949).

4. Wilbur Schramm, 'How communication works' in Schramm (ed.), *The Process and Effects of Mass Communication* (US: University of Illinois Press, 1954).

5. Harold Lasswell, 'The structure and function of ideas' in Lyman Bryson (ed.), *The Communication of Ideas* (US: Harper & Row, 1948).

6. George Gerbner, 'Towards a general model of communication' in *Audio-Visual Review*, 4 (1956).

7. Ferdinand de Saussure's *Course in General Linguistics* (UK: Fontana, 1974). The first edition, in French, was published after de Saussure's death. A translation by W. Baskin appeared in the USA in 1959. De Saussure is generally acknowledged as a founding-father of *Structuralism*.

8. C.S. Peirce, *Collected Papers 1931–58* (US: Harvard University Press, 1961).

9. C.K. Ogden and I.A. Richards, *The Meaning of Meaning. A Study of the Influence of Language upon Thought and of the Science of Symbolism* (UK: Routledge & Kegan Paul, 1923; 10th edition, 3rd impression, 1953).

10. John Fiske, *Introduction to Communication Studies* (UK: Methuen, 1982, second edition, 1990, reprinted 1995).

11. Edmund Leach, *Culture and Communication* (UK: Cambridge University Press, 1976).

12. Gillian Dyer, *Advertising as Communication* (UK: Methuen, 1982).

13. John Fiske, *Television Culture* (UK: Routledge, 1987).

14. Roland Barthes, *Mythologies* (UK: Granada/Paladin, 1973 and subsequent editions).

15. Erving Goffman, *The Presentation of Self in Everyday Life* (US: Anchor, 1959; UK: Penguin, 1971).

16. Madan Sarup, *Introductory Guide to Post-Structuralism and Postmodernism* (UK: Harvester Wheatsheaf, 1993).

17. Jean Baudrillard, a leading light in the so-termed Postmodern movement, has argued that truth, or meaning, are notions which can be dispensed with altogether as a result of the signifier, in the modern world of image-bombardment and image-recycling which audiences are subjected to, being detached from that which is signified. Basically he is saying that anything can be made to mean anything. See Nick Stevenson's chapter, 'Baudrillard's Blizzards', in Stevenson, *Culture: Social Theory and Mass Communication* (US/UK: Sage, 1995) where he is critical of 'Baudrillard's irrationalism'. Also, see Baudrillard's *Selected Writings* (UK: Polity Press, 1988) edited with an introduction by Mark Poster, and *Symbolic Exchange and Death* (US/UK: Sage, 1993), translated by Iain Hamilton Grant with an introduction by Mike Gane.

18. Robert Hodge and Gunther Kress, *Social Semiotics* (UK: Polity Press, 1988).

19. Gunther Kress, *Linguistic Processes in Sociocultural Practices* (UK: Edward Arnold, 1977).
20. Stanley Cohen and Jock Young (eds), *The Manufacture of News* (UK: Constable, 1973), one of the seminal texts of the period.
21. Aberrant decoding. Umberto Eco, 'Towards a semiotic enquiry into the television message' in *Working Papers in Cultural Studies* No. 3 (UK: Birmingham University Centre for Contemporary Culture Studies, 1972).

The Audience for Media: Perspectives on Use and Response

3

AIMS

➤ To examine the often conflicting perspectives on audience response to media communication.
➤ To relate the uses to which audiences put their experience of media to changing patterns of production and consumption.
➤ To provide a brief account of some of the most influential theories of audience response.
➤ By emphasizing the significance of the structures – in particular those of corporate ownership and control of media – out of which the media operate, to assess the potential for audience resistance to the shaping power of mediated communication.

The central part which audience analysis plays in media studies is identified in this chapter and the differences of opinion over the relative power of media and audience examined. Reference to the pessimistic views held by the Frankfurt School about the apparent powerlessness of audience is followed by summaries of Uses and Gratifications Theory, Dependency Theory and Cultivation Theory. Mention is made of emancipatory/repressive uses of media prior to media performance being discussed in Chapter 4.

Non-media influences – IVs (intervening variables), Significant Others – are discussed and active audience theory related to ethnographic perspectives which recognize diverse responses to media on the part of audience. The role played by the great corporations in all aspects of culture, and the implications for audience are given due note prior to further discussion in later chapters.

The advent and exponential growth of network communication is, of course, having a profound impact on traditional modes of transmission and reception, to the point, perhaps, when the concept of audience requires constant redefinition. Networking will be the focus of Chapter 9 so here, while acknowledging changes taking place practically by the minute, I hold to the view that pronouncements concerning the imminent demise of audience for mass communication are premature. 'Audience' may fast be becoming a myth, but that does not mean that audience as an icon of media faith has become disempowered.

Identifying the complexities of audience response to media

Proof of how and to what extent audience makes use of media is hard to pin down, but basically researchers are in the business of analyzing audience use and response with a view to measuring the *power* of media. Do the media have the power to shape, modify or alter our attitudes? Do they teach us ways of thinking; create consensus amongst us; stir in us alarm; make us more anxious, more security-minded? To what extent are they agents of change?

The trouble with seeking this Holy Grail of media studies is that our perceptions of audience response are difficult to disentangle from the actual facts of audience. Indeed while 'audience' is a word constantly being employed in media practice and media study, arriving at a definition is not unlike defining what 'friends' are: you may be able to count them, but people can be 'friends' in many different ways and to different degrees.

A person may be unmistakeably a member of an audience, in Seat 10 of Row G at the theatre. He or she may actually be seen to clap at the interval and the end of the play – but how can we be sure this member of the audience actually does appreciate, understand, enjoy the performance or is just relieved to have the thing come to an end so that there can be a timely retreat to the bar?

In *Audience Analysis*[1] Denis McQuail refers to 'the mystery of the audience'. The problem of definition is that 'a single and simple word is being applied to an increasingly diverse and complex reality, open to alternative and competing theoretical formulations'. In the Introduction to *Rethinking the Media Audience: The New Agenda*[2] Pertti Alasuutari states, 'there isn't really such a thing as the "audience" out there; one must bear in mind that audience is, most of all, a discursive construct produced by a particular analytical gaze'; in short, audience exists in the mind's eye of those seeking to define it for a particular purpose.

Having raised doubts about 'audience' as anything more than a general term for an infinite number of variations, we must nevertheless acknowledge that there have been plenty of people who consider they have a very good notion of what audiences are, what they 'do' with media and how media affect them, even to the point of predicting audience reaction. A glance at Appendix 1 (A Brief ABC of Perceived Media Effects) will show just how many and diverse theories there are, all attempting to catalogue the influences of media upon the public generally, and audiences specifically.

In relation to 'effect', the pendulum of great effect/little effect has swung backwards and forwards over the years. What one might term the 'down-play' school of analysts has not been convinced that the media have very much power over us. In *Watching People Watching Television*[3] Peter Collett and Roger Lamb summarize their findings from experiments they conducted in which people were filmed while watching television.

Selective attention

It seems that we as audience do an amazing number of things while watching TV, from eating dinner to knitting jumpers, from listening to music or doing homework to kissing and vacuum cleaning. On the face of it this would seem to indicate that, because we are not concentrating hard – at least some of the time – we are not being strongly influenced.

Collett and Lamb's research findings are interesting and perhaps more surprising to media professionals than to ordinary viewers. But do you have to be concentrating all the time to be influenced? There may be moments, perhaps when the news comes on, or a programme which seems especially relevant or fascinating, when the kissing has to stop and even the knit-one, purl-one has to be interrupted.

At the other end of the spectrum are commentators who have believed that the media exert a considerable influence over audience and this belief is usually linked with a view that the influence is often a bad one. For example, there are the pessimistic visions of the Frankfurt School of theorists, early exponents of *critical theory*; that is, critical of the downside effects on audience of mass communication.

The Institute for Social Research, founded in Frankfurt in 1923, became the meeting point of young Marxist intellectuals such as Theodor Adorno, Max Horkheimer and Herbert Marcuse.[4] When, in 1933, Hitler came to power in Germany, the Institute moved to New York (returning to Germany in 1949). Profoundly influenced by what they judged the successful brainwashing of the German people by Nazi propaganda, the Frankfurt scholars considered mass media a malevolent influence, a power against which the public was virtually defenceless.

They believed, and the belief continues to win adherents to this day, that modern culture has been commandeered by the moguls and institutions that own and control the media; that culture is in thrall to the requirements of company profits.

By being commercialized, culture has been somehow contaminated: the essential oppositional value of, for example, the arts has been in the view of the Frankfurt School appropriated and transformed into a tame, obedient and time-serving adjunct of big business.

Uses and gratifications theory

Several writers on media in the 1960s and 1970s, including Denis McQuail and Jay Blumler, countered the critical theory view that audiences were easily brainwashed, that they always believed what they were told and seemed, somehow, to have no mind of their own. What came to be termed Uses and Gratifications Theory shifted attention from the message-makers of the mass communication process to the message-receivers: the audience.

How, the dominant question became, did audiences *use* the media to *gratify* their needs? This gratifications approach worked from the premise that there is a plurality of responses to media messages; that people are capable of making up their own minds, accepting some messages, rejecting others, using the media for a variety of reasons and using them differently at different times. A crucial factor, given especial emphasis by Jay Blumler and Elihu Katz in *The Uses of Mass Communication*,[5] published in 1974, is the influence upon members of the audience of the cultural and social origins from which their needs arise.

Four categories of need

The nature of these needs had been examined a couple of years earlier in 'The television audience: a revised perspective', published in *Sociology of the Mass Media*.[6] Blumler, Denis McQuail and J. R. Brown posed four major categories of need that the media serve to gratify:

- Diversion;
- Personal relationships;
- Personal identity;
- Surveillance.

Diversion

We use the media to escape from routines, to get out from under problems, to ease worries or tensions. Of course a programme does not have to be escapist for us to escape. Crime series generally strive after realism; they address serious problems, but thankfully they are other people's problems. The key, we might remind ourselves, is the safety of our own living-room. If you are about to go to hospital *Casualty* might be worth giving a miss; while enjoyment of particularly brutal movies will be somewhat muted if the cinema is just around the corner from where muggings, knifings and shootings are regular occurrences.

Personal relationships

We often begin to know characters on TV as much as we know people in real life; in some cases more intimately. To watch soaps regularly is to enter worlds as closely detailed, as fully documented as our own. We observe many lives as they unfold and interact; we are granted knowledge of characters and situations that even the most gregarious individual in real life could scarcely match.

We are even permitted to know what is going to happen to characters before they know themselves, and before it happens. We are privileged through the magic of editing to observe developments that occur simultaneously. In short, we know more about *Neighbours*, the Australian soap, than we do about our own neighbours. This process of identification is given the term *parasocial interaction*.

As we watch, we may take note. These people have become our friends and neighbours. If not friends, they are our companions. What is more, they are our friends' and companions' friends and companions. We go to college or to work, and the topic of conversation may well be what has happened in last night's soap. If you are not a fan you may find yourself an outsider to the dominant social communication of the day. We weave our media experience into the pattern of our actual relationships: it serves as a 'coin of exchange' (rather more effectively than just talking about the weather).

Personal identity

We may be safe from the turbulences that buffet the lives of soap characters, but we may also share some of those troubles. We accept the convention that in soaps crises come thick and fast. We may look to soaps to help resolve our own crises: how do the characters resolve life's struggles – unemployment, illness, disappointment, loss of loved ones, rejection, falling out?

We explore life, test it out via characters in 'real life' fictional situations. We may look to reinforce our confidence about something: 'Yes, that's right, it's what I'd do' or 'Is that the sort of thing that I should be doing?' We may seek reassurance about our own lifestyle, our own decisions, even our own values. And we can be sure that despite all these speculative responses, they are being shared by millions of other people across the world.

Identification as adulation

In India an estimated 650 million people watched the 78 instalments of *Ramayan*, a tale of gods and goddesses, and such was the adulation bestowed by the population upon the writer-director, Sagar, and the cast, that people touched the floor in reverence when the TV soap came on; turned up in thousands to greet Sagar when he made a public appearance; and elected to Congress in 1991 the actress who played the goddess Sita.

Surveillance

Blumler, McQuail and Brown quote a viewer as saying, 'Television helps us make up our minds about things'. We use the media to gain information, to keep an eye on the world and to clarify what we think about it. At election times we may be in doubt as to who to vote for. Politicians come under particular public surveillance. In turn the public comes under the surveillance of pollsters eager to gauge voting intentions.

Along with other campaigns of persuasion, elections highlight both media performance and audience reaction. Which party is winning, getting its message over; how is this occurring? Elections are focal points for asking questions such as, which particular medium is most persuasive; which medium do people rely on for objectivity; do people believe what they are told?

Yet the very coherence of uses and gratifications theory, its neat tabulation of response following stimulus, raises queries concerning its tendency towards prescriptiveness. True, it liberates audience from being classified as a lumpen mass, and it offers us structures on which to base our investigations into audience reaction. Its problem is that it perceives *use* as largely a matter of individual rather than interactive or communal experience; not in the sense that it ignores interaction between individual and text, but in the interaction which goes on *outside* of the text.

For example, in a family of five watching TV each one may be 'using' the programme for a different purpose, to gratify a different need. Uses and gratifications theory can cope with that situation; but the crucial extra dimension is the influence of the interaction *between* members of the family and how this affects media use; for each interaction has its antecedent as each family has its own history.

With hindsight we can fault a number of theories of effect because of their over-concentration on one aspect of the communicative process to the neglect of others. The matter is well summarized by Tamar Liebes amd Elihu Katz in *The Export of Meaning: Cross-Cultural Readings of* Dallas:[7]

> As critical theorists became aware that they were studying texts without readers, gratifications researchers came to realize that they were studying readers without texts. The idea that readers, listeners, and viewers can bend the mass media to serve their own needs had gone so far [with the gratificationists] that almost any text – or indeed, no text at all – was found to serve functions such as social learning, reinforcing identity, lubricating interaction, providing escape etc. But it gradually became clear that these functions were too unspecified: these studies did not specify *what* was learned, which aspect of identity was reinforced, what was talked about, where one went to escape etc.

Nevertheless, the convergence on reader decodings of media placed audience at the centre of interest as never before, clearly implying as Liebes and Katz confirm 'an active reader – selecting, negotiating, interpreting, discussing or, in short, being involved'.

Lull's listing

In an article entitled 'The social uses of television' in the *Mass Communications Yearbook* of 1982 American researcher James Lull identified, and stressed the importance of, *social* uses of media.[8] His findings, based upon participant observation of families using TV, apply equally to the use of other media, such as reading newspapers. *Structural* use refers to the ways in which we frame the day, often ritualistically, by media use. We tune in to the early morning TV show or the news on the radio, we scan the morning paper with religious regularity. Structural use marks off – structures – our day.

Relational use matches personal relationships mentioned above. We use media as a currency of intercommunication, as an aid to companionship. We relate to each other by relating our experiences of media. *Affiliation* and *avoidance* suggest that at some times we want to get together with others, share watching a TV programme or join with others in going to the cinema (affiliation). At other times we wish to be left to ourselves (avoidance).

Social learning refers to our use of media in terms of behaviour, seeking for instance role models, guidance in the day-to-day performance of ourselves both as individuals and members of groups. *Competence/ dominance* is about control – who is competent to control the means of communication (programme the DVD recorder, for example) and who has the power to decide which programme is to be watched.

As more and more families multiply the amount of new-age media technology they possess, and as kids accumulate their own TVs, mobile phones, iPods and spend hours in front of computer screens, game-playing, texting their friends or exploring the possibilities of MySpace or YouTube, the 'family-together' element of Lull's typology of uses is the one most in danger of obsolescence – but only in Western contexts. In many parts of the world, such as the Middle East, families watching together is still the norm.

Issues of dependency

Observers of audience reaction to the mass media during the 1950s brooded over the power of the media to create in the public mind a degree of dependency; and Dependency Theory has had considerable influence on attitudes since that time.

If we are truly in the age of mass-produced information, well into Marshall McLuhan's definition of the world as an electronic global village, becoming *Netizens* as well as citizens, media analysts will be constantly attempting to measure the degree to which we, as audience, are dependent upon media for the information, and possibly guidance – clarification – with which to form our concepts of the world.

In an article 'A dependency model of mass media effects' in *Inter-Media: Interpersonal Communication in the Media*[9] published in 1979, two American researchers, Sandra J. Ball-Rokeach and Melvin DeFleur cite the following media role functions in relation to audience dependency:

- The resolution of ambiguity or uncertainty – but in the direction of closing down the range of interpretations of situations which audiences are able to make;
- Attitude formation;
- Agenda-setting;
- Expansion of people's system of beliefs;
- Clarification of values – but through the expression of value.

The media, the authors argued, are capable of activating audiences but they are also capable of *de*activating them. They believed that the fewer the *diverse* sources of information there are in the media world, the more likely the media will affect our thoughts, attitudes and how we behave. The authors were of the view that media influence will increase 'when there is a high degree of structural instability in the society due to conflict and change'.

Of course Ball-Rokeach and DeFleur were writing prior to the explosion of network communication which has clearly altered profoundly aspects of dependency. Yet it is perhaps too early to consign dependency theory to the museum of communicative antiquities. As audience, we may be distracted from mainstream mass communication by the allure of the blogosphere, but traditional media's power to command attention, define reality and drive ideology, remains formidable; and what rivalry there is faces its own struggle to have more than trivial impact; equally, to survive and prosper in face of mass media competition.

The emancipatory use of media

Ownership and control remain, and will continue to be, key elements in the relationship between the structures, the operative elements of communication, and *agency*, the response patterns of audience.[10] The relationship concerns the audience's potential to choose and make the best use for themselves of that choice – what Hans Magnus Enzensburger refers to as the *emancipatory use* of media.[11]

Enzensburger sees 'use' as being what enlightened or repressive media actually allow, make possible. In his view the nature of media output conditions the nature of reception, the emancipatory mode, for example, being characterized by *decentralization* of programme control.

Each receiver is conceived of as a potential transmitter as well as receiver. Audiences are mobilized as individual members of communities rather than treated as isolated individuals making up a mass. Emphasis is placed on feedback from audience and interaction through participation.

A process of political and cultural discourse is encouraged, of sharing as contrasted with indoctrination or depoliticization. Production rests in the hands of the community rather than being confined to specialists. Control resides in the public sphere rather than with property owners, bureaucracies, media barons or multinational corporations.

Repressive versus emancipatory use of media

Repressive	Emancipatory
Centrally controlled programme	Decentralized programme
Single transmitter, various receivers	Each receiver a potential transmitter
Immobilization of isolated individuals	Interaction from participants through feedback
Inactive behaviour of consumers	Politicizing (a learning process)
Production by specialists	Collective production
Control by owners or bureaucrats	Societal control through self-organization

Enzensburger's model is useful as a device for the analysis of media in all parts of the world. Of course it tells us only about structures of control and performance, for even under repressive political regimes – indeed *especially* under such regimes – the power of audiences to subvert texts, to read between the lines, must not be underestimated.

On the public stage – in the media, on the streets, through laws and policing – the repressive state may create a repressed public in part by means of a 'repressive' media. In the privacy of people's lives, however, in their families, in their work places, in their social meeting, aspirations to be released from repression are unlikely to have been extinguished.

Even a cursory glance at the Enzensburger model suggests that, as far as mass media are concerned, emancipation remains an ideal rather than a reality; yet applying that same model to agency as made possible by new media diversity does suggest a potentially more convincing 'fit'.

Cultivation theory

The fear that dependence on media has made for dependent people emerged from the large-scale researches conducted by scholars at the Annenburg School of Communication at the University of Pennsylvania into the ways that media, television in particular, influence our visions of reality, the world out there; the way TV *cultivates* those visions in certain directions.

For example, research has been directed at audience perceptions of the connection between the portrayal of violence on the screen and people's visualization of violence – the amount of it – in the real world. During the Annenberg researches stretching over three decades from the early 1970s, Professor George Gerbner and his team explored the links between heavy viewing of TV and perception-cultivation.

They detected a process occurring which they termed *mainstreaming*, whereby television creates a confluence, a coming-together, of attitudes. According to Gerbner, audiences use TV to confirm fears and prejudices about the 'way things are'. In their article 'The "mainstreaming" of America: violence profile number 11', published in the Summer 1980 edition of the *Journal of Communication*, Gerbner, Larry Cross, Michael Morgan and Nancy Signorielli write, 'in particular heavy viewing may serve to cultivate beliefs of otherwise disparate and divergent groups towards a more homogenous "mainstream" view'; and this view tends to shift, politically, towards the right.

TV's images 'cultivate the dominant tendencies of our culture's beliefs, ideologies and world views'. What occurs, according to the Annenburg research, is a *convergence* of people's concepts of reality to that which is portrayed on TV.

Blurred, blended and bent?

In an article entitled 'Television's populist brew: the three Bs' published in the Spring of 1987 in the American periodical *Etcetera*, Gerbner follows up the notion of convergence by identifying three things which happen to audiences for TV – at least in America. The three Bs are the stages through which mainstreaming occurs. First, television blurs traditional social distinctions; second, it blends otherwise divergent groups into the mainstream and thirdly it bends 'the mainstream in the direction of the medium's interests in profit, populist politics, and power'. Gerbner's research will be revisited in Chapter 10. See also Appendix 2, Screen Violence as Influence and Commodity: An Ongoing Debate.

These views tune in with Bad News forecasters generally. The findings of the Annenburg School gave some credence to the more sensationalist opinions of writers such as Neil Postman who, as the title of his best-known book suggests, believed that audiences are, by the ill-graces of TV, amusing themselves to death; brain-softened by too much mindless entertainment.[12]

In the Age of Showbusiness, writes Postman, focusing on the TV diet as served up in the United States, all discourses are rewritten in terms of entertainment. Substance, he believes, is translated into visual image to the detriment of political perspectives and the capacity of audience to seriously address the issues of our time. No student should miss reading Postman's *Amusing Ourselves to Death* for its own entertainment value; at the same time readers should be aware that the author's views are *impressions* – albeit very often convincing ones – rather than evidence drawn from research findings.

The resistive audience

Audiences can be a nuisance. They are prone to doing things that the communicators do not wish them to do; or, to be more precise, what the communicators wish audiences to do with their publications or their programmes is not always what audiences actually do with them. The editorial team of a newspaper would clearly wish readers to follow the paper's agenda, that is take note of the major stories of the day as signalled by the front-page headlines.

However, many readers may have their own agendas; their own priorities. They may turn straight to the sports page or the TV schedules. They ignore the *preferred reading* and by ignorance, cussedness or inadvertence, *aberrantly decode* the messages aimed at them.

It is this 'untidiness' of people, their unpredictability that helps substantiate claims that audiences are less vulnerable to media influence and more proactive consumers of media than some commentators believe; and we do well to take note of the cautionary words of Ien Ang in *Living Room Wars: Rethinking Media Audiences for a Postmodern World*[13] when she says that 'reality is always more complicated and diversified than our theories can represent', and this applies to the 'reality' of the relationship between audience and media.

Ang argues that television consumption is, 'despite its habitual character, dynamic rather than static, experiential rather than merely behavioural'. She goes on:

It is a complex practice that is more than just an activity that can be broken down into simple and objectively measured variables; it is full of casual, unforeseen and indeterminate moments which inevitably make for the ultimate unmeasurability of *how* television is used in the context of everyday life.

This is not to deny that audiences are influenced by what they read or see, but that measuring influence or effect is problematical. In any case, the effect may be positive as much as it might be negative, prompting us to respond in a similar way to any event in life, by agreeing, disagreeing, challenging, rejecting as well as accepting. We respond according to our differences – cultural, social, educational, professional; according to our age, gender, race and according to our tastes and values.

Denis McQuail in *Audience Analysis*,[1] supporting Ien Ang's position, says available research evidence serves to 'discredit the notion of the audience as a sitting "target" for media manipulation and influence'. Members of audience are capable of what McQuail terms a 'critical distance', operating through 'a strong, even determining influence of social and situational factors'. Context, as this book frequently stresses, is first base for understanding the workings of media and the responses of audience.

Persistent perceptions

The temptation is to dismiss 'effect' but this would be as risky as opting for the scenario that casts the mass media in the role of George Orwell's Big Brother in his novel, *1984*.[14] In a media-saturated world it continues to be legitimate practice to express concern about the influence of media on audience and to research into this influence.

One focus of attention among researchers has been the capacity of audiences to retain and recall mediated information. As long ago as 1986 media researcher Colin Berry in an article 'Message misunderstood' in the *Listener* of 27 November wrote:

> The evidence from both laboratory research and studies of audiences for live broadcasts, is sobering. People seem to be failing to grasp much of what it has been assumed is getting across … My colleagues and I found, in work supported by the IBA [Independent Broadcasting Authority], that knowledgeable, well-motivated grammar school sixth-formers retained little more than 60 per cent of news information they were tested on minutes after viewing.

The finding seems to accord with the assertions of Neil Postman and those of commentators who subscribe to the so-called *three-minute culture* hunch-theory, the one which fears that the attention span of the average member of audience is only three minutes (or less). My own response as a teacher to Berry's 60% finding would be that if this were achieved in class it would be pretty marvellous: my problem would be to discover which 60% that was (the beginning, middle or end) and whether that 60% was destined to last an hour, a day or for ever.

Plainly not all items of information have the same significance or salience. A news bulletin that carries items such as a major rail strike, the latest GATT talks in Venezuela and a skateboarding duck would probably have me scoring two out of three on a retention scale, particularly if I had to get to work by rail in the morning. As for the duck, I would probably remember its exploit for the rest of my life, without it having any significance for me other than its oddity.

Another researcher, Greg Philo, in *Seeing & Believing: The Influence of Television*,[15] has taken an opposing view to Berry. Referring to his own researches into people's responses to media coverage of the miners' strike in Britain (March 1984 to March 1985), Philo writes, 'I found that many details of news coverage (times, dates, places etc.) were not retained by the audience groups. But they could reproduce some of the key explanatory themes'. Once more, complexity: plainly audiences pay selective attention. Some researches indicate that we retain more about people and places than causes and consequences (see Note 16).

Consonance, dissonance

Media texts can be put to many uses; often, as we have seen, unpredictably: solace, identification, surveillance, escape, clarification, problem-resolution or just plain routine. Emphasis has been placed in analysis upon how these uses arise from cognitive and affective needs.

Sometimes we read, hear or watch things that upset or contradict our expectations. Our attitudes, beliefs and values might be suddenly given a jolt and we experience *cognitive dissonance*, a sense of uneasiness, of discomfort. How this operates in our responses to messages is analyzed by Leon Festinger in *A Theory of Dissonance*.[17] He argues that people will seek out information that confirms existing attitudes and views of the world. Such a shift replaces dissonance with congruence, a sense of at-oneness, of expectations and perceptions fulfilled.

Those elements of information or attitude that are in line with existing attitudes, beliefs and values, are selected in in order to deliver consonance, while those elements likely to increase dissonance are selected out, down-graded or simply rejected. What is happening is a process of reinforcement or confirmation.

If people are (cognitively and affectively) against blood sports, they are likely to derive strength for their standpoint by seeing an anti-blood sports documentary on television. Their position will have been reinforced. They may pay less attention to those speakers on the pro-gramme who might be in favour of blood sports.

In examining the nature and quality of the attention that audiences pay to the media we must realize such attention has to be won in the first place: no stimulus, no attention and therefore no response, affirma-tive or otherwise. Once alerted, our interest is in a state of readiness, to assess the content and presentation of media texts; to go with the flow of messages being received or to subject them to critical attention.

Ideally, our prior knowledge and experience assist us in maintaining an independent viewpoint with regard to media discourse; equally we are often vulnerable to the sheer professionalism and weight of the media's position on matters of fact and opinion.

The gun on the table

In *Seeing and Believing* Greg Philo reports on how he presented groups with a series of 12 pictures from the miners' strike. Picture 1 showed a shotgun on a table, its double barrels facing camera. When asked to write a news bulletin based on the pictures, the groups persistently opted to associate the gun with the striking miners. In fact, the gun belonged to a non-striking miner concerned to defend his family.

Philo's point, to which his experiments seem to add weight, is that media coverage of the strike had implanted in the minds of many a link between strikers and violence, a pairing which he considered had be-come a stereotype. Now it is true that the strike involved many scenes of violence, but this was meted out quite as much by the police as the striking miners. In other words the miners could have been visualized according to an alternative paradigm or classification, as *victims* of vio-lence rather than its perpetrators. Philo discovered that even people sympathetic to the strike were identifying the gun as the possession of a striking miner.

According to Philo's research the media, by their own selectivity and emphasis, have the potential to translate that take-up position to audi-ence perceptions of reality; of what 'really happened'. By a process of closure, of limiting audience access to a particular paradigm, the reading by audience of the event has been syntagmically defined: a story has been imposed through a particular arrangement of the 'facts'.

'Reality', the 'truth' of what happened, has been affirmed through the reiteration of certain patterns of interpretation (and not other patterns of interpretation), by a constant focus on some aspects of physical conflict (as opposed to others, not made explicit).

The media create pictures in the head – streams of signifiers linked by various forms of explanation, by newsreaders or reporters – that prompt expectations of similar pictures and explanations in the same mode. In this sense media can be said to act as agents of consonance. Having created a set of expectations, the media have then, by the *nature* of their coverage, induced a *self-fulfilling prophecy*:[18] striking miners, were, in this case, liable to violence. The pictures proved it and predicted it.

Frames of reference

In *The Export of Meaning*,[7] Liebes and Katz refer to two basic types of framing used by audiences for TV, the *referential* and the *critical*. The first connects media with reality: 'Viewers relate to characters as real people and in turn relate these real people to their own real worlds.' The second, the critical reading, goes beyond assessing the way TV reflects reality and examines how this is done:

> Referential readings are probably more emotionally involving; critical readings are more cognitive, dealing as they do with genres, dynamics of plot, thematics of the story, and so on.

The authors affirm that the status of audience 'has been upgraded regularly during the course of communications research':

> In short, the reader/listener/viewer ... has been granted critical ability. The legendary mental age of twelve, which American broadcasters are said to have attributed to their viewers, may, in fact, be wrong. Dumb genres may not necessarily imply dumb viewers.

From their research findings Liebes and Katz identify two main types of readers, those who remain almost exclusively in the referential frame and those who commute between the referential and the critical.

Significant others

It is vital to remind ourselves that audiences have their own *lived experience* to connect with the *mediated experience* derived from reading the papers, listening to radio, watching TV or going to the cinema; and an important part of that lived experience is other people who make up a context of influences equal to and often more powerful than those of the media themselves.

We use media referentially and critically in our everyday exchanges with others and in those exchanges media messages, media 'truths', media influences, undergo modification and reshaping at a personal or group level. The media are forces for social mediation but in turn they are themselves socially mediated.

When we are in doubt about something, in need of clarifying our views or our feelings, of sorting things in our minds, in the surveillance mode, we turn to *significant others* – parents, teachers, work colleagues, friends, and, in increasing numbers, we consult the Net, visit chat-rooms, hunt down websites for information, advice and links to others with a common interest. We scan weblogs for information and comment not always, and sometimes never, available through traditional media sites.

The crucial role of significant others in influencing opinions and attitudes was confirmed by research conducted as early as the 1940s. In *The People's Choice* published in 1944,[19] Paul Lazarsfeld and his colleagues described their study of public reaction to media coverage of the 1940 election in the United States. They found little evidence of the direct influence of the media; rather people seemed to be more influenced by face-to-face contact with others. Opinion leaders, the authors found, tended to be more interested in media, better informed, more up with events than average. Lazarsfeld identified a two-stage, or two-step, process of influence.

Step one took the message from media to audience; step two involved opinion leaders. The model was eventually developed into a *multi-step* process (see Figure 3.1), in which interaction, and reprocessing of the messages of media, undergo further mediation. The reader may wish to consider what adjustments might have to be made to the multi-step model in the light of the sheer volume and extent of mediated experience available today.

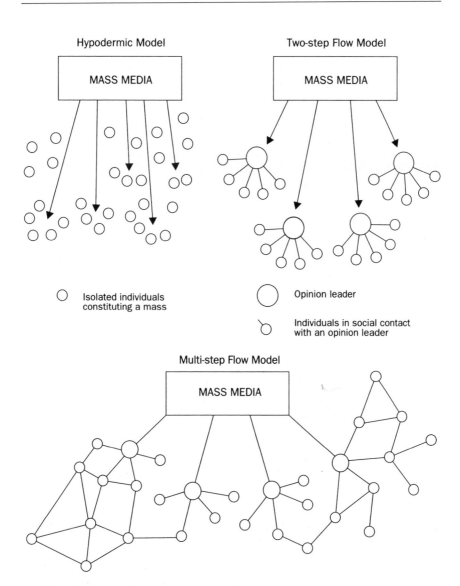

Figure 3.1 One-step, two-step, multi-step flow models of communication

From *Communication Models for the Study of Mass Communications* (UK: Longman, 5th impression 1998) by Denis McQuail and Sven Windahl. The one-step model suggests the hypodermic needle view of media's connection with audience – linear, one-way, powerful, each member of the audience perceived as an isolated individual. The two-step model acknowledges the role of significant others, opinion leaders as mediating factors between transmission and reception. The multi-step flow version acknowledges that once a media message has been received it may, at an interpersonal level, pass through any number of phases of summary, interpretation, re-formation and onward transmission.

In times of peril

There are occasions when even the opinions of the most independent significant other are dimmed or silenced. Wartime is often a case in point. Those who argue against war are usually drowned out by the cacophony of pro-war enthusiasm, when most media are likely to speak as one voice. On the national or world stage, opinion leaders may cease to count if their views run against dominant media opinion. Their words of caution or remonstrance may no longer be published or broadcast. Protest itself, and those who protest at war, are soon labelled by terms of insult designed to neutralize their message – 'pacifist', 'enemy within' and 'traitor'.

Individual opinion can rarely avoid being influenced by public opinion, the opinions that are dominant, that are asserted and which at least appear to represent a consensus. When public opinion is running in one direction it takes nerve and sometimes valour to express contrary opinions in public.

Yet however dangerous speaking out becomes, someone, somewhere, some time will risk it; not alone, perhaps, but given strength by the support of others, with a voice which may turn silence into voluble protest. In such circumstances, power often lies in groups, in the bonds that unite them, in their commonality of values. The group's solidarity provides individuals with the courage to resist, and sometimes against all odds.

Resistance through the small ads

Journalists on the Korean newspaper *Dong-A Ilbo* in October 1974 incurred the wrath of government by issuing a Declaration on Practising Freedom of the Press. They won widespread public support. In retribution the government forced advertisers to withdraw their ads from the paper, risking financial ruin. The public in turn responded by taking out thousands of small ads to counteract the advertisers' boycott. Even though the advertising ban led to the loss of 150 reporting and production jobs on *Dong-A Ilbo*, its sister paper the monthly *Sin Dong A* and the Dong-A Broadcasting system, a precedent had been set for future struggles for a free press.[20]

In democratic countries, it is no longer as easy as in the past to unite the public behind military enterprise. It may be premature to conclude that the events concerning the invasion of Iraq in 2003, based upon false claims that Saddam Hussein possessed, and intended to use, weapons of mass destruction, have created in the public a cynicism capable of resisting both the 'spin' of government and media.

The signs are both auspicious and depressing. It is true that a million protestors marched through London and many thousands through New York prior to the invasion of Iraq; it is also true that both in the United States and Britain the governments that had taken their countries to war were returned to power in general elections. Despite the horrendous carnage that has characterized the military occupation of Iraq, public sympathy has been muted, public attention all too easily distracted by a media impatient to 'move on' from stories of mayhem and disaster.

The 'project of self'

This is an appropriate moment to ask the question who 'we-as-audience' are and what 'we-as-audience-within-contexts' hope for ourselves as we encounter media communication. John B. Thompson in *The Media and Modernity: A Social Theory of the Media*[21] perceives individuals as being involved in a constant process of *self-formulation*. We are creating, as it were, the *project of self* and in this process we negotiate a route between our lived experience and mediated experience. It is a process which calls for, and stimulates, a condition of *reflexivity* – that is, constant scrutiny and adjustment of self in relation to experience, lived and mediated. Thompson writes:

> Individuals increasingly draw on mediated experienced to inform and refashion the project of self … The growing availability of mediated experience thus creates new opportunities, new options, new arenas for self-experimentation.

With new mediated experience 'we find ourselves drawn into issues and social relations which extend well beyond the locales of our day-to-day lives'. Potentially our concerns as well as our horizons are extended; and, to a degree, what happens to others outside of our spatial zones ceases to be 'none of our business'.

From being *localites* we are encouraged to become *cosmopolites*. Thompson says, 'We find ourselves not only to be observers of distant others and events, but also to be involved with them in some way'. Not infrequently, having been 'released from the locales of our daily lives', we 'find ourselves thrown into a world of baffling complexity'. In consequence, living in a mediated world 'carries with it a new burden of responsibility which weighs heavily on the shoulders of some'.

In working at the project of self, Thompson argues, we have choices:

> Some individuals turn away from [the 'claims and responsibilities stemming from mediated experience'] and seek to maintain their distance from events which are, in any case, distant from the pressing demands of their day-to-day lives. Others, stirred by media images and reports, throw themselves into campaigns on behalf of distant groups or causes.

Thompson sees this as 'relatively new as a widespread phenomenon'. Clearly it is of considerable significance in examining the active audience paradigm.

Ethnographic perspectives

An approach to the exploration of audience use of media that has had a considerable impact upon the way we decipher response comes under the heading of ethnographic research. Ethnography, according to dictionary definition, is the scientific description of the races of the earth; that is, it investigates the history, customs and lifestyles of people in their social, cultural and environmental contexts; and with express regard for the native point of view.

Ethnography seeks to understand the particular meaning-making processes of those it studies and it is characterized by its acknowledgement of the complexities of these processes. Research methods vary but generally favour *participant observation*, investigating cultural interaction from the inside; the researcher becoming a part of the activities he or she is studying.

I discuss ethnographic research into the audience for media in Chapter 10, but it is useful to mention here aspects of *cultural resistance* which ethnographic research has highlighted. There is general agreement amongst the observers of culture, society and politics that in most societies there is an eternal conflict between dominance and resistance. Only the degree of that conflict varies, for dominance never entirely dominates as resistance is never entirely extinguished.

We are familiar enough with such conflict in the work situation where dominance is typified by a company sacking its staff and its staff protesting by going on strike. Such resistance, being dramatic, is newsworthy, but ethnography reveals significant and often fascinating patterns of resistance in what has been termed the 'politics of pleasure'.

While critical theorists might view the Consumer Age as one in which dominant economic forces tantalize the public with consumer goodies, and by doing so ensure a docile population, other commentators have actually seen in consumption a potential area of resistance. At first sight, the public flocking to a sparkling new shopping mall is a clear indicator of corporate influence at work; an indexical sign of consumerism.

However, John Fiske has argued in his chapter 'Shopping for pleasure' in *Reading the Popular*[22] that 'the department store was the first public space legitimately available to women' and the 'fashionable commodities it offers provide a legitimated public identity and a means of participating in the ideology of progress'.

Resistance through style

Fiske contends that 'the meanings of commodities do not lie in themselves as objects, and are not determined by their conditions of production and distribution, but are produced finally by the way they are consumed'. Style and fashion have long had the potential for subversion of their preferred reading as two seminal works of the 1970s explained – *Resistance Through Rituals: Youth Subcultures in Post-war Britain* edited by Stuart Hall and Tony Jefferson in 1975[23] and Dick Hebdige's *Subculture: The Meaning of Style* first published in 1979.[24] Hebdige examines Punk culture and its expression in dress, body ornament and music and perceives them as forms of self-empowerment:

> The punks wore clothes which were sartorial equivalents of swear words, and they swore as they dressed – with calculated effect, lacing obscenities into record notes and publicity releases, interviews and love songs. Clothed in chaos, they produced Noise in the calmly orchestrated Crisis of everyday life in the 1970s.

'True,' the cynical might say, 'But where are the Punks now? And what difference did they make?' It has to be admitted, as Fiske readily agrees, that resistance from the bottom up is difficult and rarely likely to be effective beyond the micro-level of everyday life; that is, it does not alter the structures through which dominance is organized.

This is not, however, a reason to deny its existence as resistance or its potency. As Fiske cautions, 'Scholarship that neglects or devalues these practices seems to me to be guilty of a disrespect for the weak that is politically reprehensible'.

In Chapter 1 of *Reading the Popular*, 'Understanding popular culture', Fiske responds to the argument that resistive activity only operates at the micro-level by stating that such practices (what he calls *semiotic power*, of people forging their own meanings out of the signifiers available to them) 'may well act as a constant erosive force upon the macro, weakening the system from within so that it is more amenable to change at the structural level'.

Corporate intrusions

An author who has taken issue with the optimistic view of the resistive audience is Herbert Schiller. In *Culture Inc.* [25] Schiller launches a frontal assault upon the way big corporations have colonized culture in the USA and with it the communications industry. From that base, of cultural sponsorship and media control, direct and indirect, they have set out to further their transnational interests by enculturalization on a global scale.

According to Schiller, 'the Corporate voice, not surprisingly, is the loudest in the land' and it also rings around the world. He takes a cultivationist position, believing that consumerism 'as it is propagated by the transnational corporate system and carried to the four corners of the world by new information age technologies, now seems triumphant'.

Schiller talks of 'corporate pillaging of the national information supply' and the 'proprietory control of information'. Even the museum has been 'enlisted as a corporate instrument': history is adopted for corporate use through sponsorship. Thus eventually museums become reliant on corporate 'approval' of the past. The pressure upon them is to choose to record the kind of history that suits the corporate purpose.

Corporate power in the field of communication is so great, Schiller argues, that the active audience paradigm is called into question:

A great emphasis is given to the 'resistance', 'subversion', and 'empowerment' of the viewer. Where this resistance and subversion of the audience lead and what effects they have on the existing structure of power remain a mystery.

What Schiller is saying, in contrast to Fiske's more optimistic view, is that if resistance does not make inroads upon that which it is resisting then it cannot really be said to be resistance at all. It is not his intention to demean the notion of an active audience, rather to question just how, in the face of massive competition from the transnational Media Masters, people can hold on to and project their own agendas:

> It is not a matter of people being dupes, informational or cultural. It is that human beings are not equipped to deal with a pervasive disinformational system – administered from the command posts of social order – that assails the senses through all cultural forms and channels.

Schiller asserts that the ethnographic position tends to overlook *power-value*: if information is the central commodity of the modern age, then its 'possession' will be struggled over. Who dominates, counts:

> Theories that ignore the structure and locus of representational and definitional power and emphasize instead the individual's message transformational capacity present little threat to the maintenance of the established order.

With this position, Ien Ang concurs. In her chapter 'Global village and capitalist postmodernity' in *Communication Theory Today*,[26] she recognizes that 'the negotiations and resistances of the subordinate, confined as they are *within* the boundaries of the system, unsettle (but do not destroy) those boundaries'. What resistance does exist is inevitably fragmented. It would seem to be a matter, as Michel de Certeau has neatly put it in *The Practice of Everyday Life*,[27] of 'escaping without leaving'. De Certeau does, however, believe that audiences 'resignify' the meanings which are presented to them.

Schiller challenged

Before we give too much ground to Herbert Schiller's pessimistic views concerning empowerment and the resistive audience it needs to be pointed out that his arguments have been challenged by a number of authors, of whom John B. Thompson, already quoted in this chapter, is one. In *The Media and Modernity: A Social Theory of the Media*[21] Thompson says that 'even if one sympathizes with Schiller's broad theoretical view and his critical perspectives, there are many respects in which the argument is deeply unsatisfactory'. In particular, Thompson (in Chapter 5, 'The globalization of communication') counters Schiller's view that American cultural imperialism has wreaked havoc with indigenous cultures throughout the world, and that it is a seemingly unstoppable force.

Thompson is of the opinion that 'Schiller ... presents too uniform a view of American media culture ... and of its global dominance'. Even if we concede American cultural dominance in terms of media products and media reach, it does not follow that people are, as it were, 'subdued', especially as we have already established the point about the complexity of the audience and of the individuals who make up that audience.

Resistance through appropriation

It needs to be pointed out here that the project of self is not something that, once formed, remains constant. Equally we must recognize the possibility of a number of selves rather than one. In *Modernity: An Ethnographic Approach*,[28] Daniel Miller, investigating response-patterns to media in Trinidad, speaks of 'multifaceted forms of identity' demonstrated by the subjects of his research in their use of imported goods, ideas and traditions.

Two major events on the Trinidad calendar – Carnival and Christmas – exemplify the multifaceted nature of identity: Carnival elicits responses from participants that express individuality through differences of style and self-display. The consumerism as typified by fashion is *appropriated* for the purposes of imaginative expression. In contrast, Christmas, essentially an imported tradition, stresses other aspects of identity.

In examining the 'Trini' Christmas, Miller identifies a second cultivationist oversimplification concerning *individuality*. The belief that individuality has been defined and nurtured by mass communication and the consumerist ethic is firmly held by cultivationists and interpreted as having the effect of undermining community. Miller discovered that while Carnival is all about individuality (and is 'most effective' at countering the legacy of Trinidad's colonial past), the Trini Christmas emphasizes 'the cult of domesticity and respectability rather than of spontaneity and display' characteristic of Carnival. It was found that far from being individualizing, the process of consumption represented by Christmas is one of gradual but increasing incorporation of the community.

Miller argues from his research that 'the more knowledge people have of other societies, the more specific their own appears to be'. He says, 'I would argue there are positive consequences for the advent of mass consumption and plural cultures, wealth in materials and in imagery'.

He is saying 'lighten up': people will appropriate the messages and artefacts of consumerism and negotiate their own meanings.

He is confident that 'ethnographic exploration of the strategies by which contradiction can be lived and culture appropriated may have some advantages over an endless dialectic of nihilism'. Mediated experience does not take over from lived experience; it is absorbed, adopted and transformed by it.

Perchance to dream

A similar argument, that people are more appropriating than appropriated, is put by Colin Campbell in *The Romantic Ethic and the Spirit of Modern Consumerism*.[29] Campbell usefully positions modern trends in consumerist behaviour in a historical context, arguing that modern consumerism does not represent a radical break with the past.

For Campbell consumption is less about acquisition (thus fulfilling corporate targets) and more about providing the material for internalized fantasy or day-dreaming (thus fulfilling personal agendas). Such responses come under the heading of hedonistic behaviour; hedonism being the doctrine that pleasure is the highest good.

Campbell refers to 'the habit of covert day-dreaming'. He believes that 'individuals do not so much seek satisfaction from products, as pleasure from self-illusory experiences which they construct from their associated meanings'. This is a more complex reading of the relationship between product, image and consumer than that of the cultivationist position. Campbell argues:

> The visible practice of consumption is thus no more than a small part of a complex pattern of hedonistic behaviour, the majority of which occurs in the imagination of the consumer … the 'real' nature of products is of little consequence compared with what it is possible for consumers to believe about them, and hence their potential for 'dream material'.

The key to understanding 'modern consumerism and, indeed, modern hedonism generally,' writes Campbell is the 'dynamic interaction between illusion and reality'.

There is not the space here to do more than pay cursory attention to this affirmation of audience's power to consume the messages, images and artefacts of the dominant and appropriate them in imaginative ways, but the work of Campbell and other ethnographically-sympathetic commentators deserves to be analyzed alongside the work of those who fear the all-embracing influence of corporate culture. Campbell declares that 'no two individuals' experience of the product will be the same, just as no two people ever read the same novel'.

Domestication

Whether people are consuming cultural artefacts or actually producing them, a process of *domestication* seems to take place, of audiences making things their own. Research findings by Akiba A. Cohen and Itzhak Roeh published in *Mass Media Effects Across Cultures*[30] indicate that the domestication process – of adapting to local perceptions, needs and requirements – works along a continuum with strong intervention (or domestication) at one end and weak intervention at the other. While fiction can be located at or near the 'weak' intervention end of the continuum, imported news material is at the 'strong' end:

> From the start and throughout all stages of the process [of news broadcasting] there is organized and institutionalized mediation... Although the global market applies pressure toward uniformity, by providing the same material to all its subscribers, the individual stations press for parochialism in terms of language, culture, ideology, politics, and censorship.

Fictional content is subject to less intervention. Obviously imported programmes may have to be translated into the language of the home country and thus the scope for 'reconstruction' of texts is greater than if the original text were screened or broadcast in its original form. Selection and scheduling are other forms of intervention. 'However,' say Cohen and Roeh, referring to imported fiction programmes, 'the main burden of domestication... is borne by the recipients. Viewers interpret the messages according to their predispositions, schemas, repertoires, social locations, and life history.'

The authors believe researchers ought not to view effects from a strong–weak perspective but should take 'a rather "weak" culture-bound "circular" view, where the process of media production and consumption are necessarily contextualized':

> Message analysis, both in fiction and news, must be done in a dynamic contextual framework, taking into account the sociocultural ecology where meaning is produced and reproduced.

Global–local axis

Effects theory all too often seems to accentuate the negative, profer-
ring a cast of characters limited to exploiters and exploited. Yet there
are undoubted effects that deserve at least a cautious degree of celebration. One of these is posed by Thompson in Chapter 5 ('The
globalization of communication') of *The Media and Modernity: A Social
Theory of the Media*,[21] and which he terms *symbolic distancing*. Thompson
refers to the 'axis of globalized diffusion and localized appropriation'
which is a key feature of the electronic age.

He believes that as the 'globalization of communication becomes
more intensive and extensive, the significance of this axis increases'
(see Note 31 for reference to 'travelling cultures'). Consumers of media are both citizens of the world and of their locality: as the global
becomes available to us, we render it local – *domesticate* it, and very
often make meaning out of the global within our own lived contexts.
Thompson writes:

> As symbolic materials circulate on an ever-greater scale, locales be-
> come sites where, to an ever-increasing extent, globalized media
> products are received, interpreted and incorporated into the daily
> lives of individuals.

Consequently, '[t]he appropriation of symbolic materials enables individuals to take some distance from the conditions of their day-to-day
lives – not literally but symbolically, imaginatively, vicariously'.

Thompson refers to work done by James Lull in his study of the impact of TV in China.[32] For many of the Chinese interviewed by Lull in
Shanghai, Beijing, Guangzhou and Xian symbolic distancing was a critical aspect of their lives. Television made available to them new vistas,
lifestyles and ways of thinking. Lull quotes a 58-year old accountant
from Shanghai: 'TV gives us a model of the rest of the world.'

Such images of how other people live, says Thompson, 'constitute
a resource for individuals to think critically about their own lives and
life conditions'. The author does not pretend that this or other forms of
appropriation do not have their own problems. Nor does he deny that
they can work as much against as for individuals and communities.

Localized appropriation of globalized media products is plainly a
'source of tension and political conflict'. However, Thompson seeks
to stress that 'given the contextualized character of appropriation, one
cannot determine in advance which aspect (or aspects) will be involved
in the reception of a particular symbolic form'.

The fragmented audience and problems of measurement

In the chapter 'Tracking the audience' in *Questioning the Media: A Critical Introduction*,[33] Oscar Gandy Jr remarks how the fragmentation of audience for media, rendered possible by new technology, has resulted in a desperation among programme-makers that has led to two strategies aimed at survival. These Gandy identifies as *rationalization*, that is 'the pursuit of efficiency in the production, distribution, and sale of goods and services'; and *surveillance* which 'provides the information necessary for greater control'. Increasingly, says Gandy, 'the surveillance of audiences resembles police surveillance of suspected criminals' and people are less and less aware that their behaviour as audience is being monitored.

Gandy expresses a widely held concern:

> Perhaps the greatest threat these computer-based systems for audience assessment represent is their potential to worsen the balance of power between individuals and bureacratic organizations. Personal information streams out of the lives of individuals much like blood out of an open wound, and it collects in pools in the computers of corporations and government bureaucracies.

Resistance is, in Gandy's view, 'almost nonexistent, and what little there is may be seen as passive and defeatist'. While recognizing that a 'nearly invisible minority simply refuses to enter the system of records, giving up the convenience of credit cards and acquiring goods and services under assumed names or aliases', Gandy fears that 'to escape the information net means to become a nonperson'. It is a high risk, for one 'maintains privacy through the loss of all else'. For further discussion on surveillance, related to the Internet, see Chapter 9.

Desperately seeking…

Ien Ang in her book *Desperately Seeking the Audience*[34] examines the penchant of audience to resist being categorized, pinned down, subjugated to segmentation by those agents of dominance who dream of an age when audience, its composition and its tastes, is cut and dried. The author's doubts concerning audience definition and the measurement of audience response in her later work, *Living Room Wars*,[13] have already been referred to.

In *Desperately Seeking the Audience*, Ang details the work of the ethnographic investigator operating in micro-situations where attention is trained upon family habits and interactions of which television-viewing is an integral part. She points out that close scrutiny by ethnographic (qualitative) analysis often produces findings at odds with the (quantitative) findings of the media industry itself. The hunger for certainty about audience – about what produces healthy ratings – rarely derives much sustenance or help from ethnographers whose findings are as likely to subvert theory as reinforce it.

Watching television, Ang states, 'is always behaviour-in-context'. If this is the case, there is a 'fundamental undecidability' about reliable audience measurement. Where the media industry is desperately in search of consistency and therefore of predictability, the true condition is variability.

Ang believes that in the process of audience measurement two kinds of knowledge are in operation. The first she defines as *institutional*. This is based upon the desired goals of prediction and control. The more the media institutions can predict audience response, the more they can control it; and the more they can control it, the more successful media production becomes. Appearing under the heading 'institutional knowledge' is the classification *audience-as-consumers* and the dominant discourse is that of the marketplace.

In contrast, *ethnographic* knowledge is concerned with what Ang terms 'actual audience' contrasted with the 'television audience' as defined under institutional knowledge. Ethnographic knowledge is anchored in the understanding of the infinite variability of uses and responses within contexts which are less representative of the marketplace than of the community. The ethnographic paradigm gives priority to *audience-as-citizens*.

These 'twin peaks' of knowledge, institutional and ethnographic, also represent different philosophies of communication, the one treating knowledge as a commodity, essentially a process of transmission, the other as a public service, a process of cultural exchange. The transmission model accentuates the role of sender; the exchange model the role of receiver and the complexities that involves.

A 'nonsensical category'?

Because Ang sees TV viewing as 'a complex and dynamic cultural process, fully integrated into the messiness of everyday life, and always specific in its meanings and impacts', she concludes that '"television audience" is a nonsensical category'. Such a conclusion could well provoke a crisis in audience measurement if it were to be taken to heart outside academic cloisters. If there was no more categorization of audiences, no more measurement of this segment or that, there would be no more ratings, no more ratings wars and the industry would plunge into chaos and quandary as to who was watching, when, how and to what effect. Fortunately for the industry, it takes more than facts to destroy a myth.

The audience measurement industry has enough problems on its hands currently at operational levels for worries about philosophical justification to be seriously engaged. These problems arise from audience *fragmentation* brought about by new technology; video, cable and satellite have segmented audiences; as the use of the remote control has facilitated zipping, zapping and grazing. The advent of digitization has made channel scarcity a thing of the past, rendering it more and more difficult to actually define the nature of media consumption and effect.

Most importantly, the dramatic growth of network communication has forced research and analysis into major revisionary mode, a theme taken up again in Chapters 9 and 11. Throughout, in this overview of audience and the power of mass communication to exert influence, the keynote has been caution. Perceptions are more in evidence than proof.

It is advisable, then, to heed the words of Brian McNair in *News and Journalism in the UK*:[35] 'The effects issue is one of the most difficult and contentious in media studies, despite the vast resources and energies which have been expended in trying to resolve it.'

Summary

This chapter has focused on problems of audience definition from the point of view of how, exactly, audiences make use of mass communication. Scholarly opinion about the degree of influence the media have over the nature of audience response has been seen to resemble the swing of a pendulum between perceptions of strong influence and weak influence.

Each 'school of thought' says as much about itself, the situation in which its perceptions are formed and its knowledge assembled, as it does about audience. The Frankfurt School was influenced by the propaganda of Nazi Germany which so effectively won the hearts and minds of the German nation. In America where it is a seemingly unchallenged maxim that the population turns to TV and not the press for its information, and for guidance in one form or another, researchers have acknowledged audience dependency, but further, an encultural-izing process – Gerbner's notion of *mainstreaming* for example. The emancipatory use of media, in contrast to the repressive use, is referred to here, anticipating further discussion about media performance in Chapter 4 and network communication in Chapter 9.

Researchers of the ethnographic school, penetrating the contexts – in particular, of the family – in which media are consumed have expressed optimistic views concerning the active audience and have produced convincing evidence that *negotiated* responses, if not opposi-tional or radical ones, are commonplace. Cultural resistance is possible, at least at the micro-level and sustained resistance at this level could influence the macro-domain.

Other commentators, particularly American scholars, have raised their eyes from the micro-level of consumption to the macro-level of production and control, and they are less sanguine about the ability of audiences to 'hold their own' in the face of corporate influence over and extensive ownership of the means of mass communication nation-ally and globally. The ethnographic response is that even in the face of corporate media dominance, audiences subject imported media texts to appropriation and domestication.

To obtain an overview of the many theories of media effect, please see Appendix 1, An ABC of Perceived Media Effects.

KEY TERMS

uses and gratifications theory   structures/agency   cognitive and affective
dependency theory   emancipatory/repressive use of media
cultivation theory   mainstreaming   referential/critical reading
significant others   ethnographic analysis   self-formulation   project of self
reflexivity   localites/cosmopolites   semiotic power
audience-as-consumers/audience-as-citizens   active-audience paradigm
empowerment   corporate intrusion   appropriation   domestication
symbolic distancing

Suggested activities

1. For discussion:
   (a) What recent TV shows or series have stimulated public in-terest? Identify the qualities that have made them stand out in terms of the way they have provoked interaction, that is people talking about them?

(b) 'One *is* what one consumes'. Is it possible to read a person's 'project of self' from the way he or she makes use of media?

(c) To what extent are newspaper reading, TV-watching, cinema-going and using the mobile phone classifiable as *rituals* of everyday life?

(d) Which members or sections of an audience would you consider are most resistant to the influences of media, and which the most vulnerable to such influences?

2. Conduct a brief survey into user habits within group contexts – in a family, for example, or a group of students/workers living together.

You are interested in *how* a newspaper or TV set is used rather than what is read or watched. Who gains first access; who scans the paper but does not read it fully; who hogs the paper? What are the patterns of TV viewing and what activities continue while the set is on? Is there a gender/age/class difference in the ways papers or programmes are used?

3. Ask permission to do some spot-research at a video/DVD-hire shop. Choose a busy period and note who borrows what (in terms of age and gender). Which are the most popular films in each of the categories of viewer you have selected? Supplement your findings with an interview with a counter assistant: do punters pick and choose or are they influenced by recent publicity? Ask about the role of significant others.

4. Classify the ways in which members of the public appear on TV programmes. Perhaps using a focus group, probe reactions to the involvement of members of the public in chat shows or reality TV programmes in terms of their power to manipulate and exploit.

Now read on

For readability as well as good sense and enlightenment Ien Ang's *Desperately Seeking the Audience*[33] is a priority, along with Denis McQuail's *Audience Analysis*;[1] but there are many fascinating volumes investigating different aspects of audience in its consumption of media.

Titles provide useful signposting, such as *Audience Making: How the Media Create the Audience* (US: Sage, 1994), edited by James S. Ettema and D. Charles Whitney, *Measuring Media Audiences* (UK: Routledge 1994), edited by Raymond Kent, *Audiences: A Sociological Theory of Performance and Imagination* (UK: Sage, 1998) by Nicholas Abercrombie and Brian Luckhurst, *Rethinking the Media Audience*, edited by

Pertii Alasuutari (1999) and Andrew Ruddock's *Understanding Media Audiences: Theory and Method* (2000), both from Sage. From the Open University, see *Critical Readings: Media and Audiences* (UK: 2003), edited by Virginia Nightingale and Karen Ross and from Palgrave Macmillan, *Media Consumption and Public Engagement* (UK: 2007) by Nick Coudry, Sonia Livingstone and Tim Markham.

Inevitably because of its dominance over other mass media TV takes prime focus in volumes on audience response and participation. A good example is *Talk on Television: Audience Participation and Public* edited by Sonia Livingstone and Peter Lunt (UK: Routledge, 1994). Family viewing has attracted particular attention – see David Morley's *Family Television: Cultural Power and Domestic Leisure* (UK: British Film Institute, 1980); and his later work, *Television, Audience & Cultural Studies* (UK: Routledge, 1992). See also John Tullock's *Watching the TV Audience: Cultural Theories and Methods* (UK: Arnold, 2000), in particular, Chapter 5, 'From pleasure to risk: revisiting "television violence"'.

Video Playtime: The Gendering of Leisure Technology by Ann Gray (UK: Routledge, 1992) explores the ways in which gender finds definition in the use of technology while Margaret Gallagher seeks to assess the potential for women's groups to fulfil the active audience scenario in widely varied media contexts, in *Gender Setting: New Media Agendas for Monitoring and Advocacy* (UK: Zed Books, 2001).

For a thorough but succinct account of theory, perspectives and findings, there can be no more useful source than *McQuail's Mass Communication Theory* (UK: Sage, 5th edition, 2005), by Denis McQuail. An adventurous college library will already have stocked the four-volume *Mass Communication* edited by McQuail and published by Sage in 2006.

Excellent advice on researching audience is provided by Ina Bertrand and Peter Hughes' *Media Research Methods: Audiences, Institutions, Texts* (UK: Palgrave Macmillan, 2005) and *Practical Research Methods for Media and Cultural Studies: Making People Count* (UK: Edinburgh University Press, 2006) by Maire Messenger Davies and Nick Mosdell.

Notes

1. Denis McQuail, *Audience Analysis* (US/UK: Sage, 1997).
2. Pertii Alasuutari (ed.), *Rethinking the Media Audience: The New Agenda* (UK: Sage, 1999).
3. Peter Collett and Roger Lamb, *Watching People Watching Television* (UK: IBA Report, 1985).

4. Frankfurt school of theorists. When the Institute for Social Research returned from New York to Frankfurt in 1949, Herbert Marcuse stayed in America, writing a number of influential books, the best known of which is *One Dimensional Man* (UK: Sphere Books, 1968). See *The Frankfurt School: Its History, Theories and Political Significance* (UK: Polity Paperback, 1995) by Rolf Wiggershaus, translated by Michael Robertson.

5. Jay Blumler and Elihu Katz, *The Uses of Mass Communication* (US: Sage, 1974).

6. Denis McQuail, Jay Blumler and J.R. Brown (eds), *Sociology of the Mass Media* (UK: Penguin Books, 1972).

7. Tamar Liebes and Elihu Katz, *The Export of Meaning: Cross-Cultural Readings of* Dallas (US: Oxford University Press, 1990; UK: Polity, 1993).

8. James Lull, 'The social uses of television' in *Mass Communication Yearbook* (US: Sage, 1982) edited by D.C. Whitney *et al.*

9. Sandra J. Ball-Rokeach and Melvin DeFleur, 'A dependency model of mass media effect' in G. Gumpert and R. Cathcart (eds), *Inter-Media: Interpersonal Communication in the Media* (US: Oxford University Press, 1979).

10. In *Cultural Consumption and Everyday Life* (UK: Arnold, 1999), David Storey refers to 'structures' – the production side of media – and 'agency' – the consuming side, that is 'the capacity, within structures inherited from the past and lived in the present, to act in a purposive and reflexive manner; to act in a way that at times may modify what is inherited and that which is lived'.

11. Hans Magnus Enzensburger, 'Constituents of a theory of the media' in Denis McQuail (ed.), *Sociology of Mass Communication* (UK: Penguin Books, 1972). Enzensburger's chart is taken from Sven Windahl, Benno Signitzer and Jean T. Olson's *Using Communication Theory: An Introduction to Planned Communication* (UK: Sage, 1992), itself derived from Enzensburger's 'Bankasten zu einer Theorie der Medien' in D. Prokop (ed.), *Medienforschung* Vol. 2 (Frankfurt: Fischer, 1985).

12. Neil Postman, *Amusing Ourselves to Death* (UK: Methuen, 1986).

13. Ien Ang, *Living Room Wars: Rethinking Media Audiences for a Postmodern World* (US/UK: Routledge, 1996).

14. Big Brother in George Orwell's *1984* was the disembodied yet all-seeing, all-powerful, all-manipulative Party Leader, never seen in person, his face on the TV screens that dominate the homes and public spaces of Oceania – 'black haired, black moustachio'ed, full of power and mysterious calm, and so vast that it almost filled up the screen'. Channel 4's amazingly popular Big Brother series was appropriately named, as the 'volunteers' in the Big Brother House subject themselves to 24-hour on-screen surveillance. The difference seems to be that, while Orwell's characters lived in terror of surveillance, today's victims covet and relish it.

15. Greg Philo, *Seeing and Believing: The Influence of Television* (UK: Routledge, 1990).

16. Retention concerning people and places is stronger than recall of causes and consequences according to researches conducted by O. Findake and B. Hoijer summarized in 'Some Characteristics of News Memory Comprehension' in *Journal of Electronic and Broadcasting Media*, Vol. 29, No. 5 (1985).

17. L.A. Festinger, *A Theory of Dissonance* (US: Row Pearson, 1957).

18. Self-fulfilling prophecy. Occurs when the act of predicting certain behaviour helps cause that behaviour to take place. *Labelling* people as educational failures, for example, can be the first step in prompting a self-fulfilling failure. At the *intrapersonal* level of communication we, as individuals, decide whether we are going to conform to, or reject, the expectations about us of others; and much depends upon the influence over us of *significant others*; and their power to impose their judgements upon us. The self-fulfilling prophecy has much to do with *negative* feedback, for few of us are so confident that criticism, especially if it is sustained, does not have impact on our self-view. This condition also applies to groups within society and societies within cultures.

19. Paul Lazarsfeld *et al.*, *The People's Choice* (US: Duell, Sloan & Pearce, 1944).

20. For an account of media in Korea, see 'Modernization, globalization, and the power of the state: the Korean media' by Myung-Jin Park, Chang-Nam Kim and Byung-Woo Sohn in *De-Westernizing Media Studies* (UK/US: Routledge, 2000), edited by James Curran and Myung-Jin Park.

21. John B. Thompson, *The Media and Modernity: A Social Theory of the Media* (UK: Polity, 1995).

22. John Fiske, *Reading the Popular* (US: Unwin Hyman, 1989).

23. *Resistance Through Rituals: Youth Sub-Cultures in Post-War Britain* (UK: Methuen, 1975), edited by Stuart Hall and Tony Jefferson.

24. Dick Hebdige, *Subculture: The Meaning of Style* (UK: Methuen, 1979; Routledge, 2002).

25. Herbert J. Schiller, *Culture Inc. The Corporate Takeover of Public Expression* (US: Oxford University Press, 1989).

26. Ien Ang, 'Global village and capitalist postmodernity' in David Crowley and David Mitchell (eds), *Communication Theory Today* (UK: Polity, 1994).

27. Michel de Certeau, *The Practice of Everyday Life*, translated by Steven Rendell (US: University of California Press, 1984).

28. Daniel Miller, *Modernity: An Ethnographic Approach. Dualism and Mass Consumption in Trinidad* (US: Berg, 1994). For further evidence of appropriation or *domestication* of imported texts, see Miller's examination of how Trinidad appropriated for its own cultural requirements the American-made soap *The Young and the Restless*, in 'The Young and the

Restless in Trinidad: a case of the local and the global in mass consumption' published in *Consuming Technologies: Media and Information in Domestic Spaces* (UK: Routledge, 1992), edited by Roger Silverstone and Eric Hirsch.

29. Colin Campbell, *The Romantic Ethic and the Spirit of Modern Consumerism* (UK: Blackwell, 1987).

30. Akiba A. Cohen and Itshak Roeh, 'When fiction and news cross over the border: notes on differential readings and effects' in Felipe Korezenny and Stella Ting-Toomey (eds), *Mass Media Effects Across Cultures* (US: Sage, 1992).

31. On the theme of 'globalized diffusion and localized appropriation' see also James Gifford's chapter, 'Travelling cultures' in *Culture Studies* (US: Routledge, 1992) edited by Laurence Grossman, Cary Nelson and Paula A. Treichler. Gifford writes of cultural *hybridity* brought about by the movement – the journeying – of peoples and of cultural expression. Gifford speaks of 'dwelling-in-travel' and believes, 'We are seeing the emergence of new maps [of cultural analysis]: borderland cultural areas, populated by strong diasporic ethnicities unevenly assimilated to dominant nation states'. His advice to the researcher is to focus 'on any culture's farther range of travel while *also* looking at its centres, its villages, its intensive field states'. The notion of *travelling by media* is hinted at by Gifford and taken up by Josefa Loshitzky in 'Travelling culture/travelling television' in *Screen*, Winter 1996.

32. James Lull, *China Turned On: Television, Reform, and Resistance* (UK: Routledge, 1991).

33. Oscar Gandy Jr, 'Tracking the audience' in *Questioning Media: A Critical Introduction* (US: Sage, 1990) edited by John Downing, Ali Mohammadi and Annabelle Srebemy-Mohammadi.

34. Ien Ang, *Desperately Seeking the Audience* (UK: Routledge,1991).

35. Brian McNair, *News and Journalism in the UK* (UK: Routledge, 3rd edition, 1999).

Media in Society: Purpose and Performance

AIMS

➤ To familiarize the reader with three key models relating to purposes or functions of media in society.
➤ To emphasize the fast-changing contexts, nationally and globally, in which modern media operate.
➤ To outline a number of traditional normative theories of media and to focus on crucial roles played by media in society.
➤ To examine principles of media performance.

The more prominently the media have featured in the life of a people the sharper has been the debate on what purposes the media ought to serve in society. In 19th century Britain the press were sufficiently influential to earn the title 'Fourth Estate', a part of the power structure alongside government, the church and the law. This chapter attempts a survey of a number of definitions of the purpose and role of the media, starting with three broad models of media function – *propagandist, commercial laissez-faire* and *public service.* The shift from public to private, aided and abetted by imperatives brought about by new technology, is sketched in to remind us of the rapidity of change and the volatility of definitions. Then six normative theories arising out of specific cultural/political contexts are discussed.

A core feature common to all media – their relationship with centres of political and economic power – leads us to examine the part media play in reality-definition and as agents of social control. Ultimately how the media are constituted, as private or public enterprises, governs how they perform and what principles inspire practice.

Macro-level issues such as diversity, access and plurality are examined, and micro-level criteria such as objectivity, impartiality and balance. The notion of equality as a basic value guiding performance is broached. Finally perspectives are offered on the roles mass media play as global matters increasingly affect our lives.

Propaganda, profit, power

Lord Beaverbrook (1879–1964), born in Canada but one of the most successful British media barons, owner of *The Daily Express* and founder of the *Sunday Express*, claimed that he ran his newspapers 'purely for propaganda, and with no other purpose'. That was honest, but not wholly correct. Beaverbrook was too good an entrepreneur, and too good a journalist, ever to forget that readers seek to be entertained as well as informed. The best pills come sugar-coated, though they are no less 'medicinal' for that. Beaverbrook's idea of the purpose of mass media has been classified as the *propaganda* or mass manipulative model.

We generally associate the term propaganda with brazen strategies of persuasion, with information that is distorted, partisan or untrue. The noun (propaganda) has, then, got a bad name; but the verb (to propagate) is something no society can do without. The spread of opinions, attitudes, beliefs, and the advocacy of change or reform, have been key elements of communication throughout history.

Radical newspapers of the 19th century in demanding economic, industrial and parliamentary reform were functioning in the propagandist mode. The *Poor Man's Guardian* (1831–35) carried on its title-head

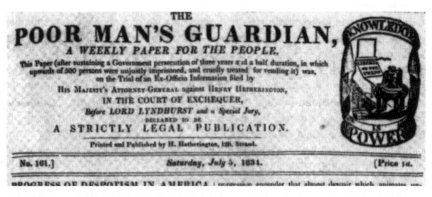

Figure 4.1 'KNOWLEDGE IS POWER'
Edited by James Bronterre O'Brien and published by Henry Hetherington, the *Poor Man's Guardian* was one of many radical 19th century newspapers, most of them equally short-lived, which defied authority's attempts to suppress them. Stamp duty was levied on every paper printed and those who evaded this and other taxes on knowledge were liable to lengthy prison sentences. The police gave a sovereign for every vendor of unstamped papers convicted.

the logo of a printing press framed by the words 'KNOWLEDGE IS POWER' (Figure 4.1). Governments, the power elite of society and those with interests or causes to advocate have concurred with that view, recognizing that knowledge is only power if it can be controlled, diffused or restricted as considered appropriate. In this sense, *not* telling is as significant as telling.

The taste of power

The Radicals were rarely able to sustain their crusade for causes unpopular with government because rival newspapers were concentrating on an alternative, *populist-profit* mode. Press barons such as Lord Northcliffe (1865–1922) in Britain and William Randolph Hearst (1863–1951) in America were no less propagandist in approach, but they were also businessmen, each with a flair for exploiting popular taste. As one of Hearst's editors said, 'What we're after is the "Gee-Whizz" effect'.

What came to be known in the States as the Yellow Press focused on sensationalism – scandals, corruption, murders. Serious news and comment were downsized if not excluded altogether. For most of the press barons the allure of power – the power to influence society and those who governed it – was a decisive factor in the content and style of their publications.

Newspapers were weapons of influence with which the press barons could attempt to impose their views on the widest possible readership. Such barons also delighted in the prestige their newspapers gained for them along the corridors of power. Yet prestige was not always forthcoming and when it was, not always sufficient for men in whom megalomania – power-hunger – was a common trait.

Advertising revenue from the late 19th century onwards gave press ownership a degree of independence that saw papers attacking government as much as supporting it, and in doing so invariably calling upon the reading public to exert their own power to influence.

With few exceptions, political power rather than political influence remained a dream for the press barons, Lord Beaverbrook being one of those exceptions. In 1911, then simply Max Aitken, he was knighted for services to the Conservative Party. In 1916 he received a peerage from George V. In 1918 Prime Minister Lloyd George appointed him Minister of Information. During the Second World War (1939–45) Beaverbrook became a member of the war cabinet of Winston Churchill, a close friend. He actually took up residence for a while in Number 12 Downing Street.

The most notable exception to the rule that media barons influence the powerful rather than join them in office is the Italian media mogul, Silvio Berlusconi. His newly-formed political party was propelled into power in Italy through the adulatory support of his own media empire. In fiction, the dream of political office eluded John Foster Kane, the larger-than-life press baron modelled on William Randolph Hearst in Orson Welles' classic film *Citizen Kane*.[1] In the stranger world of fact, Berlusconi became prime minister of his country in 1994 and again in 2000 only to fall out of electoral favour once more. What did not prove an exception to the rule was his rightist politics: Berlusconi (nicknamed in Italy, 'Sua Emittenza', His Broadcastingship) took power with the support of neo-fascists.

Purely for profit?

The *commercial laissez-faire* model has been cited as a rival to the propagandist model. This theory defines media ownership and production as being simply a financial enterprise with no other goal than to make profit; that is, there are no ideological axes to grind; readers or viewers are simply consumers whose custom has to be won and sustained.

A case might be made that the media empire of Rupert Murdoch has worked to this principle. Indeed it would be impossible to deny that profit now or profit in the future has been the primary, bottom-line purpose of News Corp, BSkyB, Fox Broadcasting Company or the Papua and New Guinea *Post Courier* – all 'power properties' in the Murdoch empire.

Yet if we recognize that profit-making not only empowers those who are successful at it, but also *requires* empowerment, then we can readily identify the ideology from which profit-acquisition springs: from the point of view of business interest, the making of profit should be as free (hence, 'laissez-faire' – leave alone), as unrestricted by regulation as possible. Whichever socio-political conditions favour profits will be reinforced by the arguments and moral support of those best able to benefit from those conditions.

For example, trade unionism has long been viewed by Murdoch as an obstacle to his vision of a viable and profitable media business. In the UK, with the support of the Conservative government of Margaret Thatcher, Murdoch took on, and defeated, the print unions. Where there are rivals, including other media moguls or competing corporations, Murdoch's News Corp has turned its firepower upon them.

In a UK *Guardian* article 'The keeper of the global gate',[2] Henry Porter quotes the *New York Times*' view that 'Mr. Murdoch does a disservice to journalism by using his media outlets to carry out personal vendettas for financial gain'. He is accused of using his papers in America, Britain and Australia, 'to advance a political agenda'.

Opportunist

Indeed Murdoch's UK tabloid the *Sun* has never been modest about its claims to influence the results of elections, proudly celebrating the victory of Tory leader John Major (it was the *Sun* 'wot won it'), and in turn (and about-face) claiming to have put Tony Blair, leader of New Labour, into Downing Street in 1997 and again in 2001 and 2005.

It would seem that the propaganda model and the commercial *laissez-faire* model are fitting bedfellows, propagating and profit-making fused into a straightforward *power* model. Further, we might classify it as a model of *control* because ultimately that is what power is about – *having* control, over self, others, situations, over knowledge itself (or at least access to it).

The media barons have notoriously exercised high levels of control over their properties. They hire and they fire. They take a direct interest in content and approach. They decide the political hue of their newspapers and broadcasting companies. Essentially, though, they are pragmatic and opportunist. Unlike many politicians, they are the controllers of ideology not its slaves. If supporting Party X is seen as good for business, Party X will receive support; yet just occasionally Party Y may seem a better bet. Practical necessities temper the fervour of ideology. And in return for supporting a particular party, favours will be expected.

Figure 4.2 summarizes to sweet perfection the willingness of media barons to meet realities head on rather than attempt to bludgeon them aside with the weapon of ideology. The *Guardian* of 8 January 2002 reproduced two front pages of the *Sun*, each presented to the world on the same day and featuring the launch of Euro currency in the Common Market.

The *Sun*'s front page available to readers on the British mainland expresses the paper's traditional antipathy to the Euro; thus the Euro symbol becomes E for Error. However, the front page of the Irish *Sun*, in recognition of Ireland's acceptance of the Euro, and in acknowledgement that the Irish people will be using the new currency from now on, offers a gesture of celebration and welcome, the Euro E representing the dawn of a new Era. The *Guardian's* headline, CAST A TWO-FACED SHADOW ON THE EUROZONE, suggests that in the *Sun's* case principle gives way, when convenient, to pragmatism.

The Sun
● "Despite the inevitable excitement generated by such a massive change, the euro's architects admitted they were not happy with its performance" (news story, page 6)
● New money means old nightmares (commentary by Iain Duncan Smith, page 7)
● "Everywhere Sun reporters went yesterday it was the same story — spenders are being taken for a ride by the euro" (page 8, January 2)

The Irish Sun
● "Over the past three years, an extraordinary amount of activity has gone into making sure that the next few weeks go without a hitch" (news story, page 6)
● A–Z of our new currency (page 7)
● "If the queues in Dublin yesterday were anything to go by, Ireland's new euro currency is set to be a huge hit with the public" (page 6, January 2)

Figure 4.2 Speaking with forked tongue?
Published in the UK *Guardian*, 8 January 2002.

The public service model: technology and competition

It is useful at this point to differentiate between the *functions* of media, the purposes to which they are directed, and their *performance*. The one I will term *normative*, the other, *performative*; a version, if you like, of the proposition that people should be judged not by what they say they do but by what they do do.

In exploring the question, *What are the media for?* we are immediately confronted by a number of other questions that need to be answered before we can progress. For example, *who* says what the media are for – a nation's citizens or its power elite; consumers or producers; public sector media or private sector media? In some countries, totalitarian in nature, government decides what the media are for. In democracies there is a *plurality* of definitions.

Clearly the dominant voices of the time assert their definitions over others; and if the dominant voices are the media themselves then those who control the media have something of a monopoly over who says what to whom and why. In countries where media are divided between public and private ownership conflicts over purpose and performance are ongoing, often bitterly fought. Each contestant has one eye on government and the other on the public.

The newspaper barons in Britain during the 1920s greeted the arrival of public service broadcasting as represented by the BBC with suspicion and later, hostility, for they saw radio as a serious threat to their media hegemony. They feared a rival paradigm of media purpose – the *public service* model. A committee chaired by Sir Frederick Sykes, set the task of making recommendations for the future of broadcasting in Britain, established a principle that was to influence the broadcasting policies of many countries throughout the world.

The Sykes Committee report declared:

> …we consider that the control of such a potential power [of broadcasting] over public opinion and the life of the nation ought to remain with the State, and that the operation of so important a national service ought not to be allowed to become an unrestricted commercial monopoly.

The BBC became the first broadcasting service in the world to be financed through an annual licence fee and it became a model for other national broadcasting systems. In contrast, the American broadcasting system was, from the start, privately owned, funded by advertising.

Yet here too the principle of public service was recognized with the foundation of the Federal Radio Commission in 1927 to regulate excesses and to encourage quality broadcasting. Today the Federal Communications Commission (FCC) serves a similar, if cautiously modest function.

The public service model centres essentially around concepts of *responsibility* working according codes of ethical and professional conduct, and in the public interest. Denis McQuail in *McQuail's Mass Communication Theory*,[3] having usefully differentiated between public interest and what interests the public, lists the following features of social responsibility theory:

- The media have obligations to society, and media ownership is a public trust;
- News media should be truthful, accurate, fair and relevant;
- The media should be free but self-regulated;
- Media should follow agreed codes of ethics and professional conduct;
- Under some circumstances, government may need to intervene to safeguard the public interest.

Like all principles, they have proved contentious over the years, posing problems of definition but chiefly because of their *regulatory* nature. Responsibility is often judged as getting in the way of freedom; and it is axiomatic that for social responsibility to survive or even prosper in a competitive world, actual regulation is often required. Without it, in public service broadcasting for example, there would be nothing to stop a TV channel excluding from its schedules any programmes that did not have mass popular appeal.

An end to control through scarcity

What protected state broadcasting systems down the years, and what ensured that public service broadcasting (PSB) continued as a central feature of cultural life was in part the desire of governments to exert control over such a powerful means of communication. Perhaps of equal significance, the limitations of existing technology restricted the number of possible broadcasting channels and therefore the number of broadcasting licences available.

Today, hostility to PSB among media moguls such as Rupert Murdoch is undiminished, and it has been aided by a significant loss of faith in the public service ethic among power elites. New technology has transformed channel 'dearth' into channel 'plenty'; and that technology has come increasingly under the control of operators in the private sector.

The 'universal' nature of PSB is under challenge from different quarters and in different ways; in the main, though, from commercial competition in a marketplace impatient of the kind of regulation that makes PSB viable. In the battle for survival, broadcasting in the public service mode, as typified by the BBC, competes on three fronts – against the predatory ambitions of the private entrepreneurs; against governments, themselves subject to intense pressure from the moguls of the private sector; and the truly daunting challenge of how to cope with the whirlwind of change in media use brought about by the advent of network communication.

The BBC's former Director General, John Birt, was not exaggerating when, in his MacTaggart Lecture delivered at the Edinburgh Festival in 1996, he declared that, 'The impact [of new technology] will be seismic'. Birt was of the opinion that 'the digital age will be marked not by openness and diversity but by dominance'. A world 'born of spectrum scarcity, a handful of channels and of regulation' was swiftly being superseded and the new age was witnessing competition 'to rival the 19th century battle for the railroad or the 20th century battle for office software systems'. For Birt the 'hallmark of the digital age must be full cultural and economic freedom'.

To survive, Birt was saying, PSB would have to compete in the marketplace, both national and global. To do this, that is to be viable commercially and also to fulfil the remit of public service, has required a skilful balancing act, whose success relies on the willingness of governments to continue to support PSB through the TV licence.

Any survey of the principles and practices of media must be conducted with Birt's 'seismic shifts' in mind. Indeed it is because of such fundamental changes in the nature of 21st century media that we need to examine the roles media play in society and the success (or lack of it) with which they perform those roles.

Not a case of either or

The temptation to see the media world in terms of a struggle between public and private should be resisted if we are then expected to take sides, classifying one or the other as preferable. The private sector does not have a monopoly of entrepreneurialism and adventure;

and the public sector does not have a monopoly of public 'virtues'. What we should worry about is one disabling the other or displacing it altogether.

Equally, it would be premature to herald the end of mass communication as we have known it. Integration and multiplication of services has become the rule rather than displacement. We watch TV and movies on our computers; we listen to the radio, summon up music and texts on our mobiles (or as Nokia terms them, *multimedia terminals*) as well as talking to each other. Print media now offer us alternatives, the newspaper from the newsstand or websites providing further information and comment, and the chance of feedback, of interactivity. A regular feature of our daily newspapers is a selection of blogs on current topics. Convergence is convenient, synergy smiles; at least for the present.

The structures, too, remain substantially in place, or to be more exact, the *networks* of control. The big fish swallow the little fish; and where the big fish are in danger of competition, they merge or enter into mutually beneficial, though often temporary, partnerships.

Six normative functions of media

All parties to the definition of the functions or purposes of media find little difficulty agreeing that the task of media is to *inform*, to *educate* and to *entertain*. Yet for the student of communication, such a trio of media goals resembles a set of holograms, appearing to have substance and meaning but reaching out to them only locates thin air. Information, yes – but what information; education, yes – but what do we mean by education; entertainment, certainly – but does its separate classification mean that it cannot also be informative and educational or that information and education cannot be entertaining? Several commentators, best known among them Denis McQuail, have sought to create a more complex taxonomy of the purposes of media as they operate in varying contexts.

By *normative* theories we mean functions as they *should* be according to dominant criteria; in some cases an ideal, in others a necessity; and they constitute guidelines to performance. In *Mass Communication Theory: An Introduction*, a 1983 precursor of *McQuail's Mass Communication Theory*,[3] McQuail posits six normative theories of media purposes:

- Authoritarian theory;
- Free press theory;

- Social responsibility theory;
- Soviet theory;
- Development media theory;
- Democratic-participant theory.

In each case the theory relates the performance of media to the position taken up by the state towards the transmission of information, comment and expression.

Authoritarian theory

The authoritarian theory describes a situation where government, in the hands of a tyrant or a ruling elite exercising repressive power over the people, lays down the law as to what the media can communicate. In this context the media are servants of state, the mouthpiece of government. If they are perceived to fail in that capacity, by showing a degree of editorial independence, they are censored or shut down.

Some media thrive in these conditions. *El Mercurio* had no difficulty getting published in Chile during the tyranny of the generals following the assassination of the Marxist President Allende in 1973. The editorial board of the newspaper would no doubt have justified its position by saying that the paper was dedicated to upholding authority (in face of Marxist chaos); that it was a force for cohesion in times when discipline – control – not liberty was the prescription for national survival.

The world is littered with examples of authoritarian theory in action: free speech challenges authority, and free speech that criticizes, or implies criticism of those in power, is seen to be subversive; the work not of a friend of the state but of an enemy of the state. Of course the rulers of democracies suffer in varying degrees from authoritarian tendencies; in opposition loudly arguing the case for liberties of opinion and expression, in office often proving reluctant to expedite those liberties.

Free press theory

On the face of it free press theory, sometimes referred to as libertarian theory, is the exact opposite of authoritarian theory: its first principle is that the free press is servant to none but its readership in its task of informing, educating and entertaining. The press of the Western world would place itself in this category. Free expression, unchecked by censorship, external or internal, is what media are about. 'Free' media claim fearlessness in the pursuit of truth; take pride in being the conscience and watchdog over the rights of the people.

It is with the free press theory – so the theory goes – that error is exposed and the truth arrived at; and, in the USA, this principle is duly enshrined in the first Amendment to the Constitution. This states that 'Congress shall make no law...abridging the freedom of speech of the press'. McQuail asks, as perhaps we all must, exactly *whose* freedom the media are expressing; and how free is free in situations dominated by competition, reliance on advertising and deeply affected by patterns of ownership, all operating in wider contexts in which there are conflicting interests and competing definitions of freedom.

Social responsibility theory

As the title suggests, key to this theory of media purpose, is responsibility. The media have obligations that amount to a form of public stewardship. The theory links with, and is part of, the democratic process, and the media operate in the role of guardians of that process, vigilant on behalf of the citizens, with a duty to be honest and fair to all in equal measure.

The theory balances the claims for freedom with the need for responsibility. Freedom to attack minorities, for example, and consequently endanger those minorities, is irresponsible and must be avoided. Public service broadcasting comes under this heading, for regulation by law or self-imposition, is seen as necessary in order to operate socially responsible checks and balances upon freedoms.

In party-political matters free press theory insists on the right to be biased in favour of one party against another, to flatter the one and disparage the other, whereas the social responsibility theory would urge that, in the public interest, and in the interests of true representation (or an aspiration to it), both sides of a case should be put.

For such a theory to work successfully there are implications for ownership and control, not just of one newspaper or broadcasting company, but across the whole spectrum of media. The theory would demand a pluralist media in a pluralist society and is only really possible through multiple ownership. Under such criteria a newspaper owner might not be permitted to move into TV, especially if the owner's paper published in the same city as the TV company he/she was interested in controlling.

The current trend towards the convergence of ownership and relaxation in restrictions on cross-media control (see Chapters 8 and 11) threatens pluralism and in consequence social responsibility. Fortunately human rights legislation goes some way to lending support to the furtherance of media responsibility.[4]

Soviet media theory

The Soviet system has passed away and with it, for the time being at least, Soviet media theory. It is still worth outlining its principles, if only to explain how it differed from authoritarian theory. In practice, of course, it didn't: the press, broadcasting, cinema, book publishing – indeed all message systems – were in the service of the state. But they were not privately run, as was the case with *El Mercurio* of Santiago. The media in Soviet Russia were the voice of the state, yes, but theoretically they were also the voice of the people.

They had the task of informing and educating the people in socialism because this was viewed as unquestionably in the people's interest. The role of the media was to mobilize and to sustain the socialist revolution, to defend it against counter-revolution and to protect it from the 'evil' influence of capitalism. Censorship was acceptable if it meant that the people were shielded from ideas and information that might contradict, and therefore undermine, the ruling ideology of communism.

With the advent of democracy in the former states of the Soviet Union, the scenario in many of them, including Russia itself, has in some parts come to resemble the authoritarian theory. Newspapers and TV stations that opt to be critical of the affairs of state are censored, journalists are attacked, censorship laws enacted; all illustrating what might be defined as a general theory of media, that governments by their very nature share an instinct for the repression of information. It follows, then, that one of the primary functions of media everywhere is to ensure that information is communicated to the people the governments are elected to serve.[5]

In some political contexts censorship may operate extensively most of the time, but no authoritarian system is 'water-tight' in that information and expression can be wholly stifled. In Soviet Russia, *Samizdat* – illegal publications produced on unregistered typewriters, carbon-copied and secretly circulated – found a ready readership through the worst days of Soviet information control; and today, while conflict between authorities and media expression is rife, there are innumerable examples of both free press and social responsibility media activity.

Current patterns of media purpose and performance in the former Soviet Union could actually be said to represent a normative category of its own – a *hybrid*, of state involvement and private enterprise; in some ways at least increasingly resembling the patterns of purpose and performance in the West.

Old habits die hard

Investigative journalist and courageous critic of Russian government, Anna Politkovskaya was murdered in the lift of a Moscow block of flats in October 2006. Her outspoken reporting, on alleged government malpractice and on the brutal civil war in Chechnya resulted in intimidation and harassment, detainment, and on one occasion attempted poisoning. In March 2007, another journalist, Ivan Safronov, correspondent of the newspaper *Kommersant*, fell to his death from a fifth-floor window. He had exposed the failure of the Russian government's new intercontinental missile system. The Committee of Journalists, based in New York, announced that 13 journalists in Russia had been murdered in contract-style killings since 2000.

Development theory

As the name implies this theory relates to media operating in developing, or so-termed Third World, nations. It has parallels with the Soviet theory because media are seen to fulfil particular social and political duties. It favours journalism that seeks out good news, in contrast to the free press position where journalists respond most readily to stories of disaster, and for whom 'bad news is good news' because it commands bigger headlines.

Development theory requires that bad news stories are treated with caution, for such stories can be economically damaging to a nation in the delicate throes of growth and change. Grim headlines can put off investors, even persuade them to pull out their investments. As an antidote to the bad news syndrome, development theory seeks to accentuate the positive; it nurtures the autonomy of the developing nation and gives special emphasis to indigenous cultures. It is both a theory of state support and one of resistance – resistance, that is, to the norms of competing nations and competing theories of media.

This is the reason why the actors in the free press system are often unhappy with and rejective of development theory attitudes and practices. They attack these as censorship. The wealthy capitalist nations, and their media advocates, see the world as their backyard. Supported by the technology with which few developing nations can compete, the West recognizes no frontiers to free enterprise; and what frontiers are set against it are simply bought away, evaded by satellite or crushed by the software of information, education and entertainment which, many critics claim, has more power than the colonizing armies of the past (see Note 6 for a comment on the New World Information Order, associated with development theory).

Democratic-participant theory

This represents the sort of media purpose the idealist dreams up in the bath. It is an aspiration rather than a phenomenon that can be recognized anywhere in practice, yet it is surely one which any healthy democracy should regard as a goal. Denis McQuail, having queried whether the democratic-participant theory warrants a separate normative classification, concludes that it deserves its identity because it challenges reigning theories and offers a positive strategy towards the achievement of new forms of media institution.

This theory places particular value upon horizontal rather than vertical modes of authority and communication. It stands for defence against commercialization and monopoly while at the same time being resistant to the centrism and bureaucracy so characteristic of public media institutions.

The model emphasizes the importance of the role of receiver in the communication process and incorporates what might be termed 'receiver rights' – to relevant information; to be heard as well as to hear and be shown. A right of reply would be a basic element of the model as would be the right, on the part of sections of the community, special interest groups or sub-cultures, to use the means of communication available.

As McQuail puts it, there is in the model 'a mixture of theoretical elements, including libertarianism, utopianism, socialism, egalitarianism, localism'. In short, *people power*. It could of course be argued that while the mass media fall short of fulfilling the aspirations of the democratic-participant model the Internet may be fast becoming 'fit for purpose' under this heading; indeed it could be further claimed that the challenge posed by networking may be pushing if not driving mass media into supporting a more participant democracy.

Functioning according to roles

If, in a first-stage analysis, we can identify a number of normative functions of media, some of them overlapping, we can further approach the task of understanding purpose by examining the *roles* the media play in society and how they perform those roles. Three such roles are of a 'canine' nature: the watchdog, the guard dog and the lapdog. In their capacity as watchdog the media are the eyes and ears of the public, its defender against possible abuses by the state or other powerful

McQuail's five basic functions of media

Having analyzed the six normative functions of media, Denis McQuail provides the reader with a useful summary of his own, under five headings – Information, Correlation, Continuity, Entertainment and Mobilization.

Information

- Providing information about events and conditions in society and the world
- Indicating relations of power
- Facilitating innovation, adaptation and progress

Correlation

- Explaining, interpreting and commenting on the meaning of events and information
- Providing support for established authority and norms
- Socializing
- Co-ordinating separate activies
- Consensus building
- Setting orders of priority and signalling relative status

Continuity

- Expressing the dominant culture and recognizing sub-cultures and new cultural developments
- Forging and maintaining commonality of values

Entertainment

- Providing amusement, diversion, the means of relaxation
- Reducing social tension

Mobilization

- Campaigning for societal objectives in the sphere of politics, war, economic development, work and sometimes religion.

From the 1983 edition of *Mass Communication: An Introduction* (UK: Sage).

organizations. As guard dogs they sit sentinel at the house of the masters. Obviously they do not recognize themselves in the role of the lapdog: such a description is left for critics of media performance.

The guard dog role is arguably most recognizable in the normative practices of authoritarian and Soviet theory but few commentators would deny its activity in democracies. The watchdog role *ought* to prevail in systems of a pluralist nature, and often does; but it is hedged about by forces whose interests demand dogs that bark only when they are commanded to do so.

We can identify many roles relative to normative requirements. A newspaper wishing to perform in accordance with democratic-participant theory will act as *advocate* of public participation in all walks of life. It will support such ideas as the representation of workers on boards of management and it will perform as *documentarist* in revealing managements that deny such representation.

Yet while this paper altruistically defends public interest it cannot ignore the fact that it is in competition with players of other roles, such as purveyors of scandal, titillation, sensation or just plain fun. It would be a mistake, however, to dismiss such roles as merely decorative, for while some observers might see the tabloid press as *court jesters*, the papers cast themselves among the world's most earnest *preachers*. Their sensationalism almost invariably has a moral if not political purpose; and if it has such a purpose, then it has an ideological intent.

In this sense a prominent role of media is that of *definer*. John Hartley argues in *The Politics of Pictures: The Creation of the Public in the Age of Popular Media*[7] that the media define what is right by describing what is wrong. He calls this *photographic negativization* 'where the image of order is actually recorded as its own negative, in stories of disorder'. 'Good grief,' one might exclaim, 'so all these stories of scandals are actually parables about how to behave properly!'

In terms of performance we can recognize here the merging of the role of *town-crier*, alerting the public to the latest news (often preferably scandalous) and that of *vigilante*. A campaign waged by the UK Sunday paper the *News of the World* against known and suspected paedophiles purported to alert the public to the extent and danger of paedophilia, but it also served to mobilize public opinion. By publishing names and addresses of convicted paedophiles the paper prompted actions generated by prejudice and ignorance against guilty and innocent alike. Here free press theory pressed ahead with its own definition of 'responsibility'.

Agents of order

A primary role played by media in society is that of *representatives of order*. This view is broached by Richard V. Ericson, Patricia M. Barnak and Janet B.L. Chan in *Representing Order: Crime, Law and Justice in the News Media*.[8] We shall be discussing news in the next chapter but it is worth quoting here points made by Ericson and his colleagues.

First, like the law, the media are agencies of policing. They produce stories 'that help to make sense of, and express sensibilities about, social order'. Things are represented in terms of correctness or incorrectness rather than in terms of truth or falsehood. The authors of *Representing Order* believe the media work towards 'legal control through compliance'. Second, it is the custom and practice of media, overtly or covertly, to define control as *institutionally* grounded within the structures of government 'and particularly its law enforcement apparatus'.

We need not confine our attention to the news to realize how deeply consciousness of law and order penetrates everyday life thanks in large part to the media. At national or local level we can be forgiven for thinking sometimes that here is not the news but the Police News. Yet this penetration extends well into newspaper columns and TV schedules marked 'Entertainment'.

How many cop series are on TV a present? In cynical moments we might wish to ask how many series are *not* about cops and criminals. Programmers might respond that audiences enjoy crime stories, that such series have high ratings, but the fascination runs deeper, perhaps feeding our own profound needs for order which are rarely as neatly fulfilled as a crime story that brings wrongdoers to book.

Essentially crime stories are about deviance from acceptable norms, from codes of conduct within the community. In their capacity as guard dogs, the media keep a close watch on the boundaries that divide conformity from deviance. By their reporting, they locate that dividing line and in doing so become the definers of deviance. They patrol that boundary, aware of course that the boundary is built of ideology not bricks.

Media in the role of mobilizers

Mobilization of public opinion in support of a cause is at its most dramatic in times of conflict when the overriding principle of performance as far as the media are concerned is to be absolutely clear which side 'we' are on. Again, this position comes under the heading of representing order. Media that attempt to give fair coverage to the enemy's point of view are soon accused of being unpatriotic.

When, during the Falklands War between Britain and Argentina in 1982, the *Daily Mirror* raised questions about the wisdom of fighting such a war, her rival, the *Sun*, mobilizer-in-chief of the war effort with its ardent support of 'our boys', was outraged and accused the *Mirror* of treason. Generally in times of crisis – which the media will have also been instrumental in identifying (hence the term *crisis definition*) – the media take on the duty of uniting public opinion in support of the government, the 'war effort' and the nation.

At such times, questions of identity, of 'nationhood', are robustly asserted: our eyes and ears are blitzed with images that reinforce patriotism – flags, uniforms, weapons, library pictures of our past victories on land, sea and in the air. What is occurring is a nurturing of public approval and support; what Edward Herman and Noam Chomsky have famously termed the *manufacture of consent*.[9]

The public is desperate for information, for reassurance, for guidance, for leadership. Consensus, the feeling of togetherness, means something: differences tend to be forgotten or minimized. We become dependent upon the media who, in their turn, are dependent upon the authorities giving the signal as to how much information is to be made public.

If there is a scarcity of information there are still pages to fill; the TV news has still to go out. What rushes to the aid of performance is conjecture, or guesswork. Experts are wheeled in by the busload to clarify, to predict; and the less hard news there is – for in wartime censorship is usually at its most rigorous – the more *human stories* have to be produced. Personalization, always a key feature of media performance, sweeps to the top of the agenda, and the cast of characters is divided between heroes (us) and villains (them).

Hartley in *The Politics of Pictures* calls this *Wedom/Theydom* and it quickly succumbs to the darker practices of *demonization* accompanied by suitable literary bombast. Thus, when NATO forces decided to unleash the dogs of war (including British Harriers) upon Serbia (and its leader 'Serb monster Slobodan Milosevic') in 1999, the *Sun* was in its element – sensational, patriotic, mobilizing. On Thursday 25 March the paper's front page printed in giant letters above the picture of a Royal Navy missile CLOBBA SLOBBA, declaring in super alliteration that 'Our boys batter Serb butcher in Nato bomb blitz'.

Come the invasion of Iraq in 2003, the *Sun* on 6 February featured the portraits of Saddam Hussein and Osama Bin Laden, presumed architect of 9/11, under the headline MONSTERS INC. announcing 'Clinching proof of the link between Saddam Hussein and Al-Qaeda'. This conveniently ignored the fact that no reliable evidence of such a link existed. It followed, as page 4 of the same edition asserted, that the Iraqi president 'was finally nailed as a massive threat to humanity'. Passion, not facts, ruled the headlines as the guard dog snarled and the watchdog remained mute.

Banging the drum for national consensus

Consensus definition and the manufacturing of consent operate in more subtle ways in times of peace. It was something of a surprise to witness the assembly of over a thousand American journalists from over a hundred news organizations at the official transfer of sovereignty of Hong Kong to China in July 1997.

Here was a case of the reporting of Other within the frame of the ideology of Self; Other in this case being the most prominent rival of the United States following the demise of the Soviet communist system, that other 'red under the bed' – China.

In a *Journal of Communication* article, 'Through the eyes of the U.S. media: banging the democracy drum in Hong Kong'.[10] Chin-Chuan Lee and colleagues perceive America's reporting of the event as a process of renewing, as well as affirming, national consensus. The transfer of Hong Kong, a paradigm in American eyes of capitalism and freedom, to the Republic of China, paradigm of state authoritarianism and the repression of liberty, was too good an opportunity to miss – an opportunity to sing the discourse of freedom while at the same time defining the 'deviance' of America's global rival.

Lee and his co-authors saw the US media's response as one of *domestication*, of framing a foreign event according to domestic norms and values, 'participating in the discursive battle among a confluence of modern "issues": West versus East, democracy versus authoritarianism, as well as capitalism versus socialism'. What is implied is 'American exceptionalism', that is, the USA's superior difference linked to its mission to protect and extend American-style democracy.

However, national and world events can suddenly change, modifying antipathies. The stand-off between America and China experienced a degree of easement following 9/11, for China responded with sympathy to the tragedy, proffering moral support for America's subsequent war on terrorism.

Principles of media performance: possibilities and problems

Let us now examine a number of principles that seek to define normative, or 'best', media performance. At the macro-level these can be identified as *diversity* of sources and outlets and *accessibility* on the part of the whole public to information; both of these contributing to a *plurality* of opinions in society.

To diversify is to make different, to give variety to. Relatedly, to *diverge* is to tend from a common point in different directions; to vary from the standard. Media provision should, then, be both diverse and capable of divergence. In our use of media we should have the option of the serious and the amusing, the challenging and the relaxing and we should be able to experience through the media a diversity of viewpoint.

At the same time we as audience should be able to access information and comment without always having to have recourse to the Murdochs and the Berlusconis of the world. Consequently, diversity applies to channel as well as content and style; and that would mean a diversity of channels as well as a diversity of ownership and control. To ensure diversity of channels there must be regulation. Who controls the airwaves, the print works, the distribution networks, the telecommunications systems, who commands the fibre-optic cables and the satellites, exerts power over choice.

In addition to the benefits of channel diversity 'best' performance would be to require diversity of *source* – that is, where information originates; where newspapers, radio and TV get their information from. Much raw material for news emerges from sources that are essentially in the business of *news management* aimed at putting over the source's position in a favourable light.

Governments are the most substantial suppliers of information in any society, followed by transnational corporations (TNCs) among whose portfolios are news agencies. The American, Herbert Gans, has pointed out that '[j]ournalists get most of their news from regular sources which, as study after study has shown, are usually speaking for political, economic and other establishments'.[11]

Diversity and freedom

The case is often put that deregulation and privatization encourage diversity: where there are more channels, more programmes to choose from, diversity inevitably follows. In another *Journal of Communication* article, 'Deregulation and the dream of diversity',[12] D.R. LeDuc is less than impressed by this argument. He comments, in reference to claims of increased over-air channel choice, 'it resembles the degree of diversity in dining opportunities experienced when a McDonald's restaurant begins business in a town already served by Burger King'.

We need to assess both *vertical* and *horizontal* diversity, the one being the number of options offered by a single channel, the other, options available at any time across the range of channels. We might conclude that more sometimes means less.

We might be equally hesitant in concluding that diversity where it exists ensures plurality of opinions. One of the legislative glories of history, the First Amendment to the American Constitution, guarantees the freedom of the press (and consequently of broadcasting and other forms of media communication). We can sit back and admire, but before we rejoice and uncritically recommend the American approach to the liberties of expression, we should recognize that the First Amendment awards the media a mighty power over which neither individuals nor the community has much influence.

Indivisible or unlimited freedom, as some commentators have pointed out, does have its drawbacks, for the First Amendment also protects the 'voice' of the great corporations who, in law, are deemed to have the rights of individuals. Hence media barons and corporate media empires have the freedom – indeed the *right* – as well as the capacity to dominate the public discourses of the time. The American scholar, Harold Innis, writing in the 1950s, in works such as *The Bias of Communication*,[13] was of the view that the First Amendment to the American Constitution, so lauded as a human right, actually served as an obstacle to free speech.

Few, however, failed to welcome the incorporation on 1 January 2001 of European human rights legislation into UK law (see Note 5, including reference to the UK government's reining in of the Act following 9/11). For the first time in British history the right to freedom of expression was enshrined in black and white. For the media, the complications are in the small print of the Act:

> The exercise of these freedoms [to hold opinions and to receive and impart information and ideas without interference by public authority and regardless of frontiers] since it carries with it duties and responsibilities, may be subject to such formalities, conditions, restrictions or penalties as are prescribed by law and are necessary in a democratic society, in the interests of national security, territorial integrity or public safety, for the prevention of disorder or crime, for the protection of heath or morals, for the protection of the rights of others, for preventing the disclosure of information received in confidence, or for maintaining the authority and impartiality of the judiciary.

It's worth asking, in view of the 'formalities' and 'conditions' serving to check freedom of expression, whether a good lawyer or even an alert spin-doctor could drive a coach and horses through this set of rights.

Further, in 2005, the UK at last had its own Freedom of Information Act (FOI), yet once more cluttered with exemptions. The demand for information from media, organizations and members of the public proved overwhelming and many previously concealed issues came to light, such as the lobbying of government by drugs companies and the varying success/failure rates of heart surgeons.

As far as the Blair government was concerned this was not a cause for celebration. Soon obstacles to access were being placed like road blocks in the way of enquiry. Not the least of these has been the charges made for the time it takes for officials to dig out information, and the limits placed on the number of requests that can be made in any given period.

Media resistance to government sabotage of freedoms of access and expression is a prime function, but matters become complicated when one freedom – of speech, publication or broadcasting – comes into conflict with the assertion (in the Rights Act) that 'everyone has the right to respect for his private and family life, his home and correspondence'. The collision of rights might be seen to be head-on: the media function as 'bringers of light' to matters that are deemed of public interest; at the same time, the right to privacy serves to protect individuals from intrusion and disclosure.

We return to the conundrum of definition: who defines and by what criteria? Have celebrities who spend much of their lives courting media attention the right to opt in certain circumstances for privacy? As for those pre-eminently public figures, politicians, how far is it possible to mark off their public functioning from their private activities?

Golden triangle or lead weight?

At the micro-level of operations three related and interconnecting goals can be identified. These are *objectivity*, *impartiality* and *balance* (see Figure 4.3). They comprise what we might, initially, call a golden triangle of public service principles, and would apply as much to the press as to regulated broadcasting.

Once more we are confronted with the difficulty of definition, not so much the words themselves – the signifiers, but their operation: their signifieds. Objectivity, it might be said, is about giving the facts as they are, without subjective slant, colouring, innuendo or the expression of personal opinion. But then, what is a 'fact'; and how does such a syntagm or chain of syntagms fit into the choice of paradigm?

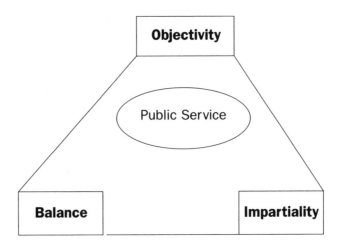

Figure 4.3   Criteria of public service communication

Insistence on definition can of course verge on the pedantic; after all we could challenge the meaning of most words (from bias to choice, from justice to sin). John Fiske, in his chapter on 'Popular News' in *Reading the Popular*[14] rejects objectivity as a goal in decisive manner:

> Objectivity is authority in disguise: 'objective' facts always support particular points of view and their 'objectivity' can exist only as part of the play of power. But, more important, objective facts cannot be challenged: objectivity discourages audience activity and participation.

Fiske incidentally implies a significant criterion of performance, that it should stimulate audience activity and participation. His position concerning objectivity is that at best there are only 'objectivities'; in which case they are for all intents and purposes 'subjectivities'. However, efforts have been and will continue to be made to both define objectivity and insist on it. A fair shot at definition has been made by J.H. Boyer. Writing in the American *Journalism Quarterly*[15] on 'How editors view objectivity', Boyer suggests the following criteria:

1. Balance and evenhandedness in presenting different sides of an issue;
2. Accuracy and realism in reporting;
3. Presenting all main relevant points;
4. Separating facts from opinion, but treating opinion as relevant;

5. Minimizing the influence of the writer's own attitude, opinion or involvement;
6. Avoiding slant, rancour or devious purposes.

After citing these in *Media Performance: Mass Communication and the Public Interest*,[16] Denis McQuail poses a number of queries as to the possibility of attaining all or any of the Boyer Six. He lists the difficulties: first, in news, items have to be selected; all reported events have to be presented in wider frames of reference; omissions, gaps and silences are unavoidable and may reflect implicit judgements about relevance and assumptions about society and its values; and news is always produced within a context of numerous powerful internal and external pressures.

The most telling argument, taken up in Chapter 5, is that underpinning the notion of objectivity is an assumption that out there is an identifiable reality about which to report. 'No account of reality,' says McQuail, 'can be uniquely correct or complete, except in the most trivial instance.' He goes on to question the desirability of objectivity as a governing principle, arguing that it is misleading to offer something which cannot be delivered.

All accounts are *versions*; thus the dominant power to express will generally, if not always, have the advantage, for this power is better placed, better resourced and quickest at getting over its 'version' to the public. An over-scrupulous insistence on objectivity would, in any event, impede some of the media's most important performances – in the reporting of human interest stories, the occasionally-stirring partisanship and in investigative journalism where subjectivity can be so trenchant and revealing.

It will have already struck the reader that objectivity, impartiality and balance are not very different ways of saying the same thing, each springing from the idea that communicators can step out of the contexts in which they find themselves. To do this they would also have to step out of their skin, shed a lifetime's 'project of self'; a striptease which public sector communication often demands of its reporters and presenters, insisting on them playing the 'golden triangle' game.

This would be a reasonably acceptable scenario if all communicators played by the rules of objectivity, impartiality and balance. The press patently do not, which arguably gives them an advantage in terms of influence if TV and radio are committed through regulation to strict neutrality. Rules of engagement that apply to some media and not others make for an uneven playing field.

Accuracy and sincerity

Jackie Harrison in *News*[17] cites two cardinal principles posed in the last publication of the philosopher Bernard Williams, *Truth and Truthfulness*. While the truth itself may be eternally evasive, truthfulness, argues Williams, is achieveable through *accuracy* and *sincerity*. For Harrison, the principles hold good for media performance. It is possible, she writes, affirming Williams, 'to accept truth as an aspiration':

> Accuracy as a core value of news consists of more than reporting the facts and figures in an accurate way, but requires that accurate judgements are made by those reporting the news...The development of trust between news (mediated by the news organizations and news journalists) and the audience is dependent upon the extent to which news is perceived to have the quality of accuracy.

As for sincerity, Harrison quotes Williams' view that it entails 'a disposition to make sure that one's assertion expresses what one actually believes'. She concedes that 'a sincere aim to be accurate and therefore truthful can...be frustrated by a variety of factors beyond the newsroom and the news medium, such as the insincerity of sources, news management by vested interests, a political culture which attempts to "spin" stories and so on'.

Pressures on accuracy and sincerity are constant and unavoidable. Not the least of these, in a highly competitive world, is the drive to 'sex-up' content and presentation in order to command audience attention. Accuracy and sincerity suffer when information, ideas and analysis, are forced into the mould of entertainment.

Media performance and human rights

As we have seen, in modern society the media may be regarded as a contemporary equivalent of the ancient Greek agora, usually the city or town square in which the population gathered to discuss the affairs of state. At their most altruistic, the media can lay claim to be the voice that speaks up for the public interest, arguably promoting and protecting *equality* above all other human rights.

The argument is not that all men and women are equal, rather that they should be treated equally; that they should have equal opportunities, equal access to information; to be fully and fairly informed of matters of public concern, that their voice should be heard in the agora or forum in whatever form it exists.

In a chapter entitled 'Mass media in the public interest' and published in *Mass Media and Society*,[18] Denis McQuail talks of public communication values. Equality he subdivides into *access, diversity* and, yes, *objectivity* as exemplified by neutrality, fairness and truth. He makes the point that equality supports policies of universal provision where information is seen as a right not a privilege.

In the same volume, James Curran, in 'Rethinking the role of media', sees that in an age where the power giants of government and the corporations have shared the spoils of the Communication Age, the media have ceased to be an agency of empowerment and become an accomplice by which the public has been sidelined.

It is the job of media, says Curran, to facilitate and protect the public sphere. One of their roles must be defender of public rights against encroachment by state and corporate powers by performing the role of watchdog, not guard dog. Curran writes, 'The media should be seen as a source of redress against the abuse of power over others'.

Models of performance

Ultimately, the practice of media ethics begins, even though it does not rest, with the practitioner. What model of behaviour should inspire the would-be journalist, photographer, cameraperson or editor? In 'The crisis of the sovereign state' published in *Media, Crisis and Democracy: Mass Communication and the Disruption of Social Order*,[19] John Keane offers a cogent and inspiring definition. First, he cites what it isn't:

> Quality journalism rejects tabloid newspaper tactics, whose golden rules are: please the news desk; get front page coverage and stay in front of everyone else; reflect the prejudices of readers; defend nationalist hype and page three pin-ups; fight for 'the scandal of the gay vicar' and other sensational exclusives with as little legal comeback as possible; remain emotionally uninvolved in any and every story; if necessary, invade privacy on a scale that would impress a burglar; all the while explaining to the interviewees that their willingness to cooperate will help others in a similar plight.

It might be argued that Keane, an academic commentator, being an outsider, can afford to be so harshly critical. However, printed in the box below is what an insider, journalist John Swainton, said to his colleagues on the *New York Times* at his retirement 'bash' in September 2000.

> There is not one of you who would dare to write his honest opinion. The business of the journal is to destroy truth, to lie outright, to pervert, to vilify, fall at the feet of Mammon and sell himself for his daily bread. We are tools, vessels of rich men behind the scenes, we are jumping jacks. They pull the strings; we dance. Our talents, our possibilities and our lives are the properties of these men. We are intellectual prostitutes.
>
> Quoted in *Index on Censorship*, 1, 2001

Did Swainton jest; or after a lifetime of falling at the feet of Mammon and selling himself for his daily bread, was he at last confessing the truth? Certainly the judgement is sweeping and largely unfair, as John Keane now confirms:

High quality investigative journalism lives by different rules. It seeks to counteract the secretive and noisy arrogance of the democratic Leviathan. It involves the patient investigation and exposure of political corruption, misconduct and mismanagement. It clings to the old maxim of American muck-rakers – 'the news is what someone, somewhere, *doesn't* want to see printed'. It aims to sting political power, to tame its arrogance by extending the limits of public controversy and widening citizens' informed involvement in the public spheres of civil society.[20]

As the world changes, so do the purposes, roles and performance of media. Today the issues the public needs to address, through the mediation of mass communication, are global as never before. In *Understanding Media Cultures: Social Theory and Mass Communication*,[21] Nick Stevenson speaks of 'citizenship entitlements' and the concept of citizenship 'has to be applied to local, national and more transnational levels'. Appropriately at each level the public needs to be served by its governments as well as its mass media in four major ways:

1. By being informed about 'the operation of expert cultures';
2. By being helped towards an understanding of 'the desires, demands and need interpretations of others who are distant in time and space';

3. By being nurtured into an understanding of ourselves 'as a social community'; and

4. By being participants in 'aesthetic and non-instrumentally defined cultural experiences'.

Stevenson writes:

> Modernity has witnessed the increasing specialisation of certain forms of expert knowledge. Most citizens do not understand the workings of complex global economies, are perplexed by the scientific debates on global warming and are unsure of the exact precautions they should take in order to prevent themselves becoming infected with the HIV virus.

The media have a role to play in explaining such matters to publics worldwide 'within a decommodified zone and outside the control of state power', providing 'a space where irrational prejudices could be challenged and an informed and genuinely democratic debate could take place'.

Functions 2 and 3 are especially crucial in conditions 'of cultural and psychic fragmentation'. The first relates to our obligations to others, not only to those within our own cultures but to those beyond our cultural and geographical boundaries whose lives, nevertheless, are impinged upon by our own behaviour. Stevenson says, 'Given the global risks of ozone depletion, global warming, toxic dumping and the long-term effects of nuclear power, local decisions would have to be tied into an appreciation of global frameworks'.

The media, because of their capacity to 'shift information spatially, are uniquely positioned to make such information available to us'. In Stevenson's view, the systems best able to provide such a service are public media because they are likely to 'put the communicative needs of citizens before the interests of powerful economic and administrative structures that maintain the status quo'.

Recognition of difference

Communities also need to be reminded of who they are, of their need to 'form identities in common with others' while at the same time guaranteeing tolerance of alternative identities and cultures. This does not mean unquestioningly honouring 'timeless forms of myth, ceremony and ritual'. Rather, a mature public and a mature media should be concerned to identify needs 'based upon reflexivity, ambivalence and cultural questioning': we reflect upon ourselves, our cultural condition (and conditioning) and we seek to live with, and tolerate, differences and contradictions. It is all part of the process of self-formulation referred to in Chapter 3.

Stevenson's fourth criterion also relates to the upholding of public interest in the face of private invasion. The aesthetic dimension is that part which exceeds the instrumental. The look, feel or sound of a thing is a criterion separate from its function or its market value. It works cognitively and affectively; it is about feelings, emotion and sensation and as such we can recognize it, enjoy it but rarely quantify it.

The author quotes the British TV playwright Dennis Potter who, in his last interview before his death in 1994, said that without the backing of a public broadcasting system his work – challenging, unnerving and often difficult – might never have flourished.

A system whose first principle was profit and therefore demanded optimum-size audiences for its programmes would draw back from the risk of broadcasting Potter's ground-breaking work. That would have been a loss to the canon of TV drama but also arguably a loss to the community in terms of cultural richness.

Stevenson argues that '[c]ultural forms of communication that challenge mass entertainment agendas should be given access to the media'. At the same time acknowledgement must be made of 'wider sets of responsibilities and obligations', for 'freedom of expression is never absolute'. Such recommendations as Stevenson makes have a special urgency at a time when 'public service is being undermined by more globally orientated commercial networks' and in contexts in which cultural differences command news agendas.

Stevenson's is a timely list of moral obligations, but one that has to be honoured and shared by all those who inhabit what Roger Silverstone terms the Mediapolis, both a physical and a conceptual space, a cultural territory which, in late modernity, is inescapable. In his Preface to *Media and Morality: On the Rise of the Mediapolis*[22] Silverstone writes of a 'crisis in the world of communication', which is 'ethical as well as political'.

He worries about the 'pollution of this mediated environment', fearing that it 'is threatening our capacity to sustain a reasonable level of humanity…it is only by attending to the realities of global communication, but also and even more so to its possibilities, that we will be able to reverse what otherwise will be a downward spiral towards increasing global incomprehension and inhumanity'.

We will return to Roger Silverstone's concerns about the Mediapolis in Chapter 11.

Summary

This chapter set out to examine the propaganda, the commercial *laissez-faire* and the public service models of media purpose, going on to discuss a number of normative functions arising out of social and political structures. The picture is broadened by identifying some key roles that the media play in society, as definers of reality, agents of control, mobilizers of public opinion and manufacturers of consent.

Media performance is viewed in relation to such guiding principles as diversity and access and operational level goals such as objectivity, impartiality and balance. The need for accuracy and sincerity is discussed and equality is seen as key to the media's capacity to advocate and support public rights within a fair and democratic society. Finally, markers are laid down concerning the responsibilities of the media within changing global situations.

KEY TERMS

Propaganda/commercial *laissez-faire*/public service models   plurality
public service broadcasting (PSB)   power elite   inform/educate/entertain
normative theories   hybrid correlation   mobilization   watchdog/guard dog
photographic negativization   diversity   vertical/horizontal   source
deregulation   objectivity/impartiality/balance   accuracy/sincerity   equality
agency of empowerment   citizenship   entitlement   decommodified zone
aesthetic dimension

Suggested activities

1. For discussion:

    (a) 'Commercial it may be, but *laissez-faire* it isn't'. Discuss this judgement of private sector media.

    (b) What does public service broadcasting (PSB) have to offer that is not already available on commercial TV channels?

    (c) How might democratic-participant modes of mass communication be developed in the face of dominant free press modes?

    (d) In what ways might the media help mobilize moves towards equality in society?

    (e) Jackie Harrison[17] supports Bernard Williams' views on *accuracy* and *sincerity*. What would be a test of media sincerity?

2. Examine copies of the tabloid/popular press with a view to identifying how they see their functions in society, what duties and responsibilities they seem to have with regard to readership.
3. Scrutinize TV or radio programmes for a week in search of evidence of 'global commitment' to the understanding of others.
4. How are the media behaving/misbehaving at this moment? Using the Internet, key into a range of websites that scrutinize media performance; make a note of these for future reference.

Now read on

Media Performance: Mass Communication and the Public Interest (UK: Sage, 1992) by Denis McQuail referred to in this chapter remains a key text. The citizenship theme is admirably dealt with by Peter Dahlgren and Colin Sparks in *Communication and Citizenship: Journalism and the Public Sphere* (UK: Routledge, 1993). The role of media in a democracy, and their duties to serve it, can be explored in John Keane's *Media and Democracy* (UK: Polity Press, 1991). More recent publications – Eric Louw's *The Media and Political Process* (UK/US, Sage, 2005) and *Media and Morality: The Rise of the Mediapolis* (UK: Polity, 2007) by Roger Silverstone – are recommended.

Nicholas Garnham's *Capitalism and Communication* (UK: Sage, 1990) examines media in relation to the power-value of capitalism while Brian McNair in *The Sociology of Journalism* (UK: Arnold, 1998) examines theories of journalistic production, focusing on case studies in the USA and UK.

The media's role as rooter-out of deviance is vividly illustrated in *The Enemy Within: MI5, Maxwell and the Scargill Affair* by Seamus Milne (UK: Verso, 1994). Also in this mode and offering fruitful insights and useful evidence, see Daniel Hallin's *'Uncensored War': The Media and Vietnam* (US: Oxford University Press, 1986), David Miller's *Don't Mention the War: Northern Ireland, Propaganda and the Media* (UK: Pluto, 1994), *Defending the Realm: MI5 and the Shayler Affair* (UK: Andre Deutsch, 2000) by Mark Hollingworth and Nick Fielding, Sheldon Rampton and John Stauber's *Weapons of Mass Deception: The Uses of Propaganda in Bush's War on Iraq* (UK: Constable & Robinson, 2003) and *Reporting from the Front: The Media and the Military* (US/UK: Rowman & Littlefield, 2005), edited by Judith Sylvester and Suzanne Huffman.

One of the most readable books on the theme of the risks public service media take when, performing the role of public watchdog, they challenge the activities of government is Roger Bolton's *Death on the*

Rock, And Other Stories (UK: W.H. Allen, 1990), an account of Thames TV's *This Week* investigation into the shooting in Gibraltar by the SAS (Special Air Service) of three members of the IRA in March 1988. See also Julian Petley's *Media: The Impact on Our Lives* (UK: Hodder Wayland, 21st Century Debates Series, 2000). Finally, for a focus on the role of economics in the practice of media, see Gillian Doyle's *Understanding Media Economics* (UK: Sage, 2002) and for a guide to performance, Richard Keeble's *Ethics for Journalists* (UK: Routledge, 2001).

Notes

1. Directed in 1941 for RKO pictures, *Citizen Kane* is the most famous 'media picture' and in the view of many critics one of the best films ever made. It is the story of a newspaper tycoon, John Foster Kane, an alias for the American newspaper baron, William Randolph Hearst (1863–1951). It is a film which according to Leonard Maltin's *Movies and Video Guide* (UK: Penguin, published annually) 'broke all the rules and invented some new ones'.
2. Henry Porter, 'The keeper of the global gate', *Guardian*, 29 October 1996.
3. Denis McQuail, *Mass Communication Theory: An Introduction* (UK: Sage, 1983). This contains items not included in *McQuail's Mass Communication Theory* (UK: Sage, 4th edition, 2000).
4. The European Convention on Human Rights and Fundamental Freedoms (ECHR) became law in the UK on 1 January 2001. The rights to freedom of expression, including freedom of the press; freedom of thought, conscience and religion, to be secured without discrimination on any ground 'such as sex, race, colour, language, religion, political or other opinion, national or social origin, association with a national minority, property, birth or other status' became enshrined in British law for the first time.
5. The question whether all information should be made available to the public is key to the debate on freedom and censorship. Arguments are put that some information, say about the defence system of a country, should be kept secret on the grounds that it would prove useful to an enemy. Most governments keep that information under lock and key. They are by nature inclined to extend existing censorship legislation, usually to control information which, made public, would expose government inefficiency, corruption or malpractice. The UK Official Secrets Act is one of the most catch-all censorship laws in the 'free' world.
6. In 1972, the General Conference of the United Nations Educational, Scientific and Cultural Organization (UNESCO) reported with concern how the media of the richer nations were not only increasingly dominating world opinion but were too often 'a source of moral and cultural

pollution'. Six years later UNESCO set up an international commission for the Study of Communication Problems under the chairmanship of Sean MacBride, former secretary-general of the International Commission of Jurists. The MacBride Commission's remit was to investigate the media information interaction between Western and Third World nations. The 484-page report arising from MacBride's 16-strong commission (which included the Columbian novelist Gabriel Garcia Marquez and Marshall McLuhan, the Canadian media guru), urged a strengthening of Third World independence in information-gathering and transmission and measures to protect national cultures against the one-way flow of information and entertainment from the West. The aim was to create a New World Information Order, which would entail a degree of 'control' over 'freedom'; and which, predictably, got a very bad press in the West. Out of MacBride emerged the International Program for the Development of Communication (IPDC), which was – again predictably – to prove a frail defensive wall against the floodtide of Western media imperialism.

7. John Hartley, *The Politics of Pictures: The Creation of the Public in the Age of Popular Media* (UK: Routledge, 1992).
8. Richard V. Ericson, Patricia M. Barnak and Janet B.L. Chan, *Representing Order: Crime, Law and Justice in the News Media* (UK: Open University Press, 1991).
9. Edward S. Herman and Noam Chomsky, *Manufacturing Consent: The Political Economy of the Mass Media* (US: Pantheon, 1988).
10. 'Through the eyes of the U.S. media: banging the democracy drum', by Chin-Chuan Lee, Zhongdang Pan, Joseph Man Chan and Clement Y.K. So, *Journal of Communication*, Vol. 51, No. 2, June 2001.
11. Herbert J. Gans, 'Reopening the black box: toward a limited effects theory' in *Journal of Communication*, Autumn 1993.
12. D.R. LeDuc, 'Deregulation and the dream of diversity' in *Journal of Communication*, Vol. 32, No. 4 (1982).
13. Harold Innes. See *The Bias of Communication* (Canada: Toronto Press, 1951) and *Concepts of Time* (Toronto Press, 1952).
14. John Fiske, *Reading the Popular* (US: Unwin Hyman, 1989).
15. J.H. Boyer, 'How editors view objectivity' in *Journalism Quarterly*, 58 (1981).
16. Denis McQuail, *Media Performance: Mass Communication and the Public Interest* (UK: Sage, 1992).
17. Jackie Harrison, *News* (UK/US: Routledge, 2006), and quoting Bernard Williams' *Truth and Truthfulness* (US: Princeton University Press, 2000).
18. McQuail, 'Mass media in the public interest' in James Curran and Michael Gurevitch (eds), *Mass Media and Society* (UK: Edward Arnold, 1991).

19. John Keane, 'The crisis of the sovereign state' in Marc Raboy and Bernard Dagenais (eds), *Media, Crisis and Democracy: Mass Communication and the Disruption of Social Order* (UK: Sage, 1992).

20. Leviathan. John Keane refers to 'the secretive and noisy arrogance of the democratic Leviathan'. Originally 'leviathan' was the Hebrew name for a huge sea monster, of terrible strength and power. It was adopted as a metaphor for the power of the state. The English philosopher Thomas Hobbes (1588–1679) gave his most notable treatise the title of *Leviathan* (1651). He argued that only absolutist government could ensure order and security. However, though the population were required to demonstrate total obedience to their monarch, they had the right to his/her protection in return.

21. Nick Stevenson, *Understanding Media Cultures: Social Theory and Mass Communication* (UK: Sage, 1995).

22. Roger Silverstone, *Media and Morality: On the Rise of the Mediapolis.* The word *polis* is Greek for city, a reality and a concept, indeed a state of mind. In this broad sense it is used by the philosopher Hannah Arendt whose ideas Silverstone discusses. In *The Human Condition* (US: University of Chicago Press, 2nd edition, 1998), Arendt writes, 'The *polis*, properly speaking, is not the city-state in its physical location; it is the organization of the people as it arises out of acting and speaking together, and its true space lies between people living together for this purpose, no matter where they happen to be...' Having quoted Arendt, Silverstone writes that '[t]he media provide in their full range of narratives and images...a tangible manifestation of the space in which men and women make their appearance to each other'.

5

The News: Gates,
Agendas and Values

AIMS

➤ To present the case that by its nature and practice the news is the product of the cultural contexts in which it operates: and, rather than mirroring reality, constructs ritual formulations of it.
➤ To explain with reference to landmark theories three core features of news production – gatekeeping, agenda-setting and news values and to examine their interactivity.
➤ To reflect on the role of ideology in the news process.

Sooner or later in every study of media communication we must descend from the high ground that offers us an overview of the terrain to examine texts and practices – the specifics that provide evidence to substantiate theories. So far attention has been trained on generalities such as the nature of audience and audience response and the roles and functions, within context, of mass communication.

More than any other message form, the news provides us with documentation that illustrates and illuminates key connections, between public communication and the exercise of power, between freedom and control, between reality and representation. It is, by its content and its shaping, a *discourse* which purports both to present reality and to explain it.

This chapter puts the case that the news is inevitably slanted because a culture's views of the world at large are coloured by a primary interest in 'its own kind'. This we call ethnocentrism, manifesting itself substantially, though not entirely, in nearness, or proximity. We note also that 'slant' is demonstrated by a preference for featuring Knowns as against Unknowns: the elite are visualized as not only being in the news but making it.

Strategies of news construction, of *framing* the news – gatekeeping and agenda-setting – are examined in relation to the underpinning criteria of news selection, which we call news values or newsworthiness. Acknowledgement is made of the powerfully competing agendas in contemporary society that strive to attract and manipulate public attention and in doing so affect the nature of news production.

The cultural orientation of news

An old adage has often been cited as a definer of what makes 'Western' news. It asserts that a fly in the eye is worse than an earthquake in China. Though ethically indefensible, the adage nevertheless pinpoints two crucial factors in the selection of events to be reported – the *ethnocentric* nature of news coverage (its culture-centredness); and the significance of *proximity*, or nearness.

What happens to 'us' is considered the prime principle of newsworthiness; and if a number of us are killed in that earthquake in faraway China reports of those deaths will guarantee that the tragedy will be more fully reported. Geographical proximity does not automatically qualify as a value demanding news attention. Events in the United States are more readily and substantially reported in Britain, for example, than events in Europe, despite the ties that bind the British to Europe; and the difference is more than one of language. Australia, New Zealand, Canada and India share with the British and Americans the English language but command far less media attention in Britain.

The difference is one of *power-value* arising from key economic, political and cultural interactions, in which America has been the dominant partner. The high profile granted to the USA in the British media, it needs to be said, is at best only modestly reciprocated in American media.

The news is as much about the perceived importance of self and other as it is about 'reality'. As perceptions of importance – significant events, occasions, developments – change, so does reality definition. At a primitive level we might envisage news as the view a sentry has at the mouth of our communal cave: who or what out there is for us or against us, and what threat might they pose? The purpose here is one of *surveillance*.

From the beginning, then, news as a version of reality is skewed by a cultural bias and conditioned by the specifics of situation: the guard dog barks, the sentinel geese cackle and we take action to protect our-selves, whether the 'invader' is a foe from across the water or a scare about salmonella in pre-cooked meals.

Cultural ritual

The surveillance function affirms the *tribal* nature of news. It is part of the rituals that dominate our lives. As our ancestors took guard when dusk fell and watched the night hours for signs of danger, so the Eye of News reports to us daily in the papers, on the hour on radio and several times daily on TV. It is as ritualistic as changing the guard; and in the nature and ordering of its content the news resembles a ceremony. Indeed we are so familiar with content and style that it might be said that the news is actually *olds*: what by precedent has been counted as news continues to be classified and used as news.

The conventions of news production are often so formulaic that they hint at a rightness born of hallowed tradition which in turn, when queried, is righteously defended. In this sense, the news is not in the business of telling us about reality; rather it is privileged to inform us about what is *important* or salient about reality. And importance is key: people or institutions featuring regularly in the news do so because they are judged to be important to society.

They are primary actors in the ritual of cultural reinforcement and renewal, lords and ladies of the dance. Thus a media bias towards re-porting their doings and sayings is, convention decrees, only natural and proper. Herbert Gans in *Deciding What's News*[1] says that Knowns are four times more likely to be in the news than Unknowns. He gauged that fewer than 50 individuals, mostly high-placed federal officials, regularly appear on American TV news.

The ritual of news is characterized both by its ethnocentric nature (its 'us-centredness') and what might be called its 'powercentredness'. Both aspects of the ritual demand a considerable degree of selection, of inclusion and exclusion. The same criteria for selection seem to ap-ply to news *sources*. According to Allan Bell in *The Language of News Media*,[2] 'News is what an authoritative source tells a journalist...The more elite the source, the more newsworthy the story'.

In contrast, says Bell, 'alternative sources tend to be ignored: indi-viduals, opposition parties, unions, minorities, fringe groups, the disad-vantaged'. As far as our opening adage is concerned – about the fly in the eye – selection depends on which fly and in which eye.

News as construct

We are seeing, then, that the news is culturally positioned, and we view reality through a cultural prism. That the rendition of reality is so convincing is partly explained because the news, framed for us by the media, is usually all that we have to go on as a portrait of realities beyond our known environment; and partly because the news is constructed with such professional skill.

Television news suggests that what we see is what there is, that we are being presented with mirror images of reality. One of the best books on 'life seen through a media prism' is edited by Stanley Cohen and Jock Young. It captures the point being made here in its title: *The Manufacture of News*.[3] Contributors to this volume examine the reporting of events and issues in terms of a process of assembly, of construction according to dominant cultural-political criteria. Among subscribers to *The Manufacture of News* are Johan Galtung and Mari Ruge, and Professor Stuart Hall whose work is referred to later in this chapter.

As audience our attention is not, however, drawn to the 'constructed' nature of news. Rather we have grown so accustomed to the modes of news presentation that we are, unless especially cautioned, likely to accept that it is at least a close encounter with reality. Yet journalists provide us with a cue to their trade as 'assembly-workers' when they refer to news reports as 'stories', thus implying a process of invention. As Allan Bell puts it, 'Journalists do not write articles. They write stories' (a theme taken up in the next chapter).

We begin to recognize the artifice of news only when we come face to face with the real thing through lived experience: disasters, riots, protest marches, strikes, demonstrations – news media have filled our heads with visions of how these things 'look'. Just occasionally we encounter such events personally and the shock of the real to our mediated experience can be devastating.

Selecting the news: gatekeeping

In studying the news we need to explore three linked features of production – *gatekeeping*, *agenda-setting* and *news values*. The operation of the first two depends upon the demands of the third which in turn regulates the *conventions* of news presentation. Gatekeeping is about opening or closing the channels of communication; it is about *accessing* or refusing access. In an article 'The "Gatekeepers": a case study in the selection of news', published in *Journalism Quarterly*, 27 (1950),

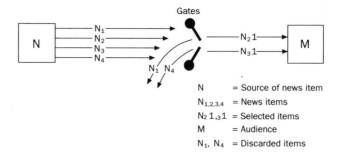

Figure 5.1 White's simple gatekeeping model (1950)

David M. White presents a simple model of the gatekeeping process (Figure 5.1).

White had spent a period of research observing the activities of a 'Mr. Gate', a telegraph wire editor on an American non-metropolitan newspaper. The notion of 'gate areas' had been posed three years earlier by Kurt Lewin in 'Channels of group life' in *Human Relations*, 1 (1947). Lewin's particular attention was focused upon decisions about household food purchases but he drew a comparison with the flow of mass media news.

While the term 'gatekeeping' originates at this time, the practice of it is as old as history and is identifiable in many areas of communication. Students who have done any research will have already experienced gatekeeping: you want some information or you would like to talk to someone, perhaps to interview them for a project you are preparing. Some gates open, some are ajar and need pushing and some are firmly closed against you: why?

Students doing projects or dissertations know why. Those whose say-so rules the opening and closing of gates may be too busy; they are more likely to open the gate – like the news – to Knowns rather than Unknowns. As one of my own students put it in a project log, 'The people I wanted information from didn't think I was important enough to bother with, being a mere student. And I had nothing to exchange with them for their advice and their time'.

At a personal level, gates can sometimes be prised open through sheer determination and persistence, but ultimately the gate swings on hinges of reward; of purpose and worthwhileness. White's model features a number of competing news items (N). At the gate, the sub-editor, 'Mr. Gate', selects those items considered of sufficient interest and importance to be passed through to the next stage of news production. Thus N_2 and N_3 have been selected and have undergone the first stage of transformation, hence White's use of the 'to-the-power 1' at this point (indicating that the 'assembly' process of shaping and selection has already begun).

N_2^1 and N_3^1 are no longer raw information: they are *mediated* information. White's model does not give the criteria for selection and rejection of news items, nor does it acknowledge the fact that in the general process of mediation there are many gates and that gatekeeping in one form or another is taking place at all levels and at each stage of the news manufacturing process.

In 1959 J.T. McNelly produced a model of news that reflects the many-gated reality of news processing. It also indicates that modifications take place to the story as it passes through each gate (Figure 5.2).

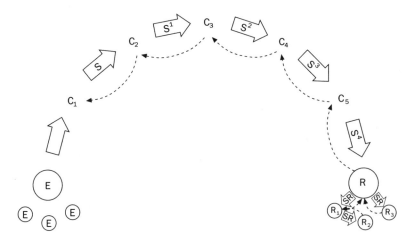

McNelly's model of intermediary communicators in news flow, showing news passing different 'gatekeepers' (after McNelly 1959)
Key to symbols in diagram:
E = Newsworthy event
C_1 = Foreign agency correspondent
C_2 = Regional bureau editor
C_3 = Agency central bureau or deskman
C_4 = National or regional home bureau editor
C_5 = Telegraph editor or radio or TV news editor
S, S^1, S^2, etc = The report in a succession of altered (shortened) forms
R = Receiver
R_1, R_2, etc. = Family members, friends, associates, etc.
SR = Story as modified by word of mouth transmission
Dotted line = feedback

Figure 5.2 McNelly's model of news flow (1959)
An important feature of the McNelly model is the SR feature that recognizes the part audience plays in the mediation of news. The model originates in J.T. McNelly's article, 'Intermediary communicators in the international news', published in *Journalism Quarterly*, 36 (1959).

At every stage in the mediation process, decisions are taken, not only about what events to cover, but how these might be covered and by whom; and gatekeeping is far from having the monopoly of media operators: audience too exercises the powers of selecting and rejecting.

We are all gatekeepers: we self-censor. We decide to say something to another person. The comment passes through the gate. But we may decide *not* to say anything; or we might need to summarize, modify, spruce up, distort, even 'sex up' that which passes through our communicative gate. Yet again, we see the importance in the process of communication of purpose or *intent*.

Reporters with leftish political leanings, working on a rightish newspaper will, if they wish to stay on the payroll, gatekeep pre-emptively; that is, they will be selective about the stories they submit for publication, knowing that certain stories (sympathetic to the left, for example) would simply not be published: so why waste time and effort in submitting them?

Self regulation of this kind is essential if the gates of access to sources of information are to be kept open. In most countries the chief supplier of information is government, and most governments regularize (even ritualize) the provision of information to the media, in particular to what are termed 'lobby correspondents'.

Here, a degree of reciprocal gatekeeping is often a condition of access. Government will provide a certain amount of information in return for the journalist using that information 'properly'. 'Improper' use of that information may lead to the exclusion of a newspaper's lobby correspondent from the privileges of daily access to government news sources.

News gathering, news editing

As we have seen, selection operates at every stage of the news production process. It varies, however, in its nature and concentration. A.Z. Bass poses a 'double action' model of internal news flow (Figure 5.3). This identifies two stages of production, Stage 1, *news gathering* and Stage 2, *news processing*. In Stage 1, reporters and photographers encounter raw news directly, or at least more directly than editors and sub-editors back at the newspaper or broadcasting station. They are usually employed on one news story at a time. By the very fact that they are 'at the scene', they have a degree of choice on what features of an event they will select, and how they will report on them.

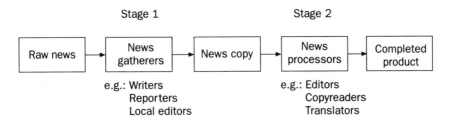

Figure 5.3 Bass's 'double action' model of international news flow (1969)
The model appears in 'Refining the gatekeeper concept' published in *Journalism Quarterly*, 46 (1969).

Once their report reaches the news organization pressures of selection mount. The editorial team has many stories to deal with. They have to balance the demands of one story against another and, as Bass points out, they have to work in accordance with the organization's norms and values. Far more than are reporters in the field, the editorial team is influenced in its decision-making by the cultural climate of the institution which in turn operates more centrally in the eye of government and the public.

Gates in times of crisis

The sound of gates slamming to, in times of crisis such as war, can be as loud as the enemy's artillery. During the Falklands War of 1982, between Britain and Argentina, it became nearly impossible to breach the walls of Fortress Information. Press and television were obliged to queue up at a drawbridge manned by the Ministry of Defence. During the second and third Gulf Wars in 1991 and 2003 (the first was between Iraq and Iran, 1980–88, with Britain and the USA giving tacit support to Iraq), the situation was different in a number of ways. First, the authorities realized that denying media access to the conflict was both impossible and undesirable. It was seen to be important that news reached home populations, albeit in a positive form. The task was to offer access without releasing control.

The strategic answer was *embedded reporting*. Reporters and photographers would be encouraged to get as close to the war front as possible, so long as they were in the company of military units. This was not a new arrangement, for reporters had been 'embedded' with British troops in the First World War (1914–18). In Iraq, it worked to good effect.

As intended, reporters developed an understandable empathy with the troops whose lives and dangers they shared. The threat to independent reporting of the news in these situations proved a source of considerable anxiety to many reporters. There were divided loyalties, between showing respect and gratitude for comrades, and reporting the true facts of war. As John R. MacArthur neatly puts it in *Second Front: Censorship and Propaganda in the 1991 Gulf War* (with a 2004 preface), embedding is 'a kind of censorship by envelopment'.[4]

Gates operate for and against media personnel, depending on whether they can be 'trusted'. It is significant that Don McCullin, one of the world's best photographers of war, was gatekept throughout the Falklands War. While other reporters and photographers were permitted at least into the outer courtyard of Fortress Information, McCullin was not even allowed to cross the moat.

The British Ministry of Defence was, according to its own lights, making the correct decision: McCullin's pictures would not have differentiated between Britons and Argentinians in portraying them as victims of war. His imaging of war as hell would not have sustained the war effort, nurtured consensus about its necessity; rather his pictures might have been instrumental in turning the public against the war.

This is always the risk in allowing the media close to battle stations. In a number of circumstances it has given rise to 'war' within war, in which the media emerge as a justifiable target: the subterranean impression that by shooting the messenger you will obliterate the message has been manifest on more than one occasion as conquest in Iraq turned to the quagmire of occupation, with reporters as much at risk from 'friendly fire' as from the bullets of Iraqi resistance fighters (see Note 5 on the death of reporter Terry Lloyd from friendly fire).

Setting the agendas of news

An agenda is a list of items, usually in descending order of importance. Meetings have agendas that have to be worked to. If an item is not on the agenda prior to the meeting there is only one point at which it can be raised during the meeting – under Any Other Business. The agenda for a meeting is normally drawn up by the secretary to the meeting in consultation with the meeting's chairperson. This gives them some power, to decide what will or will not be discussed at the meeting.

At the meeting itself, the chairperson controls the agenda. He or she may extend or curtail discussion on topics. The skilful chairperson will usually rule by consent, without the need to resort to voting. In

Japan it is a tradition that decisions must already have been tacitly settled prior to the meeting. This is to avoid loss of face resulting from disagreement in public. Meetings conducted in Western countries may seem to be different, open rather than closed texts, as it were. Yet appearances can beguile. For every overt or public agenda there is a covert or hidden one.

As far as the media are concerned one might say that the overt agenda is synonymous with public agendas; that is, what is of most importance to the public appears top of the media agenda. Yet it has to be acknowledged that wherever there are competing interests, rival ideologies, conflicting priorities, agendas are arenas of struggle. Those whose discourse dominates also choose the agenda and order its items. In the media industry reporters may wish to pursue certain agendas, but their activity will be reined in by agendas of ownership and control.

The link between media agendas and public perception of what constitutes news is a vital one to explore. If the public look to the media for news, what the media decides is news is what the public

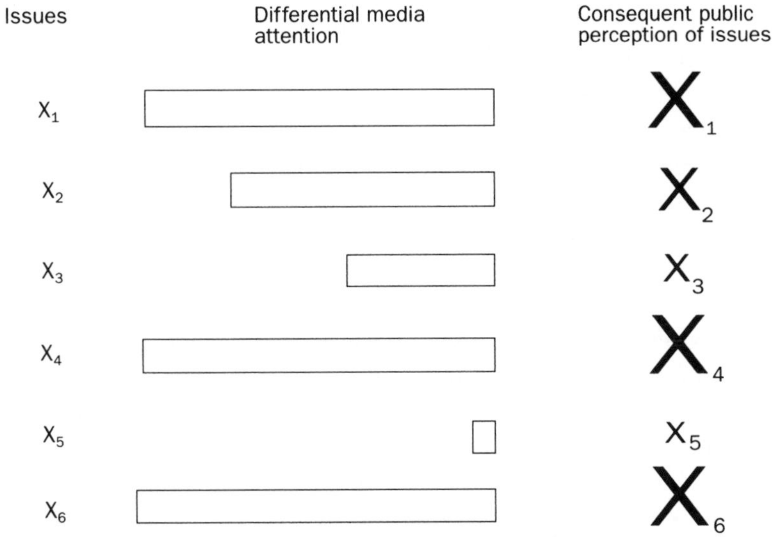

Figure 5.4 McCombs and Shaw's agenda-setting model of media effects (1976)
Each X represents an issue whose importance is amplified by coverage in the media. Even issues of considerable importance may remain of modest or negligible significance in public perception if they suffer media neglect. Maxwell E. McCombs and Donald L. Shaw first discussed agenda-setting in an article 'The agenda-setting function of mass media' published in *Public Opinion Quarterly*, 36 (1972), following this up with 'Structuring the "unseen environment"' in the *Journal of Communication* (Spring, 1976).

recognize as news. What is emphasized by the media is given emphasis in public perception; what is amplified by media is enlarged in public perception. This is illustrated by Donald McCombs and Malcolm Shaw's agenda-setting model of media effects (Figure 5. 4).

In 'Structuring the "unseen environment"' the authors state:

> Audiences not only learn about public issues and other matters through the media, they also learn how much importance to attach to an issue or topic from the emphasis the mass media place upon it. For example, in reflecting what people say during a campaign, the mass media apparently determine the important issues. In other words, the mass media set the 'agenda' of the campaign.

Amplification of issues

McCombs and Shaw argue that the agenda-setting capacity of the media makes them highly influential in shaping public perceptions of the world: 'This ability to affect cognitive change among individuals is one of the most important aspects of the power of mass communication.' The model is an oversimplification, of course. It assumes one agenda – that purveyed by the media which then becomes the agenda of the public. It can be argued that members of the public have their own agendas, shaped by their own personal circumstances.

There are plenty of *intervening variables* that influence our perceptions and our judgements other than media coverage, though it has to be said that none may be quite as powerful as the full force of media definitions, especially if the media are promoting the same definitions in similar ways. A single newspaper claiming that Party Y at an election will put up taxes may not sway public opinion, but ten newspapers saying the same thing, and TV channels reporting what ten newspapers are claiming, may well, through a process of amplification and reinforcement, drive the tax issue to the top of the public agenda.

The McCombs and Shaw model does not tell us whether effects are direct, or, from the point of view of media, intentional. Also, as Denis McQuail and Sven Windahl point out in *Communication Models for the Study of Mass Communication*,[6] the model leaves us uncertain 'whether agenda-setting is initiated by the media or by members of the pubic and their needs, or, we might add, by institutional elites who act as sources for the media'.

A later model of agenda-setting is posed by Everett M. Rogers and James W. Dearing (Figure 5.5). This identifies three interactive agendas. The *Policy* agenda is that propagated by government and

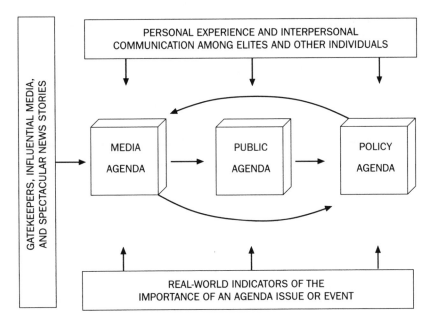

Figure 5.5   Rogers and Dearing's model of the agenda-setting process (1988)
This model was first published in an article 'Agenda-setting: where has it been, where is it going?' in *Communication Yearbook*, 11 (US: Sage, 1987).

politicians. It is one often riven by counter-agendas – the right of the party, the left of the party. Appropriate emphasis is placed in this model on contextual factors: influences pressing in from national and world events.

The Rogers and Dearing model is a useful update of McCombs and Shaw, but one might ask why the three agendas are presented as being of equal size and presumably equal power. Because the model is still a linear one, it does not sufficiently indicate the dynamic relationship between the agendas or the potential for conflict. The policy and media agendas seem to be operating as *balancers* with the public agenda as being central (which of course is what it should be but rarely is). The model conveys balance, thus it is normative.

To focus on the actual distribution of influence one would have to add an extra agenda, that of the corporations which dominate contemporary life (Figure 5.6). Corporate agendas often work in alliance with, and occasionally in competition with, the policy agendas of government, aiming to influence if not order public agendas. The reader may be justifiably tempted to add further arrows to this model to emphasize the interactive nature of the agendas.

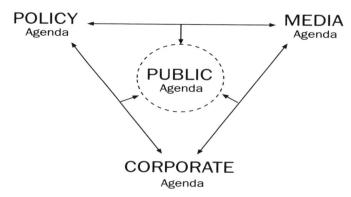

Figure 5.6 Tripolar model of agendas: policy, corporate and media
The public agenda is the only one that does not arise from consciously formed and articulated aims and objectives. Governments, corporations and media largely know what they want from the public and how to go about it. The first two are also aware that in order to create and influence public opinion they have to do it through cultural apparatuses of which the media are arguably the most important. On the other hand, pressure groups in society are instrumental in influencing public opinion with a view to using the force of that opinion to influence government or the corporations.

Agenda, discourse and climate of opinion

We have seen that just as there are many gates there are several agendas; so any analysis of agenda-setting must start with the question, *Whose* agenda, and articulated through which *discourse?* What is obvious is that there is much more to the agenda-setting process than merely listing what is important and what is less important.

Having been placed in a hierarchy of importance, stories are shaped into a discourse, a way of defining and presenting information and ideas; of creating preferred meanings out of which will hopefully arise preferred readings. Let us remind ourselves of the nature and importance of discourse by recalling a definition offered by Gunther Kress in *Linguistic Processes in Sociocultural Practice*:[7]

> Discourses are systematically-organized sets of statements which give expression to the meanings and values of an institution. Beyond that they define, describe and delimit what is possible to say (and by extension – what is possible to do or not to do) with respect to the area of concern of that institution, whether marginally or centrally.

Kress continues:

> A discourse provides a set of possible statements about a given area, and organizes and gives structure to the manner in which a

particular topic, object, process is to be talked about. In that it provides descriptions, rules, permissions and prohibitions of social and individual action.

News is a discourse, and news production is a discourse anchored by the ideology of the news producers or those who employ them, particularly if we are talking about the press. However, no news production is independent of the values that shape and drive the players at all levels. The degree to which the media agenda is also that of the public, its discourse an influential part of public discourse, depends in large part upon the *standing* of the media in public perception; its credibility as a source of information; its reputation for accuracy and sincerity.

In an article 'The future of political communication research: a Japanese perspective' in the *Journal of Communication*,[8] Youichi Ito discusses the relationship between media, government and public in Japan. He speaks of *extracted* information, that which the public draws from sources other than the mass media, from personal experience and observation, for example, and talking to others.

Professor Ito introduces the Western reader to a concept shared by the Chinese and Koreans as well as the Japanese – *kuuki*. This can be translated as a *climate of opinion requiring compliance*. It may be nurtured by the media or by those in government or be the product of extracted information on the part of the public; in other words, it becomes the force of public opinion.

The tripolar model of agendas illustrated in Figure 5.6 helps us keep in mind the potential for *alliances* of influence in the public arena. Media revelations about government corruption, for example, might create an alliance between media and public. Government, now the odd one out in the threesome, may feel pressured into moving into line – responding to the climate of opinion requiring compliance – by taking action over that corruption.

Similarly, gross intrusions into privacy on the part of the media might lead to an alliance between government and public and pressure upon media to put its house in order. Ito writes:

Mass media have effects only when they stand on the majority side or the mainstream in a triadic relationship that creates and supports the kuuki that functions as a social pressure on the minority side.

He is of the opinion that '[s]cholars should pay more attention to the conditions under which mass media credibility is or is not maintained'.

Levels and attributes

A further dimension of the agenda-setting process is suggested by Maxwell McCombs, Esteban Lopez-Escobar and Juan Pablo Llamas in an article, 'Setting the agenda attributes in the 1996 Spanish general election' published in the *Journal of Communication*, Spring 2000. The authors talk of agenda *levels* and *attributes*. Level 1 comprises the central theme of the news story, its most salient aspects; added at Level 2 are particular characteristics and traits that fill out the picture of each object. Some of these attributes are emphasized, 'many are ignored'. McCombs and his colleagues explain:

> Just as objects vary in salience, so do the attributes of each object. Just as there is an agenda of public issues, political candidates, or some other set of objects, there is also an agenda of attributes for each object. Both the selection by journalists of objects for attention and the selection of attributes for detailing the pictures of these objects are powerful agenda-setting roles.

Level 2 helps position or 'frame' Level 1. In fact it is useful to remind ourselves that agendas are *framing devices*. The authors point out that '[a]lthough object and attribute salience are conceptually distinct, they are integral and simultaneously present aspects of the agenda-setting process'. In research conducted into public attitudes to election candidates at the 1996 election in Spain, the following attributes of the major contenders were measured:

- Ideology/issue position;
- Biographical details;
- Perceived qualifications;
- Integrity;
- Personality and image.

In the same edition of the *Journal of Communication* Holli A. Semetko and Patti M. Valkenburg further explore agenda-setting as a framing device. In 'Framing European politics: a content analysis of press and television news', the authors identify five frameworks within which news is most regularly located; in other words, five principles of agenda-setting. These are listed as:

- Attribution of responsibility;
- Conflict;

- Economic consequences;
- Human interest;
- Morality.

Semetko and Valkenburg find that the biggest divergences in framing issues are not between press and television but between serious and sensational types of news outlet; the 'serious' papers and TV focusing on responsibility, the tabloids on human interest.

In a period when the so-called 'quality press' is being accused of increasing *tabloidization*[9] the distinctions between serious and popular are less marked than in the past. Today the celebrities who parade in the tabloids are as likely to feature just as largely in the broadsheets.

Agenda-setting research

Research studies into agenda-setting take two forms: *hierarchy* studies survey all the issues on the media agenda at a given time; *longitudinal* studies investigate fewer issues, possibly two or three, tracing their rise and fall over a period of time. In *Agenda-Setting* (US: Sage, 1996) James Dearing and Everett Rogers note that 'there are strengths and weaknesses of both the hierarchy and longitudinal approaches' but believe that the latter 'can provide explanatory insights into the often intricate process of agenda-setting'.

Longitudinal studies tend to counter the notion that events spring dramatically from the media to the public agenda. Dearing and Rogers speak of the 'cumulative effect of media messages about an issue' working through 'the relentless, accumulated impact of a repeated message topic'. Slowly 'the public agenda for an issue builds up. Sometime later, it will melt away'.

The authors are of the view that '[h]ow an issue is reported is as important as whether the issue is reported at all' and this may in part gain in momentum through what they refer to as *triggers*, that is particular incidents, or personal involvements by usually well-known people, whom Dearing and Rogers call 'issue champions':

> Charismatic or issue proponents seem to be necessary for launching certain issues, such as rock musician Bob Geldof for the 1984 Ethiopia famine and former *San Francisco Chronicle* reporter Randy Shilts for the issue of AIDS in San Francisco.

Would such issues have progressed through the agenda-setting process, Dearing and Rogers ask, without these issue champions? What is for certain is that celebrities are usually part of the frame and may well dictate its nature. This gives emphasis to the point made by Dearing and Rogers about *how* an issue is reported; and we might add, in what *frame* it is reported. It is important to realize that the same event, or issue, will very likely be transmitted through different frames and thus may have varying impact upon public perceptions and the public agenda.

News values

The complexities of gatekeeping and agenda-setting may at this point appear to be sending us every which way. We sense, however, that somewhere in the scrummage there is at least a vague set of rules of combat as far as media performance is concerned. Such rules we refer to as *news values*.

The names of two Norwegian scholars, Johan Galtung and Mari Ruge, have become as associated with news value analysis as Hoover with the vacuum cleaner. Their Model of Selective Gatekeeping of 1965, while not carrying quite the romance of the apple that fell on Newton's head, is nevertheless a landmark in the scholarship of media (Figure 5.7).

Galtung and Ruge were not the first to assemble a list of criteria for news selection. As early as 1695 a German writer, Kaspar Steiler, wrote about news values in his book *Zeitungs Lust und Nutz*, roughly translatable as *Uses and Gratifications of Newspapers*. Steiler discusses *importance* as a news value and the *proximity* – nearness to home – of events. Also, he identifies events that are *dramatic* and *negative*. The American

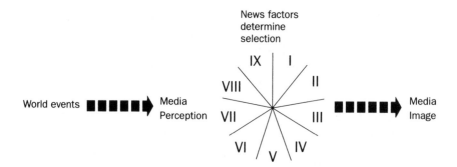

Figure 5.7 Galtung and Ruge's model of selective gatekeeping (1965)
The model suggests that until a world event is *perceived* as being newsworthy by the media, it will not qualify for consideration for transformation into a media *image* of that event.

Walter Lippman produced his own analysis of news values in 1922, in *Public Opinion*.[10]

The now-famous taxonomy, or classification, of news values by Galtung and Ruge was first proposed in an article in the *Journal of International Peace Research*.[11] This was reprinted in *The Manufacture of News* (see Note 3) and elsewhere. Of equal note when news values are being discussed is another contribution printed in *The Manufacture of News* – Stuart Hall's seminal article, 'The determinations of news photographs', a must-read for any student of media.

In the Galtung and Ruge model potential items of news resemble guests arriving at a hotel. Standing sentinel is the doorman, Media Perception, who lets some visitors pass through the revolving door of news values while others end up back in the street. As the privileged guests emerge from the revolving doors they do so with the shape and gloss of media images. They have been processed as well as selected.

A number of values the authors define as being culture-free, others culture-linked, although it has to be said that attempting to describe any activity as being unaffected by the culture that surrounds it is a knotty problem and one which may not really warrant the effort. Indeed the authors acknowledge that 'what we choose to consider an "event" is culturally determined'.

Events, argue Galtung and Ruge, will be more likely to be reported if they fulfil any one or more of a number of conditions, particularly if they fulfil these conditions in combination. Below, I have listed and then enlarged upon 11 of the news factors that Galtung and Ruge identify.

Frequency

If the event takes a time to occur approximate to the frequency of the medium's output of news – hourly, four times daily, daily or weekly – it at least initially qualifies for inclusion in news rather than if it has an 'awkward' timescale (usually, long). A murder, for example, is more newsworthy than the slow progress to prosperity of a Third World country. The completion over months or years of a dam that will aid irrigation and thus improve crops is less likely to be reported than if the same dam is blown up by terrorists.

Amplitude

The bigger, the better, the more dramatic, the more likely the event is to achieve what the authors call 'threshold value', meaning poised to pass through the gate; and 'the more violent the murder the bigger the headlines it will make'. Amplitude alone may not necessarily constitute a news value. In order to qualify it will be subject to regulation by geographical or cultural proximity. Three hundred people can die in a plane crash in Nepal and this *may* warrant an inside story in the Western press. However the presence of 'our own' people on board, however few in number, is likely to drive the story up the agenda.

The suggestion here is that *numbers* have significance only for the value placed upon them. In other words, numbers are manipulated ideologically. During the third Iraq War and occupation, the Allied forces of the USA and Britain made no attempt to assess the number of Iraqi deaths. To do so, one might conjecture, would be a self-defeating exercise: gathering the figures and publishing them might result in a greater awareness on the part of the public of the enormity of the slaughter; and those figures could be used as a weapon against the allies' purposes and actions.

BBC foreign correspondent Jeremy Bowen, discussing the 'sums' of news in *War Stories*[12] writes, 'A traditional British newsroom follows a terrible arithmetic. Generally speaking, the further away from London, and the poorer the people, the more deaths it takes to qualify as a big story'. He concedes, however, that the 'arithmetic is changing now, because round-the-clock news services have much more airtime to fill, and because technology makes it easier to cover stories in remote parts of the world'.

Unambiguity

Galtung and Ruge speak of *clarity*. The more uncomplicated the events, the more they will be noticed and reported. A number of qualifications attach to this value. Some events are of sufficient amplitude to warrant coverage even though they may be complicated. Industrial disputes often fall into this category. What may happen is that the dispute is reported but freed from the complexities that surround it.

We are seeing here the link between value and the process of news construction. Finding an event complicated or ambiguous, the media will generally work towards simplification; and one approach is to single out those items (or attributes) within a complex story that actually are unambiguous, such as actions, which may be direct and clear-cut, whereas the causes of those actions are more complex.

Marc Raboy and Bernard Dagenais in their introduction to *Media, Crisis and Democracy*[13] speak of a 'tendency to flatten a complex and multi-textured phenomenon into simple formulations' and such a tendency they see as value-loaded. They cite the case of the second Gulf

War (1991), but could equally be discussing its successor, when they say the Western media 'blackened Saddam Hussein [the Iraqi president] and his regime, obscuring all possible consideration of the real meaning of the war, of US designs and motives, of the manipulation of public opinion and disinformation'.

Oversimplification on the part of the media has less to do with the pressures of time (deadline-meeting) than with value-judgements, manifested by the collusion that occurs between authority and media in times of crisis. Indeed Raboy and Dagenais see *crisis* as a news value in its own right because it provides dramatic stories.

Familiarity

Emphasis has already been placed upon *ethnocentrism* as a news value: that which is familiar to us, about which we know something, whether it involves neighbours, neighbouring communities or neighbouring nations, is considered important because events affecting them could also be events affecting us. We are more 'at home' with what is familiar to us, generally more interested in people and places we know than those strange to us.

Galtung and Ruge state that while 'the culturally distant will be passed by more easily and not be noticed' an exception to normal practice will come about through *relevance*: a 'remote country may be brought in [to the news] via a pattern of conflict with one's own group'.

Predictability

Drawing upon a work by Bernard Berelson and Gary A. Steiner, *Human Behaviour: An Inventory of Scientific Findings*,[14] Galtung and Ruge refer to a 'hypothesis of consonance' where news is what is expected to happen, a fulfilment of predictions. News operators 'know' what news is: when events conform to this expectation, they are reported, largely in routine ways, reflecting routine thinking. Galtung and Ruge contend:

A person *predicts* that something will happen and this creates a mental matrix for easy reception and registration of the event if it does finally take place. Or he *wants* it to happen and the matrix is even more prepared, so much so that he may distort perceptions he receives and provide himself with images consonant with what he has wanted. In the sense mentioned here 'news' are actually 'olds', because they correspond to what one expects to happen...

In short, this is a version of wish-fulfilment: the event or issue fits into a pre-existing frame which in turn will shape the way the event or issue will be reported. It is a practice seen by a number of media observers to result in stereotyping of people and situations. Reporting of race often stands accused of allowing expectations to become predictions, and predictions in turn to become self-fulfilling prophecies.

If black youths are associated in the minds of the media operators with violence, then, the hypothesis of consonance would suggest, those operators will actively look for violence to occur. This theme is analyzed by Christopher P. Campbell in *Race, Myth and the News*.[15] The author writes of 'a kind of tunnel vision' that contributes to contemporary racist attitudes in the media.

Since 9/11 and the London bombings in July 2005, race and religion have all too predictably become grounds for stereotyping – blaming the whole for the few, to the point where Islam has frequently been portrayed, by politicians as well as the media, as a metonym for divisiveness and violence.

Surprise

News values compete with one another and the value of surprise runs counter to that of predictability. That which is unexpected may well prove a vital news value. Thus dog biting man (especially if he is a postman) is scarcely news; but man biting dog, that is newsworthy. As Galtung and Ruge say, 'Events have to be unexpected or rare, or preferably both, to become good news'.

Youth gangs terrorizing neighbourhoods is news because the action might be deemed predictable. Yet the same youths might qualify as news if their behaviour contradicts the stereotype: if they surprise media expectations by, for example, campaigning on behalf of a multi-ethnic society.

Surprise can also reinvigorate or reposition the coverage of current news events. Following bombing attempts in London and Glasgow in the summer of 2007, the arrest of hospital doctors opened press headlines to fresh codas of concern, incredulousness and outrage (*Daily Mirror* headline, 3 July: DOCS OF WAR).

Correspondence

Once a story is up and running it will often continue to be covered even past its sell-by date in terms of its headline potential. Galtung and Ruge say:

The channel has been opened and stays partly open to justify it being opened in the first place, partly because of inertia in the system and partly because what was unexpected has now become familiar.

It is in the interest of the media to keep stories simmering because there is always the potential to give an old tale a new twist. For example, it is common practice to link stories on similar themes, for such links strengthen news value. Old stories are regularly dusted down and given new life where they are perceived to clarify or reinforce – and amplify – the significance of new stories.

Composition

This value arises from what Galtung and Ruge term a 'desire to present a "balanced" whole'. A diet of really bad news cries out for some balancing good news: the grim needs to be matched with the cheerful, the horrific with the heart-warming. Television news often rounds off with a human interest story – light, humourous, oddball.

The cynic might see even in this practice a degree of manipulation: let people go to bed thinking the world is an entirely horrible place and in future they might switch off the news altogether. The danger is of distraction or *deflection*, where what we remember of a news bulletin may not be the headline story about government corruption but the end-of-bulletin 'filler' about a yodelling parrot or a baseball team which has won its only game in 25 years.

Eliteness

The term 'eliteness' is actually used by Allan Bell in *The Language of News Media* (see Note 2) in offering his own variation on Galtung and Ruge; but the authors count as a primary value the importance of elite people, elite institutions and elite nations in the news. The elite are Knowns. They have titles, positions. They are easily referenced; enabling stories to be *personified*, to be shifted from the theoretical and the general to the specific, the focused and the colourful. And of course having qualified for coverage the elite increase their public profile by being featured in the media.

Galtung and Ruge believe that '[e]lite people are available to serve as objects of general identification, not only because of their intrinsic importance'. Being the influentials in society, its leaders and leader-makers, the power elite possess symbolic value; hence their words as well as their actions are reported. Their opinions are more sought after and recorded. The most banal utterances of presidents and prime ministers will be reported even though they do not qualify under any criterion other than that they issue from 'top' people.

Personification

The *potential* for personalizing a story, by emphasizing its human interest, is a critically important news value, one invariably operated by the popular press. For every issue or event there has to be a person to associate with it, to encapsulate it, to symbolize it. Personality becomes a metonym for the story and its theme, and the characteristics – the attributes – of both become interchangeable.

There seems to be the need for somebody to blame, to shoulder responsibility, to be answerable: after all, you can't take a picture of an issue. Matters of political, economic, industrial or environmental importance; issues concerning gender, race, crime and punishment may involve thousands or millions, but they are swiftly re-presented in person-form: a general becomes the epitome of the war effort; the complexities of an industrial dispute are boiled down to the features of the leading protagonists.

Personification serves as an antidote to ambiguity: it simplifies as it clarifies. Further, it can add dramatic edge by matching personality with precedent. In reporting the 1991 and 2003 Gulf wars the tabloids made clear to readers the *resemblance* between Saddam Hussein and Adolph Hitler; while during the conflict in the Balkans Serb president Slobodan Milosevic was varyingly linked with Hitler and the devil. On 1 April 1999 the UK *Sun* ran a headline NAZIS 1999: SERB CRUELTY HAS CHILLING ECHOES OF THE HOLOCAUST. The effect of such historical allusion adds, by means of *demonization*, to the news value of the story.

Negativity

The only good news, it has often been said as far as news gatherers are concerned, is bad news. If immigrant workers in Germany are being terrorized by fascist gangs; if their houses are being fire-bombed; if they are beaten to death on the streets of Bremen or Stuttgart, then Germany will feature on the agenda of British or American news media more readily than that nation's successful incorporation, politically and economically, of (formerly communist) East Germany.

What Anthony Smith has termed 'aberrant news values'[16] are especially assertive in a free press system. This point hardly needs stressing, but the effects of bad news reporting are of critical and ongoing importance in our analysis of media performance. Bad news creates bad impressions: what is treated negatively, placed within negative frames, risks being thought about negatively.

Because the media are preoccupied with outcomes, we, as audience, rarely acquire information beyond the bad news. We are told *what* but rarely *how* or *why*. Explanation and analysis, the tracing of effects back to causes, do of course feature in media coverage; but the media operator might argue that sensation rather than analysis sells newspapers and boosts TV ratings.

Operational factors

Having produced their list of news values that set the agenda that controls the media gates; having provided advice which might enable us to at least know how lived events become mediated events in the news, Galtung and Ruge suggest three hypotheses of process under the headings *selection*, *distortion* and *replication*.

The more an event satisfies news values, the more it is likely to be selected. Once an item has been selected what makes it newsworthy will be accentuated. This is what the authors call the distortion stage; and the process will recur at each phase of production as the item passes to audience. Replication is what happens when a 'version' reaches a new step in the process.

Television's news values

Gantung and Ruge base their taxonomy of news values on criteria operated by the press. In *Journalists at Work*,[17] Jeremy Tunstall applies Galtung and Ruge to news values that govern TV news selection, suggesting four points of difference:

1. In TV the visual is given pre-eminence.
2. News items which include film of 'our own reporters' interviewing or commentating on a story are preferred.
3. TV makes use of a smaller fraction of the *number* of stories the newspapers carry, and even major items are short compared with newspaper coverage.
4. There is preference for *actuality* stories which film of actual events makes possible for TV.

It is the *version*, not the reality, which is being worked upon: the 'longer the chain [of processing activities], the more selection and distortion will take place ... every link in the chain reacts to what it receives ... according to the same principles'. In other words, once the features of a story have been assembled, the attributes identified, once the construction is under way, the subsequent phases of the operation build on the construction, not on 'reality'.

The status of source

In *The Language of News Media*[2] Allan Bell, making some useful additions to Galtung and Ruge, writes of *attribution* as a value. Attribution in this instance refers to the *source* of a news item, its reliability, status or prestige: organizations are, for example, characterized as being more 'reliable' sources than individuals, unless of course those individuals are elite persons.

'The more elite the source,' says Bell, 'the more newsworthy the story.' He refers to those who 'wear a general mantle of authority and are part of the institutional network where journalists expect to get information'. This value applies not only to what people do, but to who is saying what: 'Talk is news only if the right person is talking.' In this sense, the elite not only *are* the news, they *make* it. Bell is voicing similar sentiments to those of the American analyst David Barsamian who refers to journalists as 'stenographers to power'.[18]

The exception that proves the rule

If what Allan Bell says is true, that some sources of information – like trade unions, for example – suffer from media neglect; and if proximity – cultural, geographical or commercial – is a prime value for news selection, why is it that in the 1980s Poland hit the headlines in the British press and was regularly reported on TV?

After all, Poland is classifiable as a faraway country of which we know little. And yet in the early 1980s the activities of the Polish trade union Solidarity sprang into British headlines. British trade unionists must have looked on in amazement as a Conservative government and a Conservative press turned the Polish workers into heroes and not demons.

What was going on? Had news values suffered a rush of blood to the head? Was the world of values being suddenly inverted? These questions had extra pertinence in the light of what was happening to trade unions in Britain where workers' rights were being drastically restricted by new legislation. There is a plausible answer:

Ideology

This is not exactly the missing piece from the news values jigsaw because the assumption is obvious enough that the power elite come with their values, their ideology, attached. Nevertheless, any taxonomy that does not include reference to ideology is failing to offer a basis for explaining the 'Poland conundrum'.

The explanation for Solidarity suddenly becoming the headline flavour of the month in Britain lies not in the fact that here was a trade union fighting for the good of its workers; rather it was because its struggle was seen to be part of a grander conflict between Western nations and the Iron Curtain countries, between capitalism and communism.

Any force, even a trade union, standing out against the ideology of communism, for that is what Solidarity was perceived to be doing, would stimulate Western interest, western support and media coverage. In this case, the news values of importance and proximity were secondary to ideology.

Ideology and the news

Stuart Hall in 'The determinations of news photographs' (in *The Manufacture of News*, see Note 3) perceives two levels of news value. The first he describes as *formal*, the other *ideological*. Formal news values belong to 'the world and discourse of the newspaper, to newsmen as a professional group, to the institutional apparatus of news-making'. Ideological news values 'belong to the realm of moral-political discourse' in society.

This 'double articulation' as Hall terms it 'binds the inner discourse of the newspaper to the ideological universe of the society'. In practice 'there is probably little or no distinction between these two aspects of news production,' believes Hall. Ideology is essentially hidden, representing a '"deep structure" whose function as a selective device is un-transparent even to those who professionally most know how to operate it'. Hall believes '[e]vents enter the domain of ideology as soon as they become visible to the news-making process'.

Figure 5.8 Westerståhl and Johansson's model of news factors in foreign news (1994)

It would seem appropriate, then, that the model of news values suggested by Jorgen Westerståhl and Folke Johansson in the *European Journal of Communication*, 1994[19] places ideology in the centre of the news-making process (Figure 5.8).

Although the model relates specifically to foreign news, it has a general application. *Drama* enters the picture and, with news stories as well as fictional ones, the drama is bad news for someone. Stuart Hall is more specific. For him, in the domain of political news, the most salient news value is *violence*.

In the Westerståhl and Johannson model recognition is given to *access*, as much a circumstance as a value. If journalists have easy access to events, as they had during the Vietnam War (1959–75), they are obviously more able to use the evidence of their own eyes, their own direct experience, than if they are herded together far from the war zone and fed information by officials as they were during the 1991 Gulf War or if access was both geographically difficult and particularly dangerous for journalists and photographers.

This was the case with the Chechen civil war in the Soviet Union from 1994, a largely unreported conflict resulting from hazards of access to the Chechen capital, Grozny, and other parts of the country. The McCombs and Shaw model (Figure 5.4) is apposite here, for minimal media coverage of the Chechen war meant that public interest in or knowledge of the fate of the Chechen people was limited where it existed at all (see Note 20 referring to power agenda attitudes).

Very often, at home as well as abroad, the only information available is from official sources. Westerståhl and Johansson speak in their article of 'reporting coloured by national interest'. As far as Western nations are concerned, that interest is coloured by a 'common Western ideology'; in short, capitalism of the 'free market' variety, characterized by policies of privatization, deregulation and commoditization.

Ideology: absence

Where ideology appears to have no particular purchase, nations and the media that report them tend to take no sides. An example given by Westerstähl and Johansson is the first Gulf War, between Iraq and Iran which 'represented a case where the readiness in the Western world to identify with either side was at its lowest level'. For this reason, few news values were activated: 'in terms of news coverage, the death of, let us say, one Israeli soldier counted as much as the death of hundreds of Iranian or Iraqi soldiers'.

In this sense, as far as Western nations were concerned, the Iran–Iraq conflict was an 'absent war'. Absence also plays a part in events that *are* covered. While prior to and during the Gulf wars the public in the West were being informed of the necessity to vanquish Saddam Hussein, tyrant over his own people, and while America's amazing high-tech weaponry was being demonstrated on world TV screens, very little was being said about the hidden guest at the feast – oil; an 'untransparent' feature of Gulf War coverage; lubricating the wheels of ideology. It is similarly claimed by critics that the war against the Taliban in Afghanistan, headlined as a war on terrorism, has featured another public 'absence' – information about the route of vulnerable oil pipelines crossing Afghanistan from Uzbekistan.

Ideology and cultural identity

As the Millennium approached and passed, the old fault-lines between capitalism and communism became less marked than conflicts of a cultural/ethnic/religious nature. The break-up of the Soviet Union resulted in numerous set-tos, struggles for independence of which the Chechen war was only one example. Yugoslavia split and was engulfed in war along ethnic lines – Catholic Croats versus Christian Orthodox Serbs versus Bosnian Muslims.

The media both within former Yugoslavia and in the rest of the world became proponents of these ideological differences, by taking sides and influencing power agendas. For example, of Western nations, Germany was the first to recognize Croatia's breakaway from the state of Yugoslavia; and it did so as a result of public and media pressure at home. Flora Lewis in 'Between TV and the Balkan War' published in *New Perspectives Quarterly*, 11 (Summer 1994), writes:

> Bavarian TV, much weighed upon by the very conservative Bavarian government and the strong assertive Catholic church which had close connections with the church in Croatia, provided the television reports for all Germany when the war [with the Serbs] began in earnest. The coverage was very one-sided.

Here was a good example of the power of alliances with shared agendas, in this case between public opinion in Germany and the dominant media. Harried by TV, stalked by the *Frankfurter Allgemeine Zeitung* and other media, government responded to kuuki, a climate of opinion requiring compliance. Support for the recognition of Croatia in Germany was, as Lewis says, 'opinion-pushed not government-pulled'.

In turn, alliances between public opinion and media in Christian orthodox countries – Russia and Greece for example – placed support for Christian Orthodox Serbia at the top of the power agenda, just as Muslim nations rallied round the cause of Bosnian Muslims.

A significant influence affecting Croatia's ranking as a news value was the residence in Germany of some 600,000 Croatians. It might be argued that a factor that has largely been overlooked in assessing news within national frameworks has been the 'diaspora element',[21] the degree to which cultures, having travelled to new climes, exert powerful influences upon their adoptive homelands. Thus the Jewish and Irish diasporas to the United States may be seen to reflect American attitudes to, for example, Israel and Ireland; and to command favoured media attention.

News values and the pressures of time

A further criterion of newsworthiness that warrants a mention here is one posed by Philip Schlesinger in the 1970s and which seems to be even more apposite now: *immediacy*. The emphasis on the importance of time in industrial societies, highlighted in the Preface to this edition and discussed in Chapter 1, has embedded itself in the exercise of news values: the world is in a rush; time is ideological.

In an article entitled 'Newsmen and their time machine' in the *British Journal of Sociology*,[22] Schlesinger defined immediacy as the time that has elapsed between the occurrence of an event and its public reporting as news. It refers to the speed with which coverage can be mounted; and the model example would be a 'live' broadcast: 'News is "hot" when it is most immediate. It is "cold", and old, when it can no longer be used in the newsday in question.'

Immediacy is embodied in every newsperson's mental script: it shapes and structures his or her practices. It exercises a powerful influence over the format and running order of news presentation. Related to this is *pacing*: 'Each news bulletin is structured according to a concept of the right pace'; and this pace is dictated by the need to 'move things along' in order to keep the audience's attention.

The news value of immediacy can be linked to an addition Allan Bell makes to the Galtung and Ruge taxonomy – that of *competition*. What dictates choice and treatment is the competition from other newspapers, from other broadcasting channels. If, as Herbert Gans says in *Deciding What's News*,[1] the chief criteria for news presentation are clarity, brevity and colour then news producers will compete to be clear (unambiguous), brief (so as not to lose audience interest) and colourful (in order to capture and hold attention).

The news has, therefore, to be entertaining and immediacy is perceived to be an essential ingredient of entertainment. Yet Schlesinger argues that immediacy creates situations in which news is all foreground and too little background; where the emphasis on *now* obscures the *historical* sequence of events. He speaks of 'bias in the news against the long-term, and it is plausible to argue that the more we take note of news, the less we can be aware of what lies behind it'.

Tabloid news values

The tabloid press lives by popular appeal, cynical for the most part about what constitutes 'public interest' but reverential and wholehearted about 'what interests the public'. They are constantly accused of sensation-chasing, their clarity perceived as oversimplification, their brevity and colour resulting from favouring action over explanation, the emotive over the rational. The tabloids would argue in their defence that their success proves that they gratify the needs of their readers, and that this success is achieved by understanding and appropriately catering for those needs.

This they believe qualifies them to speak up for their readers' interests, to be the accredited voice of the 'silent majority'. Armed with a role seen often as a mission, the tabloids know neither fear nor self-doubt. They often display the righteousness of zealots, intolerant of contradiction, dismissive of those whose opinions, attitudes or lifestyles vary from the norms and values paraded daily in their pages.

Of course, just as the tabloids are exponents of flak they have also to put up with it from unforgiving critics. In *Sex, Lies and Democracy: The Press and the Public*,[23] Michael Bromley and Hugh Stephenson speak of tabloid reporting as 'intrusive, offensive, quasi-pornographic, arrogant, inaccurate, salacious and unprincipled'.

The true 'colour', ideologically, of the tabloid press is predicated on two factors, ownership and market competition. The stance of the UK *Sun* or the *News of the World* on matters political, social, cultural, economic and environmental has reflected the *intent* of their owner, Rupert Murdoch.

The transfer of the News Corp portfolio to Murdoch's son James in December 2007 will only result in a change of face or direction should circulations dip and advertising revenues fall.

A tabloid formula: C+5S

For brevity's sake, and on behalf of clarity and colour, tabloid news values might be summarized as follows:

CELEBRITY

SEX

SENSATION

SCANDAL

SLEAZE

SOAPS

If celebrity does not already exist, the five Ss are means to achieving it. Once achieved, Celebrity will qualify as news value to the degree that it is served by one, two, three or all of the initiating and sustaining S-values.

The tabloids' preoccupation with soaps is of special note because soaps provide all the ingredients the taboids look out for, on a plate, day in day out. Forget that they are fictions. They give us the works – sex, sensation, scandal and ample dollops now and again of sleaze. They come ready-formed, familiar to readership; and they offer a double-take, tall tales about the actors who play the fictional characters until

Hypocrisy and figleaf sermons

When Iran released the 15 British sailors and marines from brief captivity in April 2007, Britain's popular press competed to publish the experiences of 'our boys' and one girl. The *Sun* got one prize, the memoir of Fay Turney, and the *Daily Mirror* the trembling tale of the youngest member of the party, Arthur Batchelor.

Also prominent in the bidding were the *Daily Mail* and *Mail on Sunday*, the former offering, by email, 'a very substantial sum'. The *Mail on Sunday* joined with the *Sunday Mirror* to triple the £30,000 offer from the *Daily Express* while the *News of the World* proposed to outbid them all.

Its overture rejected, the *Mail* leapt indignantly upon a high moral horse. In its 12 April issue, it reproduced pictures of the coffins of soldiers recently killed in Iraq, with this mordant accompaniment: '*They* won't be selling their story, minister. Their silent homecoming from Basra in coffins draped with the union flag could not have been more different from the return last week of the 15 sailors and marines held captive in Iran – with goody bags and a green light to hawk their stories for cash'.

 Having done 'the biz', the *Sun* was not slow to point out the double standards of its competitors, touting for memoirs one minute, reacting in disgust the next. Columnist Polly Toynbee in a UK *Guardian* article, 'Our press, the worst in the west, demoralises us all' (13 April 2007), called the chequebook combat between Britain's popular press, 'heart-stopping hypocrisy… What is so squalid about these newspapers is their use of figleaf sermons to cover the real business, done with corrupting chequebook, threat, intimidation, invasion of privacy, paparazzi aggression and vicious cruelty'.

what's real and what's imagined is blurred; and somehow it doesn't matter. Not, that is, if it boosts circulation and also increases the viewing figures of soaps.

However, the embrace between the Red Tops and TV, a seemingly ideal example of synergy, of activity of mutual benefit, may in the long term prove the opposite. In his 'On the press' column in the *Media Guardian*,[24] ex-national newspaper editor Andrew Neil, referring to the inexorable decline of tabloid sales, had this to say about the likely fate of the tabloid press:

The rise of multi-channel TV and the internet have done for the tabloids. In the days of the old BBC–ITV duopoly the red-tops provided what it didn't: sex, scandal, celebrity, gossip and sport. To-day there are scores of channels devoted to these pursuits and what TV cannot provide, the internet can.

Neil is of the opinion that 'the name of the game for tabloid editors now is the successful management of decline'. It would seem that the formula C+5S does not guarantee profit or long-term survival. Could this possibly be the opportunity for the tabloids to reconsider the news values and news practices they live by?

Summary

The cultural orientation of news, its ethnocentric nature and its resemblance to ritual have been stressed. However effectively, through professional skill, the news convinces us that it replicates reality we have to keep in mind that it is only a *version* of reality; and that it is highly constructed.

The process has been examined by which an event is transformed into news. Decisions concerning the content and presentation are governed by news values that manifest themselves through agenda-setting – giving priority to some events or issues rather than others.

Every potential news item passes through a number of media 'gates' and at each gate further selection – and *mediation* – takes place. The importance of the study of agenda-setting is emphasized and reference is made to potentially competing agendas – those of governments (policy) and corporations as well as public and media agendas. Just as agendas may conflict they may also enter into alliance.

News values classified by Galtung and Ruge have been explained and linked to Stuart Hall's two *levels* of news value, formal and ideological. Selection, distortion and replication are seen to confirm the notion of news as a *construct* and a number of other values, such as crisis, immediacy, access and attribution are discussed.

Ideology is viewed as a key feature of news production. It operates within cultural and institutional contexts, influencing the ways in which news represents reality. There is recognition here of the shifting ground of ideology over which the media are important commentators and interpreters. Finally, tabloid news values are touched upon and tabloid practices related to fictional narratives such as soaps, a theme taken up in the next chapter when the forms and features of *narrative* are explored.

KEY TERMS

ethnocentrism   proximity   power-value   reality   definition   surveillance
conventions   knowns/unknowns   manufacture of consent   discourse
mediation   self-regulation   news gathering/news processing   consensus
news management   overt/covert   amplification/reinforcement
public perception   intervening variables   ideology   extracted information
kuuki   alliances   tabloidization   levels/attributes
hierarchy/longitudinal studies   threshold value   hypothesis of consonance
selection/distortion/replication   formal and ideological news values
diaspora element   attribution   immediacy   clarity/brevity/colour

Suggested activities

1. Discussion:
   (a) What strategies might non-elite persons or groups devise to improve their chances of having their voice heard on local and national news agendas?
   (b) Consider the view that the news is an agency of social control.
   (c) Compare the effectiveness as news media of newspapers, television and radio.
   (d) How far do you consider the media are prone to 'judging by appearances'?
2. Study a TV news bulletin (or bulletins) and gauge the number of stories involving elite and non-elite persons. Document the time devoted to such stories and indicate the particular news values which have 'opened the gate' to such stories. How much attention has been paid to what the actors in the story *say* compared to what they *do*?
3. Examine tabloid newspapers in search of examples of Wedom/ Theydom; their references to minorities, foreign nationals, other countries. How are they described, categorized? What difference is there in coverage of stories of 'other' between the tabloids and the so-called quality press?
4. Video record a TV news broadcast and play it to a group of viewers, half of whom you blindfold (or have sitting with their backs to the screen). When the bulletin is over, conduct a test on how much non-visual information the participants can remember. Who scores best, those who could see the on-screen images or those who couldn't?

5. Do a gender-count of a day's news, in the papers and in broadcast news. Do women feature as prominently as men; and with what kind of stories are women/men most familiarly identifiable?
6. A longer-term task would be to conduct a comparison of news values manifested in the media of different countries. How similar are they, how contrasting? Do all or any of the criteria of Galtung and Ruge have universal application?

Now read on

It is risky to fall into the trap of believing that the latest volume renders earlier books out of date. Roger Fowler's *Language in the News: Discourse and Ideology in the Press* (UK: Routledge, 1991) still provides an invaluable read concerning the way news is assembled into discourses through language. A classic of the genre is James Curran and Jean Seaton's *Power Without Responsibility* (UK: Routledge, 6th edition 2003) giving a very readable background to press and broadcasting in the UK); also from these authors, Curran's *Media and Power* (UK: Routledge, 2002) and Seaton's *Carnage and the Media: The Making and Breaking of News About Violence* (UK: Allen Lane, 2005).

This is a good time to read of first-hand reporting experience. War correspondents have produced some excellent recollections of their work. Try *News from No Man's Land* (UK: Pan, 2003) by BBC correspondent John Simpson, *War Stories* ((UK/US: Simon & Shuster, 2006) by Jeremy Bowen, already mentioned in this chapter and, perhaps the classic of its kind, Phillip Knightley's *The First Casualty: The War Correspondent as Myth-Maker from the Crimea to Kosovo* (UK: Priam Books, revised edition, paperback, 2000).

The propaganda of war is dealt with in such varying tomes as Sheldon Rampton and John Stauber's *Weapons of Mass Deception: the Uses of Propaganda in Bush's Iraq War* (UK: Robinson, 2003), *Tell Me No Lies: Propaganda and Media Distortion in the Attack on Iraq* (UK: Pluto Press, 2004), edited by David Miller and *The Record of the Paper: How the* New York Times *Misreports US Foreign Policy* (UK/US: Verso, 2004) by Howard Friel and Richard Falk.

The issue of how being poorly informed or uninformed by media affects our perception of international situations, in particular conflicts, is examined by Greg Philo and Mike Berry in *Bad News from Israel* (UK: Glasgow University Media Group, 2004). To escape being fixated on Western perspectives of media events, see *Al-Jazeera:The Story of the*

Network That Rattled Governments and Redefined Modern Journalism (US: Westview, 2003) by Mohammed El-Nawawy and Adel Iskander.

Finally, on the topic of gender and news, the following are recommended: Anne Sebba's *Battling for News: The Rise of the Woman Reporter* (UK/Australia/NZ: Hodder & Stoughton/John Curtis Books, 1994), *Women and Media: International Perspectives* (UK: Blackwell, 2004), edited by Karen Ross and Carolyn M. Byerly, and Michelle Elizabeth Tusan's *Women Making News: Gender and Journalism in Modern Britain* (US: University of Illinois Press, 2005).

Commentaries on the news, and media coverage of the news, can be found on numerous websites. Try openDemocracy.net, mediaguardian. co.uk and indexoncensorship.org.

Notes

1. Herbert J. Gans, *Deciding What's News* (US: Pantheon, 1979).
2. Allan Bell, *The Language of News Media* (UK: Blackwell, 1991).
3. Stanley Cohen and Jock Young (eds), *The Manufacture of News: Social Problems, Deviance and Mass Media* (UK: Constable, 1973).
4. John R. MacArthur, *Second Front: Censorship and Propaganda in the 1991 Gulf War* (US: University of California Press, 2004).
5. 'Friendly fire'. Not so friendly, of course. It refers to the military firing on their own side, or on their allies. On 31 March 2003, ITN reporter Terry Lloyd – a 'unilateral' rather than embedded reporter – approaching Basra, having been caught and wounded in cross-fire was then shot dead by US marines as he was being taken away in a civilian vehicle. At an inquest conducted in Oxford in October 2006, the deputy coroner, Andrew Walker, concluded that Lloyd had been killed unlawfully. The US authorities refused to allow its military personnel to be named or to give evidence. The killing of journalists working in war zones is not a crime under international law.
6. Denis McQuail and Sven Windhal, *Communication Models for the Study of Mass Communication* (UK: Longman, 1986; 5th impression, 1998). This book should be on the shelf of every student of media and communication. It identifies the models, describes their function and offers a critical appraisal of each one.
7. Gunther Kress, *Linguistic Processes in Sociocultural Practice* (Australia; Deakin University Press, 1985).
8. Youichi Ito, 'The future of political communication research: a Japanese perspective' in *Journal of Communication*, Autumn 1993. Professor Ito points out that the term 'climate of opinion' finds a parallel in the German expression 'zeitgeist', spirit of the times. He also acknowledges an important link with Elisabeth Noelle-Neumann's notion of a *spiral of silence*. (See her article 'The spiral of silence: a theory of public opinion'

in the *Journal of Communication*, Issue 24 published in 1974.) Kuuki can work for good or ill. When it is driven by the fervour of nationalism, it can, writes Ito, be 'undemocratic and destructive ... The most dangerous case is when kuuki is taken advantage of by undemocratic groups or self-ish and intolerant political leaders'.

9. Tabloidization generally refers to news and features as presented by the tabloid (or 'Red Top') press; but more specifically it describes the trend in the serious broadsheets towards tabloid preoccupations and practices; for example their relish for covering the lives of celebrities.

10. Walter Lippmann, *Public Opinion* (US: Macmillan, 1922).

11. Johan Galtung and Mari Ruge, 'The structure of foreign news: the pre-sentation of the Congo, Cuba and Cyprus crises in four foreign news-papers', in *Journal of International Peace Research*, 1 (1965), reprinted in Stanley Cohen and Jock Young (eds), *The Manufacture of News* (see Note 3).

12. Jeremy Bowen, *War Stories* (UK/US: Simon & Schuster, 2006).

13. Marc Raboy and Bernard Dagenais (eds), *Media, Crisis and Democracy: Mass Communication and the Disruption of Social Order* (UK: Sage, 1992).

14. Bernard Berelson and Gary. A. Steiner, *Human Behaviour: An Inventory of Scientific Findings* (US: Harcourt, Brace, World, 1963).

15. Christopher P. Campbell, *Race, Myth and the News* (US: Sage, 1995).

16. Anthony Smith, *The Geopolitics of Information* (UK: Faber, 1980).

17. Jeremy Tunstall, *Journalists at Work* (UK: Constable, 1971).

18. David Barsamian, *Stenographers to Power: Media and Propaganda* (US: Common Courage, 1992).

19. Jorgen Westerstähl and Folke Johansson, 'Foreign news: news values and ideologies' in *European Journal of Communication*, 9(1) (1994).

20. Chechen war coverage. Another essentially political reason why the civil war was under-reported was that the governments of nation states them-selves tended to 'look the other way', considering the conflict to be an internal matter, the business of Russia and her former satellites and not affecting the interests of the international community. This could be classified as the power agenda.

21. Diaspora: dispersal, spreading or scattering; specifically refers to the dis-persal of the Jews after their captivity in Babylon, generally to peoples living in varying locations outside their traditional homelands.

22. Philip Schlesinger, 'Newsmen and their time machine', *British Journal of Sociology*, September 1977.

23. Michael Bromley and Hugh Stephenson (eds), *Sex, Lies and Democracy: The Press and the Public* (US: Longman, 1998).

24. Andrew Neil, *On the Press*, 'The red-top editors' job to manage decline', *Media Guardian*, 20 August 2007.

Narrative: The Media as Storytellers

6

AIMS

➤ To highlight the role played by narrative in human discourse.
➤ To examine the process of framing in the creation of narratives.
➤ To discuss genre, narrative codes and character.
➤ By comparing news and fiction narratives to explore how they interact in contemporary modes of media storytelling.

Although Mr. Gradgrind, the highly opinionated schoolmaster in Charles Dickens' novel, *Hard Times*, insisted that the most important things in life, as in education, are facts! facts! and more facts! stories are what we remember the most. They arise out of our historical and cultural contexts. They are signifiers of it but they are also modes of explanation: by our stories, as it were, shall we be known; and sometimes such stories have the power of myths to leave all facts behind, and often reality itself.

This chapter works from the premise that humans are storytelling animals and that the story, the narrative, is central to the recounting of facts (in the news) as well as in fiction. The information mode in message communication is compared to the story, or ritual mode, and the two are seen to be overlapping and interactive.

Elements of stories – rhetoric, metaphor, symbol, for example, are illustrated; and processes of storytelling examined, the way narrative is used to frame content and meaning. The purposes of framing suggested by Robert Entman, Roland Barthes' five narrative codes, Vladimir Propp's archetypical story features and Milly Buonanno's criteria for fictionworthiness are briefly described. The 'newsness' of fiction, the role of facts, is touched upon in relation to popular TV drama such as soaps, while the fictional properties of news are highlighted.

Throughout, news as narrative is kept in steady focus, as are those factors external to the storytelling process that powerfully influence it – pressures to win and retain audiences, conventions of production and the possibilities opened up by new technology.

Homo narrens: the storytelling animal

The more we examine news production the more it resembles the process which produces fiction; that is, the creative process. Drama? It's what the news is about. Fascinating characters? – watch the news. Slice of life? The unfolding of meanings? Humour, pathos, tribulation, revenge, madness, lust, sacrifice? Saw it on the box last night!

A colleague I once worked with on teacher training courses always used to query matters of educational import with the words, 'What's the story?' He was a philosopher and the word 'story' had a number of meanings: on occasion, the word might mean 'angle': what's the angle? Or it could suggest something that was not apparent, that needed rooting out, as in a murder mystery – a hidden agenda; but most of all the word seemed to be used in relation to the significance of the matter in hand: okay, these are the facts, but what do they amount to?

Storytelling – narrative – has always been an entertaining way of exploring and communicating meaning. One might say that, along with music, itself so closely associated with stories through song, the story is both the oldest and the most universal form of interactive expression; and it is almost as natural and familiar to us as breathing.

Arthur Asa Berger writes in *Narratives in Popular Culture, Media, and Everyday Life*:[1]

> We seldom think about it, but we spend our lives immersed in narratives. Every day, we swim in a sea of stories and tales that we hear or read or listen to or see (or some combination of all these) from our earliest days to our deaths.

Stories do more for us than merely keep us entertained. In talking about our 'hunger for information about the historical world surrounding us', Bill Nicholls in *Blurred Boundaries: Questions of Meaning in Contemporary Culture*,[2] argues that 'our hunger is less for information in the raw than for stories fashioned from it'. Stories, says Nicholls, 'offer structure; they organize and order the flux of events; they confer meaning and value ... and inevitably more than one tale can be told for any one occurrence'.

The Autumn 1985 issue of the *Journal of Communication* looked in depth at the notion of *homo narrens*, humankind the storytelling animal. The theme, addressed by a number of authors, was that storytelling is a key human discourse. Frequently in these *Journal* articles it is acknowledged that while telling a story the narrator is also communicating a story about him or herself in terms of attitudes, beliefs and values. For example, the resistance among many researchers, particularly in America, to hard-line theories on the power of media to manipulate audiences can be interpreted as a 'story' about humane people determined to see in their fellows similar traits of principle and independence.

In his *Journal* article 'The narrative paradigm: in the beginning', Walter Fisher[3] believes that rationality, the capacity to work things out from a standpoint of experience, is determined by the nature of persons as narrative beings, by 'their inherent awareness of *narrative probability*, and their constant habit of testing *narrative fidelity*, whether the stories they experience ring true with stories they know in their lives'. Probability here suggests that a story is 'likely', that it answers real experience; fidelity that there is sufficient truth in the tale to be convincing.

We look to stories for verification, and we relate them to our personal stories. In news terms, we ask ourselves, do the stories in the papers or on TV ring true? 'Storyness', or the story format, can be seen as an alternative mode of communicating experience to that which claims essentially to transmit information.

Transmission mode, story mode

In 1926 George Herbert Mead defined two models of journalism, the *information* model and the *story* model, stating that 'the reporter is generally sent out to get a story not the facts'.[4] What Mead poses as models of journalism, Jerome Bruner sees as ways of thinking, the one the *analytical* mode, the other the *story* mode.[5] Both are deeply inscribed in our mental script as individuals and as communities.

The storyness theme is taken up by Peter Dahlgren in his Introduction to *Journalism and Popular Culture*.[6] He writes: 'Storytelling ... is a key link which unites journalism and popular culture ... narrative is a way of knowing the world ... Journalism officially aims to inform about events in the world – analytical mode – and does this most often in the story mode'. In his own contribution to *Journalism and Popular*

Culture, 'Truly awful news on television', John Langer argues that 'the world of fact and the world of fiction are bound more closely together than broadcasters are prepared to have us believe'.

On the one hand, then, we have the goal of information transmission underpinned by such guiding principles as objectivity, impartiality and balance; on the other we have the much more *subjective*, ritualistic nature of the story, which, as Dahlgren notes, both 'enhances and delimits the likely range of meanings' and which, like social rituals generally, has the power to bring about a sense of shared experience and of shared values. This, it might be said, is actually the 'story' of news: it is about cohesion-making as much as it is about information-transmission.

Symbol, rhetoric, myth

Stories are built around protagonists who are archetypal, with character-traits or attributes that are readily recognized – heroes, heroines, villains and victims. Something happens, an event producing a state of *disequilibrium*, of imbalance, which has to be corrected or resolved; and in the resolution we may read a message, a moral – about valour or self-sacrifice. A parable creates out of the specific (a story about a good Samaritan, for example) a message of universal significance; and a case could be put that most stories are parables, however much they disguise their 'message'.

As consumers of stories we like both novelty and familiarity, for after all there is a limited number of story formats. These are recycled to our profound gratification, especially the old tale given a new twist. We like to be teased, scared, taken down a cul-de-sac of narrative yet we are content to retrace our steps knowing that by doing so we will eventually reach the climax, the resolution, the one part of narrative which news stories cannot always, or even often, deliver.

Fantasies exist side by side with realism. In stories we meet our dreams and nightmares and often these have symbolic significance for the community at large. American professor Ernest Bormann, also writing in the *Journal of Communication* of Autumn 1985, refers in 'Symbolic convergence theory: a communication formulation' to *rhetorical fantasies* that 'fulfil a group psychological or rhetorical need'.

By rhetorical we mean the use of language – spoken, written, visual; of sign systems – in order to persuade; and rhetoric presumes the use of rhetorical devices, among them symbolism and metaphor. The more skilfully, the more artfully, these are employed, the more likely they are to achieve their goals. When members of a mass audience share a fantasy, writes Bormann, 'they jointly experience the same emotions, develop common heroes and villains, celebrate certain actions as laudable, and interpret some aspect of their common experience in the same way'. The story-within-discourse is essentially a conveyor of value, articulating meaning symbolically, most vividly through metaphor.

As the French philosopher Roland Barthes (1915–80) argued, such stories possess power through simplicity (and often simplification), which amounts to *myth* (briefly discussed in Chapter 2); and myth, according to Barthes, renders truths *natural* and therefore too 'commonsensical' to challenge. Myths are essentially stories about community: they are stories writ large, usually on a macro- rather than micro-scale.

The mythical element is not so much the *action* of the story but the meaning behind it, the assumptions about certain truths that are seen to be self-evident, at least to those who sustain the myth and subscribe to it. The myth-driven narrative, writes Barthes in *Mythologies*,[7] 'purifies' things. It 'makes them innocent, it gives them a clarity which is not that of an explanation but that of a statement of fact'.

If unambiguity is a news value then the power of myth to make the complicated clear and accessible might be deemed a production value. This power, Barthes believes, can mislead as it simplifies, for myth 'abolishes the complexity of human acts' – in Galtung and Ruge's terms, it distorts through selection (see Chapter 5, Note 11) – and 'establishes,' Barthes believes, 'a blissful clarity: things appear to mean something by themselves'.

In the light of these comments readers are invited to focus on certain Hollywood movies as establishers and purveyors of myth: examples might be *Independence Day* (1996) or *Pearl Harbor* (2001), each a discourse on visions of nationhood (with the home team coming out triumphantly on top). Presented with my colleague's question, 'But what's the story (behind the story)?' Barthes might have answered (should he have lived long enough to see the movies mentioned here) – *order*, or to be more precise, *dominant* order.

Once again we are seeing communication functioning as control. Historical fact, or narrative fidelity, is subverted by the need to tell a story that reinforces the myth of dominance while at the same time acknowledging that to make propaganda effective it has to be entertaining. The values of myth and entertainment fuse to mutual benefit, not only working to make things 'appear to mean something by themselves' but serving to modify, even re-write, collective memory.

Explanations, by being released from historical and cultural contexts, are thus protected against contrary or alternative readings. After all, this is what rhetoric sets out to do. By artifice in one form or another, it distorts by selection, defining itself, its ideological positioning, by what it includes and by what is absent.

Narrative frames

Every story has its narrative format or frame. In some stories the narrator, the storyteller, is evident. First-person narrative is admitting that the story is to be told from a single point of view. It is a subjective account. Third-person narrative distances the author from what goes on in the story. The author is like a deity, intangible but ever-present. We are aware that this is a contrivance. Yet if our disbelief is suspended by artful storytelling we forget authorship and find ourselves adopting the 'real' world of characters and action 'free' of authorial strings. In fact, that is one of the criteria of effective narrative, to make the strings invisible.

Writing in *Channels of Discourse: Television and Contemporary Criticism*,[8] Robert C. Allen differentiates between what he calls the *Hollywood narrative mode* and the *rhetorical mode*. The first hides the means by which the text is created. It invites audience to believe that what they are seeing is real: one is absorbed into the text without being, as it were, addressed by it. In contrast, the rhetorical mode directly addresses the viewer. Allen sees the news presented in this way: the newsreader looks directly out at us. Similar formats can be recognized in cooking, sports and gardening programmes on TV: 'The texts are not only presented for us, but directed out at us.'

Differentiating between these two modes proves problematic. In the one, the rhetorical is concealed, in the other it is exposed. Perhaps we might be better advised to recall what was said in Chapter 2 about *closed* and *open* texts, the Hollywood mode tending towards the closed text – the closure of meaning – and the rhetorical mode tending towards providing room for wider interpretation. For example, in the opening sequence of Michael Curtiz' *Casablanca* (1942) a voice-over sets the scene. Little is left to guesswork on the part of audience. *Closure* has occurred. That is, we are told exactly how to read what we are seeing. There is a preferred reading, very much the Hollywood mode.

In contrast, *Paris, Texas* made by German director Wim Wenders in 1984 offers us, at least in its initial stages, a more open text. During the first few moments of the film we see, in longshot, a man emerging from a rocky desert. We watch him take a desperate last swig from his water bottle. An eagle gazes down on him from the foreground and an atmosphere of mystery tinged with menace is created in our minds by a single guitar accompaniment.

In a sense, the guitar replaces the voice-over, yet we as audience are given the space to muse on who this man might be, where he has come from and what circumstances have brought him to this sorry pass. Curtiz is essentially mediating communication in terms of a model of transmission; indeed he employs newsreel in the opening of the film, along with traditional newsreel-format graphics. In the Wenders film there is an emphasis on *symbol*, an attempt to reach, obliquely, beyond explanation to meaning.

Though different in their use of narrative form, both of the films mentioned here subscribe to the classic *structure* of stories: something occurs that creates disequilibrium. This prompts actions and reactions that work towards resolution and the restoration of equilibrium. We see this occurring in some TV narratives and not in others.

Soaps: resolution delayed

A television sit-com concurs with the disequilibrium–equilibrium process. Generally each 'upset' has to be 're-set' by the end of the programme. With soaps, however, disequilibrium is a constant. Though some story-lines are resolved, the 'whole' story of the soap remains in a permanent state of disequilibrium – of new dramas, new crises, new twists of fate.

For a soap opera *time* is a key element in the framing process. There are 30-minute slots to be filled, each to conclude with unfinished business, preferably dramatic and suspenseful, while not being so dramatically 'final' that the series cannot continue into an endless blue yonder. Soaps need time, to bed down, unfold, and in their own time they reflect the timescales of audience. In some cases, the timeframe *of* the soap is as important as the timeframes *within* it.

The soap 'frame', thus presented with time in largesse, requires many characters and many plots. Soaps are full of talk, of gossip; we generally learn of action by report rather than see it occur. The action is largely in the cutting, the quick-bite scenes that frame both the story and the time in which it takes place. Soaps move through time but they also suspend it to suggest simultaneity, of actions taking place at exactly the same moment.

One suspects that the template or mould out of which soaps emerge is not all that different from the one which produces popular narratives of all kinds, including the news. They must attract and hold attention.

They must gratify both *cognitive* (intellectual) and *affective* (emotional) needs. They must facilitate *identification* and *personal reference* as well as *diversion* (see Uses and Gratifications Theory in Chapter 3); and they must convince us of their *fidelity*.

As long ago as 1996, Bryan Appleyard, in a contribution to the UK *Independent*,[9] declared that '[t]elevision is foaming with soaps as never before'. He was critical of the increasing dependence of soaps on realities portrayed in news narratives: 'the deluge of incident is taken from the headlines'. Relevance was being confused with reality, causing soaps to become 'closed worlds, feeding off every passing sensation'. The author worried that excessive ratings consciousness 'warps' the frame until both content and style are disengaged from the aesthetic criteria that give soaps their value as stories. Transmission, as it were, was trumphing over ritual.

Purposes and locations of framing

Writing in a *Journal of Communication* article, 'Framing: toward clarification of a fractured paradigm',[10] Robert Entman believes that a crucial task of analysis is to show 'exactly how framing influences thinking...' for 'the concept of framing consistently offers a way to describe the power of a communicating text'. Essentially, framing constitutes *selection* and *salience* – what is most meaningful.

Entman suggests that framing serves four main purposes, to:

1. Define problems
2. Diagnose causes
3. Make moral judgements
4. Suggest remedies

These, he argues, will function varyingly according to the text, but they operate in four locations in the communication process:

1. The communicator
2. The text
3. The receiver
4. The culture

Communicators, says Entman, 'make conscious or unconscious framing judgements in deciding what to say, guided by frames (often called schemata) that organize their belief systems'. Before we frame, we are *in* a frame. The text will not only be framed by the framer within a frame it will be shaped by a number of factors – requirements concerning format and presentation, aesthetic considerations, notions of professionalism and pressures to meet the expectations of convention.

When the text comes to be 'read', the frames as presented may be at variance with the frames that guide the receiver's thinking. For Entman the culture is 'the stock of commonly invoked frames ... exhibited in the discourse and thinking of most people in a social grouping':

> Framing in all four locations includes similar functions: selection and highlighting, and use of the highlighting elements to construct an argument about problems and their causation, evaluation and/or solution.

This approach is useful in the study of the encoding of messages and gauging their effectiveness. It emphasizes the subjective nature of encoding by recognizing the 'invisible' schemata – psychological templates – which, however hard we try to be objective and impartial, deeply influence our responses.

For successful communication – that is, winning the interest and attention of audience, and perhaps even going beyond that in terms of gaining the audience's assent or approval – there seems to be a need for a meeting of schemata; a common ground (or to refer to Wilbur Schramm's model illustrated in Chapter 2, an overlap in *fields of experience*). The communicator selects, then attempts to give salience (special importance) to those parts of the story that might fit with the existing schemata in a receiver's belief system.

The power of the frame rests both in its capacity to exclude and to structure the 'storyworld' in terms of dramatic contrasts; what is termed *binary framing*. Things are defined in relation to their opposite – heroes–villains; good–evil; kind–cruel; tolerant–intolerant; beautiful–ugly. In *Narratives* Arthur Asa Berger talks of 'central oppositions'.[1] The parallel with news narratives is strong here. Binary differences are a prevalent attribute of news formats, as we have seen; and they reflect in the main the viewpoints of the dominant. (For more on *binary framing*, see Note 11.)

Genre, codes and character

In the maelstrom of available stories narrative modes interact and overlap as never before, but for convenience they continue to be classified under the term *genre*. The word originates from the French, meaning a style, a form. Westerns comprise a film genre. There are horror movies, road movies, musicals, sci-fi movies and crime thrillers, all genres. Still-life paintings, historical novels, romances and who-dunnits constitute genres; and in TV we are familiar with genres such as soaps, sit-coms, chat shows, quiz shows, wildlife documentaries and 'reality' TV. Genres share common characteristics and are governed by codes that regulate content and style.

Variety works within a frame of sameness. In some genres the frame is tight, highly restrictive to the point of being ritualistic. Other genres have 'flexible' framing and offer the potential for change and development. Soaps have this potential, sit-coms less so, contends Jasper Rees reviewing, in the UK *Independent*,[12] the second festival of sit-coms run by the UK's Channel 4:

> In a play, events take place which irrepressibly alter the relationship between the characters. Whatever happens in a sitcom, you always go back to square one at the start of a fresh episode; the idea of stasis is built into the design.

No doubt sooner or later a writer will come along and create a sit-com that breaks new ground, though this will depend as much upon external framing mechanisms such as programming and popularity as the nature of the genre itself.

Each genre contains a range of signifiers, of conventions that audiences recognize and come to expect while at the same time readily accepting experiment with those conventions. Knowledge of the conventions on the part of audience, and recognition when convention is flouted, suggests an active 'union' between the schemata of the encoder and that of the decoder.

Audience, as it were, is 'let in on the act'; and this 'knowingness' is an important part of the enjoyment of narrative genres. When the hero in a Western chooses not to wear a gun (a great rarity), audience (because we are familiar the traditions of the genre) recognizes the salience of this decision. Such recognition could be said to constitute a form of participation.

We use our familiarity with old 'routines' as a frame for reading this new tweak of narrative. We wonder whether convention will be flouted altogether as the story proceeds or whether the rules of the genre will be reasserted by the hero finally taking up the gun to bring about a resolution to the story.

Barthes' narrative codes

We can explore the difference between narrative forms and we can assess their similarities. In his book *S/Z* Roland Barthes[13] writes of a number of codes, or sets of rules, which operate in concert in the production of both 'real' and fictional stories; and he argues that all stories operate according to these five codes 'under which all textual signifiers can be grouped' in a narrative.

S/Z is a singular and highly readable volume. It takes the form of a detailed deconstruction of a 23-page story, *Sarrasine*, written by Honoré de Balzac (1799–1850) in 1830. Each line in the story is linked, by Barthes, to one or more of the five codes of narrative.

Action (or prioretic) code

This portrays the events that take place in a story. It is the code of 'what happens', detailing occurrences in their sequence.

Semantic code

Barthes talks of the code of the *seme* which Richard Howard in the Preface to *S/Z* calls the semantic code. It deals with character; with characterization. Barthes calls this code the Voice of the Person. Actions are *explained* by character. Essentially the semantic function is to make clear, to explain, to bring about understanding; and thus in a story it can be instrumental in bringing about revelation. A character may reveal features about him/herself that carry the story forward, creating new events or new developments (for a parallel with news, see comments on *attribution* in Chapter 5).

Enigma (or hermeneutic) code

Under this code, termed by Barthes the Voice of Truth, 'we list the various (formal) terms by which an enigma [a mystery] can be distinguished, suggested, formulated, held in suspense and finally disclosed'. This code involves the setting up of mystery, its development and finally its resolution. A good detective story usually contains many enigmas, some of them deliberately placed there by the author to mislead – clues which take Sam Spade or Inspector Morse on a wild goose chase, enjoyable to the audience, before further clues bring them back into the 'frame' of discovery (of who committed the murder) and resolution.

Referential (or cultural) code

This, the Voice of Science, as Barthes terms it, functions to inform or explain. Such codes 'are references to a science or a body of knowledge' – physiological, medical, psychological, literary, historical etc. In a historical drama the referential code operates to explain to us how people dressed, what their homes looked like, how they travelled from place to place. The French film term, *mis en scène*, meaning 'placed in scene', detailing the 'staging' of the story, is an equivalent of the referential code.

Symbolic code

As the term suggests, this code works at the connotative level of imagery where elements of the story – character, incident – are transformed into symbolic representations such as justice, reward, love fulfilled, good triumphant. Symbol works at every level of the story. In a Hollywood-style gangster movie of the 1940s and 1950s, the gangster's (invariably blonde) moll symbolizes in her dress, speech, body language, not only her own relationship to a patriarchal world, but to that of all women 'under the thumb' of males. In Westerns (almost invariably) the dress, hair and demeanour of women, and the context (bar or chapel) in which we encounter them, will symbolize what their ranking order is in the social milieu of the story.

They will also signify the woman's fate: in George Marshall's *Destry Rides Again* (1939) the saloon-bar singer Frenchie, played by Marlene Dietrich, falls in love with the hero, played by James Stewart (who doesn't wear a gun). Love is not permitted to overcome her dubious past and her criminal present except by sacrifice. Frenchie is shot in the back while protecting Destry/Stewart. She fulfils destiny and at the same time opens the way for the hero to marry the 'nice' girl in the story.

Symbols employing metaphoric forms illuminate and enrich the texts of stories and they work in unison with semantic codes. The TV Inspector Morse drove an old red Jaguar. This symbolized the kind of person Morse was – cultured, somewhat oldy-worldly, resistant to the more traditional brashness of policing. It also helps to explain how such a detective, from whose car stereo emerged the strains of opera, never pop or jazz, went about his profession.

Symbolic coding not only fills out our view of character, it propels the action. In a Western, when the hero buckles on his gunbelt, we know that the villains have pushed their luck one notch too far.

Confrontation lies ahead: resolution will be brought about by violence exercised in the name of justice.

The gun may additionally serve a referential function. In an age when women have ostensibly proved parity of treatment with men it can be seen as symbolically apt for women to be as ready to aim straight and pull the trigger as their male counterparts; officially, as cops, or out of self-defence.

How we decode such a story is another matter, and this will obviously depend, among other things, on who we are, male or female, what our attitude is to the use of guns and the degree of openness or closure that the text of the story permits us: are we intended to cheer when the heroine blows away the villain, or are we to be left with the nagging doubt that there might have been another way to arrive at a resolution of the situation?

A case can be made for an addition to the codes Barthes discusses – a code of *aesthetics*, that is, the artistic, compositional, stylistic element of expression. We talk of writers or artists finding their *voice*, their uniqueness manifested in the artefacts they create. For example, the work of the Russian film director Sergei Eisenstein (1898–1948) is recognizable not only for its politically oriented narratives but because of his narrative style, characterized by innovative editing or *montage*. At the same time we wonder at films such as *Battleship Potemkin* (1925) or *Alexander Nevsky* (1938) for the sheer beauty of the composition, of lighting, of the handling of movement. It is fact, it is drama, but it is also poetry.

The exercise of a code of aesthetics enriches narratives. Of course an emphasis on the aesthetic might distract audience attention from the essence, the core meaning of a narrative. The problem is often faced by the news photographer: does he or she snap the truth exactly as it is, or is there a temptation to allow aesthetic considerations – composition, colour, lighting – to intervene in the recording process?

Gender coding

Being aware of different narrative codes helps us in our study of texts. The action code in a number of genres (and in real life too) is traditionally associated with male characters. Maleness equals action suggesting decisiveness that may further indicate dominance. Enigma codes relate more to women: femaleness is associated with mystery; often suggestive of a secret, victimized past. The obvious alternative for a novelist, playwright, film maker, creator of a comic strip, TV commercial or story for children is to switch the conventions so that females appropriate 'male' codes.

This generally means breaking with social conventions, shaking a subversive finger at the rules. The outcome may underline cautionary messages as happens in Ridley Scott's movie *Thelma and Louise* (1991) where the two protagonists' rebellion against a world dominated by men's demands, men's expectations and men's abuses is resolved only by their suicide: cold comfort for such a spirited lunge for personal freedom.

It is important to note that Barthes, in positing his five codes, is not claiming to fix narratives within prescriptive rules. On the contrary; he writes in *S/Z*, 'The code is a perspective of quotations, a mirage of structures; we know only its departures and returns'. Just when we think we understand the symbolism of 'blondeness' in narratives, we find that it has been extended or transformed by new encoding. In Alfred Hitchcock's *To Catch a Thief* (1955), the blonde Grace Kelly is the epitome of refinement, sophistication and distinction.

Indeed attempts to link blondeness with dumbness have often turned out to be witness to the opposite. Marilyn Monroe was often cast 'dumb' and often *played* dumb, but we know she was an altogether more complex personality, and an altogether more talented actress than the stereotype allowed.

Propp's people

In a study of Russian folk tales, Vladimir Propp classified a range of stock characters identifiable in most stories. These may be individualized by being given distinguishing character traits or attributes, but they are essentially *functionaries* enabling the story to unfold. In *Morphology of the Folk Tale*,[14] Propp writes of the following archetypal story features:

- the *hero/subject* whose function is to seek
- the *object* that is sought
- the *donor* of the object
- the *receiver*, where it is sent
- the *helper* who aids the action and
- the *villain* who blocks the action

Thus in one of the world's best-known folk tales, Red Riding Hood (heroine) is sent by her mother (donor) with a basket of provisions (object) to her sick granny (receiver) who lives in the forest. She encounters the wolf (villain) and is rescued from his clutches, and his teeth, by the woodman (helper).

This formula can be added to and manipulated in line with the requirements of the genre, but it does allow us to differentiate between *story level* and *meaning level*, between the *denotive* and the *connotative*, between the so-termed *mimetic plain* (the plain of representation) and the *semiosic plain* (the plain of meaning production).

The tale of Little Red Riding Hood, examined at the connotative level, is rich in oblique meanings and in order to tease these out we begin to examine the characters and events as symbols. We may perceive the story as a parable; that is, a tale with a moral: little girls should not be allowed in the forest on their own, however great their granny's needs. But then we begin to ask more questions – why did Red Riding Hood's mother send her on such a perilous journey in the first place; does the wolf stand for more than a wolf, granny more than a granny; and what is the significance of the stones which in some versions of the story end up in the wolf's stomach?

We are seeing that even the simplest of stories, long part of the cultural heritage of many countries, is a moveable feast, its connotative richness varying from reader to reader and context to context; and stories produced in contexts are significantly modified by new contexts. *Ring-a-Ring-a-Roses*, for instance, alluding to the onset of the plague in England – the Black Death – became over time a 'harmless' children's nursery rhyme; in this case the horror of the real being subsumed by the rhythmic charm of language itself.

It would be instructive to select a number of popular narrative forms to see how far they conform to Propp's formula, then turn to the primary folklorists of our age – the advertisers. In a commercial, the *subject* is the character who stands in for the consumer. The *object* is what the product being advertised can *do* for the subject/hero/heroine, such as bringing happiness, satisfaction, fulfilment, glamour, enviability. The *donor* or giver is the originator of the advertisement. And the *villain*? – any factor that deprives the subject of his/her desires (like dandruff, bad skin, obesity, thirst, hunger or irritable bowel syndrome).

Newsworthiness, fictionworthiness

Certain parallels can be discerned between the narrative approaches of news and folktale; and also, of their function. The Cold War of the 1950s onwards was often reported, particularly in the popular press, as a cautionary folktale in which heroes (us) were on guard against the villains (the Russians): Wedom/Theydom was the dominant narrative structure. In our Red Riding Hood basket were nuclear weapons and granny in the forest might varyingly have symbolized democracy or the free world in peril.

We recognize once more how narrative can be used to bring about socio-cultural cohesion, uniting audiences. In *Visualizing Deviance: A Study of News Organization*[15] Richard Ericson, Patricia Baranak and Janet Chan speak of news journalists as a 'deviance-defining elite' who 'provide an ongoing articulation of the proper bounds to behaviour in all organized spheres of life'. In stories, order is disrupted: things happen and then there is usually resolution. Order is restored.

For John Hartley, *disorder* is a news value. Writing in *The Politics of Pictures: The Creation of the Public in the Age of Popular Media*,[16] he says that the 'fundamental test of newsworthiness is disorder – deviation from any supposed steady state'. A first principle of news media performance is to alert the public mind to *visions of order* by portraying the opposite: binary framing in action. Hartley's view, already touched upon in Chapter 4, is that visions of order are 'photo-negativized into stories of disorder'. The sequence is predictable and seems inevitable:

Vision/Perception $\longrightarrow$ Selection $\longrightarrow$ Distortion $\longrightarrow$ Fiction

---

Hartley says, 'Journalism, in short, makes sense by inventing the real in the image of vision'.

If, then, 'the fact of fiction', as Ericson, Baranak and Chan put it, can be seen as central to the news, it comes as no surprise to learn that this mode of 'fact-fiction' has proved an influential model for 'fiction-fiction'. In a paper published in the *European Journal of Communication*,[17] Milly Buonanno links newsworthiness with what she terms *fictionworthiness*. She examines the ways in which Italian TV fiction has increasingly used the news as a model for its own themes and approaches.

The attraction of the news is obvious: it is dramatic, contemporary, relevant and familiar. Also, it is often stranger than fiction. As Buonanno puts it, 'we live today in a reality which surpasses and challenges every fantasy'. Noting the mutual reinforcement one text gives another, she speaks of:

> a circle of intertextual references substantially self-referential, that is to say, within the very media system: just as television seemingly becomes ever more a highly 'newsworthy' subject for the press, equally news becomes ever more 'fictionworthy' for television.

Buonanno's criteria for fictionworthiness

1. *Substantive* criteria: that is, factors concerning 'the prerequisites likely to confer importance and interest on a story'. These could be major issues of the day.
2. Criteria relevant to the *product*: that is, factors 'concerned with specific elements of story content, in particular aspects that are considered more interesting and appealing and which maintain viewing enjoyment'. Buonanno believes that 'in the same way that one says of journalism: "Bad news is good news" one could say of fiction that a "bad" story – that is to say a sad and tearful, violent and criminal story – is a good story'.
3. Criteria relevant to the *media*. The kind of news stories that have always fascinated the press – tales of crime and misdemeanours – have long proved fictionworthy and are a staple diet of TV drama.
4. Criteria relevant to *audience*.
5. Criteria relevant to the *competition*.

Shared values

On the casting-couch for fictionworthiness are some old favourites from Galtung and Ruge. At least on Italian TV those characters of high social status, the elite, find themselves fictionworthy. Buonanno cites *Dallas* as an American parallel while confessing that 'the exceptions are mainly to be found in British productions, where more often working-class environments are presented'. Proximity is a fiction value as it is a news value. A story is 'considered to be much more interesting if it possesses accessibility – geographically, temporally and culturally'.

Perhaps the dominant fiction value arising out of news practices is *topicality*. Buonanno writes:

> A story of topical interest is not simply a story set in the present, but a story which aspires to recount and testify to the reality of the present in its most relevant and significant form.

The image of TV as a mirror of society, a true reflector of realities, also appears to prevail in fiction values. As audience, we have an appetite to know 'how things are now', either by revelation or confirmation while a dominant aim of those assembling 'realities', in fictional or news form, is one of legitimizing one definition of 'truths' against another.

Crime series often provide us, in addition to dramatic stories, with visualizations of contemporary urban society driven by poverty, unemployment and the loss of community values. Cops often have the role thrust upon them of social workers and social psychologists as well as law-keepers.

What such series draw back from doing is offering any formula for solutions, an *institutional* remedy for the socially rooted crimes they so effectively highlight. The producers will honestly and justifiably say that is not their job. Yet whose job is it? We seem to be witnessing an uneasiness with the social status quo but no determination to alter it; and, of course, it has to be acknowledged that if the causes of the crimes dealt with in crime series were energetically addressed there might be no series to dramatize them.

In his chapter on narrative in *The Media Studies Book: A Guide for Teachers*,[18] edited by David Lusted, Adrian Tilley remarks that:

> narratives are about the survival of *particular* social orders rather than their transformation. They suggest that certain systems of values can transcend social unrest and instability by making a particular notion of 'order out of chaos'. This may be regarded as the ideological work of narrative.

The implication here is that narrative is about rendering things 'natural' – Barthes' myth-making. What happens on screen is 'the ways things are'; natural, and therefore to be expected, put up with, coped with: *c'est la vie!* Such a standpoint deserves to be analyzed and challenged, hence, in Tilley's view, the importance of *narrative analysis* which 'can make the "natural" relations between narratives and social orders not only less natural but possibly even open to change'.

Fiction and public debate

This is a moment to remind ourselves that the 'work' as Barthes defines it only becomes 'text' when it is 'read' by audience. Whether texts are straight fiction, straight documentary or docu-dramas, audiences respond both to narratives and to the issues framed by those narratives. Soaps in particular prompt individual, group and public responses that modify or alter attitudes and certainly raise issues higher on public agendas.

Few stories alerted public interest in Britain during the late 1990s as much as the 'Jordache Story' which unfolded in the British soap

Brookside between February 1993 and May 1995. This brought incest to public attention perhaps more dramatically than ever before. After serving in prison for domestic violence, Trevor Jordache persuades his family to take him back. Once more he is violent towards his wife Mandy. He has in the past already sexually abused his elder daughter, Beth. Now it is 14-year-old Rachel's turn. Mandy and Beth plot his death. They bury his body in the garden. Prison follows for both of them. Beth takes her own life. Rachel gives evidence of how Trevor raped her. Mandy is released from prison.

Such was the interest, controversy and serious debate which the Jordache Story provoked that Channel Four Television commissioned Lesley Henderson of the Glasgow University Media Group to investigate public responses. Her approach to this task is described in Chapter 10, but the Conclusion of her report *Incest in Brookside: Audience Responses to the Jordache Story*,[19] is relevant here. She affirms the significance of contemporary popular storytelling in relation to issues of social importance:

> This study reveals that *Brookside's* child sexual abuse storyline communicated complex and important messages about the issue … [it] increased knowledge and understandings about the language, reality and effects of abuse … By addressing the difficult topic of child abuse *Brookside* illustrates how a traditionally 'entertainment' genre can be used to enhance knowledge and understandings about a social problem.

Lesley Henderson's research also identified important areas of audience resistance, to the way the events were handled, to the way characters responded to those events; and also to the way other media, in particular the press, attempted to 'get in' on the story. By announcing beforehand what was going to happen next in the story, the press provided an additional 'frame' around the actual drama as it appeared on screen.

This served as a *secondary text* to the *primary text* of the programme itself and inevitably influenced the 'reading' of the story. The *Daily Mirror* (23 June 1995) reported that Beth would commit suicide. Under the headline BETH US DO PART, the *Mirror* declared:

> Beth, jailed in the body-under-the-patio cliff hanger, can't face another five year sentence. Although an appeal is pending, she decides to end it all.

The *Mirror* became part of the story, and its sensationalist announcement, Henderson points out, 'provoked distress and anger' particularly among those groups tested in research who themselves were 'survivors' of child abuse. That Beth should not face things out, and thus fail to prove an inspiring example, was bad enough; but to be told so bluntly in the press made matters worse. Indeed the reports in the press, Henderson says, 'sparked protests and demonstrations'.

The interaction between primary and secondary texts and the audience must be a constant focus of media study because the ideological thrust of secondary texts may well rework the ideology of the primary one in the minds of audience: we have, then, yet another *intervening variable* between encoding and response. In the case of the reporting of the Jordache Story, the negative news values of the press intruded between the *Brookside* story and its audience.

Not only did newspapers 'give the game away' by telling readers what was going to happen, they imposed their own judgemental attitude. *TV Quick* (22–28 July 1995) announced – BETH: A WASTED LIFE. 'Such coverage,' believes Henderson, 'presented "Beth's" death in a way which undermined all the positive strengths of the character and placed her firmly in the category of "victim scarred for life".'

Spotlighting hidden histories

Soap narratives serve a range of community purposes. In Uganda, *Ngom Wa (Our Land)*, modelled on the British radio serial, *The Archers,* has told the stories of civil war victims. Set in a fictitious refugee camp, *Our Land* allows listeners to learn about the horrors of war – the kidnappings, the murders, forced marriages – and has encouraged the community to come to terms with the suffering caused by the rebel Lord's Resistance Army.

In Spain, the traumas of the Civil War (1936–39) and the fascist rule of General Franco have been revisited in a highly popular soap, *Cuentame Como (Tell me How It Happened)*, first produced in 2002. What had, until the transmission of the soap, been a closed and often prohibited book for the majority of the population, suddenly became a national talking point.

In a news report 'Spain gripped by soap set in the dark years of Franco's rule' (UK *Independent*, 9 August 2002), Elizabeth Nash wrote, 'The series has caught the imagination of all generations of Spaniards: those who remember Franco relish the authenticity of every detail; youngsters who never knew him are fascinated by this window on their otherwise silent and invisible history'.

News as narrative

If much TV fiction takes its lead, at least in terms of content, from the news, we have to recognize that news as narrative breaks the golden rule of fiction by surrendering the *code of mystery* at the very beginning. In the Jordache Story, as we have seen, press announcements proved a 'spoiler' and dismayed many in the audience. The decision to put the ending first is plainly based upon the notion that news is information, fact not fiction; that news is about transmission, not ritual: news is *not* a story and it is definitely not an invention. It is for real.

Understandable though it is, this insistence on departing from the sequential narrative of traditional story modes, or what is termed *diachronic structure* (A comes before B and B leads on to C) poses problems. Justin Lewis in *The Ideological Octopus. An Exploration of Television and Its Audience*[20] argues that news is a 'form that, by abandoning narrative, abandons substantial sections of the viewer's consciousness':

> If we study this narrative structure in more detail, we can see just how strange news 'stories' are. The hermeneutic code is not only ignored, it is turned inside-out. History inevitably has an enigmatic quality – we do not know how the future will unfold. Television takes this history and squeezes the sense of mystery right out of it.
>
> The main point of the story does not come at the end, but at the beginning. It is like being told the punchline before the joke, or knowing the result before watching the game, or being told 'whodunnit' at the beginning of the murder mystery.

As audience, we do not 'have our interest awakened by enigma and gratified by a solution' as in traditional stories. In researching the capacity of audience to recall the gist of news programmes, Lewis found that:

> most respondents had great difficulty recalling 'stories': their discussion tended to revolve around discrete moments in each item. If they did not already know details of events leading up to the item (which applied to most of the audience most of the time) they were extremely unlikely to remember anything the item told them about the historical context.

Lewis is of the opinion that the format of news narrative relies on viewers making links, relating item to item, comprehending references which have a history that is rarely explained, largely assumed. In short, to make sense of the news a viewer has to be highly *news literate*. Any student of media can test this by scrutinizing news bulletins for their capacity to make sense of the news process itself, never mind what the news contains.

Swarming signifiers

The jump-cutting, the contortions with time; the inserts of materials related to other stories; the joining of one story to another because 'it connects' in some way, all require a combination of prior knowledge and skill in reading the news text which only the most sophisticated news addict is likely to possess.

What happens when the average viewer loses track or concentration and then attempts to make sense of a shot where the Australian prime minister is talking about relations with Indonesia while attending a world leaders' conference in Washington at which a delegation of Aborigines has interrupted his address with questions about ancient land rights can only be guessed at. Lewis argues that the narrative structure of news 'for most viewers cannot sustain the links and development necessary to go beyond crude association'. While TV news 'does not necessarily ignore historical details, it simply fails to persuade the viewer to fit these details together'.

It is difficult for the reader or the viewer to resist what Lewis terms 'associative logics' unless we, as audience, have an alternative mind-set – of knowledge, reference points, personal experience and ideological framework. Lewis believes that 'in the absence of any other information, it is the media's framework or nothing' for most viewers. If this framework is communicated in the disjointed narrative style characteristic of news presentation, problems of comprehension on the part of audience are compounded:

> The consequences of this are profound. It suggests that many viewers find it difficult to place those views of the world that are repeatedly put forward on the news, in any critical or qualifying context.

The danger arising from the insistence on treating news as information, and presenting it through a predominantly transmissional mode, is that it risks leaving the majority of people behind. This is an argument posed by S. Elizabeth Bird in a chapter entitled 'News we can use: an audience perspective on the tabloidization of news in the United States' in *Critical Readings: Media and Audiences*.[21] 'Much of the news that readers and viewers are exposed to,' writes Bird, 'is either ignored or forgotten almost immediately' and this situation arises 'from a difference in the way journalists/critics and audiences define news and how it is used'. The former 'tend to define news in terms of how effective the texts of news stories are at conveying information about the world to readers and viewers'.

True, 'Audience definitions also include this "informing" function' but the author believes that the 'cultural pressure to be informed is felt less and less today … from the audience perspective, relevant news consists of stories that take on a life of their own outside the immediate context of the newspaper or television broadcast'.

Such stories, tending to be dramatic and personal, presented vividly, with a moral point and according to the chronological narrative rather than the traditional 'inverted pyramid' of news, are the ones 'people actually remember'. Bird states that there is 'certainly a case for seeing the increasing move to the personal as a democratization of news, a chance for all voices to be heard, and thus an opening up of public discourse'.

Why can't news be more like soaps?

Elizabeth Bird's perspective on news affirms that of John Fiske in his chapter on 'Popular news' in *Reading the Popular*.[22] Fiske challenges the notion of objectivity in traditional news narratives, arguing that '"objective" facts always support particular points of view and their "objectivity" can exist only as part of the play of power'. News, he suggests, the way it is framed, structured and presented for audience consumption, is a story about power. Fiske contends:

> Rather than being 'objective' therefore, TV news should present multiple perspectives that, like those of soap opera, have as unclear a hierarchy as possible: the more complex the events it describes, the more the contradictions among the different social positions from which to make sense of them should be left open and raw.

The author believes that news narrative should be 'less concerned about telling the final truth of what has happened, and should present, instead, different ways of understanding it and the different positions of view inscribed in those different ways'.

By seeking to emulate popular narratives, news would be acknowledging that 'people cope well with contradictions'. Of course Fiske duly admits such moves would prove 'a risky business, for the meanings that people will make will often evade social control'. He also argues that news should resist its currently all-pervading tendency towards *narrative closure*. News should, 'like soap opera, leave its multiple narratives open, unresolved ... for that is television's equivalent of the oral narratives through which we make sense of our daily lives'.

Technology and news narrative

In news narratives, and indeed in most story narratives on TV and in the cinema, a do-or-die function is to attract and retain audience attention. Increasingly the wonders of technology are employed to fulfil this function. What has long been a key narrative feature is the *sound-bite*, administering to what communicators perceive to be a fickle, inattentive audience, a high dosage of JPMs – Jolts Per Minute.

Daniel Hallin in an article 'Sound-bite news: television coverage of elections, 1968–1988', published in the *Journal of Communication*[23] and summarizing his researches into American news reportage, says that the length of the average sound-bite shrunk from 40 seconds in 1968 to less than ten seconds in 1988. Readers are invited to check out tonight's offering: is ten seconds beginning to look like slow-motion?

There was a time when a political advocate could expect to string a number of coherent sentences together before being interrupted by someone else talking or by inserts of action film. Hallin argues that this trend – of the quick-fired edited sound-bite, driven by technological possibilities – has made the news more *mediated*. If the narrative rule has become, 'After ten seconds, cut!' then the description of news as an assemblage, a *construct*, is all the more apt: content is manipulated by style which in turn is technology-determined. Hallin writes:

> Today's television journalist displays a sharply different attitude towards the words of candidates and other newsmakers. Today, those words, rather than simply being reproduced and transmitted to audience, are treated as raw material to be taken apart, combined with other sounds and images, and integrated into a new narrative.

In this manner technology and ideology are working in partnership. Like Justin Lewis, Hallin expresses unease about sound-bite treatment of the news, and concern whether as a result audience possesses the capacity to keep up with the pace demanded of it. We may recall the 'highlights', the nuggets of information conveyed in dramatic pictures – but do we grasp the whole story?

Cybertales

Yet as we shall see in Chapter 9, Network Communication: Visions and Realities, technology has become less and less under the control of privileged media minorities; indeed in many instances mass communication has become indebted to members of the public, armed with pocket-size media stations. The transmission of texts and pictures, still and moving, has become two-way, multiple-way, as never before.

Arguably we are becoming less and less a silent majority, our opinions confined to our domestic situation. Suddenly we are all storytellers. New media trechnology, at least to a degree, has empowered us as *homo narrens*, as storytelling animals, to narrate via the Internet our own stories; with a realistic possibility of being heard, even heeded, beyond our front door, beyond our street; town, city or nation.

And just occasionally our stories tune in to grander narratives, more far-reaching discourses, in which the power elite discover that communicative dominance is no longer their private, uncontested territory. It is a tantalizing question: bearing in mind the exponential growth of the blogosphere, where cyberspace and 'my space' have become synonymous, could it be that citizen stories pose a potential threat to existing structures of hegemony?

Summary

Whether information is factual or fictional it has, as this chapter suggests, to be assembled into a narrative; and in the telling of stories, whatever their format or genre, meanings are made and communicated.

This chapter has stressed the importance of stories, and their symbolic significance, to society. Narratives are examined in relation to the frames which give them structure and direction. Robert Allen's differentiation between the Hollywood narrative mode and the rhetorical narrative mode, and Robert Entman's analysis of the purposes of framing are noted.

Genre and the codes that govern the construction of differing genres such as sit-coms and soaps are discussed prior to focusing on Roland Barthes' five narrative codes – action (or prioretic), semantic, enigma (or hermeneutic), referential (or cultural) and symbolic. Vladimir Propp's taxonomy of archetypal characters in narratives and Molly Buonanno's study of the way modern popular fictional narratives borrow from news modes and news content are outlined.

Reference is made to critiques of news values by Justin Lewis, Elizabeth Bird and John Fiske, and concern expressed by Daniel Hallin that the 'sound-bite' approach to news narrative, facilitated by new technology and driven by the need to win and sustain audience attention, has made the news more mediated than ever before and therefore more subject to closure and control.

The importance of narrative arises from the notion that ultimately all stories are framed by ideologies prevalent in the cultural contexts in which they are told. As the Greek philosopher Plato (c.428–347 BC) believed, those who tell stories also rule society.

KEY TERMS

homo narrens   storyness   narrative probability   narrative fidelity
information model, story model   disequilibrium
rhetorical fantasies   social cohensiveness   myth
Hollywood narrative mode, rhetorical narrative mode
open/closed texts   closure   binary framing   action/semantic/enigma/
referential/symbolic codes   code of aesthetics   story level/meaning level
visions of order   primary, secondary texts   diachronic structure
fictionworthiness   news literate   sound-bites

Suggested activities

1. Discussion
    (a) 'By our stories shall we be known'. In the light of this statement, discuss a range of American/British/French/German etc. narratives from the point of view of what they tell us about national characters/cultures.
    (b) Consider the argument that soaps are a 'woman's genre'.
    (c) Breaking the basic rules of a genre may stretch it creatively; but what are the dangers?
    (d) What might be the effects of reformulating the news (as John Fiske suggests) along the lines of the first principle of storytelling, suspense concerning what happens next?
2. Select a single episode of a TV soap, sit-com, cop series etc. and attempt a detailed deconstruction according to Roland Barthes' five codes of narrative.

3. Attempt a similar exercise using Propp's archetypical story features:

    - the *hero/subject* whose function is to seek;
    - the *object* that is sought;
    - the *donor* of the object;
    - the *receiver*, where it is sent;
    - the *helper* who aids the action and
    - the *villain* who blocks the action.

4. You may wish to investigate sport as storytelling, using Propp as a starter. Sports coverage, in the press or on TV, provides us with fascinating insights into stories about heroes and heroines, victories and defeats; and they vividly illuminate the social, cultural and national contexts in which they take place.

5. Consult the Internet with a view to summoning up comments on *trends* in TV storytelling worldwide. What are the most popular soaps in Brazil, India, Israel and Japan?

Now read on

A glance at the film/media/sociology/television shelves of the best bookshops will indicate a steady stream of new volumes on the media as storytellers and myth-makers. *Mass-Mediated Culture* (US: Prentice-Hall, 1977) by Michael R. Real and *Story and Discourse: Narrative Structure in Fiction and Film* (US: Cornell University Press, 1978) by Seymour Chatman are unlikely to be among them but will reward patience in waiting for your librarian to obtain them on loan.

Also be sure to try *Myths, Media and Narratives: Television and the Press* (UK: Sage, 1988) edited by James W. Carey, John Ellis's *Visible Fictions: Cinema, Television, Video* (UK: revised edition, 1992) and, for specific studies of film narrative, recommended are David Borwell's *Narration in the Fiction Film* (UK/US: Routledge, 1986) and *Closely Watched Films: An Introduction to the Art of Narrative Film Technique* (US/UK: University of California Press, 2004) by Marilyn Fabe.

Lively and readable is Arthur Asa Berger's book, mentioned in this chapter – *Narratives in Popular Culture, Media and Everyday Life* (US: Sage, 1997). Also deserving attention are *Making Meaning of Narratives* by Ruthellen Josselson and Amia Lieblick and a volume edited by Lieblick, *Narrative Research: Reading, Analysis and Interpretation*, both from Sage (US/UK: 1999).

If narratives prosper from having catchy titles then there deserves to be a responsive readership for Sherrie H. Inness's *Tough Girls: Women, Warriors and Wonder Women in Popular Culture* (US: University of Phila-delphia Press, 1999), a detailed analysis of the changing roles of female 'heroes' in popular film and TV drama. For an examination of Western narratives as myth, see Will Wright's *Wild West: The Mythical Cowboy and Social Theory* (US/UK: Sage, 2001). For practical advice on writing news narratives see Anna McKane's *News Writing* (US/UK: Sage, 2006).

Notes

1. Arthur Asa Berger, *Narratives in Popular Culture, Media, and Everyday Life* (US: Sage, 1997).
2. Bill Nicholls, *Blurred Boundaries: Questions of Meaning in Contemporary Culture* (US: University of Indiana Press, 1994). Nicholls believes that, 'The global reach and structural complexity of late twentieth-century reality calls for storytelling than can appear to encompass it. We hunger for news from around us but desire it in the form of narratives, stories that make meaning, however tenuous, dramatic, compelling, or paranoid they might be. What kind of world do we inhabit, with what risks and with what prospects?'
3. Walter R. Fisher, 'The narrative paradigm: in the beginning' in *Journal of Communication*, Autumn 1985.
4. George Herbert Mead, 'The nature of aesthetic experience' in *International Journal of Ethics*, 36 (1926).
5. Jerome Bruner, *Actual Minds, Possible Worlds* (US: Harvard University Press, 1986).
6. Peter Dahlgren and Colin Sparks (eds), *Journalism and Popular Culture* (UK: Sage, 1992).
7. Roland Barthes, *Mythologies* (UK: Paladin, 1973).
8. Robert C. Allen (ed.), *Channels of Discourse: Television and Contemporary Criticism* (UK: Routledge, 1987).
9. Bryan Appleyard, 'If there's too much soap, it won't wash', *Independent*, 11 July 1996.
10. Robert C. Entman, 'Framing: toward clarification of a fractured para-digm' in *Journal of Communication*, Autumn 1992.
11. Binary frames. Arthur Asa Berger (see Note 1) refers to 'central opposi-tions' and these relate back to ideas posed by the Swiss linguist Ferdi-nand de Saussure in *A Course in General Linguistics* translated into Eng-lish and published after his death by McGraw-Hill in 1966. Meaning, believed de Saussure, is derived from relationships, of one feature set against another, of one term set against another. 'The most precise char-acteristic' of concepts, de Saussure believed, 'is in being what the others

are not.' Berger quotes Jonathan Culler's *Structuralist Poetics: Structuralism, Linguistics, and the Study of Literature* (US: Cornell University Press, 1975) which discusses de Saussure's ideas in detail and those of the linguist Roman Jakobson from whom structuralists have taken 'the binary opposition as a fundamental operation of the human mind basic to the production of meaning'. Berger follows this up by saying, 'That is why when we read or hear the word *rich*, we automatically contrast it with *poor* and when we read or hear of the word *happy* we think of the word *sad*. If everyone has a great deal of money, *rich* loses its meaning; *rich* means something only in contrast to *poor*'.

12. Jasper Rees, 'Slap "n" tickle', *Independent*, 30 July 1996.
13. Roland Barthes, *S/Z* (UK: Jonathan Cape, 1975).
14. Vladimir Propp, *Morphology of the Folk Tale* (US: University of Texas Press, 1968).
15. Richard V. Ericson, Patricia M. Baranak and Janet B.L. Chan, *Visualizing Deviance: A Study of News Organization* (UK: Open University, 1987).
16. John Hartley, *The Politics of Pictures: The Creation of the Public in the Age of Popular Media* (UK: Routledge, 1992).
17. Milly Buonanno, 'News values and fiction-values: news as serial device and criteria of "fiction worthiness" in Italian television fiction' in *European Journal of Communication*, June 1993.
18. Adrian Tilley, 'Narrative' in David Lusted (ed.), *The Media Studies Book: A Guide for Teachers* (UK: Routledge, 1991).
19. Lesley Henderson, *Incest in Brookside: Audience Responses to the Jordache Story* (UK: Channel Four Television/Glasgow University Media Group, 1996).
20. Justin Lewis, *The Ideological Octopus: An Exploration of Television and its Audience* (UK: Routledge, 1991).
21. S. Elizabeth Bird, 'News we can use: an audience perspective on the tabloidisation of news in the United States' in *Critical Readings: Media and Audiences* (UK: Open University Press, 2003), edited by Virginia Nightingale and Karen Ross.
22. John Fiske, *Reading the Popular* (US: Unwin Hyman, 1989).
23. Daniel C. Hallin, 'Sound-bite news: television coverage of elections, 1968–1988' in *Journal of Communication*, Spring 1992.

The Practice of
Media: Pressures
and Constraints

7

AIMS

> ➤ To survey the personal, social and institutional pressures that media practitioners have to cope with in their working lives.
> ➤ To examine the principles and practice of media professionalism in the light of rapidly changing circumstances.
> ➤ By focusing on information sources, to address the problem faced by news practitioners of attempts by influentials in society wishing to 'manage the news'.
> ➤ To briefly outline the position of women and of ethnic minorities in media professions.

The first part of this chapter uses Maletzke's model of the constituents of media production to examine the pressures and constraints upon media practitioners, focusing on the communicator as an individual within a production team which in turn operates in a media organization. Idealism is seen to be unavoidably modified by the necessities of circumstance and context – by the law, by institutional norms, values and practices and by market forces.

A key theme of much research into media practices is the heavy reliance of media upon drawing information from official sources, thus exposing practitioners to accusations of complicity. Problems concerning the under-representation of women and of ethnic minorities are linked to habits of exclusion and stereotyping that have proved to be deeply ingrained at all levels of media.

Media communication and the 'project of self'

In Chapter 3 on the audience for media I quoted from John B. Thompson's *The Media and Modernity: A Social Theory of the Media*,[1] in which he refers to 'the project of self'. He is speaking specifically of how members of audience seek to connect up personal development with both *lived* and *mediated* experience. The media practitioner – journalist, broadcaster, photographer, advertising copywriter or film-maker – is even more directly involved in this process of self-formulation; in the 'project of self', negotiating a passage between personal needs and aspirations, the demands of the media world in which he or she is active, and the realities of the lived experience of social, cultural, political and economic life.

Many prospective students of media express an ambition to become journalists, for the perception they have of the profession seems relevant to their personal vision: it is congruent with their developing project of self. The attractions are obvious: you are out and about rather than stuck at a desk; you rarely know what reporting job you will be on from day to day. There is the possibility of travel, danger, of meeting interesting people; and journalism is widely held by young people to be a service to the community.

Young people with a keen eye on a profession in the media have often already fixed themselves work experience in newspapers or local radio, usually by sheer persistence. They are driven not only by interest and enthusiasm, but by idealism. They see news-gathering and presentation as important features of a country's mental and physical health. They recognize that journalism is the eyes, ears and voice of the public in a democracy.

Well, perhaps it would be if it could be. In the West, where free press criteria are the norm, informing and speaking up for democracy would on the face of it appear to offer a smoother ride for the journalist than in systems where authoritarianism dominates, or where the practices of development theory veer towards the repressive. But *free*, as we have seen, is a relative term. To be free from pressures is not written into any code of practice.

The young idealist will encounter pressures and constraints soon enough, of time and competition; the need to expand circulation and oblige the advertisers; the insistence on personalizing issues; the temptation to put entertainment rather than information on top of the daily agenda; the sensationalization that so often obliterates the truth and the fear that judgements concerning a universal 'dumbing down' might be well-founded.

A framework for analysis

A useful model highlighting the features of producers, production and consumers of mass communication is that of German Maletzke published in *The Psychology of Mass Communications.*[2] A selection of the elements of the Maletzke model will be discussed, beginning with the 'communicator arm' of the model shown in Figure 7.1. Here Maletzke identifies a range of pressures and constraints affecting the journalist's communicative behaviour.

The communicator's self-image

Let us imagine that you, the reader, have been taken on to a regional newspaper as a trainee reporter. Your self-esteem, as a result of the appointment, may well be high. You have a clear idea of your self-image as a result of the way people treat you; their respect for you. You will have produced some efficient and interesting reports in order to have gained your place. Much will depend, in the new environment, on how others recognize your abilities and demonstrate that they recognize them by, for example, giving you increasingly challenging tasks to do.

You will be moving to a clearer appraisal of your role as a *professional*, part of which will be the notion of 'doing a good job'. Sooner or later there will come a time when you are asked to do something you

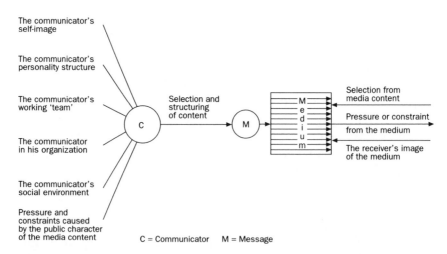

Figure 7.1 The 'communicator arm' of Maletzke's model of the mass communication process (1963)

Six major factors have exerted influence on the communicator and therefore affect the way he/she selects and structures messages for media consumption.

consider *un*professional if not unethical. It may simply be a request that is not so much unprofessional or unethical as simply distasteful, like intruding upon the grief of a bereaved family in order to get a story.

You may feel varyingly acute degrees of dissonance, of unease. You ask yourself, conscious of the image you hold of yourself, 'Is this the sort of thing *I* ought to be doing?' To refuse the particular task is to put your job at risk. Either way, you will attempt to shift your feelings from those of dissonance to consonance. If you are to stay in the job this dilemma will recur: will you attempt to 're-educate' self or should you try some other profession?

The communicator's personality

Some psychiatrists hold that the 'script' of an individual's personality is written in the early years of childhood. Socialization and experience shape attitudes and values and these will continue to affect behaviour throughout life. If, for you, kindness and compassion are values that dominate over competition and acquisition the work you produce as a journalist will, if permitted, reflect these values.

Equally you may be a person of commitment who wishes to act – get involved – rather than as a reporter must do, observe and record. The values of a journalist like John Pilger, determined warrior against injustices worldwide, express with eloquence and passion his personal vision. Getting angry, turning that anger into the communication of analysis and protest is the hallmark of Pilger as a crusading journalist; key to his personality.

A young reporter might say, 'Yes, but Pilger is famous. He has more freedom to express his views and therefore himself than the rest of us'. The 'rest of us' have, the argument might continue, to strive after such professional values as objectivity, balance and impartiality even though we may not believe any of them to be really possible. As Pilger says in the preface to *Heroes*,[3] a collection of his journalistic writing, neutrality is a 'non-existent nirvana'. Attempting something you do not believe in will prove an intolerable strain unless the inner voice of self – conscience – can be squared by argument or rationalization.

The communicator's working 'team'

Objectivity and neutrality may or may not be crucial norms for a media work team, but whatever norms have been engendered by people working together will be the ones most difficult to ignore. The dynamics of groups tend to demand a measure of conformity to group rules and practices and the reward for this conformity is the satisfaction and pride of belonging.

Students of communication will be familiar with teamwork and will recognize that individual initiative and group norms often come into conflict and have to be resolved, usually in the group's favour. Either that, or the group's performance will be impeded. In a successful group what counts for the team member is the respect and admiration he or she is held in by other members of the group. The more habitual the work of the group and the more its efforts are given status and recognition by those in important positions outside of the group, the tighter will be the bonding.

Some commentators argue that media people are performing to impress other media people, with audience response a secondary consideration. As Allan Bell puts it in *The Language of News Media*,[4] 'Mass communicators are interested in their peers not their public'.

The communicator in his/her organization

The independence of a working group survives only as long as the organization to which it belongs tolerates that independence and only as long as the working group fulfils the greater aims and objectives of the organization. The bigger the media organization the more likely it is to be hierarchically structured; a bureaucracy. There will be normative ways of doing things; procedures and regulations; and communication between the levels of the hierarchy will be strictly controlled.

Joining a major national newspaper group, a young reporter would have to attune to the political, social, economic and cultural standpoints of the organization. You would be unlikely to succeed in your new job if you submitted stories that regularly ran counter to the ideology of your employers.

The communicator's social environment

A person's education, upbringing, social class and social expectations will all affect communicative behaviour within the work context. The media workforce – certainly in the Western media – is predominantly middle class; and its collective script is influenced by middle-class expectations and values. Many commentators have argued that a substantially middle-class workforce will, consciously or unconsciously, report the world according to middle-class assumptions and perceptions.

Pressures and constraints caused by the public character of the media

Your ambition might always have been to move on from a local report-ing job into public broadcasting. You will discover that being employed by a corporation answerable to government is to experience constraints arising from the organization being one which itself is under public scrutiny. You may decide that working for state-linked media is too inhibiting: you want to throw caution to the winds, so you opt to switch to the private sector. In all probability the local commercial station's output is livelier, possibly a lot more fun. Yet once more there is a 'reg-ulatory' body ever-prepared to exert influence over content and style – the advertiser.

A constant pressure upon media operating in the public domain is the law. Should you intentionally or inadvertently write or broadcast something defamatory about a member of the public or a company or institution proof of slander (spoken defamation) or libel (written defa-mation) could result in enormous fines for you or your employer.

You could be landed in court for obscenity, for incitement to reli-gious or racial hate, for breach of commercial confidentiality and per-haps most seriously in the UK for divulging information covered by the Official Secrets Act. The dangers are not confined to punishment after the event. Perhaps the worst form of censorship for a journalist is what is termed *prior restraint*. The subject of a proposed report or programme hears that it is about to go out. In certain circumstances a decision in court may ban or at least postpone the broadcast or the publication.

At least in the West journalists are unlikely to end up in prison, a fate lurking in the wings for, sadly, media workers in a majority of countries in the world where penal codes protect the powerful and the privi-leged from media criticism.

Let us now look at the Maletzke model in full (Figure 7.2). It is at first glance rather formidable but careful examination of its parts will indicate how useful it can be as a reminder of the complexity of the encoding-decoding process. It is complex but helpfully comprehen-sive. It acknowledges a structure of response on the part of the receiver corresponding to that of media performers and media performance.

We might read into it an indicator that successful media communi-cation requires each axis of the model to take into consideration the pressures and constraints the other experiences and expects. The basic formula would appear to be that the news values held by the commu-nicator should produce the news that the receiver/public values.

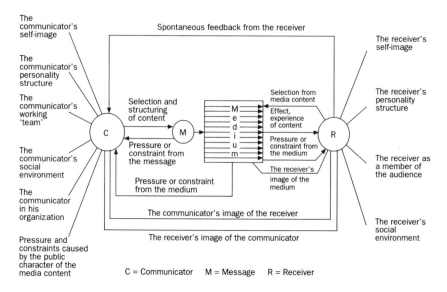

Figure 7.2 Maletzke's full model of the mass communication process (1963)

The communicator's image of the audience

The popular press prides itself in having its finger on the public pulse: it knows its readership and takes into careful consideration the factors on the right hand side of the Maletzke model. It therefore speaks for its reading public in discourses likely to be understood and appreciated; and in language – *tabloidese* – which is as accessible as it is lively.

Colin Sparks in his chapter 'Popular journalism: theories and practice' in *Journalism and Popular Culture*[5] says that it is not 'a particular mystery as to what the nature of the news values of this "popular journalism" is' and thus how it is designed to fulfil the perceived needs of readership:

> Relatively speaking these newspapers will tend to give more space to sport than to politics, stress more that extraordinary category 'human interest' than economic life, concentrate heavily upon individuals rather than institutions, upon the local and the immediate rather than the international and the long-term and so on.

Above all, Sparks believes, the 'structure of the "popular" in modern journalism is…one which is massively and systematically "depoliticized"'. This does not, of course, mean ideology-free. On the contrary, believes the author, there is 'a conception of politics which concentrates

Risking life and limb

2006 proved a bad year for the safety of media workers. According to the World Association of Newspapers (WAN), over 100 were killed, 44 of them in Iraq. In covering the news journalists risk being kidnapped (BBC reporter Alan Johnston spent 114 days in captivity in Gaza in 2007), shot (sometimes by so-called 'friendly fire'), blown up, hit by shrapnel or beheaded. They can expect to be attacked, beaten up and poisoned – as happened to Russian journalist Anna Politkovskaya on her way to cover the school massacre in Beslan. She survived only to be shot dead in the lift of her apartment on 7 October 2006.

In March 2007 another Russian journalist, Ivan Safronov, fell to his death from a 5th-floor balcony. He was found sprawled in snow surrounded by the oranges he had just bought. The official explanation was that Safranov had committed suicide, an explanation scorned by fellow journalists. The 51-year old father of two had been delving into the failure of Russia's experimental Bulava intercontinental ballistic missile. He was the 13th Russian journalist to be murdered, or die in 'mysterious circumstances' since 2000.

In the 19th century radical editors and journalists such as Joseph Swann, Richard Hassell, Henry Hetherington, William Hone, Richard Carlile, George Julius Harney, James Watson and William Cobbett were imprisoned in Britain for their writings. When they were released they went on attacking the injustices, inequality and corruption around them. Above all they demanded progress towards democracy.

James Curtis in a Net posting of the International News Safety Institute (INSI), 'In the firing line' (1 September 2006), quotes Chris Cramer, managing director of CNN International, 'Is it a more dangerous time for journalists worldwide? Yes, fact. Historical fact, numerical fact. Forget Vietnam, forget the 2nd World War – it's more dangerous than ever before'.

on the everyday at the expense of the historical' and avoids generating 'a picture of the world in which social classes are capable of transforming the fundamental structures of social life through their own self-activity'.

The young journalist coming from media education in which the purposes, roles and performance of media have been closely scrutinized is unlikely to be surprised by the expectations of popular journalism and its vision of audience. Yet the pressure to conform to institutional norms, values and practices will constitute an ongoing challenge.

The receiver's image of the communicator

We do well to bear in mind the figures quoted earlier about the dangers faced by journalists in the pursuit of news when 'journos' come in for public criticism in, say, intrusion cases. Unfortunately for the profession, examples of intrusions into privacy, muck-raking and sexational titillation loom larger in the public image of the media than journalistic skills or courage. Yet it is in the nature of news coverage that reporters appear, with notebooks and a headful of questions, at times of disaster and distress. They probe and they harry. Sometimes they will not let a matter alone.

Their performance may become despised, but that does not diminish the public's appetite for what they produce. The presence of reporters and photographers at a disaster is often unwelcome but the public is hungry for information about that disaster. Equally there is a seemingly insatiable public appetite for tittle-tattle as much as for hard news. Disapproval there may be, but there is also a degree of public dependency: the audience needs news but it also *wants* stories – dramatic, stirring, exemplary, reaffirming.

Journalists may be unpopular, but that does not diminish the importance to the public of their function in the community. In an article 'Has communication explained journalism?' in the *Journal of Communication*,[6] Barbie Zelizer writes of the way 'publics let reporters present themselves as cultural authorities for events of the "real world"'. Journalists do what they do, good or bad, because they are confident of public acceptance; and this constitutes, says Zelizer, 'one of the outstanding condundrums of contemporary public discourse'.

We, as public, are accepting of journalism's claim to be the key mediator of reality: 'Audiences tend to question journalistic authority only when journalists' versions of events conflict with the audiences' view of the same events.' Just occasionally the journalistic view is so at odds with the public's perception of reality that general acquiescence turns to positive and determined resistance.

The tasteless and sensationalist coverage by the *Sun* newspaper in Britain, of the tragedy of spectators crushed to death during the Football Association Cup Semi-Final between Liverpool and Nottingham Forest (15 April 1989) at Sheffield's Hillsborough stadium, created such outrage among the people of Liverpool that the newspaper was banned throughout the city; not by the City Council but by the people themselves who arguably felt affronted in relation to every feature of the receiver arm of Maletzke's model.

Pressures and constraints of message and medium

Journalists are generally perceived to be the first gatekeepers. The decision as to who to send on a story lies with the news editor but from that point on the journalist is at the front line of mediation, deciding what information to include and what to leave aside; what points to emphasize and which to minimize. First, there is pressure to find an angle, a key notion (or message) to hang the story on. Second, the pressure is likely to be one related to the news value of *amplitude*.

No reporter wishes to cover a story when little of significance appears to have occurred. If storylines are not evident the reporter's instinct for a story will resemble the detective's hunt for clues. There is a particular satisfaction the journalist experiences when his or her story hits the front page; and the pressure to 'make the front page' is as much personally-driven as institutionally-required.

In fact the determination to write a highly newsworthy story may well conflict with institutional constraints. If you are working as a reporter on a local newspaper you may stumble on a case of local government corruption or serious pollution caused by a local firm. The adrenalin flows. Your notebook bulges with damning information. It is full of juicy quotes given to you by members of the public. Then why are you suddenly greeted back at the office with blank stares and shakes of the head?

Your story, or at least most of it, is on the 'spike': 'This,' you might be told, 'isn't the sort of paper that prints that sort of story. We have our advertisers to think of. Are you aware that Company X takes a full-page spread twice a month?' This is a constraint brought about by the perceived role of the paper within its community. On a broader canvas, media must take heed of commercial or political giants – companies or states, home or away – whose interests may impact on editorial policy.

Stories about human rights abuses in nations such as China, Indonesia or Saudi Arabia, for example, have to be weighed in the balance against their commercial goodwill as important trading nations; and the temptation to trade silence for lucrative business contracts is ever-present.

It can be argued that we are not talking here about the constraints of the medium as a mode of communication; rather the point is that while the medium shapes the message it is the constraints upon message and content which limit the possibilities of the medium. Equally it might be said that the *possibilities* of the medium are both a challenge and a constraint.

Today, technology not only makes for speed of output, it is a driving force to the point that speed becomes a principle of operation. As Jo Bardoel describes the situation in a *European Journal of Communication* article, 'Beyond journalism: a profession between information society and civil society',[7] journalists have to cope with 'a whirling communication carousel of immediate action and reaction'.

Indeed as Bardoel recognizes, digitization is scarcely destined to slow down the 'communication carousel', for it threatens to rewrite the 'story' of mass communication in that each member of the public will have the capacity to be his or her own journalist, his or her own programme planner. Bardoel does, however, see a future for serious, analytical journalism, in *making sense* of the whirling carousel of information. In future, the journalist's task may be to help unload the overload.

The receiver's self-image and personality

All their lives students of media have also been receivers of media. Self-image will in part have been affected by exposure to media in its many forms and this experience is reflected in comments such as 'I wouldn't be seen dead reading/watching/wearing/listening to ...' and so on. What we read, watch, wear, listen to is what we are, or like to think we are. The advertiser concentrates in particular on the self-image of the prospective consumer.

An advertising campaign many years ago for *The Times* of the UK called it the paper for Top People. The covert message was that by reading *The Times* you could rank yourself among the Top People even if you weren't one. The problem was that if successful advertising boosted sales of the paper beyond the constituency of Top People, Top People would stop subscribing to it.

Self-image is essentially about individuality, a cherished and highly marketable personality trait; and tailoring messages that address the individual-in-the-mass is a prime challenge for the communicator. A key strategy is *segmentation* according to a number of personal, social and cultural criteria. Such a strategy depends for its success on communicators *knowing* their audience, its doubts and anxieties as well as its dreams and aspirations; its tastes and its preferred lifestyle.

The problem for a journalist is that there exist contrary and often contradictory images of receivers. Pete Hamill, former editor-in-chief of the *New York Daily Post* in an account of his years working on New York tabloids, accuses publishers, guided by the profit motive rather than the principle of producing quality journalism, of dumbing down content because basically they see readerships as dumb, or at least happy to be infused daily with what Hamill terms the 'virus of celebrity'.

In *News is a Verb: Journalism at the End of the Twentieth Century*,[8] Hamill, writing about the American press, argues that this attitude damages the status of newspapers in the eyes of readership, for '[t]rue newspaper professionals have learned that the readers have immense common sense'. Hamill states:

> Publishers and editors who wouldn't consider for a minute the purchase of a third-rate car or a third-rate suit of clothes are too often engaged in making a third-rate product of their own and knowingly sending it out to the public. Sooner or later, the readers wise up. Sometimes sooner. Always later.

Where, in the American press, there continues to be true 'commitment to excellence', as in the *New York Times*, the *Washington Post* or the *Los Angeles Times*, quality proves good for business. Readers 'feel respected by the writers, columnists, and editors':

> They sense that the newspaper has made a genuine attempt to discover, within the limits of time and space, what was knowable about an event or a person in the news. They know that the newspaper tries to verify stories, to determine what is true and what is not. They know that their newspaper doesn't pander or attempt to inflame cheap emotions. Those readers don't expect perfection; they know that mistakes will be made and that they will be admitted in published corrections. They can quarrel with the newspaper, but it will be on an intelligent level.

Media communicators who respect their audience will respect themselves, those for whom they work and the profession to which they belong. In the UK the BBC has, since its inception, had a reputation for respecting the truth as it has respected its audience; and this respect has been reciprocated by listeners and viewers throughout the world. In countries where communications are heavily censored, there has been a long tradition of tuning into the BBC's overseas services in order to learn from a reliable source what is happening at home and abroad.

Politicians who have been stung by the BBC's role as a critical observer as well as a balanced news-provider might not agree that the Beeb is The Best of British. There are those who would relish a night of the long knives in which the rich carcass of the BBC were carved up and distributed to the private sector. If this happened, it would represent a grievous loss to quality information, education and entertainment globally as well as nationally. Further, the demise of such an exemplar of public service broadcasting would be to the detriment of the British nation's own project of self.

The receiver's social environment

The receiver as member of readership/audience has been documented in Chapter 3, and is a recurring theme throughout the book, so this tracing of the Maletzke model concludes with brief observations on the social environment in which reception takes place.

The producers of mass communication messages are part of the context in which audiences use those messages. They are themselves audience in the sense that they are subject to the pressures and constraints placed upon society generally. Sit-coms of the 1990s contained a duly proportionate share of unemployed characters and, in Britain, financial hardship resulting from free market policies and the rolling back of the welfare state, has never been far away from the families that have populated long-running soaps such as *Eastenders* or *Coronation Street*.

Such powerful narratives dramatize problems. Solutions to those problems are left for audiences to conjecture upon; which is perhaps as well, for solutions on screen, unless matched by solutions in real-life situations, only diminish audience trust in the integrity of media communication; in narrative fidelity.

Of course in countries where normative practices are ruled by the authoritarian theory of media (as discussed in Chapter 4), the power of media communicators to reveal to a community the nature of its own social environment is strictly censored if not forbidden altogether. All that is permitted are visualizations that conform to the requirements of those in total authority. For example, in Saudi Arabia the audience for media is denied any public reference to politics, religions other than Islam, pork or pigs, alcohol or sex (see Note 9).

Official, state censorship often produces alliances between communicators and receivers, both media and public dodging authority in ingenious ways. Though many governments rule, or seek to rule, through disinformation, and insist that the media purvey that disinformation, that does not mean that publics are necessarily misinformed.

Ducking and weaving become the order of the day. Censorship is a barrier to be overcome, to be circumvented; and in many instances audience itself becomes part of the act of defiance as the box below illustrates.

'Arise! Refuse to be enslaved!'

Under decades of strong ideological control, many among the Chinese within the country, and China watchers in the outside world, can skilfully read between the lines of censored media texts and come up with esoteric signals and subversive readings. It is 'common sense' among Chinese that the real truth is probably closer to the opposite of what the official papers claim...

After the June 4th Tiananman Square incident in 1989, the Chinese government adopted restrictive media measures and engineered an official interpretation of the event. However, all sorts of oppositional encoding and decoding activities transgressed against the official lines. At times journalists planted esoteric messages against the government. One poem in the overseas edition of *People's Daily* said 'Down with Li Peng' if read diagonally.

Another instance is a story about the symbol of the 1990 Asian Games hosted in China. People could find very strange ways of reading the symbol: looked at sideways, it was a 6, and on the left, it was a 4. It contained, as the story went, a commemoration to the democratic martyrs of June 4th (6/4). Another extraordinary instance occurred in a political prison in which prisoners were required to sing the national anthem. Surprisingly, they sang it with gusto, 'Arise! Refuse to be enslaved!'. The authority sensed the irony and dropped the ritual.

Eric Kit-Wai, in *De-Westernizing Media Studies*[10]

The dilemmas of professionalism

Framing all the aspects of Maltetske's model as far as the media communicator is concerned is the notion of professionalism and the principles and operational conventions which shape that professionalism. We encounter once more that awesome threesome – objectivity, impartiality and balance. A feature common to these, however precisely we define their differences, is that journalists must not take sides; must not reveal their personal bias, show favour, sympathy or antipathy.

In other words, journalists must position themselves outside the action. They are observers, not participants. This is a convention hardened by tradition, and occasionally regulation. To breach it is to commit the worst of crimes, to be unprofessional. The dilemma is real, profound and largely unexamined.

Just occasionally the role of impartial observer is rejected for a 'higher good'. This painful but arguably enobling choice is well exemplified in one of the best feature films about journalism, *Under Fire* (1983) directed by Roger Spottiswoode and set in Nicaragua, when a news photographer played by Nick Nolte puts aside professionalism and involves himself in political events.

The People's Army, struggling against the repressive machinery of state, suffers a terrible blow. Their charismatic leader is shot dead on the verge of sweeping the tyrants out of office. Nolte is asked by the revolutionaries to fake a picture of the leader to make him appear to be still alive. By every rule in the professional book, Nolte must refuse. On the other hand, the situation cries out that he bend the rules in the name of the people's struggle against oppression. As audience for *Under Fire*, we are expected to respond affirmatively to this potential act of 'professional suicide' and to celebrate its successful outcome for the revolutionaries.

Here the journalist has taken the side of the underdog rather than stayed aloof; and Spottiswoode's message seems to be that where issues of right or wrong, democracy or repression are involved, the power of the word or of the image should be wielded by journalists as 'part' of life rather than their behaving as though they are somehow disengaged from it.

'Bystander journalism'

This point was given heartfelt support by a 'real' journalist, Martin Bell of the BBC, in the Autumn of 1996. The veteran foreign correspondent's speech to News World '96, a conference in Berlin of 500 news broadcasters from all over the world, called for an end to '"bystander journalism" based on the old tradition of detached, cool and neutral reporting'.

Four years earlier Bell had been badly wounded reporting the civil war in Bosnia. While acknowledging the need to honour fairness and the meticulous concern for facts, for accuracy, Bell declared in his Berlin speech:

> I do not believe we should stand neutrally between good and evil, right and wrong, aggressor and victim…It is a real problem we should address: my answer is what I call journalism of attachment, journalism which cares as well as knows.

In some reporting situations neither attachment nor neutral intent amount, as it were, to a hill of beans. According to another BBC foreign correspondent, Jeremy Bowen, in his book, *War Stories*,[11] 'in the Middle East being an honest journalist is not a particularly good way of making friends', such is the complexity and sensitivity of the Israel–Palestine conflict: if journalists 'just describe what has happened, on anything but the most straight-up-and-down stories, they can end up raising more questions than they answer'. Any attempt to explain things 'can get you into trouble, because it involves making choices and assessments'. Bowen goes on:

> Even if you work so hard to be fair that people cannot tell what your real or imagined views are, they still try to deduce things from that. A British Jew, a supporter of Israel, congratulated me on something I had written. He could not tell, he said, which side I was backing, but he assumed it must be the Israelis, because I sounded reasonable and only Israel's supporters were reasonable.

Bowen asks, 'How can a journalist make sense of it all in a few hundred words or in a couple of minutes of airtime?' He confesses that the 'depressing answer to the question is that it is very difficult; the best reporters who try the hardest do not always succeed, and the clueless get lost very quickly'.

Professionalism at the level of myth

A fascinating and exhaustive study of the institutional norms, values and practices of the British Broadcasting Corporation was conducted by Philip Schlesinger. In his book *Putting 'Reality' Together: BBC News*,[12] he explores what he terms 'myths of professionalism' that held sway in the corporation. First, Schlesinger identifies the *micro-myth*. Here, the *autonomy* of the production staff is held to be self-evident, responsibility being fully delegated downwards from the Director General.

Second is the *macro-myth* which enthrones the view that the BBC is socially unattached. In spite of the myth of independence, Schlesinger found that an 'invisible framework of guidance is omnipresent' – the institutional *ethos*. Of the newsroom, Schlesinger writes:

> The style of control is one which relies upon responsible editors, who have been thoroughly socialised by long exposure to the mores [essentially, norms and values] of the Corporation that they will 'instinctively' make the right decision.

Claims to independence, Schlesinger argues, have validity only within the notion that the 'value framework...has already, largely been developed at higher levels of control, to which most newsmen have no access'. Most journalists, whether working in broadcasting or for newspapers, will probably recognize this state of affairs. They will have at least a nodding acquaintance with the *control features* listed by Schlesinger such as the hierarchy of positions and (not least, or to be belittled) the attraction of a secure, well-remunerated job; factors that 'tend to ensure conformity in the newsrooms'.

Perhaps the most familiar control feature, and the one by which careers rise or fall, is the senior editor's power to assign news staff to stories. Few pressures can be greater for the journalist than the one which starts everything off, being chosen to cover one story rather than another; being favoured (or not favoured) in what Schlesinger calls a 'pecking order'. Much depends on track-record: how well did you manage last time?

Schlesinger cites *reliability* as a prime criterion for selection. This does not simply mean reliability to come back with a good story, fully documented and well told. People tend to be chosen for their proven record for saying 'what one wanted in an acceptable (ie. inconspicuous) way'. In other words, what counts is a safe pair of hands; or to supplement one useful cliche with another, horses for courses.

This situation is illustrated in another thought-provoking movie about media people, Karl Francis' *Giro City* (1982). Glenda Jackson as film director and Jon Finch as reporter for a commercial TV station are scheduled to cover two stories, financial corruption in Wales and the conflict in Northern Ireland. Finch is a top-class reporter, independent but suspect, likely to put his pursuit of the truth ahead of his responsibility to appear 'evenhanded'.

He is about to crown a fine investigative story about Ireland with an interview with a British cabinet minister. At the last moment, he is substituted as interviewer. A 'safer pair of hands' is put in his place to give the minister an 'easier ride'. As for the Welsh story, the truth is struck silent as the law renders the 'case' *sub judice*. Few films illustrate the pressures and constraints upon journalists as effectively as *Giro City*.

Schlesinger explodes the micro-myth of autonomy, of independence, believing that the news, with its 'flagship' – highly prestigious, high-profile – function, is 'the home of the conformist'. True, official ideology stresses autonomy, but this 'does less than justice to the substantive controls which actually constrain production'.

Ideological keynote

'Impartiality,' believes Schlesinger, 'is the linchpin of the BBC's ideology: it is a notion saturated with political and philosophical implications'. Yet impartiality can only have meaning 'in the context of an existing set of values, and in the case of the BBC the relevant complex of values is that of the "consensus"'. To be impartial, it is necessary to be uninvolved in that which is being reported. However, the BBC, and most other news-producing organizations, are not floating islands above the fray. They are actors in the drama of social, cultural, political and economic events; influenced and influencing.

Schlesinger says that what the BBC produces as news is 'structurally limited by the organisation's place in Britain's social order'. The main consequence of that position is that 'the outputs of broadcasting are, in general, supportive of the existing social order'. Pressures to conform to dominant norms and practices exist in every organization, media or otherwise. As far as the BBC is concerned, Schlesinger states:

> I was faced with a mass of conformists. Their conformity lay not in their personal style, dress or lack of sexual peccadillos, but rather in their adoption of the model of corporate professionalism provided for them by the BBC by degrees varying from unreflecting acquiescence to the most full-blown commitment.

Schlesinger quotes a senior news and current affairs editor as saying, 'Every time a man reveals a personal commitment he reduces his professional usefulness, until the moment arrives when he may be said to have used up all his credit-worthiness'. For personal 'commitment' we can also read personal *value*. It seems that survival in the institution would depend upon a practitioner being value-*free*. Schlesinger calls this the 'myth of value-freedom'.

The bottom line of the institutional message might be, either subscribe to the myth or get out. The myth is 'essential for public consumption' and thus it must be 'believed by those who propagate it' as 'a condition of employment'. Such beliefs, argues Schlesinger, 'anchor news production in the *status quo*'.

Since Schlesinger published his conclusions the media industry has seen substantial job losses (some three thousand at the BBC in the early years of the new millennium), circumstances that understandably make for caution and second thoughts over risk-taking. And when risks are taken, such as when BBC correspondent Andrew Gilligan, on the early morning *Today* programme, suggested that the government had been exaggerating claims that Saddam Hussain possessed weapons of mass destruction (see Box), all hell breaks loose, heads roll, official apologies are swift and abject; a blanket of caution and circumspection descends.

Dodgy dossier?

Pressed to justify the invasion of Iraq in 2003, the UK government published a dossier claiming that Saddam Hussein's WMDs could, in a matter of 45 minutes, be turned on the British people. Early on a May morning, reporter Andrew Gilligan, in an unscripted broadcast on the BBC's Radio 4 *Today* programme, voiced the opinion that the government 'probably knew' that the 45-minute figure was wrong. The government responded in fury, suspecting, as was the case, that Gilligan had received insider briefing.

The 'mole' turned out to be Dr David Kelly, a government weapons expert. Gilligan later admitted that he had wrongly inferred that Kelly was the direct source of the 'sexing up' claim. However, he insisted in his resignation speech that Kelly's information concerning WMDs (which did not exist) was correct.

Kelly was 'outed' as source. On 17 July he was found dead, allegedly having taken his own life. In August, the government's appointee, Lord Brian Hutton, conducted a swift enquiry into the Gilligan/BBC/Kelly affair, taking evidence from 74 witnesses in 25 days. He cleared the government of wrong-doing, though Gilligan, in his resignation statement, asserted 'I did not accuse the government of fabrication, but of exaggeration. I stand by that charge and it will not go away'.

In his report, Lord Hutton criticized the BBC for 'defective' control over Gilligan's broadcasts. Hutton was in turn widely criticized for a 'whitewash' of government while at the same time pillorying the BBC. In Gilligan's view, the report cast 'a chill over all journalism, not just the BBC's. It seeks to hold reporters, with all the difficulties they face, to a standard that it does not appear to demand of, for instance, government dossiers'.

The fall-out from the affair involved more than Andrew Gilligan's job. Following the publication of the Hutton report, the BBC's chairman, Gavyn Davies, and Director General, Greg Dyke, both resigned. The 'unreserved apology' by the BBC's acting chairman, Lord Ryder, prompted protest rallies by BBC staff in London, Glasgow, Cardiff and Bristol.

News management and the hazards of source

Maletzke's model offers us a comprehensive framework for investigating the variables working at the stages of message formulation and reception. The audience's perception of the communicator as message-producer is recognized, but in our survey of pressures and restraints we need to pay critical attention to the journalists' own sources, for it is an old axiom that a story is only as reliable as its source.

The central criticism levelled at the reporting fraternity is that they rely too heavily upon official sources, that is, briefings in one form or another by those in authority. In Chapter 3, I quoted Allan Bell as saying in *The Language of News Media*[4] that news 'is what an authoritative source tells a journalist'. He refers to those who 'wear a general mantle of authority and are part of the institutional network where journalists expect to get their information'.

Obtaining information that does not come from official sources is a genuine problem even for the journalist determined to cut through the protective cordon of those 'authoritative sources' whose purpose is the *management* of news. The pressure to 'get a story' is such that the official account is considered better than no account. In an ideal world journalists would resist attempts by official sources to write their stories for them. In practice, perceived necessities can often serve as an alibi for merely reworking official briefings.

Journalists are rarely short of information – provided by all the agencies in a society who wish their story to be told. What they are always short of and desperately in need of is the kind of information people in authority do not want them to print or broadcast. There are occasions when a reporter looks out on the world and sees plenty of news management, but pitifully little news.

Spin-doctoring

Let us be clear about the meaning of *news management*. This does not refer to news teams involved in news production; rather it describes the myriad forces in society that want to get a story about themselves, preferably favourable, into the news. News management is to be expected; it is a necessary function of governments and organizations. Where it has met with legitimate criticism is when management becomes 'spin' in the sense of 'spinning a tale' with intent to deceive, mislead and simply to deflect attention away from the truth.

Martin Moore in *The Origins of Modern Spin: Democratic Government and the Media in Britain, 1945–51*[13] refers to the term as having become 'ubiquitous and is normally used pejoratively'. He writes:

Modern spin evolved from information management but is distinct from it. It involves the deliberate distortion of information and manipulation of the independent media in order to achieve government objectives. In modern spin the information itself is no longer considered to have inherent value but is regarded as malleable raw material in the service of an eventual goal. How it is perceived and its predicted response are considered more important than any ideals of objective truth.

The 'spin-doctors' are operatives in the public relations machine, usually former journalists who, working for political parties, corporations or pressure groups, strive to get their patrons' message across via the mass media, asserting the 'good' news, suppressing the bad. They are there to ensure that preferred readings are answered by dominant responses. The effect the message has on the public takes precedence over whether it is true or not.

In the Glasgow University Media Group's 1993 publication, *Getting the Message: News, Truth and Power*,[14] David Miller reports on the way that the Northern Ireland Information Service controlled – news managed – the information coming out of Northern Ireland and how it did this by exercising what Miller terms a 'hierarchy of access'.

Working under the direction of the Northern Ireland Office, the Northern Ireland Information Service, according to *Hansard* of 7 May 1991, spent £7.2 million in the year 1989–90 on press and public relations in a campaign to define the situation in Northern Ireland according to the requirements of the Westminster government. Specifically the strategy was to emphasize two themes: terrorism as an assault on democracy and the fact that Northern Ireland's commercial and industrial progress ('carrying on regardless') was making terrorism irrelevant. Miller writes:

Because of the perceived difficulty of getting good news [about Northern Ireland] into the media, the information service itself has two staff who produce 'good news' stories for the international market…They attempt to 'place' these stories in suspecting and unsuspecting magazines and newspapers.

We are witnessing here an example of practices often termed *disinformation*; and such practices are exercised worldwide. Of course journalists are themselves guilty of this but they are often as much victims of disinformation (or 'plants') as perpetrators (and perpetuators) of it. More usually, journalists and their editors 'let through' official information either without checking it out or challenging it.

Miller quotes an unpublished disssertation by Eamon Hardy for Queen's University, Belfast, on the Northern Ireland Information Service and its link with the Northern Ireland press.[15] In a three-month period Hardy discovered that Belfast's three daily papers used between 57% and 68% of Northern Ireland Office press releases as the basis for news stories. Channel 4's *Hard News* programme picked up on the fact that very little of the original briefing was altered, Hardy telling them that:

> Attached to each press release there are things called Notes to Editors, which are supposed to be a government analysis of its own facts and figures and quite often I found that, in fact very often, you have journalists using these Notes to Editors as their own analysis.[16]

According to Miller, the Northern Ireland Office operated selectivity as to how much information reporters would receive. There seemed to be a pecking order: the more *influential* reporters were (that is, the more important their paper or country of origin), and the more likely they were to use NIO information favourably (that is favourable to the arguments of the government), the more they would get the red carpet treatment. London-based media outlets, particularly television, featured high up in the hierarchy of access. Miller says:

> Journalists from Western countries are seen as more important than journalists from what was the eastern bloc or the Third World ... Even among Western journalists degrees of access can depend on the importance to the British government of the country they are from. French and German journalists, for example, are higher up the priority list than their counterparts from Norway, Denmark, Sweden or Finland ... But the main target for information efforts overseas has long been the United States of America.

Competing for control

News management in its modern guise is about two things, attempting to control the content of the news that reaches the public and, through such control, exerting influence upon public and media agendas. In *Journalism in the 21st Century: Online Information, Electronic Databases and the News*,[17] American media commentator Tom Koch challenges the view that the media set public agendas, or even their own. He reminds us of the general situation journalists find themselves in, that is, as employees of corporate institutions:

> Mainstream reporters and editors directly serve not the public at large but, rather, the economic necessities of those corporations that hire and pay them. [In turn] [t]hose news corporations...exist to provide advertising space for the advertisements whose sale may guarantee sustaining financial returns.

Profitablity, then, exerts a firm grip over agenda-setting. The principle of objectivity (what Koch calls 'journalism's instrumental myth') encounters the obstacle of business bias. Koch believes that 'journalists do not set the agenda they publish and broadcast. Instead they affirm and reflect the decisions of others':

> The traditional assumption has been that reporters, or at least their editors, determine what events will be covered, and, therefore, are conscious contributors to any bias in the news. In reality, news professionals are almost totally dependent on press releases and the public statements of sanctioned 'experts' and officials.

Koch sees journalists in the USA not so much as producers of disinformation as casualties of it, condemned to reproduce elite messages for want of other sources of information. In an earlier work, *The News as Myth: Fact and Content in Journalism*[18] he defines two forms of event, the *boundary event*, that is, the actual occurrence – accident, death, disaster – and the *journalistic event* that follows it, in which a report is based upon what journalists glean from officials. In *Journalism in the 21st Century* Koch writes, 'Editors assign reporters to follow publicly sanctioned, journalistic events and not investigate their antecedent boundary occurrences'.

They will, for example, report a presidential speech on the dangers of drug dependency, and by reporting it they will turn presidential opinion into fact, rather than investigate the reality of what is claimed:

> Reporters rarely question independently the legitimacy of the speakers' statements, and truth is reduced to the reasonably accurate reportage of what an official says in press conference or a similarly public forum.

The result, Koch believes, and this goes some way to explaining the ingrainedness of stereotypical images, 'is a compliant press whose job is to report and relay what officials tell them to write' and the power of these officials to set the news agenda and control the media 'is increasingly evident the higher one goes on the political or economic ladder'.

Bucking officialdom: an online route

If the 'middleman' intrudes so assertively in the production of news narratives, then, Koch suggests, cut out the middleman. Digital technology closes the gap between boundary event and journalistic event as never before. The Internet, with its scores of browser services permitting fast access to vast stores of data is radically altering the information-seeking process. Koch believes that databases 'efficiently place an enormous amount of information at the command of the reporter or the writer':

> Further they do so with incredible specificity. Data available from online sources is so vast that it would take an expert months or years to search through them manually for the pertinent fact or the seminal article.

Any field can be narrowed 'to the appropriate and crucial information within minutes by a competent data researcher'. Koch sees in electronic databases the possibility of greater objectivity and less bias in reporting because more fundamentally '"complete" information may enter the public forum on a regular basis'.

This liberation of journalism (and consequently of the public it serves) from traditional information sources and therefore from the ideologies which those sources protect and project may not be welcome to power elites, but, Koch concludes:

> ... it is a lesson of the printing revolution that officials find it difficult or impossible to prevent the resulting flow of information when technology and economies combine to make a new level of dissemination both possible and profitable.

All this, of course, relies on the continuing independence of online services from the control of the great corporations and of the state (see Chapters 8, 9 and 11).

'Flak' as constraint

The media are subject to spin and they also suffer from what Edward Herman and Noam Chomsky, in *Manufacturing Consent: The Political Economy of the Mass Media*,[19] term 'flak' – 'a negative response to a media statement or programme'; and this may well resemble flak in its wartime sense: a blitz taking the form 'of letters, telegrams, phone calls, petitions, lawsuits, speeches and bills before Congress, and other modes of complaint, threat and punitive action'.

Herman and Chomsky state, 'If flak is produced on a large scale, or by individuals or groups with substantial resources, it can be both uncomfortable and costly to the media'. Used by the powerful, such as the great corporations, flak is designed to protect self-interest by bringing the media into line, by heading off potentially damaging media coverage that, as the authors put it, is not deemed *useful;* and the power of flak grows through alliances, often between corporate and policy agendas (see Chapter 5).

The authors speak of the guard-dog role of seemingly independent institutions 'organized for the specific purpose of producing flak'. They cite the example of Accuracy in Media (AIM) whose funding was contributed to by eight oil companies in the 1980s. The authors declare that, 'The function of AIM is to harass the media and put pressure on them to follow the corporate agenda and a hard-line, right-wing foreign policy'.

Uneven playing fields 1: gender imbalance

What constitutes both a constraint and an issue in the world of media communication is the treatment of women and of ethnic minorities *by* media and their under-representation in terms of media employment. If my experience of the quality, drive and commitment of the women applying for media studies degrees has been anything to go by, the future may demand the exercise of positive discrimination – in favour of men.

This impression is given weight by surveys in the United States, Britain and the Netherlands which record substantial increases in the number of women entering schools of journalism or enrolling for other communications courses, to the extent that reference has been made to a 'gender-switch'. Yet this trend is unevenly reflected in the media profession itself.

Public relations, advertising, magazine production and publishing appear to offer better opportunities for women than other specialist media fields. In *Feminist Media Studies*,[20] Liesbet van Zoonen, discussing the position of women in media towards the end of the 20th century, writes that, 'One of the factors explaining why some areas of communication provide more opportunities for women than others is the status of the medium'.

Where this is low, she argues, opportunities for women increase. She cites the example of radio, displaced in importance and status by television: 'The resulting loss of prestige may have decreased male competition for job openings enabling women to fill the gaps.' On the other hand, 'in many developing countries radio is still the mass electronic medium and dominated by men'. Van Zoonen adds that 'local (low prestige) media almost invariably employ more women than national (high prestige) media'.

Once employed, women have had further problems to deal with, in particular the attitudes of male colleagues and decision-makers:

> Gruesome anecdotes of women encountering blatant sexism abound, and can be found in any number of popular press cuttings, biographies and research reports … Whatever particular cultural form they may take, discriminatory attitudes towards women on the workfloor seem to be common practice in media production world wide.

Women's domestic and parental responsibilities constitute the toughest hurdle of all to their careers in the media. As van Zoonen points out, 'media work and motherhood have been made notoriously difficult to combine due to a lack of provision at the work place and to social values and beliefs'.

Women journalists are often expected, by male colleagues and by the organizations that employ them, to perform professionally in a manner different from men; to subscribe to expectations of 'femininity'. Van Zoonen says:

> Women are confronted by social and cultural expectations of femininity and at the same time are expected to meet criteria of professionalism. In the Netherlands, for instance, many female journalists feel that they are judged primarily as women being subjected to continual comment on their appearance and 'invitations' from male colleagues.

There is no evidence, van Zoonen argues, that women constitute a different group of professionals from their male colleagues. She refers to her own research in the Netherlands: two-thirds of the women journalists she talked to did believe that 'women journalists pay more attention to background information and are more willing to look for spokeswomen instead of spokesmen' than their male counterparts yet there was no difference 'in the actual selection of topics or issues'.

The chief problem facing women is that they generally enter an organizational culture whose *mores* and discourses are male-orientated. To survive, women must adapt; become socialized into the ways of the institution – what van Zoonen believes 'tends to reaffirm a conservative *status quo*' which she discerns already having begun at the stage of journalist training.

The 'maleness' of news

According to Sue Curry Jansen, speaking of the 1990s, conditions and prospects for women were equally disadvantaged in the United States. In 'Beaches without bases: the gender order' published in *Invisible Crises*,[21] Jansen states that the news generally, and international news in particular, needs to be viewed through the 'prism of gender'. When it is, we come to realize that news content and news gathering are 'gendered' with a profound, and institutionalized bias towards maleness:

> In the United States men write most of the front-page newspaper stories. They are the subject of most of those stories – 85 percent of the references and 66 percent of the photos in 1993. They also dominate electronic media, accounting for 86 percent of the correspondents and 75 percent of the sources for US network television evening programs.

Women, women's issues and problems are not newsworthy unless they can be labelled according to traditional female roles – wife, mother, daughter. 'Men are typically assigned to *hard* news, news that has significant public implications. Women, in contrast, cover *soft* news stories and stories related to topics traditionally associated with female responsibilities'. In international news coverage, 'women not only are marginal but also normally absent'.

Jansen quotes a term used by Robert W. Connell in *Gender and Power*[22] when he talks of 'hegemonic masculinity' which dominates political and economic life as well as media. This describes masculine relationships characterized by dominance and subservience, men to men, and men to all females; and this situation is replicated, Connell argues, in the global ordering of relationships between nations. Jansen continues:

> Under the present global gender order, policymakers and journalists find it more *manly* to deal with guns, missiles, and violent conflicts than with matters like female infanticide in China, the increased trade in children in the sex markets of Manila and Bangkok in the wake of the AIDS epidemic, the impact of the intifada on Palestinian women, or the political activism of groups such as Women in Black, Israeli women who support the intifada.

The author is angry but not without optimism for the prospect of gender-shifts in the emphasis of news content and production. Women *are* seeking empowerment in all sorts of ways but such actions do not get into the news. Jansen asks:

> How many readers of this book know that women have established a feminist radio station, Radio Tierra, in Chile? How many know that they are producing and distributing feminist videos throughout the Americas? How many know that women in Sri Lanka have formed underground media collectives to produce videos documenting human rights violations? ... How many know that the Manushi collective in India has published a successful magazine that confronts the oppression of women in that society?

Media scholars are then asked whether they are aware of the resistance among traditional media operators to such attempts to assert women's rights; for example in Kenya when similar efforts by the editorial staff of *Viva* magazine were halted by transnational advertising agencies:

> These agencies threatened to withdraw advertisements if the advertising-dependent magazine continued to address issues like prostitution, birth control, female circumcision, polygamy and sex education.

Such stories, says Jansen, ' have low or no news value within the framing conventions of mainstream objective media'. They will only be found 'at the margins of journalism'. However, 'A new journalism dedicated to breaking this code of silence is emerging in the wake of global feminism,' believes Jansen. 'As a result, the old Western journalistic establishment may be approaching the eleventh hour in its crisis of credibility if not survival.'

Not for mums

When British journalist Yvonne Ridley entered Afghanistan illegally (with the consent of her newspaper) in September 2001 and was then arrested and held by the Taliban, the press released a barrage of criticism that revolved around the assumption that female journalists with children are first and foremost mothers. Their careers are of secondary importance. Press reports of the parallel case of French journalist Michel Peyrard, also caught entering Afghanistan illegally, never referred to his actions as irresponsible, although he, too, was a parent.

Margaret Gallagher, UN Report, *Women, Media and Democratic Society*.[23]

Integrity and courage

Disapproval of the risks women correspondents take in reporting from war and other dangerous situations is becoming history, driven out by their courage and the quality of their reporting. Today, according to an estimate by the US Brookings Insitute, over a third of foreign correspondents are female, compared with 1970 where the number was under ten per cent. Wherever there is war, carnage, the bombing of towns and villages, the likelihood of TV audiences seeing women reporters ducking shells, flak and snipers to bring stories to world attention is obvious and impressive.

Not only are women correspondents matching their male counterparts in terms of the risks they take and the dangers they experience (between 1993 and 2001, 18 women journalists were killed), their approach to war reporting often adds a fresh dimension – greater attention being paid to the suffering war inflicts on the civilian populations, with particular focus on the traumas and tragedies of women and children.

Generally the position of women in media has improved and is improving, as Brian McNair in *News and Journalism in the UK*[24] affirms when he states that 'as a new generation of women enters the profession from university … young female journalists (that is, up to the age of 35) actually appear to be doing better than men of the same age'. McNair believes that while sexism survives it 'appears to be on the retreat, with consequences not just for the gender structure of the profession but the form and content of journalism'.

Awards but no parades

Following the murder of Russian journalist Anna Politkovskaya in October 2006, a rally in her honour met with official disapproval, the authorities in Ingushetia dispersing the crowd, several of whom they arrested and charged with hooliganism. Politkovskaya had been named a Press Freedom Hero by the Vienna-based International Press Institute (IPI). In its World Press Freedom Review of 180 countries the IPI named 2006 'the most brutal year in modern media's history'. Among other press freedom heroes was the Irish journalist, Veronica Guerin, shot down in the street while researching into criminal activities in Dublin. Awards to women media workers are also made by the International Women's Media Foundation. Its annual awards are for courage and for lifetime achievement. One Courage in Journalism Award winner is US freelance reporter Jill Carroll who was kidnapped and held captive in Bagdhad for three months.

Uneven playing fields 2: ethnic imbalance

If women have had to struggle to make their professional way in face of 'hegemonic maleness', a similar state of imbalance exists in terms of ethnic representation. All too often in the West, the media is a 'white person's world'. In an overview of this kind there is insufficient space to do more than touch upon the issue of under-representation of ethnic minorities in all areas of media production, or to examine the implications this has for a multi-cultural society. It ought, however, to be considered by students of media a vital topic for investigation.

Such an enquiry needs to reach back into examining traditional ways of *representing* minorities in print, broadcast and film media which have in large and distressing part been covertly (and often overtly) racist. Teun van Dijk in *Racism and the Press*[25] argues:

> From the point of view of a 'white man's world', minorities and other Third World Peoples are generally categorized as 'them', and opposed to 'us' and, especially in western Europe, as not belonging, if not as an aberration, in white society.

According to van Dijk the media do not address the problems of minorities; rather they define minorities *as* the problem (see Figure 7.3).

Figure 7.3 Another example of police prejudice

This illustration from an advertisement for the Metropolitan Police effectively illustrates the point Teun van Dijk makes on the negative stereotyping that affects public perceptions of race. The viewer of the advertisement is led to assume that a black criminal is being pursued by a uniformed policeman. In fact, the 'criminal' is a plain-clothes detective and the real criminal is out of the picture. Perceptions of police prejudice against black members of the community are turned back on the spectator. We are invited to reflect on our own prejudices.

In the reproduction of current realities, by word and image, the tendency at least in some media is to view ethnic minorities as existing only in the sense that they seem to pose problems for the white majority. When they speak out, or take action, their message is *re*-presented stereotypically; and when advocates of anti-racism object to such representation they too receive a 'bad press'.

Invisibility as an issue

Every member of such minorities, and this will include a goodly proportion of the student fraternity, many of them aspirants to careers in the media, will recognize, be sensitive to (and often deeply offended by) this situation. Van Dijk's book deals with racism in press headlines, the choice and treatment of topics related to ethnic minorities in the 1980s; yet in many ways still relevant today as a report on behalf of the UK Commission for Racial Equality, published in 2006, indicated.

Commissioned from MORI in 2005, and involving 511 British adults aged 16+, *Careers in Print Media: What People from Ethnic Minorities Think* 'found strong perceptions among respondents from the ethnic minority sample that print journalism was dominated by white men', that 'the profession was not representative of Britain's ethnically diverse society' and that 'there was a prevalence of racism'. Improving the situation, the report concluded. 'will depend on greater equality of opportunity and a more inclusive working environment'.

According to the UK Trades Union Congress (TUC) in a press release of 27 October 2006, only 1.8 per cent of broadcast radio workers are Black or Asian and it is TUC policy, in partnership with BECTU, the broadcasting union and the broadcasting industry, to remedy this serious imbalance.

It is useful to recall what has been discussed in this book on the purposes, roles and performance of media. By and large, serving the dominant elite takes priority in media practice, if not in theory, over the principle of 'full and fair coverage' for all, and *of* all. In *Racism and the Press* van Dijk draws a very clear connection between the racist attitudes often expressed in Britain's right-wing press and the view of minorities held by the general public.

Referring to the particular attention paid by the press to Vietnamese boat people and Tamil refugees, the author states that 'once defined as positive or negative by the Press (and dominant politicians), such groups are generally confronted with similar attitudes from the population at large'.

'...hideously white'?

Recognition of the under-representation of ethnic groups in the BBC was made public in January 2001 when the Corporation's Director General, Greg Dyke, interviewed on Radio Scotland's current affairs programme, *The Mix*, called his organization 'hideously white'. He said, 'The figures we have at the moment suggest that quite a lot of people from ethnic backgrounds that we do attract to the BBC leave. Maybe they don't feel at home, maybe they don't feel welcome'.

The biggest problem, admitted Dyke, 'is at the management level'. He referred to a Christmas lunch for management: 'and as I looked around I thought: we've got a real problem here. There were 80-odd people there and only one person who wasn't white.'

Dyke was reported to have pledged that by 2003, ten per cent of the BBC's workforce and four per cent of its management would be drawn from ethnic minority backgrounds. Before he could fulfil that pledge, Dyke was forced to resign following the Hutton Report (see the *Dodgy dossier?* Box earlier in this chapter).

Veil alert and sundry other minor panics

What happens, however, when those groups in society, traditionally classified and treated as marginal suddenly, by the circumstance of events become the focus of attention? Following 9/11 in the United States, the so-termed 'war on terrorism' came more and more to appear to be a 'crusade' against Muslim communities worldwide, the American media singularly failing to challenge and refute the connections made by President George W. Bush between Al-Qaida and Saddam Hussein's Iraq; or to query the claims made, in the USA and in the UK, concerning Saddam's WMDs.

In the UK at least, there were few overt media attacks on Islam or Muslim communities, even after the London bombings of July 2005. Both religion and race were subsumed beneath expressions of concern over broader, cultural issues. Comment emanated from the media and politicians over matters such as the right to be critical of another's faith; and such alarmist questions as 'Should we shelve Christmas as a national institution out of respect for those in the community who do not share this tradition?' True, as a panic-raising device this was never more than a media side-dish, but the implication was not trivial: somehow, *we* were at risk of being robbed of our tinseltide by *them*.

More significantly there was the debate kicked off in 2006 by cabinet minister and former UK Foreign Secretary, Jack Straw, MP for Blackburn. He publicly expressed unease about having to talk, in his constituency surgeries, to Muslim women wearing the veil. The media took up the story, their theme, as it was Straw's, that the veil symbolized – connoted – divisiveness and separation. Not long afterwards, there was a transposition of the issue into one of security as the press in the UK reported that a wanted terrorist had 'possibly' escaped the country in disguise, wearing a burka and veil. The language of dress was all at once a discourse on law and order and another case of WeDom/Theydom in the context of a perceived clash of civilizations.

Although these reactions did not seriously amplify into a full-scale moral panic on the part of the media, government and public, they were sufficient to stir the pot of apprehension and suspicion; and, worse, to prompt government to introduce legislation curtailing freedoms hardwon over generations (see Note 26, on the Racist and Religious Hatred Act, 2006).

Advances on the film front

While question marks continue to hover above the involvement of ethnic minorities in mainstream radio and TV, the film world has been energetically opened up by black film makers. This is in part due to new technology that has helped professionalize and individualize the home movie and not least because of the opportunities created by film festivals worldwide focusing on work by black directors.

In recent times there have been black cinema festivals in Berlin, Toronto and London (the Pan-African Film Festival at the Institute of Contemporary Arts), while Cardiff staged a Black Welsh Film Festival in 2005. In the USA *Film Life*'s Celebration of Black Cinema: Past, Present and Future was presented by Turner Network Television in 2006. In 2007 over 120 films by black directors, including 30 feature films from seven countries including the UK were screened in Beverley Hills as part of the annual Hollywood Black Film Festival.

The basic issue here, as it is for all 'alternative' media, is whether present and future developments in the mediasphere prove *enabling* – that is for creative activity at the margins to win wider attention and support. As never before, new media technology facilitates diversity. Being female or black is secondary to being 'able'. Not only are audiences being served up an almost exponential growth in choice, they are also, as the blogosphere encroaches upon the traditional mediasphere, seizing the opportunity, in increasing numbers, of becoming makers in their own right. As never before, perhaps, encoding and decoding are becoming one and the same activity.

Even so, it pays to be cautious over imminent possibilities of level playing fields, and to take note of comments made by Karen Ross in her 1996 publication, *Black and White Media: Images in Popular Film and Television*.[27] In her final chapter, 'Twenty-first century blues', she sees the picture as 'still one of strict colour-coding' because a key feature of Western media continues to be 'dominance by white people and many of the problems of black (mis-)representation are a consequence of this fundamental fact'. Ross adds that it is the 'poverty of black images rather than their frequency that constitutes the real problem'.

Summary

Media practitioners function in the world their words and images have helped to create; and they are part of the public they address. They are subject, as the Maletzke model highlights, to a formidable array of pressures, personal, professional, social and political. The discourses they project and reinforce do not 'belong' to them any more than they belong to the general public. Those who call the tune are those who pay the piper. Conformity might therefore be perceived as a condition of media performance, and examples abound of a media compliant to the demands of those in authority and those who sign the cheques.

The predicaments facing media communicators are compounded by pressures placed upon them from agencies of all kinds whose intention is to influence media agendas; to 'manage the news'. Media critics readily identify a media story in which those under the control of power elites dutifully communicate to the public visions of order while at the same time purveying myths of their own freedom. Whatever communicative freedom exists, it is not equally distributed in gender or ethnic terms. The media world is perceived by some commentators as dominated by 'hegemonic masculinity' and reluctant to accord equal opportunities to ethnic minorities, either in terms of representation or employment.

Yet in an imperfect world journalism remains, in principle and often in practice, the bastion of justice and the voice of democracy. The more globalized media communication becomes, the greater journalism's responsibilities. When it is silent, we must fear for our human rights. That is one of many good reasons for studying the media and for wanting to pursue a media profession.

KEY TERMS

Project of self   lived/mediated experience   congruent
dissonance/consonance   group bonding   defamation   prior restraint
structure of the popular   bystander journalism   journalism of attachment
myths of professionalism: micro/macro myths   institutional ethos
control features   reliability   impartiality   myth of value-freedom
news management   spin-doctoring   disinformation
boundary event/journalism event   flak   hegemonic masculinity
ethnic representation

Suggested activities

1. Discussion:
   (a) How does the technology of the media constitute a pressure on the producers of media messages?
   (b) Should journalists have any more rights of access to information than the general public?
   (c) How does competition between media institutions, channels, programmes exert pressure on those involved in production?
   (d) How does the advertising industry constitute a pressure on media production?
2. Conduct a study entitled 'Journalists at Risk'. Research the number of deaths, of reporters and photographers, worldwide during the last three years. What are the stories behind those deaths, and what (if any) is the public memory of the men and women who paid the ultimate price to bring home the news? In your researches, make use of the Internet and keep a note of useful websites.
3. Compile notes for a seminar paper, essay or talk on the following quotation:

   > Can one culture use its own terms to say something about another culture without engaging in a hostile act of appropriation or without simply reflecting itself and not engaging the otherness of Other...can we ever escape our provincial islands and navigate between two worlds?[28]

4. Look up references on 'law and the journalist': what legal constraints limit a journalist's access to and use of information? Find out what recent cases there have been in which the law has been used against journalists. Compare the situation in different countries.

5. Prepare a treatment/synopsis for a radio or TV programme to be entitled 'Gender and the Media'. Focus on issues such as pressures to conform to stereotypes, with particular reference to differences between images (what happens in the story on screen) and realities (what really happens). For example, is advertising progressive or regressive with regard to gender portrayal?

6. Carry out a survey of the representation on TV of actors, news presenters, talk-show hosts/hostesses drawn from ethnic minorities and examine the nature of that representation.

7. Examine an issue of a newspaper or a TV news edition with a view to locating the source of the information used. How often is source acknowledged? Are some sources apparently given more credence than others? How often are ordinary members of the public used as source and how is their information handled?

Now read on

For a perspective on 'how things used to be' for editors and journalists who pushed the cause of alternative media in the face of traditional values, see Tony Palmer's *The Trials of Oz* (UK: Blond & Briggs, 1971), a sharp reminder that the Swinging Sixties were also an age of repressive censorship. There are few times when freedom of speech and expression are not at risk from those in authority, as the authors contributing to *Free Expression is No Offence* (UK: PEN/Penguin, 2005), edited by Lisa Appignanesi, make clear. The UK periodical *Index on Censorship* provides a vital source of information and analysis of censorship worldwide.

Philip Knightley's *The First Casualty – From the Crimea to Vietnam: The War Correspondent as Hero, Propagandist and Myth Maker* (UK: Prion edition, 2000) is again recommended. Try also Martha Gellhorn's powerful *The Face of War* (UK; Virago, 1986) and *Reporting War: Journalism in Wartime* (UK/US: Routledge, 2004), edited by Stuart Allen and Barbie Zelizer. For a focus on individual journalists of outstanding merit, see David Randall's *The Great Reporters* (UK: Pluto Press, 2005).

Journalism in global contexts is scrutinized by Brian McNair in *Cultural Chaos: Journalism, News and Power in a Globalised World* (UK/US: Routledge 2005). An extremely useful and readable guide through the minefield of pressures, constraints and ethical controversies is Richard Keeble's *Ethics for Journalists* (UK/US: Routledge, 2001): it deals with regulation, sourcing, sleaze coverage, dumbing down (and dumbing up), reporting race and racism, representing issues of gender, mental health etc. Also, look out for Tony Harcup's *The Ethical Journalist* (UK: Sage, 2006) which includes an interview with former BBC correspondent Andrew Gilligan on his meeting with Dr David Kelly (see the box in this chapter, *Dodgy dossier?*). As for ' spin', try John Nichols and Roberet W. Chesney's *Tragedy and Farce: How the American Media Sell Wars, Spin Elections, and Destroy Democracy* (US: New Press, 2005) and the book mentioned earlier in this chapter, Martin Moore's *The Origins of Modern Spin: Democratic Government and the Media in Britain, 1945–51* (see Note 13).

More and more women are playing prominent roles in news gathering and presentation. Worth following up are three books from the 1990s, *Women in Mass Communication* (US/UK: Sage, 1993), edited by Pamela J. Creedon, *Battling for News: The Rise of the Woman Reporter* (UK: Sceptre, 1995) by Anne Sebba, and *Women Transforming Communications: Global Perspectives* (US/UK: Sage, 1996), edited by Donna Allen, Ramona R. Rush and Susan J. Kaufman.

For more recent publications, see *Women and Journalism* (US/UK/Canada: Routledge, 2004) by Deborah Chambers, Linda Steiner and Carol Fleming and Michelle Elizabeth Tusan's *Women Making News: Gender and Journalism in Modern Britain* (US: University of Illinois Press, 2005).

On the theme of gender linked with micro-media enterprise, see Margaret Gallacher's *Gender Setting: New Media Agendas for Monitoring Advocacy* (UK: Zed Books, 2001); and on the issue of racial representation Robert Ferguson's *Representing 'Race': Ideology, Identity and the Media* (UK: Arnold, 1998) is recommended along with Sarita Malik's *Representing Black Britain: Black and Asian Images on Television* (UK/US: Sage 2001).

Notes

1. John B. Thompson, *The Media and Modernity: A Social Theory of the Media* (UK: Polity, 1995).
2. G. Maletzke, *The Psychology of Mass Communication* (Germany: Verlag Hans Bredow-Institut, 1963).
3. John Pilger, *Heroes* (UK: Pan Books, 1986; new edition, 1995).
4. Allan Bell, *The Language of News Media* (UK: Blackwell, 1991).
5. Colin Sparks, 'Popular journalism: theories and practice' in Peter Dahlgren and Colin Sparks (eds), *Journalism and Popular Culture* (UK: Sage, 1992).
6. Barbie Zelizer, 'Has communication explained journalism?' in *Journal of Communication*, Autumn 1993.

7. Jo Bardoel, 'Beyond journalism: a profession between information society and civil society', *European Journal of Communication*, September 1996.

8. Pete Hamill, *News is a Verb: Journalism at the End of the Twentieth Century* (US: Ballantine, 1998). Hamill's highly personal account is a paean to good journalism. He is in no doubt that in the US press there has been dumbing down in recent years. In particular he is critical of publishers who, in pursuit of profits, have encouraged their papers to submit to 'the most widespread phenomenon of the times... the virus of celebrity'. Hamill asserts that, 'Newspaper reporters and editors know that most of these people [celebrities] aren't worth six minutes of anybody's time. Privately they sneer at them or shrug them off. But they and their publishers are convinced that the mass audience is demanding these stories, so they keep churning them out. They defend their choices by insisting they are only giving the people what they want. If they are right, the country is in terrible trouble. I think they're wrong.'

9. Stated in 'Saudia Arabia', US State Report (1995) and quoted in *Index on Censorship*, 4 (1996).

10. Eric Kit-Wai Ma, 'Rethinking media studies: the case of China', Chapter 2 in *De-Westernizing Media Studies* (UK/US: Routledge, 2000), edited by James Curran and Myung-Jin Park. The reference to the gusto with which political prisoners sang 'Arise! Refuse to be enslaved' derives from E. Friedman's contribution, 'The oppositional decoding of China's Leninist media' in *China's Media, Media's China* (US: Westview, 1994), edited by C.C. Lee.

11. Jeremy Bowen, *War Stories* (UK/US: Simon & Schuster, 2006).

12. Philip Schlesinger, *Putting 'Reality' Together: BBC News* (UK: Constable, 1978; Methuen, 1987).

13. Martin Moore, *The Origins of Spin: Democratic Government and the Media in Britain, 1945–51* (UK/US: Palgrave Macmillan, 2006).

14. David Miller, 'The Northern Ireland Information Service and the media: aims, strategy, tactics' in John Eldridge (ed.), *Getting the Message: News, Truth and Power* (UK: Glasgow University Media Group/Routledge, 1993).

15. Eamon Hardy, '"Primary definition" by the state – an analysis of the Northern Ireland Information Service as reported in the Northern Ireland press' (Unpublished dissertation, Queen's University, Belfast, 1983).

16. Eamon Hardy speaking on Channel Four's *Hard News*, 19 October 1989.

17. Tom Koch, *Journalism for the 21st Century: Online Information, Electronic Databases and the News* (US: Adamantine Press, 1991).

18. Koch, *The News as Myth: Fact and Context in Journalism* (US: Greenwood Press, 1990).

19. Edward Herman and Noam Chomsky, *Manufacturing Consent: The Political Economy of the Mass Media* (US: Pantheon, 1988).

20. Liesbet van Zoonen, *Feminist Media Studies* (UK: Sage, 1994, reprinted 2000).

21. Sue Curry Jansen, 'Beaches without bases: the gender order' in George Gerbner, Hamid Mowlana and Herbert I. Schiller (eds), *Invisible Crises: What Conglomerate Control of the Media Means for America and the World* (US: Westview Press, 1996). The title of Jansen's article is a play on what in her notes the author calls 'a groundbreaking work', Cynthia Enloe's *Bananas, Beaches and Bases: Making Feminist Sense of International Studies* (US: University of California Press, 1989).

22. Robert W. Connell, *Gender and Power* (US: Stanford University Press, 1987).

23. Margaret Gallagher, United Nations (UN) Report, *Women, Media and Democratic Society* (2002); quoted by Sheila Gibbons on Women's E-News in a posting 'European news media: AKA bastion of gender bias' (29 June 2005). Gibbons cites an International Federation of Journalists Gender Council conference in Nicosia in May 2005, calling for media owners to strengthen gender equality in their profession. She quotes European co-ordinator Annegret Witt-Barthel who talked of 'a deplorable unwillingness to support equal treatment in the workplace, including equal pay and equal right of promotion to leadership positions'.

    Yvonne Ridley, meanwhile, converted to Islam in 2001 after her release from captivity. In 2007 she became a London presenter for Press TV, Iran's state-run 24-hour English-speaking news channel.

24. Brian McNair, *News and Journalism in the UK* (UK: Routledge, 1999).

25. Teun van Dijk, *Racism and the Press* (UK: Routledge, 1991).

26. Paragraph 29B of the UK Racist and Religious Hatred Act (2006) declares that: 'A person who uses threatening words or behaviour, or displays any written material which is threatening, is guilty of an offence if he intends thereby to stir up religious hatred...A constable may arrest without warrant anyone he reasonably suspects is committing an offence under this section'. Punishment for being found guilty of such offence can land the offender(s) up to two years in jail. British TV and film comedian Rowan Atkinson described the Act as a 'sledghammer to crack a nut'. Shami Chakrabarti of Liberty was of the opinion that, 'In a democracy there is no right to be offended. Religion relates to a body of ideas and people have the right to debate and denigrate other people's ideas'. See *Free Expression is No Offence* (UK: PEN/Penguin, 2005), edited by Lisa Appignanesi.

27. Karen Ross, *Black and White Media: Black Imagery in Popular Films and Television* (UK: Polity, 1996).

28. Paul B. Armstrong, 'Play and cultural differences' in *Kenyon Review*, 13 (1991) and cited in *Representing Others: White Views of Indigenous Peoples* (UK: University of Exeter Press, 1992), edited by Mick Gidley.

The Global Arena: Issues of Dominance and Control

8

AIMS

> To examine the notion that in a media-saturated world, information has increasingly been transformed into a commodity subject to market forces.
> To identify the factors threatening public service communication in the New Information Age.
> To consider the nature and extent of corporate influence in media communication worldwide.
> To draw attention to global imbalances both in the supply of information and its flow.
> To record signs of resistance to the long march of corporatization.

What makes the study of media communication such a contemporary activity is its concern for issues that affect our everyday lives as individuals within communities, as members of groups, as consumers, voters and citizens; and on a global terrain. Issues rise and fall in importance and new trends in media create new issues. Central to this chapter is the issue of control of the means by which publics, nationally and globally, are addressed in contexts of ever-pressurized competition.

Information proved to be the most vital 'product' of the late 20th century and has advanced in 'commodity-value' in the 21st. It is therefore of maximum interest to the major players on the public stage, and instrumental to the workings of policy, media and corporate agendas. Key to our interest as media-watchers is how that information is used to shape public perceptions of reality.

The tendency towards alliances between the nation-state and big business, is explored in relation to public and private spheres of mass communication, trends in deregulation and privatization, and fears by a number of critics of cultural encirclement of the public by the great corporations.

Although new technology has facilitated the growth of information and speed of access, development globally has been uneven, with core nations seen to be information-rich and periphery nations information-poor. Yet while globally imbalances substantially remain, publics are seen to be capable of asserting themselves in the face of cultural invasion and exploitation.

Information, disinformation, 'mythinformation'

Mention has already been made of how the Bush–Blair axis persuaded Congress and Parliament that the 2003 invasion of Iraq was justified because Saddam Hussein possessed weapons of mass destruction (WMD). These did not exist, so how was it that so many people were persuaded?

The short answer is – *disinformation*, which decades if not centuries of practice have raised almost to an art form. We are back in the realm of storytelling, of truth-establishing narratives, of the making of myth, of discourses sharply coloured by persuasive rhetoric.

The apparent ease with which stories-of-explanation take on the impetus of myths lies in their past record; their success in persuading most of the people, most of the time, of their truthfulness; and that truthfulness (or otherwise) is the product of *mediation*, of the media in whatever form refurbishing past stories as framing devices for the present.

This process can be illustrated by taking one photograph as conveying the righteousness of hindsight and the power of retrospection. In the UK, the Moors Murderer Myra Hindley was never released from prison even though, after a number of years of incarceration, she qualified for parole. Every time the matter of her release came to media attention, the papers reproduced a scarifying picture taken at the time of her conviction, decades before. Such was the evocative power of that image, perfectly fulfilling the stereoype of the heartless woman capable of child-murder, that the authorities retreated in face of public opinion, that is, mediated public opinion.

A more recent photograph of Hindley, one of her smiling, would have obliged the media to re-examine the finality of their definition of what constitutes, in this case, evil – a phenomenon much bandied about, but, like myth itself, rarely defined, seldom challenged.

We all know about evil: Saddam Hussein was evil. He was compared to Adolf Hitler who was also evil. The term is a useful catch-all: there were those in the British press who drew parallels between Hitler and Arthur Scargill, General Secretary of the National Union of Mineworkers, during the strike of 1984. In Scargill's case, he was *demonized* because what he was doing ('holding the nation to ransom') made him 'Other'; one of 'Them'.

Once the comparison was made, or implied, the public saw Scargill as Public Enemy Number 1, the striking miners 'the enemy within'. Label-libelling had combined with disinformation to do their propagandist work. Any claims to accuracy as a moral duty were neatly kicked in to touch.

Should Scargill have made a significant come-back on the political stage, the demonic narrative and the images that went with it would have been dusted down once more to use against him. In short, once a demon, always a demon, until of course neutralizating (or even neuterization) has taken place.

Roger Silverstone in *Media and Morality: On the Rise of the Mediapolis*,[1] referring to such historical events of symbolic nationhood as Pearl Harbor and 9/11, speaks of stories sitting 'on the shelf ready for the next moment, the next crisis, when the personification of an alien evil can resume its strategic place in the definition of what it is to be an American'.

'I came to tell the truth … the good, the bad and the ugly'

In July 1987 Oliver North, a military adviser, was summoned to give evidence in the United States to the Iran-Contra Hearings. These concerned secret arms sales to Iran, the proceeds of which were used to supply cash for arms to the Contras, right-wing rebels intent on the overthrow of the Marxist government of Nicaragua. The affair was widely seen as a government cover-up by a deeply embarrassed Reagan administration.

The accusatory spotlight fell not upon the President or his Vice President, George Bush Senior, but upon a minor player in the drama. In the dazzling glare of public attention North chose not to play the role of victim. Instead, he reached for stardom, declaring to the American nation on TV, 'I came to tell the truth … the good, the bad and the ugly'.

Oliver North's words, borrowed from the title of a Clint Eastwood movie,[2] were not casually chosen. He did not see himself as the villain of the piece but as someone to be admired. He presented himself on TV as a hero – the proud little man taking on the faceless power of state bureaucracy. He believed, rightly as it turned out, that his

American audience would come to see him as a real-life Clint East-wood character; in their minds, fact and Hollywood heroes of the silver screen would blur and merge.

The sufferer in this melange of media and myth-making was the truth, or at least any clear path towards public understanding of it – what had actually happened, who was really involved, who gave the orders in this attempt by a big nation to subvert the sovereignty of a tiny country such as Nicaragua.

A number of commentators on the North trial believed it to be a cleverly managed piece of disinformation or to be more exact, *distraction*, on the part of the Reagan administration. North was groomed for, and achieved, stardom, in narrative that obscured the true story of events by creating in the public mind another one, more accessible, more consonant – at one with – popular expectations; a romance manufactured in Hollywood and wrapped in the Stars and Stripes.

Keep Ollie, dump Congress

This New York graffito of 1989 is quoted at the head of Robin Anderson's chapter, 'Oliver North and the News', in *Journalism and Popular Culture*.[3] Anderson argues that the whole Oliver North episode created in the public mind a preference for myth over truth in the sense that 'myth appeared more reasonable than the black world of covert policies, cynical motivations and the real lack of American values'.

Though some commentators referred to North's testimony as 'soap opera hearings' Anderson believed North 'hit the bedrock of fundamentally masculine mythologies quite removed from soap opera. He tapped into the various codes of action/adventures and war heroes deeply etched in the genres of popular culture'. In one sense North *was* the victim in that he was abandoned by authority to take personal blame for what had been a government conspiracy. ABC News made this clear on the day before North gave evidence (6 July 1987):

Almost from the opening gavel these hearings pounded home one point. In the Iran Arms sales and the efforts to arm the contras, all roads led to and from Oliver North.

By focusing on the activities of one individual, the narrative exonerated by exclusion the guilt of those who had authorized North's behaviour.

We have already noted Roland Barthes' view, expressed in *Mythologies*,[4] that the significance of myth is its ability to transform the meaning of history; and therefore of truth. The process is as follows: first the 'story' is drained of its historical truth through the restriction or reinvention of information. The empty shell awaits an ideological re-creation, as Anderson puts it, 'repackaged via the "concept", in this case American hero mythologies'. Anderson believes that the 'human cost of the Contra war which was continually denied…can be formulated into a postmodern spectacle of American values', that is a preference for image over truth, of mediated over lived reality.

Plainly Hollywood myths, almost invariably asserting the gender dominance of the male, are not confined to the Wild West of long ago; and such myths underscore, and often fuel, visions of the world as a dangerous place, one perpetually in crisis and thus demanding that the nation's 'guard' must be kept up at all times. Arising out of this stance emerged the policy that took the United States to war in Iraq in 2003 – the policy of pre-emptive action, on the face of it a military strategy though more meaningfully a manifestation of American destiny (see Note 5, on terror as the 'great evil of our time').

In Chapter 7, reference was made to Robert W. Connell's term, *hegemonic masculinity*.[6] We can see in the Contra affair and arguably in American foreign policy generally a 'gendered' picture of the world situation, often uncritically affirmed by the mass media. Sue Curry Jansen in 'Beaches without bases: the gender order' in *Invisible Crises*[7] regards gender values as having constituted the basis of Cold War mythology:

> The Cold War may be over, but the dangerous worldviews of men in power show few signs of pacification or of imaginative reconstructions. The Persian Gulf War [1991] was, among many things, a *boy thing*, in which George Bush [Senior] demonstrated – live and in colour – that his missiles were bigger, better, and much more potent than Saddam Hussein's.

Sue Curry Jansen's comments appositely describe the response of Bush Junior, newly-elected American president, to the tragedy of 9/11. Like Oliver North borrowing his imagery from the Western, George W. declared that he wanted the culprits who planned the outrage, Dead or Alive. Further, in drawing on the mythology of the West as represented by Hollywood, the story of events was joined by a willing partner – evangelical Christianity with its passionate vision of good and evil.

Together these comrade forces, aided and abetted by the ideology and practices of capitalism, constitute, in the words of Roger Silverstone in *Media and Morality*,[1] 'the ground for a culture that is quick to find evil in the other, and to accept the self-righteousness of the imperial position'. What is happening in examples like these is, to a very large extent, the substitution of the image for reality

Soon the American cavalry were heading first to Afghanistan, to pulverize the Taliban (who were sheltering Al-Qaida), then, in the spring of 2003, to 'take out' Saddam Hussein in Iraq. As for the media's war coverage, the public was treated to *useful* information (that is, useful to the war effort) but provided less generously with *damaging* information, that is, data on civilian casualties. Media that attempted to insist on balanced reporting, and sought to take up a more pluralist position towards war and occupation, were greeted by the flak (see Chapter 7) of accusations of disloyalty and lack of patriotism.

It's a conspiracy!

Myth-making is not the monopoly of power and corporate agendas. In the age of network communication distrust of government 'explanations' has bred counter-myths couched within the frame of conspiracy. *Loose Change*, a 90-minute Internet documentary film made by three young Americans, challenging the official version of the 9/11 Twin Towers disaster, found its way on to television in several countries across the world, attracting audiences of millions. Over 100,000 DVDs were sold in a short time to audiences willing to believe the theory posed by *Loose Change* that the disaster was actually staged by the US government in order to justify and win support for the invasion of Iraq in 2003.

Over-riding or ducking extensive evidence that supports the official version of events, the conspiracy posited in *Loose Change* echoes another, concerning the Japanese aerial attack on the American fleet at Pearl Harbor, in 1941 – that President Roosevelt permitted the Japanese assault in order to take America in to the Second World War. Official denials only fuel the myth.

Downsizing issues

Having seen how in the saga of the Ollie North and the Contras affair, and generally in times of emergency or conflict, a nation's media, given the choice between truth and myth, opt for the latter, let us turn to a second case study relating to the vulnerability of information in the public domain, The Tale of Sir Richard's Vanishing Report.

Using mythologies of heroes and villains is one way of manipulating or obscuring evidence in public life. Another is to treat genuine issues as if they were of marginal importance; and, by downsizing them, strike them off the public agenda. This was the strategy of the British tabloid press concerning the Scott Inquiry report of 1996.

It was another case of secret government corruption, this time in Britain. The Conservative government, its ministers and its civil servants, repeatedly denied to parliament that a 'blind eye' had been turned to the export of weapon-making technology to Saddamn Hussein's Iraq in support of its conflict with Iran (the first Gulf War, 1980–88).

Chaired by Sir Richard Scott, the enquiry set up to look in to the Arms for Iraq Affair found that officialdom had been economizing with the truth. This time government stood accused of undermining the sovereignty of its own people. 'It will be hairy for ten days,' believed William Waldegrave, Chief Secretary to the Treasury, when the Scott Report[8] was published. One broadsheet described the report's conclusions as 'the most damning indictment of the behaviour of ministers and civil servants'.

However, although the government survived a House of Commons debate on Scott by only one vote in February, it was soon to be 'greatly assisted', believed Richard Norton-Taylor in his *Guardian* article, 'Scott free?',[9] 'by the short attention span of most MPs and most sections of the media'.

Displacement by trivialization

No minister resigned from the British government following the Scott enquiry; and Waldegrave's prediction was fulfilled. While acknowledging that the one-vote victory for the government was ONE HELLUVA CLOSE SHAVE FOR THE PM, the *Daily Star* of Tuesday 27 February 1996 declared in its editorial, 'The rest of us are SICK TO DEATH of the Scott Report'. One of the most important issues of any time – corruption in government – had become a bore. The *Star* believed, 'It's time now to move on to more important things and let the Government get on with the business of running Britain'.

The UK *Sun* of 16 February was no more willing to take on the role of watchdog or protector of Parliament and public, choosing not to snap at abuse but to turn the whole business into a joke. Above their banner head, YOU'RE SCOTT FREE, the *Sun* chanted, IT'S ALL OVER ++ THANK SCOTT IT'S ALL OVER ++ THANK SCOTT IT'S ALL OVER. Readers were treated to 10 THINGS YOU CAN DO WITH REPORT, including turning it into briquettes 'and letting them smoulder on the fire', or using it as the 'perfect cure for insomnia. Reading a page or two is guaranteed to put anybody to sleep'. Finally, 'File it away in a dusty vault and forget about it – just like the Government probably will'.

The cases of Oliver North and of the treatment of the Scott Report illustrate how momentous issues are also issues about media performance discussed in Chapter 4: the role of public watchdog is sidestepped; matters of critical importance in democracies are trivialized; the evidence is marginalized, dismissed even, by myth or ridicule. Discourse is dominated and subverted; and personification rules.

Precedents such as these feed the arrogance of authority. Even when the 'Weapons of Mass Destruction Story' was revealed as a sexed-up pack of lies; when it was realized that the American and British people had been misled into an illegal war, all those that were in power (as with Scott) remained in office. There was not one resignation. The only victims were the messengers – the BBC, its Chairman and Director General driven to resign, the 'guilty' reporter Andrew Gilligan fired ,and the information source, Dr David Kelly, driven to suicide.

Power games, public relations

While the media and their masters are the most visible players in the arena of public life, they have emulators and rivals. We have seen from our examination of news values the tendency to personalize issues, sensationalize events and spectacularize presentation. Such lessons have been taken on board by advocates of all kinds.

Just as the agents of sports stars pump up their clients' asking price, so the agencies employed by governments, or potential governments, seek to assist them, using sophisticated propaganda, in winning elections. Under a headline NORIEGA'S HEIR WINS PANAMA POLL the UK's *Guardian* announced that 'Saatchi & Saatchi has notched up another election in Central America'.[10] Phil Gunson, writer of the report, noted:

> The victory of Ernesto 'the bull' Perez Balladares in the Panamanian presidential elections returns to power the party that backed Manuel Noriega's thuggish six-year rule. And it marks the second

time in a fortnight that Saatchi & Saatchi has won an election in central America.

The first of the London-based advertising agency's triumphs was in El Salvador where it advised Armando Calderon Sol of the Arena party who, says Gunson, 'steam-rolled the leftwing opposition in last month's second-round presidential poll'. Arena 'is an extreme right neo-fascist party... the party of the death squads'.

Gunson quotes Alberto Conte of the rival public relations firm McCann Erikson. He considered Saatchi & Saatchi – in its Panama campaign – had 'a very disciplined client [in Balladares] who accepted all their recommendations'. It was a 'well-structured campaign with attention to detail. The experts did their job and the "product" followed instructions to the letter'. Gunson then quotes radio commentator Fernando Nunez Fabrega who said that the 'making of the president' included advising Balladares to use his hands a lot:

> He has big hands, and apparently that has a sexual connotation. Also, they finished dyeing his grey hair white at the front to make him look more distinguished.

In public relations work the political 'hue' of clients' money counts for less than its substance. PR has always had a role to play in the commerce and the politics of developed nations. Of course presenting an image to the public, replete with symbolism, is an ancient practice. When Van Dyck was invited to paint a portrait of King Charles I he knew his duty – to flatter; so Charles is portrayed astride a charger, dominant, regal in a golden light. Today, the difference is TV, its reach and its capacity to outdo the flatterers of the past, to over-ride realities with glossy spin.

In 2001 the 'hard-man' of Israel, Ariel Sharon, about to be elected prime minister of Israel with a landslide majority, in the words of *Guardian* correspondent Jonathan Freedland, pulled off 'one of the great political con-tricks of modern times – running TV ads depicting him as a cuddly old man walking Israel's streets holding the hand of a small child'.[11]

Silvio socks it to 'em

Such imagism is the stock-in-trade of modern politics, rarely better illustrated than in the Italian election campaign of 2001, when media magnate Silvio Berlusconi stood for election with the target of becoming prime minister for the second time.

Head of a coalition of right-wing parties, Berlusconi was able to use his massive media holdings to make his case for election despite several corruption charges still in the legal pipeline. His family holding company Finvest owns and operates three TV networks, a daily newspaper, and a publishing house (not to mention AC Milan football club). During the election campaign, one of his networks, Rete 4, cancelled *Wind of Passion*, a Brazilian soap opera with high ratings, because the winsome communist hero might have influenced voters.

As part of his campaign, Berlusconi issued through his own publishing house, Mondadori, a 128-page self-congratulatory biography entitled *An Italian Story*. The UK *Guardian's* Rome correspondent, Rory Carroll, in a news-piece 'Berlusconi woos voters with the secrets of Silvio', wrote, 'Shrugging off accusations of egomania, the centre-right opposition leader has calculated that a cult of personality will sway floating voters'. The book, containing 250 photographs, all of them of Silvio, was delivered free to an estimated 20 million Italian households.

Did Italian voters resist the hype, sharing the view of *La Stampa* of Turin that the publication was an 'exceptional triumph of the ego'? No they did not. Berlusconi's own party, Forza Italia, and its alliance partners, comfortably won the May election. And one of the first things the new Prime Minister was reported to do on taking office? Conduct a purge of journalists and executives from Italy's state television, RAI. Their offence? Having been insufficiently fawning towards Berlusconi's centre-right coalition.

On 22 May 2001, a *Guardian* headline announced, 'Berlusconi to purge state TV'. Writing from Rome, Rory Carroll talks of Berlusconi's intention 'to consolidate his government's dominance of the media... extending his influence to over 90% of television news' (see Note 12 on the need to be cautious about crediting all of Berlusconi's electoral success to his ownership of media).

Mercifully for belief in an 'active audience' and thus an active electorate, the power to beguile the public is not guaranteed to last. In due course, Berlusconi's media-aided success story took a turn for the worse when real experience (his government's policies) removed the burnish of mediated experience. Silvio was ousted by the Italian electorate in April 2006 in favour of left-wing rival Romano Prodi; but only by a narrow margin.

> ### 'The Unfinished Struggle'
>
> Berlusconi has been far from alone in believing in the power of media to nurture the cult of personality. *The Unfinished Struggle* was the title of a 33-part TV soap opera based on the life of the Malaysian prime minister, Mahathir Mohamad, broadcast on successive nights through September and October 1999 – during a period of the prime minister's unpopularity and not long before the election.
>
> Lim Kit Siang, the leader of the parliamentary opposition, was quoted in response to this collusion between the media and the powerful as saying, 'It's another example of the very one-sided and unfair campaign that will be taking place. I have not had one minute of national TV news coverage in 30 years let alone a soap opera'.

Faking it

At least one can say that Balladares' hands were above the table for all to see. Modern PR prefers the covert to the overt operation. A 2006 report by Diane Forsetta for the American Center for Media and Democracy, *Fake TV News: Widespread and Undisclosed*,[13] based on her researches with Daniel Price, identified 77 TV stations in America regularly using Video News Releases (VNRs) provided by PR firms, without disclosing their source. Three broadcast PR firms were serving as many as 49 clients.

Over a ten-month period of research, Forsetta and Price found that each of the 77 stations surveyed

> actively disguised the sponsored content to make it appear to be their own reporting. In almost all cases, stations failed to balance the clients' messages with independently-gathered footage or basic journalistic research. More than one-third of the time, stations aired the pre-packaged VNR in its entirety.

In order to reach TV audiences across America, writes Forsetta, 'and to add a veneer or credibility to clients' messages' the PR industry uses VNRs, 'pre-packaged "news" segments and additional footage created by broadcast PR firms, or by publicists within corporations or government agencies'. They are 'designed to be seamlessly integrated into newscasts, and are freely provided to TV stations'.

The vast majority of VNRs are made for corporate clients; in addition to these are what are called satellite media tours (SMTs), 'actual interviews with TV stations, but their focus and scope are determined by the clients'. In effect, says Forsetta, 'SMTs are live recitations of VNR scripts'. Only in one instance 'was there partial disclosure to viewers'. While the anchor of one station said, 'This interview... was provided by vendors of the consumer trade show', the actual corporate clients were not named.

Nothing, it would seem, is safe from corporate incursion, even blogging; and there is a newish term for our media lexicon – the *flog*. This is an apparent blog, only it is a company advertisement in disguise; either a direct masquerade or via an existing blogger. In a news item on 'Blog placement', the *International Herald Tribune* of 3 December 2006 spoke of a 'growing trend in marketing, with elite bloggers receiving gifts like show tickets, laptop computers, trips to Paris and bottles of champagne'. Jaap Favier, research director of a technology research company is quoted by the *Herald* as saying, 'Who can we trust? ... What is true and what is fake?'

Struggles for dominance: private sector v. public sector

The issue of who controls the dominant means of communication, who speaks to the public, and how, can be said to be the frame within which all other issues can be seen to connect. Depending on the matters in hand, the prize is consensus – public interest, public support or merely public acquiescence.

We, as the targeted public, may sense the struggle for our allegiance and suspect that this struggle is at least as much in the interest of the communicator as in our own interest. The thoughtful community is uneasy about and seeks to resist the desire of governments, of authorities, to control message systems. We argue for rights of access and expression. We witness private-sector enterprises also wishing to dominate message systems in the name of profit; and we call for protective regulation.

The struggle is often presented in stark terms, between public and private ownership and control. However, the issue is less about the *categorization* of ownership and control, public or private, and more about the *degree* and *extent* of that control. The issue is monopolistic tendencies; the problem, the power (or lack of it) of agencies working on behalf of the public to establish and sustain checks upon those tendencies. In an age characterized by the deregulation and privatization of public utilities of all kinds as well as telecommunications and broad-casting, we see traditional checks and balances – regulatory require-ments – in retreat and at risk.

In Chapter 4, the principles and practice of public service in media production were briefly discussed. In particular, the future of public service broadcasting (PSB) will continue to be a key issue for study and debate. Indeed it was fear of commercial appropriation of public channels of communication that created PSB in the first place. Pre-sented with the task of recommending how a state broadcasting com-pany should be run, the Sykes Committee (1923–24) in the UK put the case for public service very succinctly. Its report is worth quoting again here:

> … we consider that the control of such a potential power [of broad-casting] over public opinion and the life of the nation ought to re-main with the State, and that the operation of so important a na-tional service ought not to be allowed to become an unrestricted commercial monopoly.[14]

Such principles framed the growth and development of the BBC, and a number of other state broadcasting systems, over many decades.

The role of the state has always been controversial: authority and freedom of expression have rarely made for contented bedfellows; yet nor have public service and commercial values. Sykes' belief that there should be some countervailing power to that of market forces continues to command wide support; first, because it acknowledged the difference between the public and the private sphere in the life of a nation and second because it recognized the predatory nature of the private sphere.

The public arena is where audience is located; it is also the market-place where consumption takes place. To win consumers, the private sphere needs audience. What it is not obliged to take into consider-ation is the public as citizens. Only in the public sphere – fenced off, albeit modestly, from commercialization and consumerization – so it has been believed, can certain values and practices be maintained (see the social responsibility theory of media outlined in Chapter 4).

Few would assert that public service broadcasting has fully repli-cated the agora, or fulfilled its ideal as being an example of public communication working in democratic-participant mode. But it has arguably been the best agora available. Even so, its virtues may not be sufficient to ensure its future. Three developments in the final decades of the 20th century threatened the survival of PSB:

1. The ambition in the Age of Information of the private sector to expand its interests.
2. The ideology of many governments favouring the private over the public and their policies of privatization of public utilities.
3. Smoothing the way for the other two, the possibilities of diversification brought about by new technology.

All at once, channel scarcity (on which public service regulation has so much relied) ceased to be an obstacle to expansion. The availability of hundreds of TV channels poses a formidable threat to any system of public service because, as was explained in Chapter 3 on audience and audience reception, it has become increasingly difficult to identify and define what 'public' is actually being served.

The narrowing base of media ownership

While there are many more available channels for the transmission of information and entertainment than in the past, there are fewer *controllers* of those channels. Indeed the world of media has come to be dominated by those whose growth has appeared to be exponential. Time Warner, the giant of giants, and Disney both almost tripled in size during the 1990s. Close on their heels in terms of size are media giants such as Viacom, Bertelsmann of Germany, Sony and Murdoch's News Corporation; formidable in size but in number few enough to sit around the same media table.

Issues of size and mergers and the implications for the future of media production and consumption will be reconsidered in Chapter 11. Suffice it to say here, the ambitions of the media giants are global, their strategies predatory. For example, Rupert Murdoch has been called by Christopher Browne in *The Prying Game: The Sex, Sleaze And Scandals of Fleet Street and the Media Mafia*[15] 'perhaps the most ruthless predator in the history of the world news media'. His antipathy to PSB, and to the BBC in particular, is well known, and regularly expressed in the News Corp press.

Murdoch has also proved himself a regulation-buster, rolling back Federal Communications Commission (FCC) controls in the USA, for example when he was permitted by the FCC, in contravention of its own regulatory code, to run a broadcasting station and a newspaper in the same city. Nothing, not even public interest, must stand in the way of profit. As if to cap once for all his reputation as a gifted opportunist, Murdoch gained possession in the summer of 2007 of America's media equivalent to the Crown Jewels – the *Wall Street Journal*.

'The great myth about modern proprietors,' writes Nicholas Coleridge in *Paper Tigers: The Latest, Greatest Newspaper Tycoons and How They Won the World*[16] 'is that their power is less than it used to be. The fiefdoms of Beaverbrook, Northcliffe and Hearst, often invoked as the zenith of proprietorial omnipotence, were in fact smaller by every criterion than the enormous, geographically diffuse, multi-lingual empires of the latest newspaper tycoons'. The author claims:

> The great media empires spanning the world have subjugated more territory in a decade than Alexander the Great or Ghengis Khan in a lifetime and funnelled responsibility for the dissemination of news into fewer and fewer hands.

Whether or not we consider Nicholas Coleridge to be exaggerating we might pause to consider the advantages media moguls have over the moguls of old: today their territories are restricted by neither time nor space. The next conquest is only a fax or an e-mail away; and perhaps most significantly their acquisitive instincts have been at play in a territory once celebrated as being largely free of their control – the Internet and online services (see Chapter 9).

Corporate power and the media

We have seen throughout this book the possibilities of approaching communication from different points of the compass: from the perspective of producers and production; from the point of view of media content, via the semiological analysis of the text; and from the angle of audience perception and experience. Whichever approach we choose, we encounter the proposition that communication is *power* and that power is obtained and held through *control*.

Who controls the means of mass communication has the potential power to influence the ways in which society works. Therefore it has to be a constant task in the study of mass media to monitor control and the controllers, especially when the public domain of communication has so few powerful advocates. In Chapter 5, I suggested an amendment to the agenda-setting model of Rogers and Dearing.[17] To the policy, public and media agendas a fourth agenda has been added (see Figure 8.1), that of the corporate agenda.

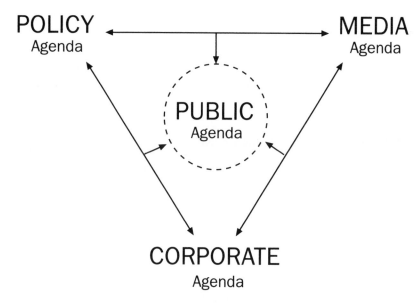

Figure 8.1 A 'tripolar' model: the dynamics of public agenda-setting

Governments work with corporations, corporations influence governments (sometimes they have bigger incomes!) and the media are very often, and increasingly, part of corporate portfolios that involve production, manufacturing and distribution across many different modes of communication. Of equal significance is the way the great corporations work with each other, to mutual advantage; what is termed *synergy*.

Media to suit the business model

In an openDemocracy posting, *Why Media Mergers Matter*,[18] William Hoynes points out:

> These media conglomerates are often more cooperative than competitive, with an increasing number of strategic alliances and joint ventures. Given the small number of major media players, there is very little competition in the media industry and the major media companies use a variety of strategies to try to reduce the limited competition that does exist.

Such policies impact on media content, the preference being for the generic rather than that which is medium-specific. Will a novel, for example, translate easily and profitably into film or TV format; and will this in turn allow for commercialization through spin-offs of one kind or another? Hoynes writes:

> The bottom line approach of media conglomerates leaves little room for those concerned about the integrity of their specific product ... it is becoming a liability for media content, even news stories, to be singular or unexploitable. It is simple, recognisable, uncontroversial and transferable brands – *Teletubbies*, *Pokemon*, *Harry Potter* – which suit this business model, not complex, medium-specific, challenging or unfamiliar media texts. In short, media conglomerates prefer content with many uses and content-providers that can supply re-usable commodities.

Scourge of the TNCs

Few authors have registered more acute concern about the 'corporatization' of public expression than Herbert I. Schiller. In *Culture Inc.*,[19] Schiller – a thorn in the side of the transnational corporations (TNCs) until his death in 2000 – examined the dangers, as he viewed them in an American context, that arise from the privatization, and thus commercialization, of information. Schiller believed, 'Transforming information into a saleable good, available only to those with the ability to pay for it, changes the goal of information access from an egalitarian to a privileged condition'.

Not only does information come at a price, the information itself is judged according to its potential commercial demand. Schiller quotes the president of an American database company, Dialog, as saying, 'We cannot afford an investment in databases that are not going to earn their keep and pay back their development costs'. Asked which areas were currently failing to pay their way, the spokesman replied, 'Humanities'.

Dialog is cited as showing discrimination of another kind, refusing to make available certain databases to trade unions who wished to use the data in their bargaining with management. Situations such as this one can be found throughout society, in matters of scientific, legal, forensic and technological data: information is for sale; and if it isn't saleable, it's not available. As Everette Dennis has neatly put it, 'What you don't know can hurt you'.[20]

Schiller writes of 'corporate envelopment of public expression' where the 'public information stockpile is transferred to corporate custody for private profit-making'. He talks of 'corporate pillaging of the national information supply', setting the scene of a power struggle where the corporations, especially in the United States, appear to be winning hands down: 'Who is in control determines the answer to the first question that faces any social order: who gets what?'

Schiller had little doubt that in the big match, Corp v. Public, Corp wins, even when it ought to be clear to the crowd that there has been some ball tampering:

How to account in an age of intensive publicity for such reticence about such a remarkable public relations achievement – the transfer of wealth from the poor to the rich without a sign of public indignation?

Culture: appropriated?

Schiller's concern does not stop at the ways information is 'corporatized' and held to ransom. He fears that cultures too have been appropriated: the corporate appetite is whetted by any cultural phenomenon – art, sport, music, festivals, parades, public celebrations of all kinds – which can serve corporate objectives. Even the museum in America 'has been enlisted as a corporate instrument'.

It is unquestionable that corporate sponsorship has provided massive and sometimes life-sustaining support for sport and the arts. The motive does not necessarily spring from a love of sport and the arts, or from altruistic notions of enriching the social and recreational life of the people. Sponsorship does two things: it brings the name of the company to public attention and it associates that name with the occasion that draws people in through the turnstiles. The *image* of the one must be appropriate to the image – the desired reputation – of the other.

Art, Schiller argues, must fit the image of something timeless (like profits), detached from social and historical contexts. Looking at the *kinds* of art sponsored by the great corporations, Schiller observes that emphasis is placed upon 'the social neutrality of art and its alleged universalistic essence'. The art object is 'abstracted from its social and historical context... lovely, perhaps, but without meaning or connection'.

Of course there is nothing new about corporate sponsorship. We owe, over centuries in the West, great architecture, music, painting and sculpture to the patronage of the church, the transnational corporation of the past. The church was circumspect about what art was created in its name and highly censorious of what it disapproved of. Schiller would doubtless argue that the difference is in scale and reach: Catholic art in Europe was dominant but escapable. Enculturalization through media artefacts is less easy to evade.

What, it might be asked, if art suddenly challenged everything the corporations stand for; if it attacked the ideology of consumption? Would corporate institutions be any more tolerant of such 'heresy' than the old Inquisition?

'Regulatory favours'

During the Thatcher years in Britain and the Reagan-Bush (Senior) era in the United States the transnationals not only expanded their control over the information industry but were substantially aided by government policies of deregulation and privatization. In America the FCC, a national regulatory body created to nurture and protect PSB, spent the Reagan years doing just the opposite.

Its officers were, in Herbert Schiller's words, 'deregulation obsessed'. One by one rules that protected the principle and practice of broadcasting in the interest of the public (rather than in the interests of consumerism) were withdrawn, largely at the behest of media owners.

In *Media Moguls*[21] Jeremy Tunstall and Michael Palmer refer to 'regulatory favours', that is, conglomerate deals with government in return, as the authors argue, for 'a good press'. For example, newspapers owned by a corporation will support government directly, mute criticism of it or withhold from the public that information which could damage or embarrass it. In return government either abolishes or waives official media regulation.

Such protective regulation may concern the nature and extent of ownership; it may stand in the way of cross-media ownership; it may be designed to exert control over programme content – such as insisting on a percentage of 'serious' programmes (documentaries, for example) being allocated prime-time rather than late-night slots. It may regulate the amount of imported material that can be shown in the interests of protecting home-produced programmes.

Tunstall and Palmer's choice of language concerning the activities of the great corporations is no less emotive than that of Herbert Schiller or Christopher Browne. 'By implication,' they say, 'media conglomerates are not independent watchdogs serving the public interest, but corporate mercenaries using their muscle to promote private interest'.

James Curran in 'Mass media and democracy: a reappraisal', published in *Mass Media and Society*,[22] echoes the concerns expressed by Schiller, Tunstall and Palmer, Hoynes and many others, declaring that the trend towards deregulation and privatization has 'resulted in television becoming increasingly embedded into the corporate structure of big business'. Curran cites an example of corporate sensitivity to 'bad' news with the case of the Toshiba corporation. A subsidiary of the company, Toshiba-EMI, had issued a record attacking Japan's nuclear programme, something the parent company was closely involved in. The record was withdrawn.

If TNCs own newspapers and broadcasting stations; if they sponsor the arts and control the music scene, the chances of their 'subsidiaries' criticizing anything the parent corporation does are slim. Curran argues: 'The free market…compromises rather than guarantees the editorial integrity of commercial media, and impairs in particular its oversight of private corporate power.'

He warns that corporate aspirations to global control have seriously reduced media diversity. He is supported in this view by Jay Blumler writing about the precarious position of PSB throughout Europe. Discussing the 'inexorable internationalization of communication networks' in a *European Journal of Communication* article,[23] Blumler believes (along with Hoynes) that 'the international marketplace is no supporter of programme range…In fact…it is structured *against* diversity'.

Limiting plurality: 'democratic deficits'

Convergence of ownership intensifies across the media terrain the ideology and practice of consumerism. William Hoynes[18] argues that such 'market-orientated systems make no distinction between people's role as consumer, which is private and individual, and their role as citizen, which is public and collective'. He adds that, 'This is why market-oriented media have a tendency to produce economic benefits while simultaneously sustaining democratic deficits'.

In *Capitalism and Communication: Global Culture and the Economics of Information*[24] Nicholas Garnham is of the view that the great corporations operate 'in the interest, not of rational discourse but of manipulation'. Plurality of opinion is, like diversity of provision, to be encouraged on corporate terms or not at all. Freedom of speech will be tolerated so long as it does not encroach upon corporate sensibility or threaten business interests and practices.

TNCs have been careful to cut with the grain of 'approved' state ideology while at the same time using that ideology for their own benefit. For example, pressure from the corporations eventually persuaded the American legislature to treat the corporate voice as having the same rights under the Constitution as an individual. Thus advertising copy, advertising discourses, are protected under the First Amendment; and so is pornographic 'communication'.

If, by the constant association of one practice with another, of one image with another, the two – corporate interest and civil rights – become blurred and merge imperceptibly, then one of the classic appropriations on the corporate record is what Herbert Schiller[19] describes as the 'incessant identification of consumerism with democracy'.

The trick is to change the preposition 'with' to the verb 'is': consumerism *is* democracy: attack consumerism, pose alternative lifestyles to consumerism and you are in danger of 'subverting' democracy itself. Thus, as Schiller argues, 'any interference with private ownership and enterprise' might be classified as 'a perilous step toward concentration camps'.

The multinationals claim through the many media voices they control that global capitalism is good for peace, good for democracy and, in any event, there is no viable alternative. It is an issue of our time that the media voices that are capable of at least providing the space and time for alternatives to be posited and discussed, rarely do so; and the matter is urgent.

Accountancy rules

The issues of corporate dominance discussed here have had an often far-reaching effect on the working lives of media people. Perhaps as never before broadcasting has become, in the free market economy, subject to the iron 'discipline' of the company accountant. Barbara Thomass in a *European Journal of Communication* article, 'Commercial broadcasters in the Member States of the European Community: their impact on the labour market and working conditions',[25] examined the impact of market forces in the 1990s on media employment in the European Community. She writes that an explicit political intent to subjugate UK broadcasting to the laws of the market and at the same time cripple the trade unions has led to the transformation of the broadcasting scene in the United Kingdom, leading critics to suggest that money, rather than programmes, is the main issue.

Companies seeking the commercial TV franchises in the UK in 1993 shed labour in order to finance their bids in a 'blind' auction. Faced with the uncertainty of knowing how much a successful bid for a franchise might be, companies cut their own costs to the bone in order to beat the competition (without ever knowing how much the competition was going to bid!). With fewer people of talent to work for them, and competition for an increasingly fragmented audience never more intense, commercial sector companies have been confronted with the question – can quality be sustained or must it be sacrificed in pursuit of maximum-size audiences to satisfy the advertisers?

The BBC too has been forced into cost-cutting. Thomass estimated that there had been over 3000 job losses at the BBC since 1993. The slimming down of the Corporation continued apace with the appointment of Mark Thompson as Director General to succeed Greg Dyke, forced to resign in 2004 following the Labour government's spat with the BBC over the reporting of Saddam Hussein's WMDs, and the Hutton Report.

A Timesonline posting of 25 October 2004 carried a cartoon in which a BBC newsflash appears on screen, with the announcement, 'We interrupt the US elections with news that I've just lost my job'. The posting reports that a quarter of the BBC's 28,000 employees faced the axe, with another 6000 at risk the following year.

The system of Producer Choice (allowing programme makers to go outside the corporation for personnel) had already created within the BBC uneasiness, distrust and insecurity, permanent contracts being replaced by casualization. Plans were already afoot to sell off parts of the BBC (for example, BBC Technology Ltd, BBC Broadcast Ltd, and BBC Resources Ltd) and to increase the quota of work by independents, thus making further inroads on programme-making by the Corporation's own staff. In-house training would be outsourced to private contractors.

The casualization of labour linked with cost-cutting, privatization and deregulation represent the market model. This may not yet have dislodged institutions such as the BBC from the public service model, but it has put irresistible pressure on it to reshape itself as an exemplar of traditional business practices, edging more and more towards the ideology of 'the user pays'.

Nicholas Garnham, in a chapter entitled 'The media and the public sphere' published in *Communicating Politics: Mass Communications and the Political Process*,[26] writes of 'an unholy alliance between western governments, desperate for growth, and multinational corporations in search of new world markets in electronic technology and information goods and services'. Garnham states that the result has been to 'shift the balance between the market and public service decisively in favour of market and to shift the dominant definition of public information from that of a public good to that of a privately appropriable community'.

Fortunately for the BBC and PSB generally, the Corporation's charter was renewed in 2006 for another 12 years; and fortunately for the future of employment in broadcasting, 'Aunty' as the BBC used to be called in calmer days, has proved itself a fierce competitor in the market of information and entertainment, increasing the number of its broadcasting channels and becoming a leader in Internet services.

Global imbalances in informational and cultural exchange

It is important for the student of media to be constantly aware of the interconnection of issues and of the interrelationship of the local and the global. An issue worthy of study and extended research is that of the uneven distribution of information in micro- and macro-contexts.

Equality of opportunity depends crucially upon an equal spread of information, for information is the hinge upon which decisions can be made to the benefit of the individual, the group or the nation. Without the necessary information – scientific, medical, technological, economic or political – protagonists in a competitive world are at a serious disadvantage.

For example, in Europe there are an average of 1400 free public libraries per country while in Africa the average is 18. America and Japan are respectively served by over 150 and over 120 daily newspapers while in 30 countries there is only one; in 30 more it is estimated there is no newspaper at all. These figures are quoted by Cees Hamelink in his chapter 'Information imbalance: core and periphery' in *Questioning the Media: A Critical Introduction.*[27]

Hamelink surveys the global communications scene, identifying core nations, the *information-rich*, and periphery nations, the *information-poor.* This information imbalance, says Hamelink, puts a great proportion of the world's population at a serious disadvantage, rendering it susceptible to exploitation, manipulation and, unless the imbalance is rectified, destined for a future of continued deprivation.

Put together, all the countries in the periphery own a mere 4% of the world's computers. Of the world's 700 million telephones, 75% are located in the world's nine richest countries. Perhaps most significantly in an age driven by technological advances, only 1% of the world's patent grants are held by countries in the information periphery.

Satellite photography has become the spy-in-the-sky that enables the user to identify crucial details of a country from an altitude of 150 miles. Thus rich nations can learn more of what is going on in a poor country, and more quickly, than the poor country knows about itself. Such technology provides early warning to core nations about vital information ranging from the movement of tuna shoals off Nigeria to detecting the quality of the coffee harvest in Brazil.

Not only is the degree of available information imbalanced, so is the information *flow*. The greater part of information flow is between core nations and where the flow is between core and periphery it is substantially one-way traffic, from core to periphery. 'Estimates suggest,' writes Hamelink, 'that the flow of news from core to periphery is 100 times more than the flow in the opposite direction'.

Information gaps

There are differences too in the nature of that flow. From the periphery comes 'raw', unprocessed – and unmediated – information, while information moving from core to periphery comes packaged, with price attached. Very often that information arrives as disinformation. Hamelink stresses the capability and the will of core nations to manipulate information for political purposes:

> Both the CIA [America's secret service] and the KGB [secret service of the former Soviet Union] have elaborate networks for deliberate distortion of political information. Disinformation employs the fabrication and distortion of information to legitimate one's own operations and to delegitimate and mislead the enemy ... Peripheral countries have little chance to correct or counter such disinformation.

Information flows, in their direction, volume and quality, are imbalanced and this imbalance is not to be lightly dismissed by the view that 'eventually the poor will catch up'. It is an axiom that by the time the disadvantaged have closed the information gap, the advantaged will have gone another step ahead. The inadequate information capacities of most peripheral countries are, says Hamelink:

> a serious obstacle to their own efforts to combat poverty and other deprivations ... Without information about resources, finance, and

trade, peripheral countries are at a continual disadvantage in negotiations with core countries, and this jeopardizes their survival as
independent nations.

When so much information on poor nations is kept in data banks
by information-rich countries, a 'peripheral' nation's very *sovereignty* is
at risk:

> …information imbalance leads to the cultural integration of peri-
> pheral countries in the culture promoted by the core. Imported
> cultural programming encourages consumerism and individualism,
> and diverts attention from any regard for the long-term needs of the
> country.

Consumerism, with its stress on individualism and personal rather
than group or communal enterprise, also tends to accentuate divisions
within a state between the haves and the have-nots. Hamelink states
that, 'Internal gaps develop as urban elites become part of the international economy while the rural poor get left behind'. Economic dependency on the part of the information-poor becomes political and
cultural dependency.

If a country does not have sufficient independence to nurture its own
language or languages, its own forms of literary, musical and dramatic
expression, its own historical and artistic heritage, then it is vulnerable
to cultural invasion; and the desire for – the need for – cultural self-
determination is jeopardized.

The public: not necessarily a pushover

Once again care must be taken to differentiate between macro-visions
– often bleak, certainly disturbing, of cultural colonialism amount-
ing to media imperialism – and micro-practices. Research findings by
Tamar Liebes and Elihu Katz published in *The Export of Meaning*[28]
indicated that the American soap *Dallas* was read in quite different
ways by people of different origins, cultures and outlooks; indeed was
appropriated by them. It was *Dallas* that was dominated, not the audience for *Dallas*.

In *The Media and Modernity: A Social Theory of the Media*,[29] our old
friend John B. Thompson also takes an optimistic view of the capacity
of audiences – cultures – worldwide to make their own meanings out
of 'core' nation texts. He talks of an 'axis of globalized diffusion and

localized appropriation'. Globalization does not eliminate the negotiation of textual meanings: 'Through the localized process of appropriation,' Thompson argues, 'media products are embedded in sets of
practices which shape and alter their significance.'

John Keane in *Tom Paine: A Political Life*,[30] a book strongly recommended to readers interested in campaigning journalists of the past,
quotes an old maxim, that the fecundity of the unexpected is more
powerful than any statesman. In other words, life is prolific with the
unpredictable. A glance at history will indicate to us that the volatility
of change is a more common feature of existence than the status quo.

For a period in the 1980s and 1990s the wind of change had all at
once altered course and seemed to be blowing from East to West. The
traditionally 'poor nations of the East' were prospering; their goods advertised in our papers and on our TV. Their new-earned wealth was
being invested in our own factories to the point where some claimed
to see a 'reverse colonialism' taking place.

The so-called 'Tiger' economies of the Pacific basin – Japan, Malaysia, Taiwan and South Korea (and potentially the most powerful of
them all, China) – were no longer 'developing' nations; they were competing nations and the balance of power was seen to be tilting in their
direction: which would be the Third World nations of tomorrow?

Then the surge towards a greater economic balance between East
and West was checked by recession in the Tiger economies, reminding
commentators that predicting trends is less successful than spotting
them, deliberating upon them and passing judgement on them. In the
dreamworld of advertising it is possible to claim that 'Coke is *it*!' In the
real world, what is *it* is uncertainty and uncertainty is the only thing
that can be confidently predicted.

Who, for example, could have foreseen the astonishing rise in the
use of mobile phones in Africa? The International Telecommunications Union (ITU) has reported that in the five years leading up to
2006 the continent's use of mobiles increased by 65%, twice the global
average and twice as fast as that of Asia. The ITU's estimate of 65 million users by 2005 has seen the number rise by 2006 to 100 million,
and not just in Cape Town and Cairo. According to an *afrol News* posting, 'Mobile Phones Revolutionise Africa',[31] the penetration of mobile
use is occurring regardless of place or circumstance, defying 'structures
hostile to investment, warfare, failed states and natural disasters'. So-
malia, 'which has not had any central government for over a decade,
has achieved a vibrant mobile industry' and '[m]obiles have steadily
advanced in Congo Kinshasha and Liberia despite warfare'.

As for the great corporations, some commentators have even argued that they contain within them, like the dinosaurs, the seeds of their own destruction; that their expansionism is as much a symbol of doubt as confidence. The case is put that for every media enterprise that is successful, for every blockbuster movie, every best-selling novel, every chart-topping hit tune there is an undertow of failures and disasters; of texts that bomb rather than blaze.

Like the Red Queen in *Alice in Wonderland*, so the argument goes, the giants of global enterprise have to run in order to stand still; they expand or die. It is no surprise, then, to observe them seeking to colonize and eventually to monopolize that as yet only partially subdued 'continent', Cyberspace.

Summary

This chapter has stressed that a primary issue concerning the media, nationally and globally, is ownership and control. We have witnessed how transnational corporations have established commanding powers over the mediated experience of consumers of media worldwide. By controlling the means of mass communication, World Managers are in the strategic position to shape the message systems of our time, to impose the image of themselves and what they represent upon global 'reality'. In the furtherance of both state and corporate interest and ambition, misinformation, disinformation and 'mythinformation' are commonplace.

The alliances that occur between governments, big business and the media are seen to be institutional rather than haphazard in nature. Corporatization of cultural life is extensive, aided by general shifts towards deregulation and privatization. Commoditized, information becomes the servant of those who produce it and, a number of commentators fear, diversity of output is seriously at risk.

Public service communication has been in retreat, its governing principles under review if not under attack. The situation has come about partly in face of privatization policies, partly as a result of new technologies leading to the widening but also the fragmentation of audience.

The case urged at every opportunity by the transnationals, that the free market is a guarantor of democracy is seen here to be a self-serving and possibly dangerous assertion. Employment in the media industry has been increasingly casualized and this trend has been accompanied by drastic cost-cutting and thus the threat to quality and diversity.

Also, in the so-called Information Age, attention has been drawn to the uneven distribution and flow of information. A few commentators have claimed to spot signs of reversal in corporate growth; of national cultures, and cultures within those nations, beginning to reassert themselves. Who knows, perhaps Murdoch's News Corp may prove itself a dinosaur after all (or will it be swallowed up by Time Warner or lock in with Disney?). Science is uncertain what factors consigned the dinosaurs to extinction and media commentators are equally uncertain as to what, other than rigorous national and international regulation, will 'tame' the corporate Leviathans.

Either way, the notion of the commoditization of information is not new. The French novelist Honoré de Balzac in 1839 wrote of the press as degrading writers into becoming purveyors of commodities. The difference between Balzac's day and now is not so much attitudes, values and behaviour as their scale and their diffusion.

Monitoring the present is tricky, predicting the future hazardous because of the speed of change brought about by info-technology; and because that technology has been so rapidly affordable. The number of libraries or landline telephone systems in African countries may not have increased substantially in recent years, but the accelerating use of mobile phones across the continent, in countries rich and poor, suggests that those traditionally classified as also-rans are fast coming up on the rails.

Vanessa Gray, spokesperson of the International Telecommunications Union is quoted by *afrol News*,[31] as saying that 'Africa has been able to leapfrog from having the most backward systems to taking advantage of the latest technologies'. The wizard in this development has been network communication.

KEY TERMS

cultural encirclement   disinformation, 'mythinformation'
demonic narrative   symbolic nationhood   distraction
masculine mythologies   useful information, damaging information
economizing with the truth   corporate incursion   flog
regulatory requirements   channel scarcity   synergy   appropriation
regulatory favours   democratic deficits   producer choice
information-rich, information-poor   core nation, periphery nation
information gaps

Suggested activities

1. Discussion
   (a) What archetypical images from the past prove of ongoing service to mass media in the present?
   (b) 'Myth is propaganda's most useful tool'.
   (c) Does who owns what really matter?
   (d) What needs to be done if public service broadcasting is to survive in the digital age?
   (e) How might the ambitions of transnational corporations be modified or controlled?
   (f) What could core nations do to bridge the information gap between them and peripheral nations?
2. Conduct a survey of the use of *product placement* in films and TV series. How often, for example, do we see cans of Coke as bit-part 'actors' in the story? What significance can be ascribed to product placement? What hidden agendas might there be in terms of collusion between product marketing and programme production? Check with the regulatory body for broadcasting in the UK, Ofcom (Office of Communications) on its policy with regard to product placement (www.ofcom.org.uk).
3. Draw up a list of references for an International Media Profile in which you plan to study all aspects of a Third World nation's media – its press and broadcasting services, its cinema industry (if it has one) and the degree to which that country 'uses' media imports from other, 'core', countries.
4. If you are looking for a subject for an extended essay or a dissertation, an under-researched area is the work of NGOs (non governmental organizations), such as Amnesty International, Friends of the Earth, Greenpeace, Liberty or Oxfam, in highlighting issues of public concern often ignored by the mass media. Online exchanges and personal interviews with NGO officials will reveal the challenges they face in achieving a foothold on media agendas; and the strategies they adopt to command public attention.

Now read on

Perhaps the most fascinating aspect of the study of media is how it impacts on culture as a whole and how culture, and cultures, respond to the part played by media in local, national and international life. Nowhere is this interplay between media and audiences more vividly at work – and more *intertextual* in nature – than in advertising, particularly as the advertising industry is so closely wedded to corporate empires. Try, then, *Advertising, The Uneasy Persuasion: Its Dubious Impact on American Society* by Michael Schudson (US: Basic Boooks, 1984; UK: Routledge, 1993), Armand Mattelart's *Advertising International: The Privatisation of Public Space* (UK: Comedia, 1991), translated by Michael Channan, and *Advertising and Popular Culture* by Jib Fowles (US/UK: Sage, 1996). *Ethics in Public Relations: Responsible Advocacy* (US/UK: Sage, 2006) by Kathy Fitzpatrick and Carolyn B. Bronstein is also recommended.

On visual culture, see *Images: A Reader,* edited by Sunil Manghani, Arthur Piper and Jon Simons (US/UK: Sage, 2006) and on the dominant phenomenon of celebrity in the modern age, try another contribution from Sage, *Stardom and Celebrity: A Reader,* edited by Sean Redmond and Su Holmes (2007).

There has not been the space in this volume to devote to alternatives to mainstream media, so Chris Alton's *Alternative Media* (US/UK: Sage, 2001) offers a wide-ranging survey of radical alternatives in the USA and the UK. Also, look out for John Tomlinson's *Globalization and Culture* (UK: Cambridge University Press, 1999), George Monbiot's hard-hitting *Captive State: The Corporate Takeover of Britain* (UK: Macmillan – now Palgrave Macmillan, 2001), *The Media and Cultural Production* (UK: Sage, 2001) by Eric Louw and Gillian Doyle's *Media Ownership: Concentration, Ownership and Public Policy* (UK: Sage, 2002). Daya Kishan Thussu's *International Communication: Continuity and Change* (UK: Hodder Arnold, 2nd edition, 2006) provides an excellent overview of the international scene, with useful case studies, including the 'Murdochization' of the media.

Notes

1. Roger Silverstone, *Media and Morality: On the Rise of the Mediapolis* (UK/US: Polity Press, 2007).
2. *The Good, the Bad and the Ugly* (1967), a 'spaghetti Western' directed by Sergio Leone, with Clint Eastwood, Lee Van Cleef and Eli Wallach; probably the best of Leone's 'Dollars' trilogy.
3. Robin Anderson, 'Oliver North and the News' in Peter Dahlgren and Colin Sparks (eds), *Journalism and Popular Culture* (UK: Sage, 1992). North became a successful radio broadcaster.
4. Roland Barthes, *Mythologies* (UK: Paladin, 1973).
5. In *An End to Evil: How to Win the War on Terror* (US: Random House, 2003), David Frum and Richard Perle, classifying terror as 'the great evil

of our time' argue that Americans must fight and fight to win: 'There is no middle way for Americans: it is victory or holocaust.'

6. Robert W. Connell, *Gender and Power* (US: Stanford University Press, 1987).

7. Sue Curry Jansen, 'Beaches without bases' in George Gerbner, Hamid Mowlana and Herbert I. Schiller (eds), *Invisible Crises: What Conglomerate Control of Media Means for America* (US: Westview Press, 1996). In her notes, Jansen refers the reader to Abuoali Farmanfarmaian's 'Sexuality in the Gulf War: did you measure up?' in *Genders*, 13, Spring 1992.

8. Scott Inquiry: Report of the Inquiry into the Export of Defence Equipment and Dual-Use Goods to Iraq and Related Prosecutions (1996). See *The Scott Report and its Aftermath* by Richard Norton-Taylor, Mark Lloyd and Stephen Cook (UK: Gollancz, 1996).

9. Richard Norton-Taylor, 'Scott free?', *Guardian*, 14 August, 1996.

10. Phil Gunson, *Guardian*, 10 May 1994.

11. Jonathan Freedland, 'Israel's dark hour', *Guardian*, 7 February 2001. Freedland writes of a 'roll-call of shame that constitutes his [Sharon's] CV' and refers to the 'brutal reprisal raids he led against Palestinian infiltrators in the 50s' and the 'blood-soaked invasion of Lebanon three decades later'. However, Freedland does not argue that the TV image of a 'cuddly old man' won the election for Sharon. He puts this down to an unpopular opponent and a deep fear among the Israeli community about its security.

12. It is probably misleading to ascribe Silvio Berlusconi's success as solely resulting from the power of his media empire. In a *European Journal of Communication* article, 'Towards a "videocracy"? Italian political communication at a turning point' (September 1995), Gianpetro Mazzoleni argues that Berlusconi's populist message 'found several ears to listen to it'. Perhaps more clearly than other media moguls, Berlusconi understood how elections today are fought out on TV, and that votes are won by grabbing attention, mixing the emotive with the entertaining.

13. Diane Forsetta and Daniel Price, 'Fake news: widespread and undisclosed', Center for Media Democracy website, posted 16 March 2006.

14. Sykes Committee. Appointed in April 1923 by the Postmaster General to review the status and future of 'broadcasting in all its aspects'; chaired by Sir Frederick Sykes, the Committee met on 34 occasions. As well as recommending a public rather than a commercial service, the Sykes Committee proposed a single receiver licence of ten shillings to be paid annually.

15. Christopher Browne, *The Prying Game: The Sex, Sleaze and Scandals of Fleet Street and the Media Mafia* (UK: Robson Books, 1996).

16. Nicholas Coleridge, *Paper Tigers: The Latest, Greatest Newspaper Tycoons and How They Won the World* (UK: Heinemann, 1993).

17. E.M. Rogers and J.W. Dearing, 'Agenda-setting: where has it been, where is it going?' in *Communication Yearbook*, 11 (US: Sage, 1987).

18. William Hoynes, 'Why media mergers matter', openDeomcracy website, posted 16 January 2002.
19. Herbert J. Schiller, *Culture Inc.* (US: Oxford University Press, 1989).
20. Everette E. Dennis, *Of Media and People* (US: Sage, 1982).
21. Jeremy Tunstall and Michael Palmer, *Media Moguls* (UK: Routledge, 1991).
22. James Curran and Michael Gurevitch (eds), *Mass Media and Society* (UK: Edward Arnold, 1991; 4th edition, Hodder Arnold, 2005).
23. Jay Blumler, 'Meshing money with mission: purity versus pragmatism in public broadcasting' in *European Journal of Communication*, December 1993.
24. Nicholas Garnham, *Capitalism and Communication: Global Culture and the Economics of Information* (US/UK: Sage, 1990).
25. Barbara A. Thomass, 'Commercial broadcasters in the Member States of the European Community: their impact on the labour market and working conditions' in *European Journal of Communication*, March 1994.
26. Nicholas Garnham, 'The media and the public sphere' in Peter Golding, Graham Murdock and Philip Schlesinger (eds), *Communicating Politics: Mass Communications and the Political Process* (UK: University of Leicester Press, 1986).
27. Cees Hamelink, 'Information imbalance: core and periphery' in John Downing, Ali Mohammadi and Annabelle Srebemy-Mohammadi (eds), *Questioning The Media: A Critical Introduction* (US: Sage, 1990).
28. Tamar Liebes and Elihu Katz, *The Export of Meaning: Cross-cultural Readings of* Dallas (US: Oxford University Press, 1990; UK: Polity Press, 1995).
29. John B. Thompson, *The Media and Modernity: A Social Theory of the Media* (UK: Polity Press, 1995).
30. John Keane, *Tom Paine: A Political Life* (UK: Bloomsbury, 1995).
31. An *afrol News* posting (update 13 May 2007) reports on statistics announced by the International Telecommunications Union (ITU) showing that Africa has been the fastest-growing mobile phone market, the increase being an annual rate of 65%, more than twice the global average. The text of Vanessa Gray's address to a Cairo conference of the ITU, *The Unwired Continent: Africa's Mobile Success Story*, providing statistics up to 2004 and 2005, can be located through the ITUs website.

Network Communication: Visions and Realities

9

AIMS

> ➤ To review how the rise and development of network communication prompted early pioneers and prophets to envisage for society new worlds of opportunity.
> ➤ To focus in particular on claims made for the Net that it is a force for liberation and empowerment.
> ➤ To put such visionary claims into perspective by considering marketization and surveillance as potential obstacles to communicative freedom and citizen entitlement.
> ➤ To discuss a number of social and psychological issues concerning the nature of Internet use.

Nowhere, except in dreams, have reality and fantasy contended for our attention more than 'on the Net'. This chapter acknowledges the potential for imaginative, if not fantastic, surfing in Cyberspace while at the same time tracking the realities of Net communication as it has evolved. Networking has become the prime means of communication across the globe; the online population of users, and the Net's online uses having grown exponentially, for good and sometimes for ill.

The Net is seen as a market with infinite opportunities. Their appetites whetted by the success of dot.com entrepreneurs the great corporations are in the process of colonization. Big deals threaten to envelop Net sourcing and control. Equally, the Net has been viewed as a force for change, capable of challenging social, economic and political structures.

It is not too far-fetched to compare the Net to the Greek agora, a place where citizens could exercise a degree of power over those that rule them; to see it as capable of transforming the ways we think and act as well as communicate; capable of a profound 'makeover' of the mediapolis, where media and reality mesh and intertwine as never before; and where traditional authority structures are challenged and occasionally evaded altogether.

Such 'people power' is rarely invited by those who make decisions on our behalf, and as the Net's possibilities have increased so have the anxieties of the power elite. What in the early days could justifiably be compared to the open prairie is now witnessing enclosure by laws, regulation and increasingly sophisticated surveillance.

Considerable critical attention is also being paid to the 'effects' of computer networking. Like traditional addictions it can become obsessive. The allure of the 'virtual' can blur the boundaries between that and reality. At worst, users give over their real lives to the virtual; they become ghosts in their own machine.

The importance of networking for research will be viewed in Chapter 10; and brief reference here to the impact of the Net on traditional media will be further explored in Chapter 11.

Cybervisions 1: dreams of freedom

The word 'cyberspace' seems to have been first used by William Gibson in his novel *Neuromancers* published in America by Ace Books in 1984, though to locate the origin of cybernetics – the study of feedback systems – we need to go back as far as 1949 to Norbert Wiener's *Cybernetics: Or Control and Communication in the Animal and the Machine*.[1] Gibson describes cyberspace as 'a consensual hallucination ... [People are] creating a world. It's not really a place, it's not really space. It's notional space'.

In this notional space we can all be cybernauts, potentially free agents who by pressing computer keys can take off into the stratosphere of seemingly infinite knowledge instantly accessed. To borrow the words from the title of J.C. Herz's book, we can exhilaratingly surf the Internet.[2]

The notion of a 'new world' awaiting new-age exploration was a dominant metaphor among Net enthusiasts and commercial enterprises alike. A Boston software computer firm once claimed in its advertising, 'Sir Francis Drake was knighted for what we do every day ... The spirit of exploration is alive at The Computer Merchant'.[3] Imagination, in the realm of simulated or *virtual reality*, recognizes no limits, as Henry Rheingold, an apostle of the Net, states in *Virtual Reality*.[4] The author speaks, with the zeal of all pioneers of change, of:

my own odyssey to the outposts of a new scientific frontier...and an advanced glimpse of a possible new world in which reality itself might become a manufactured and metered commodity.

Such sentiments were characteristic of the early days of Net use. Romance was in the air. The Net was seen to offer us psychological space which in both mental and physical terms seemed in the real world to be more and more restricted. The Net offered us exhilarating liberation from the real.

Spatial stories

In a conversation between two American academics, Henry Jenkins and Mary Fuller, published in *CyberSociety: Computer Mediated Communication and Community*,[5] Jenkins was of the opinion that the fervour with which many Americans took to the Net and to new frontier-type virtual reality games, was a response 'to our contemporary sense of America as oversettled, overly familiar and overpopulated'.

Jenkins argued that space is the organizing principle of computer games: a succession of new spaces, reached and conquered by skill and know-how, determine rather than are determined by the narrative. This view tunes in to Michel De Certeau's assertion in *The Practice of Everyday Life*[6] that '[e]very story is a travel story – a spatial practice'.

The Jenkins–Fuller dialogue drew connections between the visions and practices of Renaissance explorers, and the narratives written by them and about them, and the New World exploration of Nintendo games. Jenkins says:

> Our cultural need for narrative can be linked to our search for believable, memorable, and primitive spaces, and stories are told to account for our current possession or desire for territory.

Computer games of the Nintendo variety are, believes Jenkins, a 'playground for our world-weary imagination'. He adds:

> Nintendo takes children and their own needs to master their social space and turns them into virtual colonists driven by a desire to master and control digital space.

These 'spatial stories', as De Certeau calls them, are therefore part of a long tradition of storytelling no doubt originating long before the epic journeying of Odysseus recounted by the blind poet Homer. The intriguing irony, Jenkins points out, is that it is Japanese games creators and manufacturers, keying in to essentially Western – American – tales, embellishing them with 'eye candy' (graphics to dazzle 'world-weary imagination') who are narrating stories of modern-age exploration and colonization. In such cases, who is doing what and to whom? Henry Jenkins concludes a fascinating exchange by asking:

> Does Nintendo's recycling of the myth of the American New World, combined with its own indigenous myths of global conquests and empire building, represent Asia's absorption of our national imagery, or does it participate in a dialogic relationship with the West, an intermixing of different cultural traditions that insures their broader circulation and consumption?

Such a question prompts another, 'In this new rediscovery of the New World, who is colonizer and who the colonist?' Either way, the multi-cultural possibilities of such interaction, within a globalized setting, is intriguing, and invites the attention of the researcher as explorer.

The web is 'My Space'

In hardly any time at all the world wide web has been colonized by a vastly broader and Net-active population than could have been dreamed of a decade ago, to the point that it has floated new nomenclature: Web 2.0, a term seeking to encapsulate a 'second generation of use'. Critics have argued that it is little more than a marketing buzzword and that it merely describes an expansion of technological facility and Net use.[7]

Meaningful or not, the term is current and can be purposefully used to denote a number of characteristics concerning the storage, creation and dissemination of information, opinion and comment; and to identify *process*, which is interactive and to an increasing degree egalitarian. It constitutes software systems structured around the aim of participation, of social and cultural exchange; consequently, user-friendliness is key. It has not transformed the Net into a medium of narrative, but it has helped facilitate and extend it across communities.

Once users in their thousands discovered the ease with which they could enter the portals of MySpace, Facebook, YouTube and other typically Web 2.0 sites, once the Net became accessible to the mobile phone, or media station as it now deserves to be called, the Net began to resemble a popular revolution in which ordinary people were given a voice and seemingly limitless opportunities to make, and sustain, contact with others.

Cyberspace has become Storyville, and the stories are about Me. The 'second generation' of the Internet has, in the words of Mark Poster in his chapter 'Postmodern virtualities' in *Cyberspace/Cyberbodies/Cyberpunk*[8] edited by Mike Featherstone and Roger Burrows, become an 'explosion of narrativity':

> Individuals appear to enjoy relating narratives to those they have never met and probably never will meet. These narratives often seem to emerge directly from people's lives but many no doubt are inventions. The appeal is strong to tell one's tale to others, to many, many others.

This explosion of narrativity depends, states Poster, 'upon a technology that is unlike print and unlike the electronic media of the first age: it is cheap, flexible, readily available, quick' and, because narratives can, with ease, incorporate sound and vision, there is the potential – in such 'phenomena as "desktop broadcasting", widespread citizen camcorder "reporting", and digital film-making' for narratives to transgress 'the constraints of broadcast monopolies'.

Poster was writing these comments in the 1990s. Even he might have been surprised at the speed and the extent to which his predictions have become a reality. The Net has evolved into a stage on which, seemingly, all the world performs. In 2005 there were 46 mentions in the UK press of the video-sharing website YouTube; before the end of 2006 there were approaching a thousand. This site, along with MySpace, has gone from minority to mass with breathtaking speed.

The web has proved it can make instant stars, like the Arctic Monkeys whose MySpace page in 2005 brought the group fame and fortune. Meanwhile self-styled pop princess Lily Allen uploaded four of her songs on to MySpace in November 2005. By the spring of 2006 these had been downloaded over a million times. Parlaphone then released Lily's first single, 'Smile', which in July became the number one single.

What buzzed on the wires was not only Lily's singing, but the frankness of her views. She was, as some commentators put it, 'a breath of fresh air'. Her iconoclasm (and often harsh words about more established pop stars – Bob Geldof, 'sanctimonious prat') excited a young, vast, audience that traditional radio and TV have rarely shaken or stirred.

The vision here is liberation; it is about opening up, providing ordinary people opportunities, largely denied them in the past, to express themselves and what interests or concerns them to communities of Net users who in turn can respond with their own stories. Suddenly, interactivity is potentially a universal experience.

Cybervisions 2: the Net as agent of change

The surf is riding high. Interactive communities may for the most part confine their Net activities to the personal, but many commentators also believe that the Internet is a force for political change, one that unsettles existing hierarchies of authority and control. Since the 1990s, network communication has been often effectively used for the assertion of, and struggle for, civil rights, cultural identity and political independence, bypassing traditional local and national boundaries and power structures.

A story in the British *Independent* of 7 March 1995, written by Leonard Doyle, was headed 'Rebels use Internet to argue case'. In Mexico the Zapatista National Liberation Army was continuing revolution against what it saw as government tyranny in the age-old way, waging war from jungle hideouts and using rusty old rifles. But they had a new weapon – the laptop computer; and a new battleground, Cyberspace. Doyle writes:

> Marcos, the Mexican rebel leader, carries a laptop computer in a backpack and plugs the machine into the cigarette-lighter of a pickup truck before tapping out his now famous communiques. Copied onto floppy disks the statements are taken by courier to supporters who transmit them by telephone to computer bulletin boards.

Doyle quotes a rebel spokesman as saying, 'What governments should really fear is a communications expert'. All at once the events within one country cease to be local and become common knowledge. Networks of sympathizers across the nation, across the continent and across the globe can transmit essential information and in turn transform that information into 'bullets' which at the very least alert the many to the abuses of the few.

When Mexican president Ernesto Zedillo launched a military offensive aimed at capturing Marcos, an 'urgent action' alert was transmitted to sympathizers worldwide, and this included the president's own fax number and that of his interior minister. Doyle again: 'As a result of the campaign the president's fax machine either burnt out or was switched off according to Mariclaire Acosta, head of a Mexican human rights group.'

Doyle refers to Harry Cleaver of the University of Texas at Austin. Cleaver had become a key link in the rebels' information chain. He used in 1994 hundreds of people via the Internet to organize the translation of the book *Zapististas! Documents of the New Mexican Revolution*, completed in three weeks.

New media helped prepare the next stage of the Marcos narrative – his triumphal entry into Mexico City in March 2001. Unarmed, he and a posse of masked comrades were greeted by thousands of supporters in the Zocalo, the biggest city square in the world save for Moscow's Red Square. Marcos' safety was guaranteed by the nation's president. Ironically, it was the 'old' media – film, TV, radio, posters, placards, loudspeakers – employing the *Hollywood narrative mode* (see Chapter 6) that finally turned reality into myth.

Appropriation of this myth was instantly under way: the outlaw of the Chiapas, champion of Mexico's indigenous population, voice of the poor and genuinely downtrodden, was suddenly being commodified by street traders doing good business selling Zapatista masks, T-shirts, Marcos scarves, action dolls and recorded music. Cynics were left to wonder how long it would be before Disney made an offer to screen Marcos' life story.

Power value

The claim for the Net that it is a political force, one that might further the cause of civil liberties across national boundaries, was given top-of-the-agenda confirmation in the first edition of *Wired UK* published in March 1995. On the cover was a picture of Tom Paine (1737–1809) and a resounding quotation from this great English advocate of human rights: 'We have it in our power to begin the world over again.'

Paine was awarded the cyberaccolade of 'Digital Revolutionary'. The creative director of the magazine, Tony Ageh, talked to Jim McClellan of the *Observer*,[9] saying:

> The key word here is 'world'. It's not just about computers connected to telephones. It's about a new way of thinking. It's now no longer about who you know. It's about what you know. In a small period of time the window's been blown open. Everything's up for grabs. What we are doing is pulling people in and saying 'get a piece of this!'

Ageh echoes the sentiments of Michael Benedikt in *Cyberspace: Some Proposals*[10] when he writes, 'We are contemplating a new world'. In fact, the 'new world' of *Wired UK* survived only till March 1997 when the magazine ceased publication in the UK. The ideas of Ageh and Benedikt are the stuff of romance, at once challenging cynics while making them extra cautious.

What some pro-network commentators claim has been happening is that control, traditionally exercised by governments and powerful groups such as the transnational corporations, has been shifting away from centres to peripheries, from organizations to individuals forming their own, hierarchy-free associations.

Certainly there is plenty of evidence that in many countries of the world the electronic highway is perceived as a threat to hierarchy and authority; and hegemony itself is undermined. This, at a basic level, is a yardstick of power – that states, those in authority, take the 'threat of people power' on the Net so seriously that they are prepared to impose on network communication rigorously intrusive censorship.

Both of the visions sketched in here arise from aspirations concerning individual freedom and empowerment; and like all visions they encounter contesting realities. One of these is the *marketization* of the Net and the ambitions of profit-centred commerce, the other the anxiety of those in authority who see networking as a threat to their control.

Realities 1: the corporate embrace

As long ago as 1994, in a publication which was itself a heady voyage into cybergraphics, *Imagology: Media Philosophy*,[11] Mark C. Taylor and Esa Saarinen warned that assaults on the perceived freedom of the Internet were increasing:

> Who writes the rules and establishes the laws that govern cyberspace? So far, the regulations in this strange world are surprisingly few. Entering cyberspace is the closest we can come to returning to the Wild West. Console Cowboys roam ranges that seem to extend forever. But as feuds break out, fences are built, cut and rebuilt. Eventually, governments will step in and mess up everything. The wilderness never lasts long – you had better enjoy it before it disappears.

The Net has now passed out of its idyllic phase in which metaphors of the open prairie, or the open road, dominated expression.

Governments censor (see later); big business embraces. The signs of change were obvious and early: all at once, as we rode out under the Western sky, we began to note rising out of the dust and the cactus – billboards; we were entering, as it were, Marlboro country.

Initially corporate management was slow to see the Net's full potential, yet soon realized with a jolt that cyberspace was host to more than an aggregate of lonely hearts and electronic games players. It presented a fabulous new marketplace, a shopping mall of global dimensions.

In a phrase, big business said, 'We must have that!' Appropriation of the Net for commercial use became an increasingly aggressive strategy, a powerful variation of the game of control. The 'freeness' of the Net; the fact that information was largely provided at no cost, was of course a matter that commerce has found unacceptable. If information is available; if information is in demand, then it will have to come at a price.

During the late 1990s the Net came to be seen as an investment equivalent of the Klondike gold-rush. Dot.com companies burst like fireworks into the Internet sky, and many of them burnt themselves out, to the point where dot.coms were referred to as 'dot.gones'. These were not, however, the big operators who were anything but dot.gone. True, the corporations lost money on their initial dot.com investments but such were their profits from other sources that they were in a good position to hold on, and then extend their investments as rivals went under.

Cross-promotion

Net trading is not only about buying and selling or the distribution of information; it is about *publicity*. Economies of size favour the media giants because they are able to exploit cross-promotion more effectively than their smaller rivals. The products, activities and services of the great corporations can be publicized at modest expense compared to the cost which lesser Internet operators would have to pay to advertise their wares. In addition, top firms, being the possessors of the hottest 'brands', can exercise leverage on search engines across the board to obtain prime window positions.

'No Tolls on the Internet'

This was the headline of a Washingtonpost.com article by Lawrence Lessig and Robert W. McChesney[12] concerning perhaps the most critical issue in the life so far of network communication, that of *network neutrality*. Big business doesn't want it; Congress has had difficulty making its mind up; but what is it and why is it seen by commentators as being a make-or-break issue? Lessig and McChesney define it as follows:

> Net neutrality means simply that all like Internet content must be treated alike and move at the same speed over the network. The owners of the Internet's wires cannot discriminate.

In other words, my posting, your posting must be treated in exactly the same way as postings by corporate users. It will not be consigned to 2nd class delivery. The authors of 'No Tolls on the Internet' ask whether Net neutrality will be preserved, 'Or will we let it die at the hands of network owners itching to become content gatekeepers?' and they argue that the 'implications of permanently losing network neutrality could not be more serious'.

In 2005 the US Federal Communications Commission (FCC) removed regulations preventing cable and phone companies such as AT&T, Verizon and Comcast from discriminating against content providers. Lessig and McChesney quote Timothy Wu of Columbia University describing the new situation as 'the Tony Soprano business model':

> By extorting protection money from every Web site [write Lessig and McChesney] – from the smallest blogger to Google – network owners would earn huge profits. Meanwhile, they could slow down or even block the Web sites and services of their competitors or those who refuse to pay up…Without net neutrality, the Internet would start to look like cable TV. A handful of massive companies would control access and distribution of content, deciding what you get to see and how much it costs.

The authors detect the 'smell of windfall profits in the air in Washington' as the phone companies 'are pulling out all the stops to legislate themselves monopoly power'.

Net users fight back

Over 700 groups, bloggers by the thousand and in excess of three-quarters of a million citizens have voiced their opposition and campaigned in favour of what has been termed the First Amendment of the Internet. The website savetheinternet.com argues that 'Net Neutrality is the reason why the Internet has driven economic innovation, democratic participation, and free speech online. It's why the Internet has become an unrivalled environment for open communications, civil involvement and free speech'.

In June 2006 the US Senate narrowly rejected strict Net neutrality, while the Senate Commerce Committee tied 11–11, thus failing to approve a Democrat-backed amendment that would have guaranteed that all Net traffic would be treated equally whatever the source or destination might be.

However, following victory for the Democrats in the mid-term US elections, hope for eventual Net neutrality was restored. American's most prestigious newspaper, the *New York Times* in a news item, 'Protecting Internet democracy'[13] affirmed the principle of net neutrality:

In the last week there was a limited but important victory for net neutrality. As a condition of approving the AT&T–BellSouth merger, the Federal Communications Commission required AT&T to guarantee net neutrality on its broadband service for the next two years. The commission was right to extract this concession, but it should not be necessary to negotiate separate deals like this one. On the information superhighway, net neutrality should be a basic rule of the road.

A more sombre note was sounded a day later by Charles Arthur in the UK *Guardian* in a piece entitled 'AT & T climbdown is a victory for Net neutrality – or is it?'.[14] While some advocates of Net neutrality 'were dancing for joy,' writes Arthur, 'others think that AT & T/SBCs promises are nearly worthless – and that only a Democrat-driven bill obliging telcos [telecommunication companies] not to discriminate between sources of data will keep information flowing freely'.

Network neutrality may or may not be protected in future by regulation, but in most other Net enterprises money does the talking. In June 2005 Rupert Murdoch bought up the Intermix company, creator of MySpace, for reputedly £200m. In October 2006 Google parted with £840m to purchase YouTube from its originators, San Francisco-based Chad Hurley and Steve Chen.

In the autumn of the same year YouTube was showing a hundred million video clips, a hundred million 'personal stories' a day. Interactivity was booming as never before, yet operating within the same organizational frameworks of corporate capitalism.

Dammit, spammit

It is to be wondered whether the Internet will continue to resemble an ever-expanding universe or sooner or later begin to feel like a holiday resort spoilt by publicity to the point when it is so overcrowded it puts off users. Spam, spawned by the drive for online profit, is a serious threat to the Net's viability as a source of information exchange, as a mode of meaningful interactivity. Increasingly Net users find that windows on to the world of knowledge have become clogged up with ads. Once we have hazarded an online purchase, we are likely to feature in the electronic address-book of hundreds if not thousands of agencies eager for our custom.

What might have begun as a source of welcome interactions of one kind or another, of students e-mailing each other, contacting staff on-line, searching for assistance in the preparation of essays or dissertations, threatens to suffer a blitzkrieg of unwanted messaging.

The stories are legion of people returning from a holiday or business trip to discover so many e-mails stacked 'against the door' that they can scarcely force entry; and as for getting on with the work in hand, e-mail potentially becomes a liability, a time consumer rather than a time saver.

Legitimate advertisers can be a nuisance, but beyond them are those who roam cyberspace with mischievous or malicious intent – the wreckers, the spawners of viruses; subverters of the Net whose activities are all too familiar for them to be repeated in detail here. Fortunately, both governments and companies are working to impose limits, legal and technical, on spam; but with equal resolution, the spammers are working to circumvent these limits. The qualities that have made network communication such an inspiring source of information and exchange are put at risk, subjected to exploitation and subversion; the web environment in danger of pollution.

Meanwhile, back at Old Times Ranch

During uneasy moments when the computer screen is awash with an effluent of spam, users of a certain age cast a nostalgic glance over their shoulders at the 'old media'; at the memory of holding a *real* newspaper (despite the ink on our fingers), something to sit back with in an armchair, or while away a commuting hour on the train to work; equally to tune into radio or TV news and to be spared marketing's prefaces, punctuation and epilogues. It is reassuring, in such circumstances, to realize that while Internet use has made significant inroads into spaces traditionally occupied and dominated by the mass media, the trend has been characterized so far by adjustment rather than displacement.

The mass media have not been left behind because in true entrepreneurial fashion they have embraced the web with enthusiasm and vision, offering competitive and developing online services: you are stimulated by an article in a newspaper or magazine, you can contact the author and regularly be provided with further related texts; you enjoy a radio or TV programme, you can, using a broadcasting website, hear more and very often be able to question the programme presenter, thus entering a wider debate with pundits and other viewers who share your interest.

The media have benefited enormously as far as accessing ordinary people is concerned. What in the past were readers, listeners and viewers are now potential reporters, commentators, communicative innovators in their own right. More and more, audience is made up of *participants*. As far as Net use is concerned, this *is* good news, and it *should* be for mass communication too; yet what is worrying is whether those in thrall to the social possibilities of network communication, particularly the young, will have the motivation, interest or time to guarantee a future for traditional press and broadcasting communication.

Caution has to be the watchword for any prediction of what is in store for the relationship between mass media and the Internet. Jim Hall writes in the Introduction to his book *Online Journalism: A Critical Primer*:[15]

New media's potential for inexpensive one-to-one, one-to-many and many-to-many reciprocal communications carries far-reaching and disruptive implications for traditional news producers and journalism.

It is not simply a case of one brand competing with, or striving to complement, the other; rather Net communication is challenging verities that have served as the bedrock of mass communication since the 19th century. News values as we have defined them so far; principles of transmission (such as the need for objectivity, balance and impartiality) are threatened by the sheer plurality of Net communication and the capacity of consumers to package their own news information from a myriad sources.

At the very least in our scrutiny of traditional news values in the light of online journalism we should, as Jim Hall suggests in his chapter,

The nature of news, 'add interactivity to the short list of journalistic core values' and this in turn has to be considered in respect of 'changes in society including a levelling of its structural hierarchies and with the way we understand text':

> In using hypertext, or linked elements of text or information, the relationship between the reader and author undergoes a shift that inverts traditional understandings of the construction of meaning and reshapes some of the values that underpin it.

Realities 2: shadow of the Panopticon – the Net is watching you

There is ample evidence that in many countries of the world the electronic highway is perceived as challenging hierarchy and authority. Hegemony itself is undermined. This, at a basic level, is a measure of power – that states, those in authority, take the 'threat of people power' on the Net so seriously that they are prepared to impose on network communication rigorously intrusive censorship.

In May 2001 the authorities in Iran shut down 400 cybercafes. In the same month, Saudi Arabia, which had opened its doors to the Internet in 1999, and was witnessing an annual growth in Net use of 20%, marked 200,000 websites for closure. These were not temporary reactions till the authorities become accustomed to the face of Net communication and its commercial benefits. In December 2006 Iran shut down access to Amazon.com and YouTube, following similar edicts against Wikipedia and the *New York Times* website; this occurred despite the common knowledge that the country's president Mahmoud Ahmadinejad ran his own blog and the fact that there were over 75m surfers in Iran, the highest rate of web use in the Middle East next to Israel.

The Net poses a dilemma for those in power. It is accepted as a necessary tool of communication in an electronic age, one which governments need to invest in and promote – for approved purposes; so outright bans are self-defeating. On the other hand, the Net loosens control from the centre. Margins either are, or are perceived to be, empowered. That which by tradition, supported by authority and often coercion, was seemingly written in stone – the official version of the truth – is challenged by disparate voices; and these voices are heard and responded to without recourse to offical routes.

China: Great Wall, Fire Wall

No country has felt the 'draught' caused by Internet use more than China. After centuries of cultural isolation, the Chinese people have greeted the Net's gift of a window on the world with enormous enthusiasm. The Beijing government has licensed Internet use; it has even given the nod to the first China-based website to go public overseas (Sina.com). But it has also introduced legislation banning the discussion or transfer of all 'secret information', with punitive jail sentences for those found guilty.

It has been estimated that China employs over 30,000 officials to monitor Internet traffic. Even so, bearing in mind the millions of Net exchanges that take place day and night it might be deemed a task beyond the reach of the most determined state censorship. This would be to overlook one of the key properties of Net communication – its *specificity*.

The Chinese user need only tap in one from a list of over a thousand or so banned words, such as 'truth' or 'dictatorship', or a phrase such as 'riot police' or a location with historical or political significance, such as 'Tiananmen Square'; and there is likely to be a knock at the door which will be real, not virtual.

The Golden Shield and 'Kitchen Table Democracy'

The *Jin Dun*, or Golden Shield Project, initiated in 1998, has developed into the most ambitious system of Internet censorship by the Chinese authorities; a firewall on the scale of the Great Wall itself and, as novelist Ma Jian describes it in an online article on the project, 'more practical and impenetrable than the Berlin Wall'.[16]

The author warns of a Chinese Internet service that is 'filled with baits and traps'. The unsuspecting user is greeted with 'friendly Web page designs, easy-to-click icons and symbolized facial expressions, beautiful female stars in online ads and constantly updated internal news' and these goodies 'induce users to participate and express their own ideas. But once someone's fingertips touch the keyboard, the "Kitchen Table Democracy" of the Web no longer exists – he or she may find themselves stepping into a trap, because the Internet police monitor every word that is typed'.

Ma Jian describes the situation as Orwellian, but 'what Orwell failed to predict is that China's government has accomplished this with the aid of Western democracies' – a reference to Internet provider companies in the West desperate for Eastern custom.

Paradoxically, the software that has permitted Chinese electronic surveillance is largely the result of collusion between the Chinese authorities and Western providers determined to cash in on China's 1.3 billion population, of whom over 110 million are Net users.

And in the Western backyard

Surveillance is far from being an activity confined to so-called 'repressive states'. It is occurring increasingly in freedom-respecting democracies; and with little or no popular protest. Details about ourselves as citizens, voters and consumers have, thanks to computer technology, become a public commodity. Privacy, it could be claimed, met its Waterloo with the introduction of the switchcard, the modern version, some commentators claim, of the notorious Panopticon proposed by Jeremy Bentham (1748–1832), English philosopher, political writer and penologist.

The Panopticon – the all-seeing one – was Bentham's idea for prison design: a watchtower would be placed in the centre of an encircling building. This would enable the prisoners to be watched at all times without surveillance being obtrusive. The *knowledge* of being watched would, Bentham believed, lead to *self*-regulation on the part of the watched. In other words, they would come to submit willingly to surveillance.

Bentham's Panopticon was essentially concerned, as an idea, with correction, turning the wrongdoer into a reformed person living according to pre-established social norms. It was, then, a *normalizing machine*: through surveillance and the threat rather than the exercise of coercion, it both defined the norm and, once the wrongdoer had accepted this, returned him or her to a kind of freedom.

Discipline of the norm

With the coming of what the French philosopher Michel Foucault in *Discipline and Punish: The History of the Prison*,[17] has called the 'technologies of power', Bentham's vision would appear to be closer to realization. In *The Mode of Information: Poststructuralism and Social Context*,[18] Mark Poster comments that 'The population as a whole has long been affixed with numbers and the discipline of the norm has become second nature'. He is of the view that, 'Today we have a Superpanopticon, a system of surveillance without walls, windows, towers or guards'.

Poster fears that the 'populace has been disciplined to surveillance and to participating in the process' willingly, without coercion:

> Social security cards, drivers' licences, credit cards, library cards and the like – the individual must apply for them, have them ready at all times, use them continuously. Each transaction is recorded, encoded and added to databases. Individuals themselves in many cases fill out the forms; they are at once the source of information and the recorder of the information.

Home networking constitutes 'the streamlined culmination of this phenomenon: the consumer, by ordering products through a modem connected to the producer's database, enters data about himself or herself directly into the producer's database in the very act of purchase'.

In this sense, the population participates in 'the disciplining and surveillance of themselves as consumers'; or, as Foucault chillingly expresses it, 'He who is subjected to a field of visibility, and who knows it, assumes responsibility for the constraints of power ... He becomes the principle of his own subjection ...'

Today's Panopticon is seen by many commentators to take a number of electronic forms, closed circuit TV cameras being the most obvious example. However, rating Superpanopticon status is the mobile phone, especially in its capacity to extend our networking capability from home and work to every place we ever go. It has to be asked, is the Internet inviting a degree of surveillance that would have made even Jeremy Bentham (or George Orwell) blench?

As we have seen, the Internet offers us a galaxy of opportunities. It is also subject to abuse – exploitation for criminal purposes, for trading in pornography, racial and ethnic hatred, even for organized terrorism. Such abuses are, rightfully in many cases, seen as a threat to society. At the same time they can prompt justification (or some might claim the 'excuse') on the part of authority for censorship and punitive legislation. The fear is that what begins as surveillance of criminality becomes the opportunity to subject the whole of society to panoptic scrutiny.

Interests of state

We may not have heard of Carnivore or Echelon but we can be pretty sure that sooner or later, if 'we' are activists in any way – political, cultural, environmental – that they will soon have heard of us. In the USA the Federal Bureau of Investigation (FBI) operates a Net tapping system, originally code-named Carnivore until it was realized that the metaphor seemed menacing as well as inappropriately memorable, when DCS 1000 was substituted. Taking care of the UK, though with worldwide application, is the US-originated Echelon, a system for monitoring traffic on commercial communications satellites.[19]

We are probably just as likely not to have heard of ILETS – the International Law Enforcement Telecommunications Seminar, dedicated, over several years of secret meetings, to put in place systems that would be 'interception-friendly'. Even if we are British citizens we might be forgiven for being unfamiliar with the work of the UK government's Home Office Encryption Co-ordination Unit or its Government Technical Assistance Centre (GTAC) operating within the London headquarters of MI5 at Thames House, Millbank.

The bureaucracy, the legality and the process need not detain us here; but the objective is clear. Monitoring of e-mails is located within ISPs, Internet service providers. The spy in the ISP will work through specificity. As data from ISPs travel on shared links, the electronic spy will key into information 'packets' in ways not dissimilar to bloodhounds: words, phrases, names that are of key interest to national or commercial security are 'sniffed out' by secret encryption. As for the ISPs they have no idea just what data, or how much, are being extracted from clients' private messages.

R(est) I(n) P(eace) Freedom?

The Introduction to the UK Regulation of Investigatory Powers Act (RIPA) of 2000 states the following aims:

[To make] provision for and about the interception of communications, the acquisition and disclosure of data relating to communications, the carrying out of surveillance, the use of covert human intelligence sources and the acquisition of the means by which electronic data protected by encryption or passwords may be decrypted or accessed; to provide for Commissioners and a tribunal with functions and jurisdiction in relation to those matters, to entries on and interferences with property or with wireless relegraphy and the carrying out of their functions by the Security Service, the Secret Intelligence Service and the Government Communications Headquarters; and for connected purposes.

The Regulation of Investigatory Powers Act, while causing consternation among human rights watchers, never really engaged most news agendas in the UK. The protests of some of the broadsheets went unheard, perhaps because, for the general public, censorship was seen as justifiable if it curtailed the dissemination of race hate or the conspiracies of paedophiles on the Net. The threat to civil liberties may take time to sink in, especially as RIPA is empowered to operate in secrecy.

Surveillance and the 'War on Terrorism'

Since President George W. Bush declared war on terrorism following 9/11, there has been jihad on the freedoms of expression and access to information in a number of democracies, in particular the USA and the UK. The threat of terrorism has come to be seen as a justification for measures restricting traditional, and long fought-for, civil liberties.

The US Patriot Act of 2001 was rushed through Congress in the stunned and reeling aftermath of the destruction of the Twin Towers in New York and the deaths of over 3000 people. Among a traunch of controlling measures, the Act extended state powers to intercept electronic communication. In the words of Nancy Chang, Senior Litigation Attorney at New York's Center for Constitutional Rights, in *Silencing Political Dissent: How Post-September 11 Antiterrorism Measures Threaten Our Civil Liberties*,[20] the Patriot Act has granted 'the executive unprecedented, and largely unchecked surveillance powers including the enhanced ability to track e-mail and Internet usage...'

In addition, writes Chang, the Act grants the executive powers to conduct 'sneak-and-peek searches, obtain sensitive personal records, monitor financial transactions and conduct nationwide wiretap' and by doing so 'sacrifices our political freedoms in the name of national security'. At around the same time, and referring to the appetite of the authorities in Britain for raising the bar of censorship, Brian Appleyard in a UK *Sunday Times* article, 'No hiding place',[21] wrote:

> Our government, police and intelligence services have more legal powers to poke around in our lives than those of communist China. And thanks to new technologies from mobile phones to the internet, they can use those powers to find out where we are, whom we talk or send e-mails to, and what websites we click on.
>
> According to most experts in the field, a police state with powers of control and surveillance beyond the wildest dreams of Hitler

or Stalin could now be established in Britain within 24 hours. And guess what: MI5 probably read this article before you did...The Englishman's home is no longer his castle, it is his virtual interrogation centre.

Such comments came well before the drive during 2005, 2006 and 2007 to introduce the ultimate Panopticon to the British people – the electronic Identity Card; again justified in part by the argument that it might increase the chances of spotting existing or would-be terrorists.

Visibility works two ways

If the idea that all our private affairs are under constant surveillance by the Superpanopticon of computer databases is disturbing, we can take some comfort from the fact that another form of 'visibility' encompasses the Superpanopticonists themselves. Politicians, civil servants, business people whose activities have in the past been shielded from public gaze are now more *visible* to the public than ever before.

Once again we turn to John B.Thompson to edge us a step back from the pessimism that seems to be a professional hazard of the media critic. In *The Media and Modernity*[22] he calls into question the notion of the modern Panopticon:

> Whereas the Panopticon renders many people visible to a few and enables power to be exercised over the many by subjecting them to a state of permanent visibility, the development of communication media provides a means by which many people can gather information about a few and, at the same time, a few can appear before many; thanks to the media, it is primarily those who exercise power, rather than those over whom power is exercised, who are subjected to a certain kind of visibility.

We as the public may, through the computer data systems that threaten our privacy, feel vulnerable, but, Thompson believes, the visibility made possible by the electronic Panopticon, available to media and public alike, makes it 'more difficult for those who exercise political power to do so secretly, furtively, behind closed doors'.

Self, other and 'reality' in cyberspace

The heady visions of early commentators concerning the potential for exploring the possibilities of self and other on the Net have, like the metaphors of freedom, lost most of their gloss. We express worry now about what Mark Poster terms 'the instability of identity in electronic communication';[8] at the consequences of the opportunity to be *other* as well as self; to switch gender, age, nationality. It would seem that disembodiment liberates the psychotic as well as the free spirit.

A research project conducted by the Stanford University Institute for the Qualitative Study of Society, published in 2000, found that heavy use of the Net risks turning people into isolates, obsessively hooked up to the Net. Director of the Institute, Norman Nie, commenting on the findings drawn from a survey of 4113 net users in December 1999, believed '[w]e are moving from a world in which you know all your neighbours, see your friends, interact with lots of different people every day, to a functional world, where interaction takes place at a distance'.

In turn, critics have resisted such gloom-and-doom talk, arguing that obsessives will be obsessive whatever communicative (or other) opportunities are available to them. One might equally refer to 'couch potatoes' as obsessively glued to the TV; or people always with their heads in a book. It is a matter of lively and continuing debate whether the Internet is different in kind or degree; after all the cinema was long thought by some as likely to corrupt – juveniles in particular – and popular music has been similarly accused of being a 'bad influence'. Today we furrow brows over that other electronic Pied Piper – the computer game.

Parallels have also been drawn between Internet use and addictions such as drinking, sex and gambling. There has been much concerned literature about wrecked lives. For example, in *Caught in the Net*,[23] Kimberley Young of the University of Pittsburg and founder of the Center for On-Line Addiction, estimated that there were some eight million people seriously hooked on the Net.

She states that anyone who spends more than 40 hours a week surfing the Net is probably suspect. Her researches indicate that those most at risk, in the USA at least, are middle-aged housewives and students. According to Dr Young, signs of addiction are:

- Preoccupation with the Internet
- Always wanting to go on to the Net for longer periods
- Always unsuccessfully trying to cut back
- Restless, moody and depressed when trying to cut back
- Always staying online longer than planned
- Regularly lying to the family and therapist about time online
- Using the Internet as a way of escape.

Concern about IAD (Internet Addiction Disorder) has become widespread. In 2005 China opened its first Net addiction clinic in Beijing. In the same year, in America, a Stanford University phone survey of 2513 respondents discovered that nearly 14% found it difficult to stay away from Net use, while almost 6% felt that their Net surfing adversely affected their relationships with other people.[24]

Elias Aboujaoude head of the Impulse Control Disorders Clinic at Stanford's School of Medicine, and principal author of the study, says it was conducted as a result of an alarming rise in the number of patients seeking treatment for excessive computer use. 'We are seeing more and more people losing their jobs,' Dr. Abouiaoude told the press, 'because of too much time spent surfing the Internet during work,' and '[m]ore relationships are breaking up because of spouses sneaking out of bed to check e-mail in the middle of the night'.

Reality and illusion: the blurring of boundaries

The 'sneaking out of bed' syndrome suggests a collision of two realities, the one available in the 'real' world and the other entered through the portals of the computer screen, the Alice Through the Looking Glass world of 'virtual' reality. This would seem to possess attractions more alluring than the real bed, in a real bedroom and with a real person between the sheets (and perhaps a bevy of screaming children in the dead of night).

The purpose is escape. The real world is all too predictable. The virtual world offers a tantalizing unknown, one in which hundreds if not thousands of others are searching for, as it were, 'better company', fresh stimulus, new challenges, opportunities for adventures, risks even, all available from the safety of the user's console.

The question arises, just how efficiently do people discriminate between the real and the simulated? We know from experience of audiences for television that the characters in soaps are seen as real – at least real enough to be regarded as real; otherwise why would people protest so volubly at the death or imprisonment of a favourite character; why would the actor who plays a soap villain be at risk of vilification for the behaviour of the character he or she plays?

What's real? The Internet poses this question endlessly, its capacity for anonymity helping to blur the difference. In *War of the Worlds: Cyberspace and the High-Tech Assault on Reality*,[25] a polemic that does not hesitate, at least metaphorically, to empty both barrels into the claims of the technovisionaries, Mark Slouka writes:

Instead of exploring a local farm pond (or catching praying mantises in the park) today's eight-year-old can explore on her computer. Instead of keeping and taking care of a pet, she can spend time with her electronic pet on her computer. Instead of visiting real animals at a zoo (itself already a kind of simulation) she can visit the dodo and the passenger pigeon... All this may have its advantages – no smashed aquariums, no dog hair on the sofa – but what it lacks is inestimable: in a word reality.

Slouka deplores the 'ease with which these games blur the line between appearance and reality, the ease with which they are able to capture their users' emotions'; and what is significant 'is not the simulation [for most computer games are 'less interested in growing things than in skewering them'] but our willingness to buy into it':

> ... whether we're growing tomatoes or slicing our way through a crowd with a chainsaw, after all, we're buying into a fake, and that says something about our relationship to reality.

The attention of the student of media has constantly been drawn in this book to the role the media play in defining realities. Slouka's argument about the 'assault on reality' which he perceives as happening both in cyberspace and out of it, thus deserves discussing and exploring; for, he claims, 'reality... is beginning to lose its authority'.

Slouka asks, does this matter? And answers his question by saying, 'Of course it does, and in more ways than one'. If counterfeit technologies 'were limited to the world *inside* the computer, if dealing with them meant no more than dealing with the psychological side effects of raising virtual fish or virtual kids, or living in virtual communities... they'd be less of an issue'. He fears that 'the illusioneers or imagicians or whatever we choose to call them are introducing their hallucinations into the culture at large'.

Faking realities

To illustrate what he terms the 'culture of simulation' – aided, abetted and perfected through the technology of digitization – Slouka refers to a photograph tacked to the wall above his desk. It is a reprint of a famous and historical picture of President Roosevelt, Prime Minister Churchill and Comrade Stalin, taken at Yalta in 1945. And standing in shirt-sleeves immediately behind them is – Sylvester Stallone, the film actor, born in 1946. Slouka keeps the picture above his desk as a reminder of 'the increasingly slippery world we inhabit', a world in which the most remarkable fact about reality is the ease with which it can be faked.

Slouka readily admits that photography has since its birth been 'fakeable', that propaganda is 'as old as language' and that the 'original photograph at Yalta was staged ... But,' Slouka argues, 'it's one thing to leave something out, or rig the meaning of an image by presenting it in a particular way; it's quite another to recreate the image itself'.

The reality the image presents to us, in an age so dominated by the visual image, is being tampered with; and if the image can be so easily manipulated, so can public perceptions of it, believes Slouka. We become accomplices in illusion-making:

> Though aware, for example, of the inherently manipulative power of advertising, or the extent to which so-called reality-based television programmes are rigged, we nonetheless seem willing to buy the products (and the realities) they sell. Though aware that the photo-op of the candidate washing dishes at a homeless shelter or gazing admiringly at a redwood is staged – even directly contrary to his or her actual policies – we vote as though the images actually had some bearing on reality.

This indicates 'the enormous and abiding power of the visual sense' which more than any other 'compels our faith. We want and need to believe what we see':

> The problem with this is that our instinctive allegiance to the things our eyes show us has been transferred, largely if not entirely, to images of things as well ... [and image manipulation techniques] carry the threat of manipulating not only the images we consume, but the world we inhabit. They threaten, in other words, to make our world virtual to an extent unimaginable outside science fiction.

The manipulated image undermines our trust in all representations, says Slouka, and consequently our trust in all mediated information. He believes, and it is up to the student of media to scrutinize this view with care as well as scepticism, that 'the threat inherent in image-manipulation techniques is the threat of authoritarianism, of information control'.

Why? – because public belief in the veracity of some, if not all information, must be supported by a measure of conviction, otherwise a community risks 'nothing less than the kind of institutionalized cynicism found under authoritarian regimes'. Slouka refers to the 'blurring of fiction and reality' so characteristic of public communication in the former Soviet Union and its satellites, East Germany, Czechoslovakia, Hungary and Poland. This 'spawned a culturewide and pervasive cynicism towards all official information':

> And exposing the frauds, I suspect, even if it becomes possible, will be of little help; once the public's faith in images is shaken, cynicism will spread like a contagion to *all* sources of information.

The author advocates a firm grip on real – unmediated – life, for all its drawbacks; and he advises the reader to resist claims of the 'inevitablity' of the virtual world taking over from the real:

> If we don't, we'll grow increasingly frightened of unmediated reality; more and more isolated, we'll come to depend, first for our comfort and eventually for our very sanity, on the technologies and the people behind them who offer to stand between us and the hostile world we inhabit, who offer us platitudes, fictions, and out-and-out lies on which we've come to depend, who shield us from the increasingly terrifying aura of first hand experience.

Postmodernist resonances

In *Life on the Screen: Identity in the Age of the Internet*,[26] Sherry Turkle identifies a close 'fit' between network technology and postmodernist visions of contemporary life. She writes of a 'nascent culture of simulation' in which 'the self is constructed and the rules of social interaction are built, not received'. In consequence we 'are inventing ourselves as we go along'.

'Postmodernist theories,' says Turkle, 'suggest that the search for depth and mechanism [a systematic explanation for things] is futile, and that it is more realistic to explore the world of shifting surfaces than to embark on a search for origins and structure'.

Ronald J. Deibert in *Parchment, Printing and Hypermedia: Communication in World Order Transformation*,[27] also notes the bits-and-pieces nature of network technology and postmodernist visions of contemporary life. He compares the way the technology extracts 'bits of data in different forms from disparate sources' and pastes them together 'into an assembled whole' with the way 'postmodernists conceive of the self as a networked assemblage without a fixed centre'.

Consequently 'identities on the "net" – such as age, gender and occupation – are malleable because of the concealment that computer networks afford the user'. However, that concealment is won at the cost of surrendering to superficiality, what Diebert terms 'depthlessness'. He echoes Turkle, though with less approval, arguing that 'depth is replaced by surface, or by multiple surfaces'.

Rootedness versus attachment

As we have seen, network technology disembodies the user, releases him or her from time, place and even a prescribed identity. In the view of Darin Barney in *Prometheus Wired: The Hope for Democracy in the Age of Network Technology*[28] the Net fulfils postmodern identities by being 'fragmented, de-centred, partial, unstable, multiple, heterogenous [composed of parts of different kinds], incomplete, discontinuous, fluid and highly differentiated'. With these characteristics in mind, Barney believes that 'the network medium is itself an essentially uprooting technology'. He writes:

> Put crudely, the practice of information gathering via the World Wide Web does not root someone in the same way that withdrawing a book from the local library does. Both are mediating technologies that connect users to sources of information that are remote to their immediate experience. However, the library is rooted, by virtue of its spatial fixity and proximity to the place where those using it work and live, in a way the Web cannot be.

Barney argues that '[t]he Web exists everywhere and nowhere, and by using it people are rooted everywhere and nowhere, which is to say they are not rooted at all'. He differentiates between rootedness and *attachment*. Rootedness is 'a comparatively static condition – roots grow but seldom move', whereas attachment 'is a function of interest':

> People decide when and where to attach themselves, and they can detach themselves without vital consequences when they lose interest. The obligation in a relationship based on attachment – such as membership in a network community – lasts only as long as the parties' interests are satisfied, and so resembles that established by a contract.

On the other hand, says Barney, roots 'run deeper than mere interests, create obligations that often conflict with interests, and bind more strictly than contracts'. People who 'are interested in doing so attach themselves to communities; people who are rooted *belong* to communities'. It follows that attachment 'can only stand in for, but never adequately replace rootedness'.

Plainly Barney cherishes rootedness in the face of postmodernist theory that casts doubt on the viability in the modern age of such human properties. The author quotes Simone Weil in support. In *The Need for Roots*,[29] she lists liberty and freedom of opinion among the most primary human needs, but also asserts that 'to be rooted' is 'perhaps the most important and least recognized need of the human soul'.

Barney worries about an 'environment of escalating uprootedness', echoing the concerns of Mark Slouka and other scrutineers of the interfaces between technology and social change. He fears that as more people 'devote their finite social energies to personal and partial online communities at the expense of those offline, their attention and care for where they live and work is likely to wane'.

The Net's enabling potential

Network communication poses the dilemma that many of its up-sides are also actually or potentially its down-sides. In *Media and Morality: On the Rise of the Mediapolis*,[30] Roger Silverstone states, 'Chat rooms and bulletin boards, have, relatively speaking, long become the semi-public, semi-private spaces for a kind of intimacy and a kind of politics'; thus the 'otherwise invisible and unheard can claim an audience, different in quality perhaps but not always in significance, from the fifteen minutes of celebrity offered by the chat shows and the tabloid press'.

Albeit in a very limited sense, the Net is *enabling*. People occupying the margins, those for the most part belonging to the often unheeded, sidelined if not altogether rejected *other*, have a chance to be heard, to make their case for acceptance and inclusion.

In a world where reality is so comprehensively mediated, every effort should be made, so argues Silverstone, to accommodate other – the stranger, domestic or foreign – on equal terms in global space (and this should also be the task of mass media generally). However, says Silverstone, echoing Darin Barney, 'The strengths of such online spaces, ease of access, speed and intensity of connection, are also their weaknesses, in the fragility and ephemerality of that intimacy, and in the self-reinforcing move towards singularity rather than the plurality of voice':

> In this context the stranger emerges as an individual, but she or he is increasingly and effortlessly vulnerable to exclusion if the voice does not fit or if it does not match: exclusion or self-exclusion comes with the click of a mouse or the instant judgement of a web-master.

Silverstone remains optimistic that the virtues of network communication will outweigh its disadvantages. He sees alternative networks 'emerging to occupy the public and political spaces of the global media world'. He considers the web-log 'a phenomenon to contest the already weakening stranglehold of the national press and broadcasting systems'; it is 'a media space of global proportions with still an extant commons', that is, a platform for public participation; or, as Silverstone puts it earlier in his chapter on hospitality and justice, 'a common possession'. It is also one 'constantly at risk both of its self-violation (paedophile and terrorist networks) and its enclosure (by transnational corporations and political controls)'.

Summary

This chapter began by viewing the role of metaphor in describing network communication and its power to elevate process beyond the purely practical. The very term 'cyberspace' suggests flight; just as 'surfing' hints at activities that have nothing whatever to do with the realities of sitting in a darkened room in front of a computer or signalling up Net information on a mobile.

The Net has also been envisaged as a space that combines the public and the private, the local and the global, in which the public can contribute to discourses – political, cultural, economic and social – from which in the past they have been largely excluded. The traditional audience for media has been passive, a generally silent majority; but the Net has introduced the world to interactivity on an unparalleled scale. The talk is of freedom, equality and occasionally global inclusion; of *people power* challenging and sometimes subverting traditional structures of power.

Realities inevitably catch up with and sometimes overtake dreams. State and corporate power, political and commercial, exercise their own visions for the use and occupation of cyberspace. They strive to colonize it or consumerize it; preferably both. The Net as marketplace has already succumbed to a great degree to corporate envelopment. At the same time ruling authorities across the globe have not only recognized the benefits of Net communication, on their terms; they have become resolute in devising ways to control it.

Meanwhile reference is made to worries widely expressed about the effects, social and psychological, of Net use, of the tendency to neglect 'real' life, and real people, for the 'virtual' world at the (solitary) user's fingertips. Equally attention is paid to uneasiness expressed by Net observers at disengagement from the real, the blurring of realities, the potency of the fake, the ephemerality of identity and of relationships.

It is a relief, then, to take a walk in to town – and find the streets are not empty because the population is crouched in front of its cyberscreen; a relief to discover people still attached to their real bodies in real time and real places; and heartwarming to see people still sampling technology's greatest contribution to civilization, the book.

Perhaps for a while at least we can suspend judgement over Mark Slouka's fear that 'firsthand experience has joined the list of endangered species', and affirm Roger Silverstone's view that '[t]he internet is coming of age, and in its troubled adolescence it is throwing up significant alternatives to established forms of media practice ...'

KEY TERMS

cybernetics   virtual reality   spatial stories   narrativity   interactivity
hegemony   empowerment   marketization   economies of size
cross-promotion   network neutrality   blog   specificity
Panopticon/Superpanopticon   discipline of the norm   encryption
visibility   Net addiction   assault on reality   postmodernist visions
rootedness versus attachment

Suggested activities

1. Discussion:
   (a) Consider the opportunities and the dangers involved in surfing the Net.
   (b) What are the arguments for and against 'policing' the Internet?
   (c) How far should parents worry about the freedom of their children to wander the streets of the Netropolis?

(d) In what ways will the growing popularity of the Net world-wide affect modes of mass communication such as the press, TV and the cinema?

2. How might resistance be organized to the ambitions of TNCs (transnational corporations) to colonize the Internet?

3. Conduct a survey among your acquaintances, in life or online, with a view to identifying patterns of Net use. What constitutes the majority of their activities online; how much time is spent online, and to what extent has online activity had an effect on life offline?

4. Similarly do a study among young people of *texting* as a mode of social interaction. Explore the perceived benefits of texting and the degree of its use. It may prove useful to simply note the frequency of use by your target group, of calls and texting; and to pose questions concerning content and style. To put your direct findings into context, trawl the Net for expressions of concern about the growth of texting. For example, are standards of language, spoken and written, damaged by the 'shorthand' of texting?

5. Create a list of newspaper and broadcasting websites; assess their usefulness particularly with regard to whether information is usefully extended and interactivity encouraged.

6. Prepare a compendium of websites that focus on (a) government surveillance practices worldwide and (b) corporate ambitions and the Net.

7. Visit the following sites in a period of approximately one hour: www.oneworld.org, www.environlink.com, www.grassroots.com, www.indexoncensorship.org, www.openDemocracy.net

   What are the main topics and issues on their agendas?

Now read on

The claims and counterclaims of pundits concerning network communication should be seen in the context of the evolution of the technology of communications, at least going back to the invention and development of telegraphy in the 19th century. Look up the work of two major contributors to our thinking on society and technology, Harold Innes and Marshall McLuhan.

Then try Joshua Mayrowitz's *No Sense of Place: The Impact of Electronic Media on Social Behaviour* (US: Oxford University Press, 1979), *Media Technology and Society: A History from the Telegraph to the Internet* (UK: Routledge, 1998) by Brian Winston and Tom Standage's *The Victorian Internet: The Remarkable Story of the Telegraph and the Nineteenth*

Century's Online Pioneers (UK: Weidenfeld & Nicolson, 1998). Importantly, return to Winston to read his *Freedom, Media and the West from Gutenberg to Google* (UK/US: Routledge, 2005).

For details on 'citizen journalism' and the blogosphere see Stuart Allan's *Online News* (UK/US: Open University, 2006), which focuses on participant journalism in relation to major news events (Chapter 4, Covering the crisis: online journalism on September 11; Chapter 6, Online reporting of the war in Iraq: bearing witness, and Chapter 8, Citizen journalists on the scene: the London bombings and Hurricane Katrina).

In order of publication, the following warrant attention: *Writing Space: The Computer, Hypertext and the History of Writing* by Jay David Bolter (UK: Lawrence Erblaum and Associates, 1990); *Being Digital* by Nicholas Negroponte (UK: Hodder & Stoughton, 1995) and the following, all from Sage publications: Robert Shields' *Cultures of Internet: Virtual Space, Real Histories, Living Bodies* (UK: 1996); *Cyberspace/Cyberbodies/Cyberpunk: Cultures of Technological Embodiment* (UK: 1996), edited by Mike Featherstone and Roger Burrows; *Virtual Culture: Identity and Communication in Cybersociety* (US: 1997), edited by Steven G. Jones and Cees J. Hamelink's *The Ethics of Cyberspace* (UK: 2000).

Recommended from Routledge is *The Cybercultures Reader* (UK: 2000) edited by David Bell and Barbara M. Kennedy; *Information and Communications Technology in Society* (UK: 2006), edited by Ben Anderson *et al.* and Aylish Wood's 2007 publication, *Digital Encounters: Agency and Affect*. For a searching analysis of the hazards, moral and practical, of policing the Internet see Gordon Graham's *The Internet: A Philosophical Inquiry* (UK: Routledge, 1999). Volume 35, no. 4 (2007) of *Index on Censorship* is dedicated to 'Cyberspeech: free expression online'.

Readers are recommended in particular to sample David Weinberger's article 'Online on message'. The author has no doubt that digital communication, with its capability for instant interactivity and informality of exchange, is having a radical impact on political communication as is manifestly demonstrated at election time. Traditional speech-making survives, but it is supplemented and informalized by the blog. See Weinberger's *Everything is Miscellaneous: The Power of the New Digital Disorder* (US: Times Books, 2007).

Notes

1. Norbert Wiener (1894–1964), father of cybernetics. Wiener acknowledged that the word *cybernetics* had already been used by the French

physicist André Marie Ampère. Wiener's book, *Cybernetics; or Control and Communication in the Animal and the Machine* (US: Wiley, 1949), combines 'under one heading the study of what in a human context is sometimes loosely described as thinking and in engineering is known as control and communication'; in short, response or feedback systems. In his later, more accessible work, *The Human Use of Human Beings: Cybernetics and Society* (US: Anchor, 1954) Wiener says that, 'Society can only be understood through a study of the communication facilities which belong to it'.

2.   J.C. Herz, *Surfing the Internet* (UK: Abacus, 1995).

3.   The Computer Merchant ad appeared in *Boston Computer Currents*, September 1991.

4.   Henry Rheingold (ed.), *Virtual Reality* (US: Simon & Schuster, 1991).

5.   Mary Fuller, assistant professor of literature, Massachusetts Institute of Technology (MIT) and Henry Jenkins, director of film and media studies at MIT, 'Nintendo@ and New World Travel Writing: A Dialogue' in Steven G. Jones (ed.), *CyberSociety: Computer Mediated Communication and Community* (US: Sage, 1995).

6.   Michel De Certeau, *The Practice of Everyday Life* (US: University of California Press, 1984).

7.   The term Web 2.0 is generally ascribed to American Tim O'Reilly of O'Reilly Media, a prominent US network consultancy firm; and it arose during a brainstorming session in 2003, making its full public appearance at the first Web 2.0 conference in 2004, the aim being to find a term that would describe a stage in the Net's evolution. In a Radar website communication (10 March 2005), O'Reilly refers to the Net as 'harnessing the collective intelligence of users' and this means 'that users are continually improving the [technological] application by their very interaction with it'. The term is imprecise and its use has prompted controversy. Critics view the 'second coming' as signposted by Web 2.0 as no more than an evolutionary step, building on existing, or potential, Net characteristics. However, Web 2.0 warrants its place in the pantheon of new terminology because it could be said to describe the tipping point at which what began as a technology-driven phenomenon became a user-generated activity; in O'Reilly's words, 'definitely about people'.

8.   Mark Poster, 'Postmodern virtualities' in *Cyberspace/Cyberbodies/Cyberpunk* (US: Sage, 1995), edited by Mike Featherstone and Roger Burrows.

9.   Tony Ageh is quoted by Jim McClellan in 'It's a wired world', *Observer/ Life*, 19 March 1995.

10.   Michael Benedikt (ed.), *Cyberspace: Some Proposals* (US: Simon & Schuster, 1991).

11.   Mark C. Taylor and Esa Saarinen, *Imagology: Media Philosophy* (UK: Routledge, 1994).

12. Lawrence Lessig and Robert McChesney, 'No tolls on the Internet', Washingtonpost.com, 13 June 2006.
13. *New York Times*, 'Protecting Internet democracy', 14 January 2007.
14. Charles Arthur, 'AT&T climbdown a victory for Net neutrality – or is it?' UK *Guardian*, 15 January 2007.
15. Jim Hall, *Online Journalism: A Critical Primer* (UK/US: Pluto Press, 2001).
16. Ma Jian, 'Ma Jian on China's Golden Shield Project', online article, openflows.org, 30 May 2005.
17. Michel Foucault, *Discipline and Punish: The Birth of the Prison* (UK: Penguin Books, 1991).
18. Mark Poster, *The Mode of Information: Poststructuralism and Social Context* (UK: Polity Press, 1990).
19. Echelon is operated by the UK, USA, Canada, Australia and New Zealand, and has been estimated to intercept up to three billion communications a day and scans 90% of Internet traffic.
20. Nancy Chang, *Silencing Political Dissent: How Post-September 11 Antiterrorism Measures Threaten Our Civil Liberties* (US: Seven Stories Press, 2002).
21. Brian Appleyard, 'No hiding place', UK *Sunday Times*, 15 April 2001.
22. John B. Thompson, *The Media and Modernity: A Social History of the Media* (UK: Polity Press, 1995).
23. Kimberley Young, *Caught in the Net* (US: John Wiley, 1998).
24. The Stanford University phone survey was conducted under the auspices of the School of Medicine. Research leader Dr Elias Aboujaoude was reported by BBC News as saying, 'We often focus on how wonderful the internet is … But we need to consider the fact that it creates real problems for a subset of people'. Details of the Stanford research can be found in the October 2006 edition of the *International Journal of Neuropsychiatric Medicine*.
25. Mark Slouka, *War of the Worlds: Cyberspace and the High-Tech Assault on Reality* (US: Basic Books, 1995).
26. Sherry Turkle, *Life on Screen: Identity in the Age of the Internet* (US: Simon & Schuster, 1995).
27. Ronald J. Deibert, *Parchment, Printing and Hypermedia: Communication in World Order Transformation* (US: University of Columbia Press, 1997).
28. Darin Barney, *Prometheus Wired: The Hope of Democracy in the Age of Network Technology* (US: University of Chicago Press, 2000).
29. Simone Weil, *The Need for Roots* (UK: Routledge & Kegan Paul, 1952).
30. Roger Silverstone, *Media and Morality: On the Rise of the Mediapolis* (UK/US: Polity Press, 2007). Silverstone's concept of the Mediapolis will be briefly highlighted in Chapter 11.

Research as Exploration and Development

10

AIMS

> ➤ To make the case that research is a key feature in the study and understanding of the media.
> ➤ To examine approaches to academic research, including using the Internet, and briefly record the work of important contributors to the field.
> ➤ To overview the aims and strategies of the media industry's own market research.

Debate concerning the mass media, their power, their intentions within the context of ownership and control, rises and falls according to media performance, for in today's public arena, in the avenues and squares of the mediapolis, life *is* media for most of us, most of the time. We live with our neighbours; we live with *Neighbours*. Life is a weave of the real and the mediated, the threads difficult and sometimes impossible to prise apart. Yet it is important to try to do so, at the very least to obtain a picture of what is happening in a mediated world, why, and to what effect. In short, media activity itself invites mediation – observation, interpretation, analysis.

Opinion only carries weight when it is accompanied by evidence that has been assessed with a degree of distance and objectivity and with the caveat that research findings will be challenged, misconstrued, manipulated; and sooner or later proved wrong or inadequate. Research is always a threat in that it seeks to go beyond the apparent and the obvious. It discomfirms more than it confirms. Its subversive potential is part of its fascination.

The issues discussed in this book should prove a stimulus to research activity. Definitive proof may be impossible to find, but the process of research itself will help clear the way to greater understanding, to a balanced view of the many controversies that help to thrust the issue of media performance to the top of socio-cultural and political agendas.

Research helps substantiate theory; sometimes it dismisses or undermines perspectives that have long held sway. It checks the premature leap to conclusions. Most of the activities students of media will be involved in will include research. Finding out about things is the prelude to traditional essays and reports, but it is equally vital in the preparation of media artefacts such as radio and TV programmes, marketing assignments, the creation of advertisements or the production of newspapers and magazines.

Research is exploration. It gives practice in the skills of investigation such as questionnaire design and interviewing techniques. It nurtures persistence, risk-taking, problem-solving and it has relevance for the future: the key to successful journalism is good research; knowing where to look and how to look.

Here a variety of research approaches is discussed – content analysis, ethnography and investigation through focus groups; and the reader is introduced to some of the work of the best media researchers in the field. Their findings are landmarks in the development of our knowledge about media production and audience reception. They are stepping-stones in the evolution of a discipline.

All forms of mass communication, from advertising to broadcasting, from periodical or newspaper publication to the movies and latterly the burgeoning universe of network communication (as marketization accelerates), rely on research findings either to continue the way they are or to change to cater for new expectations and tastes. In America, a blip in the ratings for a TV show can spell the end of its run. Market research, then, is big business in its own right, a vital gauge of current success or failure; at the same time a barometer of predicted weather, fair or foul. A number of major commercial research enterprises are discussed here.

Engaging the truth: research perspectives

In the early 1980s a small advertisement appeared in the Dutch women's magazine, *Viva*:

> I like watching the TV serial *Dallas* but often get odd reactions to it. Would anyone like to write and tell me you like watching it too, or dislike it? I should like to assimilate these reactions in my university thesis. Please write to...

The researcher, Ien Ang, chose a novel approach to finding out by eliciting women's written comments on one of their favourite programmes. From the 42 letters she received, Ang produced an analysis in book form, *Watching 'Dallas': Soap Opera and the Melodramatic Imagination*.[1] Although she worked only on the comments provided by her correspondents, knew nothing of their background and did not at any time follow up the comments by interviewing the writers, she nevertheless produced a notable piece of qualitative research.

Another researcher, working on the same material – a man, for instance – might well have placed differing emphases upon the material, drawn differing inferences; even come up with differing conclusions. Thus in scrutinizing the research process we have to address the problem of objectivity. We can do this fairly swiftly by declaring that, while fairness to source is imperative, absolute objectivity could well be classified a luxury reserved only for the gods.

What Ang does in *Watching 'Dallas'*, and what all constructors of meaning must do, is 'engage' with the truth rather than promise its definition: mediation is unavoidable. Research is about information-gathering just as a journalist gathers information for a story. It involves selection and emphasis. It involves the previous experience, knowledge, interests and values of the researcher, however open-minded he or she plans to be.

The collation of data is a process of deconstruction – examining the parts – and reconstruction; and this involves turning one set, or many sets of clues into a specialist form, usually sentences in print. Putting anything observed, spoken about or experienced into words transforms it. Raw data has to be studied, organized, sifted, compared, analyzed, synthesized and finally interpreted. That is what is so absorbing and satisfying about doing it.

The rewards of research

Research can be fulfilling but also profitable in a number of ways. It may obtain a researcher a PhD; it may lead to a job or a further research commission and in some academic institutions people's competence is judged according to the quantity and quality of their research. Little, or nothing, then is selfless. Where research is of direct interest to the making of profits, in industry, commerce and medicine, for example, or where research helps define audience needs, tastes and habits in the consumption of media products, it is in demand and can often be remunerative.

We can discern two strands of research here, the commercial and the academic. The results of such research enterprise often fuse, academic research being used for commercial purposes, commercial research offering data and reference points for academic directions and preoccupations. Ultimately all media research is about *content* – its nature, assembly, presentation and purpose; and *response* – the way audiences react to, deal with, and are affected by that content. Today, in the light of dramatically expanding Internet activity, we are interested in the nature of *use* and *interactivity*.

In our role as researcher we may varyingly elect to concentrate on textual analysis or to become observers of communicative activity, sometimes actually becoming participants in that activity. We may never actually meet the people we are investigating or we might spend our days and nights with them.

The commercial researcher, for instrumental reasons, would wish to know how people 'use' a TV soap opera: is it gaining or losing popularity; what features of the programme serve to command and sustain audience attention; and what does such a programme 'do' for people which can be replicated in future programming?

The academic approach differs in that there is less pressure to come up with answers, particularly the sort of answers which those that employ researchers wish them to come up with. The academic researcher primarily wishes to arrive at a state of understanding and to communicate that understanding to others.

The rewards for this may be publication, the respect of the researcher's peers, even fame, not to mention being studied by generations of students of communication and media; but the most significant goal is discovery: the academic researcher is a modest emulator of Magellan, the first sea captain to circumnavigate the globe, with an *alter ego* of Galileo or Newton. Each of these did more than discover; they affected their world by their discoveries and influenced the course of history.

Research as change agent

The fruits of research have the power to influence and in some cases to bring about change. For example, research into gender definitions and the treatment of gender may work towards attitudinal change with regard to the portrayal of women in media. Feminist research not only wishes to uncover evidence about the continuing male-dominatedness, the patriarchy of contemporary society, it aims to use that evidence to bring about attitudinal and behavioural changes.

In a *Journal of Communication* article, 'The potential contribution of feminist scholarship in the field of communication',[2] Brenda Dervin argues that research is enabling and *empowering*, that it gives women a voice in a world that generally renders them voiceless. Such research, says Dervin, 'is transformative in that it is concerned with helping the silent speak and is involved in consciousness raising'.

Research can be militant, subversive and, of course, it can be used against those whom it is intended to benefit, through selective use of the evidence offered, or simplifications (or distortions) of complicated findings. Such offences are most often committed by the media when they, in their turn, mediate between the researcher's detailed findings and the media's audience.

What is considered newsworthy in a researcher's text is highlighted, amplified and the highlights replicated. Those original dependent clauses, the crucial academic cautions about not reading too much into limited results, tend to be marginalized or omitted altogether as eye-catching headlines and 'in-a-nutshell' summaries distort as they diffuse.

If researchers have to recognize that they can exert little or no control over the ways their research data is used once it enters the public sphere, they need also to remind themselves not to lose sight of their own interpretative role in drawing up and presenting research findings. The saying that there are 'lies, damned lies and statistics' suggests that even if the researcher relies entirely upon questionnaire data, total objectivity remains a dream, for who wrote the questions in the first place, and who will compose the sentences which summarize and generalize the findings?

Admitting the shaping force of one's own subjectivity as a researcher is essential; in which case it becomes all the more important to factor in to the research equation two other guiding principles – accuracy and and an open-minded respect for alternative or conflicting data.

Approaches to research 1: content analysis

In 1982 Angela McRobbie published an intriguing content analysis of the British teenage magazine, *Jackie*. In an article '"Jackie": an ideology of adolescent femininity', published in *Popular Culture: Past and Present*,[3] the author charts the covert ideology that was intended to influence the reader of *Jackie*. She did not merely look at the content, she examined the source from which that content emerged – the publishing house of D.C. Thompson of Dundee, whose history had been characterized by 'a vigorous anti-unionism' and 'a strict code of censorship of content'.

From such a source arose material that McRobbie saw as the 'story' of *Jackie*, 'an implicit attempt to win consent to the dominant order – in terms of femininity, leisure and consumption, i.e. at all levels of culture'. Using a semiological approach to her analysis of the magazine, McRobbie identified in *Jackie* discourses that were relentlessly encoded towards inculcating in the reader traditional attitudes and behaviour.

The view from Glasgow

Some of the most controversial, and readable, content analysis has been produced by the Glasgow University Media Group (GUMG). Their chief research target has been television news in Britain. As they studied television news bulletin by bulletin, story by story, they have asked: Is the news biased, and if so, biased in favour of what or whom and against what or whom? The GUMG's conclusions, based on research conducted in the 1970s and onwards, have been that TV news in the UK *is* biased, is *not* impartial and that bias and partiality favour those in authority against those who challenge it.

Bad News,[4] the first in the GUMG series of books on their findings, challenged the traditional view that broadcasters are substantially more objective than their counterparts in the press. 'Our study,' write the eight authors, 'does not support a received view that television news is "the news that happens".' The Group's monitoring of news bulletins over a six-month period found a bias in TV against the activities of organized labour and a preoccupation with effects rather than causes.

Understandably broadcasters reacted sceptically to the GUMG's conclusions, accusing them of bias in their own perception of news production. Did they not realize the pressures journalists and programme makers work under? Undeterred, the GUMG produced *More Bad News* in 1980, *Really Bad News* in 1982 and *War and Peace News* on broadcast coverage of the 1982 Falklands War, the 1984 Miners' Strike and Northern Ireland, in 1985. The Group's conclusions reflect what McRobbie had been saying about *Jackie*. News, the authors declared in *More Bad News*, 'is not neutral and not a natural phenomenon: it is rather the manufactured production of ideology'.

Pennsylvania perspectives

On a grand scale perhaps the best-known research expedition has been that led by Professor George Gerbner (1919–2005) from his home port at the University of Pennsylvania's Annenberg School of Communication. There are several references to Gerbner's work in this book and acknowledgment of the influence of his findings on the perceived impact of TV on audience.

The Cultural Indicators (CI) programme of research based at the Annenburg School tracked violence on TV for over 30 years, using content analysis and extensive surveys of audience reaction. The CI has accumulated in a massive computer database observations on over 3000 programmes and some 35,000 characters coded according to many thematic, demographic and action categories.[5]

Gerbner and his team constitute a good example of how researchers not only add to our knowledge, they extend our vocabulary by embodying hypotheses in new terminology. Once enshrined in language, once put to use and re-use, the hypotheses take on the substance of truth; until, that is, they are checked or overtaken by new research embodying new terminology.

It was Gerbner and colleagues who introduced the notion of *mainstreaming* in which a perceived effect of heavy TV viewing is the *convergence* of political attitudes into a centre position between right and left but ultimately with a skew towards the right. Cultivation theory (discussed in Chapter 3), with which Gerbner is chiefly associated, sees TV's images as cultivating and nurturing in the audience 'our culture's beliefs, ideologies and world views'.[6]

The size of this effect, cultivation research has indicated, is less critical 'than the direction of its steady contribution'. Subsequent research has challenged Gerbner's extrapolations, arguing, basically, that people are actually less subject to influence than the Annenberg findings seem to indicate. (For a closer look at the perceived effects upon audiences of screen violence, see Appendix 2.)

Approaches to research 2: ethnography

Arguably the most challenging and certainly the most engrossing approach to research, is *participant observation*, a method of information-gathering that is usually associated with *ethnography*, the study of people interacting within domestic and communal contexts.

It exemplifies the mode of research referred to as *qualitative* as contrasted with *quantitative* research typified by the CI project and public opinion research generally. The differences are not actually of 'quality'. Quantitative research, dealing with hundreds or even thousands of respondents rather than a handful, is as anxious to come up with reliable, objective data as those researchers working in the ethnographic mode. The differences are that quantative research is generally less personal; researcher–respondent encounters take place in the questionnaire, by phone or Internet rather than face-to-face. Qualitative research is in-depth enquiry, its tools observation and interview; and it is often an immensely time-consuming exercise.

The ethnographic researcher is concerned with more subjective understandings, involved with perceptions and interpretations. The focus is on interactions, 'namely,' as Liesbet van Zoonen puts it in *Feminist Media Studies*,[7] 'the implicit and explicit rules people employ to make sense of their everyday surroundings and experiences'.

Hazards lie in the way of ethnographic research. To participate is to risk becoming partisan; to be, as it were, 'taken over', drawn away from being the critical observer. The researcher may be viewed with suspicion or hostility, seen as an unwelcome outsider; and there may be times when meaningful progress seems to be at a standstill. William Kornblum, in the Introduction to *In the Field: Readings on the Field Research Experience*,[8] edited by Carolyn D. Smith and William Kornblum, writes:

> Usually the most trying aspect of this kind of research is the effort to obtain permission to spend time with the people one wishes to get to know. Once this is accomplished (and it is never entirely achieved), the work of observation and description can become, on the surface, quite routine and even boring … one's very presence can become a drag. From the standpoint of those being observed, the observer is ignorant of the most obvious truths and constantly exposes that ignorance by questioning behaviour that everyone else takes for granted.

Kornblum makes a point with which students of communication preparing research projects will readily identify. This concerns *reciprocation*, that is, having something to offer in exchange for the information required: 'In short, our respondents often find us tiresome unless we have something to offer them other than just our goodwill.'

Further, Smith and Kornblum in the Preface of *In the Field* describe how the experience of qualitative field research can have a 'profound effect on the researcher, who often must re-examine his or her values and attitudes and may be forced to make choices that would not be required in the ordinary course of events'.

Responding to Rocky

This aspect of participant observation is well illustrated by the field research experience of Valerie Walkerdine. In 'Video replay: families, films and fantasy', an account of her work published in *Formations of Fantasy*,[9] Walkerdine records an image of herself as observer and intruder:

> I am seated in the living room of a council house in the centre of a large English city. I am here to make an audio-recording as part of a study of six year old girls and their education. While I am here, the family watches a film, *Rocky II*, on the video. I sit, in my arm-chair, watching them watching television. How to make sense of this situation?

The family, called 'Coles' by Walkerdine, see the researcher's role as one of surveillance. 'Joanne,' Mr Coles announced to his daughter when Valerie Walkerdine arrived, 'here's your psychiatrist!'

The nature of this intrusion created in Walkerdine strong feelings of dissonance and in her report she wonders whether 'this activity of research' is not a 'perverse voyeurism'. Here was a middle-class academic subjecting a working-class family to a scrutiny that ran the risk of being judgemental. Walkerdine confesses to reacting with a degree of abhorrence to the relish with which Mr Coles cheered Rocky's last-round victory, bloody and brutal.

She felt worse as he replayed the video again and again, dwelling on every detail of Rocky's triumph. She found such pleasure shameful and disgusting. However, back at the university Walkerdine replayed *Rocky II* in order to find reasons why Mr Coles might have derived the satisfaction he did from the movie. She began to look at things in a different light:

> I recognized something that took me far beyond the pseudo-sophistication of condemning its macho sexism ... The film brought me up against such memories of pain and struggle and class that it made me cry ... No longer did I stand outside the pleasures of engagement with the film. I too wanted Rocky to win. Indeed I was Rocky – struggling, fighting, crying to get out ... Rocky's struggle to become bourgeois is what reminded me of the pain of my own.

Like Rocky, Mr Coles was fighting 'against the system and for his children' and that struggle reminded Walkerdine of her own, academic struggles as a working-class child to use education 'to get out'. The difference is that one struggle is seen in physical terms, the other intellectual, but all at once, the subject of the research and the researcher find themselves in the same 'ring'.

In *Interpreting Audiences: The Ethnography of Media Consumption*[10] Shaun Moores commends Valerie Walkerdine's 'conversion' as good ethnography:

> She makes a genuine effort to see things 'from the point of view' of her subjects, paying careful attention to the interdiscursive ties that bind Mr Coles into the film fantasy. Crucial to her reconsideration of the Coles' viewing pleasures is the detour she takes into autobiography.

Another significant difference between quantitative and qualitative research is illustrated here. By its nature, quantitative research must be specific and targeted. The key to good questionnaire-design is precision: any question, or any answer, ambiguously phrased, poses problems for the analysis of data. In ethnographic research this ambiguity is an opportunity for further enquiry; for making imaginative connections between comments and situations which, on the face of it, have no relevance to the researcher's aims.

While recognizing the value of the approach of Valerie Walkerdine, and a number of other notable field researchers, and commending it

---

Researching is also about washing the pots

Over a three-year period James Lull and his team of researchers studied the viewing habits of over 200 households in California and Wisconsin. The researchers visited homes on a number of occasions and, in true ethnographic tradition, 'ate with the families, performed chores with them, played with the children and took part in group entertainment, particularly television watching'.[11] Such participant observation was essential, Lull believed, to reduce the danger of responses being influenced by the fact of watching: after a relatively short time 'the presence of the investigator in the habitat of his subjects … need not severely disrupt the natural behavior of the family unit'.

as a 'striking alternative to the traditionally neutral and "objective" stance of social scientists', Shaun Moores suggests that identification with the subjects of research must not be pushed to the point where the critical faculties of the researcher are suspended. Some measure of distance between observer and observed needs to be preserved:

> Over the coming years, I believe that the continuing task for recep-tion ethnographers will be to examine sympathetically the 'meaning systems' of others – whilst retaining a crucial space for ideological evaluation and critique.

Crucial contacts

Ethnographic research does not have to be participant. Indeed there are many strategies of information-gathering aimed at finding out how people 'make sense of their everyday surroundings and experiences', though the most important of which is traditionally the interview in one form or another. The best research employs a number of information-gathering tools – observation, questionnaires, in-depth interviews, group discussions, role-play and the examination of documents, from letters to family photo albums, all seen as offering clues to the pursuit of greater understanding; and sometimes revelation.

The American researcher Janice Radway took an engaging journey into the realm of women's reading of romance novels. She wished to find out the role such reading played in the lives of women, to what extent the romances provided antidotes to the 'real' world of marriage and families. In *Reading the Romance: Women, Patriarchy and Popular Lit-erature*,[12] Radway used in her research structured questionnaires, open-ended group discussion and in-depth, extended, interviews.

In addition she focused on a *contact*, whom she called Dot, the woman behind the bookshop counter. Dot was able to cast the light of long-term experience on the choices women made of the books they read, and their reactions to them. The more participant is research, the more it needs a 'Dot', an insider-contact. Where the researcher wish-es to gain entry into cultural communities access may rely upon this kind of sponsor, someone known in the community, trusted and whose 'friendship' can be the passport to acceptance.

Radway not only attempted to understand the fascination romance literature had for working-class women readers, she implied that such readers could, with encouragement, do better; and this judgemental approach has invited criticism. In 'The politics of feminist research:

between talk, text and action' published in the *Feminist Review*,[13] Angela McRobbie had referred to what she termed a 'recruitist' concept of the politics of feminist research and it is this incipient *recruitism* that worries Ien Ang in discussing Radway's perspective on readers of romance.

For Ang, writing in *Living Room Wars: Rethinking Media Audiences for a Postmodern World*,[14] Janice Radway's position veers towards the coercive by appearing to push her subjects into more serious reading. Ang believes that the ethnographic researcher is better advised to take up a more 'vulnerable stance', more circumspect, for 'Radway's radical intent is drawing dangerously near to a form of political moralism, propelled by a desire to make "them" more like "us"'.

Public and popular

Research during the 1980s and 1990s generally targeted two areas of media consumption. First, what John Corner has classified as 'public knowledge'.[15] This involves news and other programmes such as documentaries, dealing with information as a public commodity, and thus concerning itself with such issues as persuasion, the manipulation of information, audience comprehension and retention of messages. The other research area concerns *popular culture.*

An example of research work spanning both areas is that of Justin Lewis. In 1985 he interviewed 50 members of an audience for an ITN *News at Ten* bulletin. His findings were summarized in 'Decoding television news' in a book edited by Phillip Drummond and Richard Paterson, *Television in Transition: Papers from the First International Studies Conference.*[16] Lewis found a surprisingly large gap between the news stories as they were presented and the way audience members re-told those stories.

Having scrutinized, through empirical study, the responses to public discourse of a cross-section of people living in or near Sheffield, Lewis turned to the 'popular brief'. He conducted a study in the United States of responses to *The Cosby Show*. Much of Lewis's *The Ideological Octopus: An Exploration of Television and its Audience*[17] draws upon the insights provided by these research probes. His findings, and those of other researcher-explorers into the public and the popular, confirm the unpredictability of people and consequently the problem research faces in understanding the workings of the human mind: for example, the apparent ease with which a person can hold contradictory visions and opinions without suffering cognitive dissonance.

True, we recognize that what might be normal in the TV world is, Lewis observes, 'rather different from the normality of the world beyond it: but since we spend so much time watching TV, we are liable to lose our grip on distinctions between the two'. Lewis believes it would help if we as analysts dispensed with 'the notion that human consciousness is a rational and coherent place for thoughts to dwell'.

This is not to say that TV has less power to cultivate responses; quite the contrary, in Lewis' view. He writes of his study of the news and of *The Cosby Show* (whose dominant characteristic seems to have been its ambiguity):

> Both studies dispel two related notions. The first is the idea that television's ideological power rests upon the ability of its authors to infuse programmes with preferred meanings. The second is the notion that ambiguity reduces a programme's ideological power, passing control, instead, to the audience.

The author believes that '[t]o comprehend the power of television ... we must appreciate its influence regardless of intention and in the face of polysemy'. In other words, TV news is powerful in ways often unintended by those who produce and present it, and popular programmes, in their *apparent* unambiguity, are more influential than they might seem to be.

Blumer's five principles of research

1. Audience studies should be carried out in the direct empirical context of media use.
2. Reception should be understood against the background of individual and collective life histories which render current events and meanings intelligible.
3. Uses and effects should be seen in relationship to other influences, not as isolated phenomena.
4. The process of interpretation of meaning by audience precedes and modifies media effect.
5. Media use should be related to the use of other communication technologies.

Herbert Blumer, *Symbolic Interactionism. Perspective and Method* (US: Prentice-Hall, 1969).

'Empirical' refers to knowledge obtained through experience and Herbert Blumer is recommending that it is preferable to scrutinize audience response in the normal situation in which respondents experience media rather than placing respondents in laboratory situations. By advising that research attention is paid to 'collective histories', Blumer acknowledges the importance of shared experiences derived from the group or community to which respondents belong, and these are a product of the past as much as an indication of the present. The author stresses the importance for the researcher of examining the integrated, interactive nature of lived and mediated experience.

Approaches to research 3: focus groups

In British reception research the name of David Morley is deservedly one of the most familiar and respected. No chapter on research and research methods should fail to mention Morley's seminal work published in 1980, *The 'Nationwide' Audience*.[18] The research arose (as much of the best research and the majority of the most challenging ideas about media have done) from the Birmingham University's Centre for Contemporary Culture Studies (CCCS).

The media group of the CCCS set out to measure audience responses to the BBC's *Nationwide* evening news-magazine programme that ran during the 1970s. The study was summarized in a 1978 monograph by Charlotte Brunsdon and David Morley in *Everyday Television: 'Nationwide'*.[19] It examined the ideological connotations of the programme and its ways of addressing audience. Stage two of the research project followed up textual analysis with a qualitative survey of readers' interpretations. Morley showed a video recording of a *Nationwide* programme to 29 groups made up of people with a range of educational and professional backgrounds; following up the screening with in-depth interviewing.

The 'Nationwide' Audience examined how members of the survey groups decoded the messages they received, how they accepted, modified or rejected the programme's preferred reading of events and issues. Morley had this to say about his approach to interviewing group members:

> The initial stages of the interview were non-directive; only in subsequent stages of an interview, having attempted to establish the 'frames of reference' and 'functioning vocabulary' with which the respondents defined the situation, did I introduce questions about the programme material based on earlier analysis of it.

Non-directive questions are those that avoid giving a hint as to what answers the researcher might be expecting or wanting. They are the opposite of *leading* questions. By 'functioning vocabulary' Morley means that the terms which will be used in the research exercise will have been made clear to respondents, to ensure that everyone is, as it were, 'talking the same language'; and to help structure proceedings.

Morley's findings rejected traditional perceptions of the passivity of audiences. The indication was that audiences make up their own minds, that there is resistance to dominant discourses both between groups with common characteristics and between people within those groups. Generalizing about the response of 'professional people' or trades unionists is unreliable and hazardous. Even when the dominant discourse was accepted, read according to communicator preference, members of the audiences did not come to that position without knowing why, without relating the message to personal knowledge and experience.

Shaun Moores[10] writes of Morley:

Despite all its shortcomings....*The 'Nationwide' Audience* has justifiably come to be regarded as a landmark in the development of critical media theory and research ... [and] an important turning point at which attention began to be switched from the narrow examination of textual forms towards an empirical examination of audience engagement with texts.

Morley drew the conclusion from his findings that the TV message is:

a complex sign, in which a preferred meaning has been inscribed, but which retains the potential, if decoded in a manner different from the way it has been encoded, of communicating a different meaning.

In later work Morley unpicked some of the oversimplifications that characterize *The 'Nationwide' Audience*. For example in *Family Television* published in 1986,[20] he writes:

There is a tendency in the *Nationwide* book to think of deep structures (for instance, class positions) as generating direct effects at the level of cultural practice. This is a tendency I would want to qualify now, to examine in detail the different ways in which a given 'deep structure' works itself out in particular contexts, and reinstate the notion of persons actively engaged in cultural practice.

Morley also says in *Family Television*, affirming Herbert Blumer's First Principle of Research, that the decision to interview groups outside of their cultural or domestic contexts was something he would have changed: the response of audience to media messages should be conducted where audience normally receives those messages, usually in the home with their family or friends around them. Later research has taken this lesson to heart.

That tell-tale shotgun

In Chapter 3, reference was made to research conducted by Greg Philo that was based on audience reaction to the coverage of the miners' strike in Britain between November 1984 and February 1985. A member (and later director) of the Glasgow University Media Group, Philo used photographs of the strike as a stimulus, asking small groups of respondents to write up news stories from what they had seen. In particular there was a photograph of a shotgun lying on a table.

This proved an arresting focus, eliciting from groups attitudes which, in the main, put the striking miners in a bad light (one in tune with, and obviously influenced by, media coverage of the strike). Philo, in *Seeing & Believing: The Influence of Television*,[21] writes:

> The actual news story which it [the gun] was taken from concerned a miner, who was breaking the strike. He stated on the news that he was prepared to use the gun to defend himself. But it was apparent that in the imaginary news stories that were written, the gun was persistently being put into the hands of *striking* miners.

Philo's research findings challenge the position Morley and other researchers take up concerning the capacity of audiences to assert their own against the preferred reading of the communicators. Philo's own students in a pilot study to the actual research project that began a year after the strike was over, opted for the dominant response concerning the gun on the table. Even students of media, ever-wary of preferred readings, nevertheless seemed all too ready to associate strikers and violence.

Philo worked with groups of on average nine respondents. These were drawn from four areas of experience: groups with a special knowledge or experience of the strike, such as senior police officers and miners' and women's support group members from Yorkshire; occupational groups – solicitors' offices in London and Glasgow and electronics employees in Harlow; special interest groups – mothers and toddlers groups in Glasgow, London and Kent; and residential groups – from southwest England, Bromley and Beckenham in Kent and Shenfield in Essex.

The groups were asked to write a typical BBC news bulletin based upon 12 pictures of the strike, including the gun on the table; and then they were asked a series of questions, such as (Question 1): 'When you first saw the picture of the gun, who did you think it belonged to?' Question 2 raised the matter of audience perception of the objectivity of BBC news: 'Does the BBC news have a point of view? Does it, for example, favour one political party over another, or is it neutral? Is it biased, unbiased, pro-establishment, anti-establishment, accurate, impartial? How would you describe it?'

As with most research, especially of the imaginatively and innovatively designed sort, this project came up with a number of unexpected findings, not the least the quality of the news content which groups produced and the clarity of recall of the incidents of the strike. Philo's conclusions give weight to the case that television has powerful effects; for example, its power to instil in viewers patterns of association:

> There was remarkable unanimity of belief amongst the groups in this sample about what had actually been shown. In the general sample, 98 per cent believed that most picketing which they had seen on television news was violent ... most remarkable is the number of people who believed that these television images represented the everyday life of picketing.

The source for these beliefs says Philo 'was overwhelmingly given as television and the press, with the emphasis on TV, because of its immediate and more dramatic quality'.

The degree of acceptance of the television image, the degree to which associations, between shotguns and striking miners, between picket lines and violence nevertheless 'depends very much on what beliefs, experience, and information' the audience 'bring to what they are shown'. Equally important was whether, as Philo puts it, people have a 'critique of television latent in their beliefs'.

It is a revealing point, for in some cases it was only when respondents were pressed on an issue that the latent critique emerged. Without being pressed, respondents were in danger of taking images at their face value; a case of a message 'being absorbed in spite of other beliefs which were held'. Philo contends, following a stronger line over effects than David Morley, that 'where no critical view of television exists, the likelihood of accepting its account may be very great'.

Factors of acceptance/rejection

Research work such as that of Greg Philo and the Glasgow University Media Group often crystallizes into theory, or at least route markers. In *Message Received: Glasgow Media Group Research 1993–1998* (UK: Longman, 1999), edited by Philo, acceptance/rejection of media messages is seen to depend on three primary factors:

- Direct experience of events on the part of audience.
- The use of logic – the ability to work things out and mobilize critical faculties.
- Cultural affinities and value systems.

Measuring response to TV's portrayal of incest

Another member of the Glasgow University Media Group, Lesley Henderson, was given the task by Channel 4 Television of gauging audience response to the portrayal of incest on the British soap opera, *Brookside*. For a brief summary of her findings, see Chapter 6. Here it is only necessary to commend to readers Henderson's research methodology, reported in *Incest in Brookside: Audience Responses to the Jordache Story*.[22]

Twelve discussion groups made up of 69 participants aged between 13 and 66 were selected from people living in the west of Scotland. The groups were pre-existing, that is the 'participants knew each other prior to the research sessions'. Lesley Henderson writes:

> This facilitated a relaxed session which was crucial given the sensitivity of the topic. It also allowed for the preservation of some of the elements of the social culture within which people discuss television, that is, with their work colleagues and friends.

Three of the groups were formed according to 'special interest' – social workers, representatives from women's organizations and teenage sexual abuse survivors. The remaining nine groups were drawn from the 'general population':

> Each session included approximately eight people, although the size of the groups ranged between three and ten. Sessions were moderated by the author and took place in schools, youth club centres, work places and participants' homes. The sessions lasted up to two hours and were all tape-recorded and then transcribed and analysed.

Sessions began with a general questionnaire about TV viewing habits, with the key question, 'Should child sexual abuse be portrayed in fictional television?':

> The group then divided into two or more subgroups and was invited to engage in a script-writing exercise. This involved giving them a set of still photographs taken from a key scene in *Brookside's* storyline and invited to write matching dialogue. The group returned to discuss these scripts, the handling of specific characters and to debate the inclusion of such an issue in TV drama.

Difference in audience decodings

Focus groups were used to particularly interesting effect by Tamar Liebes and Elihu Katz who summarize their findings in *The Export of Meaning: Cross-cultural Readings of* Dallas.[23] Their remit was to survey differences in reading the American soap opera *Dallas* between cultural sub-groups in Israel and also viewer groups in the United States and Japan (where *Dallas* had proved unpopular with audiences). Forty groups of three married couples, of similar age, education and ethnicity were selected from Israel Arabs, newly-arrived Russian Jews, veteran Moroccan settlers and members of kibbutzim. These were matched by ten groups of second-generation Americans in the Los Angeles area.

Later, eleven Japanese groups were selected and interviewed. The authors' findings give strength to the theory that an audience's cultural experience and expectations deeply influence the way texts are read and interpreted. The divergences of reading, of critical focus on varying aspects of the soap – of 'variations in decodings, involvements, uses and effects' – seemed to indicate that media texts are seen through the prism of cultural context; and their meanings are the result of negotiation arising from interactive responses. In unison with Greg Philo, Liebes and Katz speak of the 'fruitfulness of asking viewers to be critics'.

Different formats, varied responses

Response to media messages is inevitably linked to the ways those messages are communicated, to their narrative formats: change the format, research indicates, and you modify the response. This principle is well illustrated by a research project, *UK News Access*, funded by Bath Spa University College and conducted by Simon Cottle.

The results of this research are briefly summarized in Cottle's chapter 'Television news and citizenship: packaging the public sphere' in *No News is Bad News: Radio Television and the Public.*[24] Cottle examines the different formats of news, eliciting patterns of what he terms *containment* as contrasted with *participation*. The spectrum or hierarchy of formats ranges from the 'restrictive' to the 'expansive', from the presentational format of the Newscaster only (Format 1) to the Live group interview (Format 9).

Cottle identifies ten variations. Formats 1 to 5 are those most commonly used in traditional TV news broadcasts. They provide 'severely restricted opportunities' for audience to match the preferred reading with their own personal reading of, and involvement in, the news-transmitting/news-reception process. Cottle says:

> Nearly half of all TV news items ... provide few if any opportunities for direct access and discursive engagement by non-news voices, and such voices that are referenced remain the discursive prisoners of the news presenters and their informing news frame.

By discursive engagement, Cottle means the capacity on the part of audience to be involved in the news interpretatively. Certain formats of presentation counteract what Cottle terms an 'interpretative vacuum'. For example, live interviews with the public (Format 8) and live group interviews (Format 9) 'considerably improve upon the restricted and limited opportunities' presented by tighter formats:

> Live interviews afford interviewees an 'extended' opportunity to respond to the interviewer's questions, in their own terms, in chronological time, and in the ways that they feel are appropriate. They may even, on occasion, seek to challenge the interviewer's agenda and informing assumptions, and agenda-shift to different issues and interpretative frameworks and in so doing fracture the imposition of a particular news frame.

Readers may recall Roland Barthes' differentiation between the *work*, that which is produced by the communicator (in this case, the news) and the *text*, that which is decoded by audience. Cottle is suggesting that news production is often reluctant to let go of the work by opting for tight, closed, narrative frames. Consequently as 'opportunities of access' and 'discursive contestation' are disabled, 'cultural citizenship'[25] is put at risk.

The recognition of pleasure

Throughout the last quarter of the 20th century the importance of the relationship between fictions and audiences had been fully recognized by researchers. Do soaps, for example, reach those parts, like Heineken lager, not reached by other message-carriers? Considering also that soaps are claimed to be watched more by women than men, how do women react; how are they affected; do such programmes empower or do they ensnare by stereotyping?

As we have seen, at the core of the study of media is the process of *representation* and the ways in which the media represent the world provide fertile grounds for investigation. Programmes that at one time were classified as 'mere entertainment' are now given serious research attention. How, researchers in the 1980s and 1990s asked, is social class represented in popular TV fare such as soaps; to what extent are feminist issues addressed? The experience of *pleasure*, and of *popular* pleasure in particular, was brought out of the margins on to centre-stage as a target of research.

Taking pleasure was not seen as being another manifestation of the 'imposition' of preferred meanings; quite the contrary: taking pleasure was potentially liberating. This point was made as early as 1982 when Dorothy Hobson in *'Crossroads': The Drama of a Soap*[26] expressed concern that such an immensely popular series, especially among women, was consistently derided by critics; put down as worthless entertainment.

Hobson paid refreshing respect not only to popular fiction but more importantly to the audience for that fiction. She found *Crossroads* to be a 'progressive' text, raising, as do most other soaps, problems and issues seen by women to be part of their everyday lives. The soap was revived on UK television in the spring of 2001 but failed to win sufficient audience support to guarantee its survival.

Respecting the popular

Writing in *Watching 'Dallas'*,[1] published three years after *'Crossroads'*, Ien Ang, like Dorothy Hobson, considered women's responses to the soap a potential source of liberation – 'from the chafing bonds' of the pressures of everyday life. At the same time she recognized how the significance of pleasure had been underestimated; indeed until this time soaps had largely been dismissed *because* they appeared to aspire to nothing beyond entertainment.

Ang identified two contrasting ideological standpoints. The *ideology of mass culture* perceives that which is popular as being somehow harmful, damaging to higher order aspirations. In contrast, the *ideology of populism* recognizes the importance of pleasure and that it is a personal thing. It can be a stimulus to self-and-other awareness.

It is regarded by those who experience it as something to be relished because it has been earned. What researchers need to clarify is what degree of *reprocessing* of popular messages goes on in the minds of audience; what measure of interactivity exists between the popular and the 'serious'; in short to examine the numerous 'hunch' theories concerning notions of dumbing-down and ill-effects in the light of evidence.

Researching audience use of media technology

Considerable interest has been shown by researchers in the use, within the home, of media technology. Initially, this interest accelerated with the introduction of the video recorder. All at once we as audience were no longer dependent upon the schedules of the TV companies: we could even ignore these altogether and play recordings; and if we possessed a video camera we could entertain ourselves with our own creations.

Not only could we schedule our own viewing through the recording facility of the VCR (and later DVD recorder), we acquired a measure of control over time itself: we were enabled to fast-forward (skip the 'boring' bits or the adverts) and better negotiate viewing habits with those around us: you watch your programme while I record mine on another channel.

British researcher Ann Gray conducted in-depth conversations with 30 Yorkshire women about their use of the VCR during the mid-1980s and her findings were published in *Video Playtime*.[27] Like David Morley, Gray was interested in issues such as gender, the division of labour in the home, the role of leisure and the power relations exercised in family units; her theme, technology as being *socially situated.*

Gray found her subjects talking about more than their use of VCRs. Initially she wondered whether chit-chat that had nothing to do with video use had anything to contribute to her research. In fact she realized, on listening to recorded tapes of her interviews, that the prevalent 'storytelling' that characterized the women's responses to and divergences from her questions proved to be a means by which those questions were re-interpreted in a meaningful sense for the subjects themselves.

Ann Gray borrowed a colour-coding device employed by Cynthia Cockburn in research for her book *Machinery of Dominance: Women, Men and Technical Know-How*.[28] Gray ascribed the colour blue to items of technology, from kitchen to tool shed, perceived to be 'masculine' and pink to items thought to be 'feminine'. This approach, she writes:

> produces almost uniformly pink irons and blue electric drills, with many interesting mixtures along the spectrum... my research has shown that we must break down the VCR into its different modes in our colour-coding. The 'record' 'rewind' and 'play' modes are usu- ally lilac, but the timer switch is nearly always blue, with the women having to depend on their male partners or their children to set the timer for them.

Gray found in many of her respondents a sense of inadequacy concern- ing their use of equipment and this was linked to self-deprecation, of respondents running themselves down. She quotes Edna as saying, 'Oh no, I haven't a clue, no. If there's anything I want recording I ask one of the boys to do it for me. This is sheer laziness, I must admit, because I don't read the instructions'.

The sense of inadequacy Gray found among her sample of respon- dents links with one of Dorothy Hobson's findings with regard to women watching *Crossroads*: they seemed to feel they had to apologize for the pleasure they gained from watching the soap. This is not to say that Ann Gray found her respondents naive as well as apologetic. Rather she identified a strategy among her respondents that she called 'calculated ignorance'. Edna, asked about working the VCR timer in future, says:

> I'm not going to try, no. Once I learnt how to put a plug on, now there's nobody else puts a plug on in this house but me... so [*laughs*] there's method in my madness, Oh yes.

Ignorance, then, is a defence strategy against exploitation. What Edna seemed to be doing was resisting having 'blue' objects turned into 'pink' ones. It would appear that the colour to aim for in the use of the VCR, was lilac: that is, equality.

The HICT Project

The 1990s saw increased research interest in the notion of 'technology-as-text' or as British researcher Roger Silverstone put it, 'There is meaning in the texts of both hardware and software'.[29] Silverstone, along with several other well-known contributors to the field – David Morley, Sonia Livingstone, Andrea Dahlberg and Eric Hirsch – was involved in a major and ongoing enquiry into 'The Household Uses of Information and Communication Technologies' (HICT).

This investigation receives a warm commendation from Shaun Moores in *Interpreting Audiences*[10] 'because of its commitment to looking at a collection of objects in the household media environment, its efforts to elaborate an overall conceptual model for exploring the role of information and communication technologies in home life' and for its 'concern to develop a "methodological raft" for empirical research on domestic cultures'.

Such has been the enormity of the data collected that the results of the enquiry have only partially been published. However, out of data collection have emerged theoretical perspectives. For example, Silverstone along with Morley and Hirsch, speaks of a 'moral economy' that operates within the culture of the family. In a chapter, 'Information and communication technologies and the moral economy of the household' in *Consuming Technologies: Media and Information in Domestic Spaces*,[30] the authors identify four constituents of the 'moral economy'.

Firstly there is the process of *appropriation*: technology, once it crosses the threshold from shop to home, becomes a belonging (even part of the family) whose use soon reflects the relationships of those who use it, not the least the power-bases for use (who, for example, is or is not allowed to 'touch it'). At the same time, the next two constituents are in place: *objectification* and *incorporation*.

Objectification refers to display in the home, where and how the items of communication technology are arranged in relationship to other domestic objects (pride of place or tucked away in a corner). Incorporation involves the actual patterns of use of the technology and the part the technology plays in the family's day-to-day activities.

So far what has happened is that the technology has been absorbed into an environment whose perspectives are essentially domestic, inward-gazing. The fourth constituent of use is *conversion*, where the actors in this techno-drama turn from their private world to the world beyond the household. That which is cultivated in the private domain, for example knowledge or experiences derived from TV (and latterly the Internet), is 'traded in' beyond the front door as 'coin of exchange' in social interactions at the workplace, the club or pub or even in the polling booth. The authors give the example of a teenager employing his skill at computer games, developed in the home environment, as a 'ticket' of entry into peer culture.

The opportunities for research into the uses of media technology have dramatically increased as Net communication has become commonplace; while definitions of 'domestic use' have had to be re-drawn as a result of the widespread shift towards individual rather than group viewing and the massive growth in computer ownership.

The Internet as a research tool

The Internet, with its hand-held genie, the mobile phone, offers the user seemingly untold research possibilities. Out there is a vast, exponentially increasing and instantly available store of information that might, on the face of it, threaten to tip books and libraries into oblivion. In addition, users can key into communities of interest, establishing fruitful contact and, crucially, interactivity.

I can obtain information from the Net about my own contexts, local, regional or national, when other sources are closed to me either through regulation or bureaucratic decision. They are dumping some sort of toxic waste just down the road – is it dangerous? At the council offices, they're cagey. I tune into the Net, give the details of the waste. Someone somewhere will be able to identify it or direct me to where I can find the data I want; and somewhere too there will be a group of protesters who have had similar toxins dumped outside their door.

Students of media communication, concerned as they are for most of their work with developments and issues that are recent and increasingly global in significance, can use the Net to find the very latest information and comment. Once under way, research brings feedback and interaction.

A group of my own students, preparing a survey of the media in Romania, established direct contact with Romanian journalists online; out of one such contact a friendship developed whose value proved both academic and personal, extending well beyond the timescale of the course assignment.

The Net encourages interactivity and it provides specificity: you wish to look up an exact item within a particular field of information; the dictionaries and reference books have given you a modest start but to acquire the amount of information you need you would have to search many volumes, some of them either difficult or impossible to obtain; and always there is the critical timelag: you have a deadline to meet.

Your problem might not be scarcity of information but too much of it. Where do you start and how do you reduce the vast range of information available to the specific requirements of your research task? Specificity in each case is the key. You may not require, for example, access to the whole gamut of research findings on the perceived effects of screen violence on audience. Rather your interest may orientate towards particular types of violence and modes of their portrayal in relation to segments of audience. By being fed with key words, the computer does our selecting for us and at a speed unmatched by any other research method.

'Digital soup'

Tim Miller in an article 'The data-base revolution' in the *Columbia Journal Review*[31] cites an example of the advantage the database has over a publication:

> Take for example, *Who's Who in America*. In the print version each word in the two volume set is bound to one place only on a sheet of paper; the 75,000 biographies are arranged alphabetically. Thus we can find Caspar Weinburger in the Ws. In the computerized version, by way of contrast, each word swims in a digital soup ready to be dipped out in accordance with almost any criterion the researcher wants to specify.'

'Digital soup' is one of the more memorable metaphors to be found in the lexicon of network communication. Miller goes on to prove the point of specificity:

> …last year, when librarians at the *San Francisco Chronicle* wanted to find members of the secretive, men-only Bohemian Club, they went to the on-line version of *Who's Who* offered by Dialog Information Services, a vendor of more than 300 data bases. Within seconds the computer located the word 'Bohemian' each time it appeared in an entry. Among the club members found: Secretary of Defense Caspar Weinburger. A Search of this kind in the print version of *Who's Who* would have taken a reporter approximately eight years, not counting coffee breaks.

Sometimes of course specificity is not necessarily the key to research. The Net's facility for providing bulletin boards allows researchers to put out general calls for help and assistance. Two of my own students set out to investigate the press in Kenya. They soon discovered the predominant ethnocentricity of libraries and traditional databases. Information on our own press is vast but on that of Africa as a whole it was found to be meagre and largely out of date. An SOS on the Net prompted informed correspondents to make contact, including a Kenyan journalist.

It is not only the abundance of available information that can threaten to be overwhelming, but its diversity. Tom Koch in *Journalism for the 21st Century: On-line Information, Electronic Databases and the News*[32] summarizes how the formidable can become manageable:

To search only newspapers for stories on, say, addiction and habituation would, using traditional methods, require months. To absorb the technical literature on the causes of drug abuse might require weeks. The legal issues involved would demand weeks more for those unused to the very specific bibliographic system used in traditional law libraries. The mass of potential data is overwhelming. But the fears of some that computerized information would merely overwhelm the writer with extraneous information have been balanced by the system's inherent capability to tailor information retrieval to very specific requests.

For the student of media, and for the student of media with an eye on a professional future in journalism, this 'inherent capability' may be seen as a vital feature in the accessing and management of information. The online mode potentially liberates the researcher from traditional – usually restricted and often highly controlled – sources of information, while at the same time offering a plurality of sources manageable through specificity.

Issues of source

Before we celebrate the Net as the answer to all our research needs it is important to take account of its 'downside'. First, how *reliable* is Net-provided information; is it as *comprehensive* as we would like it to be? 'Digital soup' may be a memorable metaphor, but being 'in the soup' is an experience familiar to most of us. For example, many of our enquiries will find themselves directed towards the world's biggest online encyclopaedia, Wikipedia, created by Jimmy Wales in January 2001. This is a text not only open to contributors and (on the face of it) requiring no prior vetting, its entries are constantly subject to re-writing, alteration, addition and subtraction. As one might expect, such freedom has led to cases of abuse. Yet at the same time the reader cannot help but be impressed by the seriousness and care with which most – anonymous – contributors, for no payment, have penned their entries.

The researcher is advised to emulate one of the key principles of journalistic practice: never rely on information from a single source. This same advice should apply to the *mode* of information provision. Years ago I used to urge students, in preparing tasks, to broaden their researches from books and periodicals to the Internet. More recently, my advice has worked in reverse: too often students are relying entirely on information gleaned from the Net and giving short shrift to material in print.

Only so far

As we have seen, specificity is the prime virtue of Net research; but it is a very mechanistic specificity – that is, it does the sorting for you, but not the thinking. To illustrate the point, I typed into my Google box the following: *Academic research of the net advantages and disadvantages.* In 0.36 of a second Google announced access to 1,010,000 items.

On page one, I spotted a useful starter: *Advantages and disadvantages of internet research surveys – evidence from the literature.* There were two small problems, first I had to sign in, second, the material dated back to 2002. On the same page I was offered *Professional ethics, the advantages and disadvantages of a code of ethics*, at least on the face of it nothing to do with my particular quest. Inevitably one begins to doubt the value of tracking through scores if not hundreds of further items, not really knowing at what point those items will prove valuable; and, critically, whether they will carry you deeper into the subject.

If I can't remember the name of the director of a film I want to show, the Net suits my purpose swiftly and perfectly, filling me with a moment's relief. If I really wish to dig in to a subject, examine in informed detail or even get the very latest thinking on that subject, the surfing can lead me into choppy water; and it is with more than a moment's relief that I head for a well-stocked library.

Researching network communication

Paradoxically some of the best advice on using the Net as a research tool is to be found in old-fashioned book form. *Doing Internet Research: Critical Issues and Methods for Examining the Net*,[33] edited by Steve Jones, sets out in 13 chapters and 299 pages to establish principles and best practice. In Chapter 7, 'From paper-and-pencil to screen-and-keyboard: toward a methodology for survey research on the Internet', Diane F. Witmer, Robert W. Colman and Sandra Lee Katzman write of 'the exponential growth of electronic communication and its potential for democracy, culture, and workplace productivity' that is 'drawing keen interest from researchers in both industry and academia'. Topics of major Net inquiry include:

- how technology is adopted
- its role in creating culture and community
- online work and play
- group dynamics in the computer-mediated environment, and
- interpersonal relationships.

Research enterprises on and about the Net have proliferated in recent years to cover all of the above themes, and more. An early example of findings arising from Net-research is worth quoting here as it illustrates the gap between the facility of interactivity and the wariness with which it is often employed.

Jennifer Stromer-Galley conducted a scrutiny of the websites of American politicians, with a particular focus on their capacity for interaction with the public. Her findings were summarized in 'On-line interaction and why politicians avoid it' published in the *Journal of Communication*.[34] In 1996 Stromer-Galley did a preliminary study of the websites of presidential candidates Bill Clinton and Bob Dole; following this up in September 1998 with an examination of websites of gubernatorial candidates in ten states.

Prior to the primary elections in Minnesota and Maryland, she sent e-mails to candidates seeking clarification on three issues – crime, school vouchers and taxes. Only eight out of a possible 20 election candidates responded. It would seem that politicians, despite their celebration of the inter-communicative capacity of the Internet, were at that time not overanxious to use it. Stromer-Galley explains:

Human interactive channels on the Internet are not utilized by candidates for at least three reasons: they are burdensome to the campaign, candidates risk losing control of the communications environment, and they can no longer provide ambiguous campaign discourses.

The meaning, to put it more simply, was – they couldn't waffle. In this case, says the author, 'An interactive forum such as a public bulletin board could create an environment in which people would ask specific questions of candidates and make comments criticizing a position or action'. Such a possibility did not seem to candidates to be a factor that might enhance their ability to be elected.

Summarizing her findings, Stromer-Galley says, 'The possibility of citizens engaging in discussion of any kind (deliberative or otherwise) with political candidates on-line or with other citizens on a candidate's website appear risky, burdensome and problematic'. It would be an interesting piece of research for media students to run a similar survey of their national or local politicians to find out whether electioneering has caught up with networking possibilities.

Exploring 'keitai culture'

Research interest in Net communication has extended to the use of the mobile phone. Referred to as a 'gismo nation', Japan has led the field in the use of the mobile phone or 'keitai' (roughly meaning 'something you carry with you'); and fittingly Japanese researchers have produced interesting results from the study of keitai culture.

Mizuko Ito and her fellow researchers, Daisuke Okabe and Misa Matsuda have investigated the nature and patterns of use of the keitai by Japanese children and youth. The subjects of their research studies kept communication diaries of their message exchanges. These are analyzed in *Personal, Portable, Pedestrian: Mobile Phones in Japanese Life*[35] which also contains a range of useful essays from other contributors in the field.

Ito, in a japanfocus web posting, 'Personal portable pedestrian: lessons from Japanese phone use'[36] writes:

In our ethnographic studies of mobile phone use, we found that the personal dimension of the mobile phone was a central characteristic that structured usage patterns ... Much of the exchange between couples was 'sweet nothings' that functioned to affirm their connection with each other rather than explicit acts of communication... This steady stream of text exchange punctuated by voice-calls and face-to-face meetings, define a kind of 'telenesting' practice that young people engage in, where the personal medium of the mobile phone becomes the glue cementing a space of shared intimacy.

In this sense, the culture of constant social connection, seamlessly integrated into everyday life is seen to contrast with what the authors of *Personal, Portable, Pedestrian* consider the more escapist character of Internet use. The *pedestrian* element of their reading of mobile use refers to the generally commonplace content of messages, but also they see the 'street level presence' of the keitai as neatly fitting in to 'pedestrian urban ecologies'.

The exploration of mobile use highlights key features such as the multi-tasking capacity of young people: 'to read while watching TV, to eat while walking... to use the mobile phone while walking or biking'. Research attention has further centred on the use of the mobile to take photographs. Says Ito, mobile phone pictures 'are often of the more fleeting and mundane moments of everyday life – a cake that looked good at a café, an interesting but everyday scene or viewpoint, or a sudden moment of cute kid or pet activity'.

The author refers to these photo-snaps and the sweet nothings exchanges as 'brief attentional interludes uniquely characteristic of the role of portable technologies in Japanese life', and, with little doubt, in

The shrinking Net

Blogger Richard MacManus conducted a useful research exercise into trends in online traffic, and found that, while websites had increased exponentially in number (by 75% between 2001 and 2006), the *use* of websites had narrowed. By the end of 2001 the top ten websites took 31% of hits. By the end of 2006 the figure was 40% of page views. MacManus believed this convergence was due to the growth of social networks such as Facebook, MySpace and Bebo. In 2001, MySpace did not exist, but by 2006 it had cornered 16% of Net traffic. Evidence thus suggests that convergence of ownership in mass media generally is being replicated in cyberspace.[37]

the life of communities of the young wherever there is keitai access. In its publicity for *Personal, Portable, Pedestrian* the MIT Press quotes a comment by Roger Silverstone, architect of the HICT project:

> Reaching beyond Japan and beyond the mobile phone, the book provides a theoretically rich and empirically sophisticated template for all future work that seeks to understand the nature of socio-technical change in personal communications.

Segmentation: the marketplace approach

While academic researchers and commentators were tardy in acknowledging the significance of pleasure-taking in media consumption, market researchers have always had this at the forefront of their enquiries. Seeking to please is the goal; knowing how to please is half the problem: the other half is knowing how to go on pleasing. In order to do this, market research must above all things seek to know and understand its audience.

A primary strategy is segmentation, that is, dividing up the consumer population into those most likely, those potentially likely and those unlikely to consume what has been produced for them. Once segmented into groups, defined by class, age, gender or according to our purchasing power and lifestyle, we are treated as segments, encouraged to think and behave in the ways we have been defined as thinking and behaving. What we are perceived to be, we are intended to become. The more this happens, the more, arguably, George Gerbner's cultivation theory has relevance (see Chapter 3).

After all, the advertising industry is the giant among the pigmies in terms of investment in audience research: research findings are turned to account, used to shape and influence. If consumerism has its way, we will come to recognize ourselves by identifying with the images the spin-doctors have created to reflect and entice us. We are Mainstreamers perhaps, governed by a need for security; Aspirers (seeking status); Succeeders (desiring control); or even Reformers (dedicated to the quality of life).[38] In the United States, subject to the segmentation strategies of, for example, PRIZM (Potential Rating Index by Zip Market), we might find ourselves classified under 'Pools and Patios' or 'Bohemian Mix'.

If we were being segmented according to 'Needham Harper World-wide', a classification that in America divided over 3000 respondents into ten lifestyle groups, men might find themselves labelled as 'Herman the retiring homebody' or 'Dale the devoted family man'. Women can look to be classified as 'Eleanor the elegant socialite' or 'Mildred the militant mother'. Should you fail to recognize yourself in the categories, you may suspect there is something wrong – with yourself; so you must try harder. There seems to be no category for Debbie or Derek, the debt-ridden students.

Segmenting by VALS

Perhaps the best-known classification of communities-as-consumers is VALS – Values and Lifestyles. Arnold Mitchell and a team of researcher colleagues, sponsored by SRI International, published in 1983 the findings of large-scale, quantitative research in *The Nine American Lifestyles*.[39] For the researchers, lifestyle was a 'unique way of life defined by its distinctive array of values, drives, beliefs, needs, dreams, and special points of view'.

The VALS scheme linked values and lifestyles to choices, tastes and patterns of consumer spending. It examined the interaction between person, context and ideology. Each works on the others and is influenced by the others in a process subject to fluctuation and change. What is fashionable today, what boosts self-image, what is 'cool', what impresses society and sells in the marketplace is, for tomorrow, fit only for boot sales.

Of the nine segments of the consumerist population examined by Mitchell, the largest – 35% of the whole – and consequently the one that would matter most to the adworld, was named the Belonger. The equivalent of the British categorization of the Mainstreamer, the Belonger was (and probably still is) generally middle-class, middle-aged and concerned with security. While VALS' chief aim was to assist in the process of 'matching product to producer' it has obviously played a significant part in matching voters to policies, electorates to presidents and prime ministers.

Keeping up with the Satos

Researching differences in order to categorize is not just a commanding force in the West. The Hakuhodo Institute of Life and Living in Japan produced its own six-segment market typology of consumers:[40]

Crystal Tribe (attracted to famous brands)
My Home Tribe (family-orientated)
Leisure Life Tribe
Gourmandism Tribe (tempted by gluttony)
Ordinary People Tribe
Impulse Buyer Tribe

The Hakuhodo Institute shares with VALS, and indeed with the advertising industry wherever it operates, the belief that what is sold is not products but *self*. What is purchased is not hardware or services but *image*. Indeed in the Introduction to its research the Hakuhodo Institute speaks of 'life designer' as being a preferable term to 'consumer'.

Reference is made to 'hitonami consciousness', *hitonami* meaning 'aligning oneself with other people' which, rendered in consumerist terms, indicates a desire to 'keep up with the Satos'; in other words, social conformity. However, the Institute detected trends similar to those manifested in the West – away from conformity towards the need to express individuality.

What research across the affluent regions of the world seems to indicate, at least tentatively, is a *convergence* of attitudes and lifestyles. In the light of such trends, Hakuhodo produced a new typology:

The Good Old Japanese
The Silent Majority
The Confident Middle Class
The Style-Orientated Japanese
The Do-it-my-way Japanese
The Confident Theoreticians

The problem with market research is its selectivity, its focus largely on paying customers. The VALS scheme identified the Need-Driven (that is, the poorest in the community) as 11% of the population of the United States in the 1980s. However, in global terms, the Need-Driven are arguably in a majority. While in the better-off countries consumerist values can find fulfilment, in the Third World all that is often permitted the Need-Driven population are images of affluence, of the Gourmandism Tribe, of lifestyles alluring yet out of reach. Information on how such people respond to the affluence of other, what they make of such second-hand experiences, is thin on the ground; yet it ought to be an area of critical research for the future.

Ultimately segmentation ends up as just another exercise in stereotyping. Its character portrayal may often be picturesque, but the process of identification by type chases change rather than initiates it, rarely catching up with what Anthony Giddens in *Modernity and Self-Identity: Self and Society in the Late Modern Age*[41] has termed the 'pluralization of lifeworlds' requiring the individual to act out, over time, a number of identities.

Convergence of research approaches

Let us briefly return to current trends in academic research. Over the years scholars have recognized that research needs to take in all aspects of production, texts and audience responses. To focus only on one feature is to risk forfeiting discoveries about the interaction between them and with forces outside the media production/media consumption process. Whether we are researching or analyzing we need to recognize the *co-orientational* nature of these, the 'big three' (see Figure 10.1). Each element of the model acts in recognition of its relationship with the others, feeding forward and feeding back in a process of constant interaction. This was acknowledged by members of the Glasgow University Media Group, traditionally so closely associated with focusing on production and text to the exclusion of response.

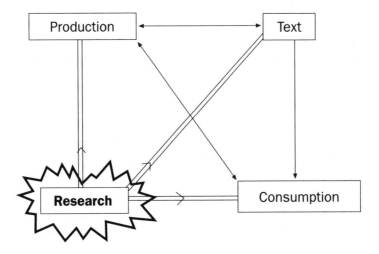

Figure 10.1 Research as co-orientation

In 1993 the Group produced a reader edited by John Eldridge, *Getting the Message: News, Truth and Power*.[42] Significantly, in the concluding chapter of the book, 'Whose illusion? Whose reality? Some problems of theory and method in mass media research', Eldridge indicates that emphasis on media production, focusing on the communicator's end of the process – what the Glasgow Group has been famous for – is not enough. Such research data needs to be analyzed in relation to documentation concerning reception, which must be investigative, critical and educational; meaning proactive, with a job to do.

It must be work that displays 'to viewers and readers and listeners the possibilities for highlighting perspectives, checking codes and interpreting messages' and places an emphasis upon 'a coping strategy of resistance to mass media'. Yet again we see research as having goals beyond those of record, where discovery is an initial step towards the possibilities of change.

Somewhere in the middle of our model, shifting, turning, forming, reshaping according to dynamics influenced by culture, class, economics, politics and new technology is *meaning*, or rather a space – an agora – in which meaning is asserted, negotiated or rejected. What the researcher is doing is attempting to go beyond common sense, to identify the ideologies that rule the dominant discourses and to measure the degree to which people absorb these, question, reject or re-form them to serve their own ends.

In particular, student researchers – readers of this book, perhaps – have much to do in terms of measuring the uneven access to TV of *minorities*, the often questionable textual representation of these minorities and the response of minorities within the audience to such representations.

Larry Gross points out in an article on the place of sexual minorities in the mass media in *Remote Control: Television, Audiences & Cultural Power*,[43] that those elites in society who define the public agenda 'are (mostly) white, (mostly) middle-aged, (mostly) male, (mostly) middle and upper class, and entirely heterosexual (at least in public)'. In the Introduction to *Remote Control*, Ellen Seiter and her co-editors say that the aim of empirical audience research should be to incorporate the perspectives of people of colour, of the elderly, gays and lesbians, women and the poor – those whose voices have not been heard in media research so far, and who do not constitute the desirable demographic groups targeted by advertisers – into the study of the media in society and the development of alternative media.

In this way the work of the researcher promises to make the invisibles visible and help create for them a *constituency* in which those marginalized by labelling, stereotyping or demonization may come to be more fairly and more understandingly represented.

Research as authentication: the picture that didn't lie

THE NOTORIOUS WAR PHOTOGRAPH THEY SAID WAS A FAKE... was the headline of an article in the UK Sunday *Observer*[44] by Rita Grosvenor and Arnold Kemp. It referred to perhaps the most famous and the most controversial war photograph in history – Robert Capa's *Spain's Falling Soldier* (see Figure 10.2).

Against a bare hillside and a featureless sky a republican soldier is hurled back by the force of the bullet that kills him. His right arm is flung outwards, his rifle slipping from his grasp. Legs buckle, neck jerks partially sideways: for him, the last moment of life, but for the photographer, a supreme moment of truth. So supreme, in fact, that critics have doubted the authenticity of Capa's picture, suggesting that the incident may have been staged for the benefit of the camera, thus casting a shadow over the reputation of one of the 20th century's foremost war photographers.

Figure 10.2   'Spain's Falling Soldier': piecing together the evidence

Capa was blown up by a mine in 1954 while he was covering the Vietnam War. Painstaking research may prove to have extinguished the shadow from Capa's reputation. Just as amateur archeologists have occasionally dug up pots of gold, so amateur researchers have 'excavated' vital evidence that challenges prevailing 'truths'.

The story of the photograph that has come to encapsulate the poignancy and tragedy of the Spanish Civil War (1936–39) was given new clarity and resonance as a result of evidence painstakingly assembled over many years by an amateur sleuth. At the age of 14, Mario Brotons was fighting in the Civil War. He was present at the same time as Capa in the Cerro Muriano front near Cordoba in September 1936.

Later in life, Brotons became haunted by Capa's picture. He felt sure he recognized the picture's terrain and the dress (not uniform) of the dying soldier – open-necked shirt and light-coloured trousers. Brotons was convinced that this soldier was a miner from Linares in Andalucia, in particular one of the 300 militiamen of the Alcoy contingent, recognisable from the cartridge belts and harnesses they wore, hand made by local leather craftsmen to the garrison commander's special design.

Brotons identified the Falling Soldier as Federico Borrell Garcia, a 24-year-old millworker from the town of Alcoy (Brotons' home town), recorded dead on 5 September 1936. Though archives in Madrid and Salamanca state that many militiamen had been wounded on the Cerro Muriana front that day, each registered only one dead – that of Federico Borrell (maternal surname, Garcia).

Questioned about the soldier in Capa's photograph, 78-year-old Maria, widow of Everisto, Federico's younger brother, confirmed that the man in Capa's picture was her dead brother-in-law: 'I knew him well.'

Sadly, Mario Brotons died in 1996 before he could publicize his discovery, though he left behind him copious documentation that was given headline treatment in the *Observer* and duly honoured in the Imperial War Museum's Spanish Civil War exhibition, *Dreams and Nightmares* (2001–2).

As this chapter has argued, and as Brotons' painstaking investigation shows, research is exploration and detective work. It demands skill in reading the signs, both present and past. Just occasionally research resembles archeology that breaks the Code of Enigma, in Brotons' case going a long way towards authenticating a unique action in a unique moment that created a media text of timeless and universal significance.

Summary

This chapter has presented an overview of landmarks in media research, detailing the differing perspectives and approaches of academic and of commercial enquiry. All research can be seen to be instrumental in purpose. Market research wishes to find out what audiences like now so that what is served up to them in future will prompt equal interest. Scholarly research has other aims, first to gain understanding, ideally to cast illumination on the path towards the unattainable – the whole truth; secondly to draw the attention of others to such illumination.

Three modes of academic research are discussed here – content analysis, participant observation or the ethnographic approach and enquiry based upon groups of respondents. Following on from Chapter 9, the Internet as a research tool and network communication as a target of researchers are briefly addressed; while due note is made of the necessity for the integration of methods of research into media production, content and consumption.

The practice of segmentation of audience/consumers is considered the prime aim of commercial research, the emphasis of interest being on *large* segments, often to the neglect of other elements of the population. Critics see, in contrast, the importance of academic research in the study of minorities both as part of mediated experience and in terms of their response to it.

KEY TERMS

change agent   empowering   content analysis
cultural indicators   ethnography   participant observation
qualitative/quantative   reciprocation   empirical   discursive
engagement   ideology of mass culture/ideology of populism
socially situated   moral economy
appropriation/objectification/incorporation/conversion
interactivity   specificity   ethnocentricity   'keitai' culture
multi-tasking capacity   segmentation
(VALS) values and lifestyles   market typology
co-orientation   authentication

Suggested activities

1. Discussion

   (a) What problems are posed for the researcher by the fragmentation of audience resulting from the impact of new media? For example, has the dramatically increased *personalization* of media made researching the mass both irrelevant and ultimately impossible?

   (b) 'The technology may change, but people remain much the same.' Consider.

   (c) In the light of new media developments, review the value of participant observation, that is, being 'part of the activity' under investigation.

   (d) How far do the media contribute to the shaping of our personal identities?

2. Research methodology is usually divided up between the *quantitative* and the *qualitative*. Itemize the specific modes of research that fall into each category (for example, questionnaires, interviews, observation) and assess what might be the strengths and weaknesses of each one.

3. 'Young people are turned off by the coverage of politics in the media.' Design a questionnaire that probes *whether* this statement is true and seeks to discover how young people could be made more responsive to such coverage. Is it the word itself that is the turn-off, its narrow definition as describing the activities (and antics) of politicians?

   The aim of the questionnaire should be to ascertain whether, by using alternative descriptors (for example, *human rights/responsibilities/obligations*) a more encouraging picture of young people's attitudes might emerge.

   Ask no more than five questions, four of them closed-ended (that is requiring an answer which can easily be turned into statistics – yes/no/don't know or a simple tick) and one open-ended question (allowing for free comment by the respondent). Remember to leave enough space on the questionnaire for this.

   Examples:
   (Closed)   Does politics bore you?
   (Open-ended) How might the media make politics more interesting for young people?

4. You have been asked to prepare a five-minute piece for a magazine programme on radio, your theme, *What do listeners think of the radio station's coverage of local issues?* Using a portable tape-recorder conduct a street survey of the opinions of members of the public.

   Questioning should avoid yes/no answers and encourage the interviewees to speak their minds freely, therefore the more open-ended the questions the better. Considering what seems to have been a renaissance in radio listening, you may wish to extend your enquiry, to deal with such questions as:

   ● Why has radio sustained and increased its attraction to listeners?
   ● What listeners are we talking about?
   ● What are they listening to and in what mode (for example, on their mobile)?

5. You wish to gauge public response to a major issue in the news. Bring together two small groups and present each with a series of pictures illustrating the issue. Ask the groups to write a short news story: how much of the original do they remember; how much of the 'angle' of treatment, in the press or on TV, do they recall; what interpretation (of their own, or the media's) do they place on the story?

6. Conduct a survey of the use of music on TV: what functions does it serve in different programmes? Examine the ways in which words, images and music interact, shaping text and influencing reception.

7. 'Going digital' will soon become obligatory for radio listeners and viewers of TV. Conduct a piece of research involving questionnaires, interviews and/or focus groups seeking to highlight how informed the public are about the switchover from analogue to digital, how prepared they are for it and what problems they see arising from the transition.

Now read on

There are practically as many books on *how* to research as volumes on *what* research has been done. Readers wishing to take advice on research methodology might like to start with Ranjit Kumar's *Research Methodology: A Step-by-Step Guide for Beginners* (UK/US: Sage. 1999). Also from Sage, excellent practical guidance is available in *Gender Issues in Ethnography* (2nd edition, 2000) by Carol A.B. Warren and

Jennifer K. Hackney, Christine Hine's *Virtual Ethnography* (2000), *Secrets for a Successful Dissertation* (1998) by Jacqueline Fitzpatrick, Jan Sacrist and *The Internet Research Handbook: A Practical Guide for Students and Researchers in the Social Sciences* (2001) by Debra J. Wright and Niall O Dochartaigh. In addition, try *Web Studies* (UK: Arnold, 3rd edition, 2004) edited by David Gauntlett and Ross Horsley.

For fruits of research, see Greg Philo and Mike Berry's *Bad News from Israel* (UK: Glasgow University Media Group, 2004) which examines the way media coverage of the Israeli–Palestinian conflict has influenced public perceptions and attitudes. Media influence is also the theme of *Tell Me No Lies: Propaganda and Media Distortion in the Attack on Iraq* (UK: Pluto, 2004), edited by David Miller. On the theme of media and political awareness and involvement, see *Citizens or Comsumers: What the Media Tell Us About Political Participation* (UK/US: Open University, 2005), by Justin Lewis, Sanna Inthorn and Karin Wahl-Jorgensen.

Chapters on items of specific research interest – such as European soap operas, lifestyle segmentation, gendering the Internet, traditions in search of audience – can be found in *Communication Theory and Research* (US/UK: Sage, 2005) edited by Denis McQuail.

Notes

1. Ien Ang, *Watching 'Dallas': Soap Opera and the Melodramatic Imagination* (UK: Methuen, 1985).
2. Brenda Dervin, 'The potential contribution of feminist scholarship to the field of communication' in *Journal of Communication*, Autumn 1987.
3. Angela McRobbie, '"Jackie": an ideology of adolescent femininity' in B. Waites, T. Bennett and G. Martin (eds), *Popular Culture: Past and Present* (UK: Croom Helm, 1982). See also McRobbie's *Feminism and Youth Culture: From 'Jackie' to 'Just Seventeen'* (UK: Macmillan – now Palgrave Macmillan, 1991).
4. Glasgow University Media Group (GUMG): *Bad News* (UK: Routledge & Kegan Paul, 1976); *More Bad News* (UK: Routledge & Kegan Paul, 1980); *Really Bad News* (UK: Writers and Readers' Cooperative, 1982); *War and Peace News* (UK: Open University Press, 1991). In 2002 the GUMG published research findings based on focus groups indicating that TV news provides less than adequate balanced information in the reporting of the Israeli–Palestinian conflict. In a UK *Guardian* article 'Missing in action' (16 April 2002), Philo observes how young viewers recalled the images of violence but not their origins or their causes. He suggests that TV's failure in this regard is because TV news 'exists in a very commercial and competitive market and is concerned about audience ratings. In this

respect it is better to have great pictures of being in the middle of a riot with journalists ducking stones than to explain what the conflict is about'. A second and more crucial reason, believes Philo, is an awareness of how controversial honest and detailed explanations might be: 'Israel is closely allied to the United States and there are very strong pro-Israel lobbies in the US and to some extent in Britain.'

5. Data on the Cultural Indicators research programme are quoted by George Gerbner in Note 1 of his contribution 'The hidden side of television violence' published in *Invisible Crises: What Conglomerate Control of Media Means for America and the World* (US: Westview Press, 1996), edited by Gerbner, Hamid Mowlana and Herbert I. Schiller.

6. George Gerbner, Larry Gross, Michael Morgan and Nancy Signorielli, 'The "mainstreaming" of America: violence profile no. 11', *Journal of Communication*, Summer 1980.

7. Liesbet van Zoonen, *Feminist Media Studies* (UK: Sage, 1994).

8. Carolyn D. Smith and William Kornblum (eds), *In the Field: Readings on the Field Research Experience* (US: Praeger, 1989).

9. Valerie Walkerdine, 'Video replay: families, films and fantasy' in Victor Burgin, James Donald and Cora Kaplan (eds), *Formations of Fantasy* (UK: Methuen, 1986).

10. Shaun Moores, *Interpreting Audiences: The Ethnography of Media Consumption* (UK: Sage, 1993).

11. James Lull, 'The social uses of television' in *Human Communication Research*, 6(3) (1980). See also Lull's 'How families select television programmes: a mass observation study' in *Journal of Broadcasting and Electronic Media*, 26(4) (1982). In 1988 Lull edited *World Families Watch Television* (UK: Sage) and in 1990 published *Inside Family Viewing: Ethnographic Research on Television's Audience* (UK: Routledge).

12. Janice Radway, *Reading the Romance: Women, Patriarchy and Popular Literature* (US: University of North Carolina Press, 1984).

13. Angela McRobbie in *Feminist Review*, 12 October 1982.

14. Ien Ang, *Living Room Wars: Rethinking Media Audience for a Postmodern World* (UK/US: Routledge, 1996).

15. John Corner, 'Meaning, genre and context: the problematics of "public knowledge" in the new audience studies', in James Curran and Michael Gurevitch (eds), *Mass Media and Society* (UK: Edward Arnold, 1991; 4th edition, Hodder Arnold, 2005).

16. Justin Lewis, 'Decoding television news' in Phillip Drummond and Richard Paterson (eds), *Television in Transition: Papers from the First International Television Studies Conference* (UK: BFI, 1985).

17. Justin Lewis, *The Ideological Octopus: An Exploration of Television and its Audience* (UK: Routledge, 1991).

18. David Morley, *The 'Nationwide' Audience* (UK: BFI, 1980).

19. Charlotte Brunsdon and David Morley, *Everyday Television: 'Nationwide'* (UK: BFI, 1978).

20. David Morley, *Family Television* (UK: BFI, 1985). See also Morley's *Television, Audiences and Cultural Studies* (UK: Routledge, 1992).

21. Greg Philo, *Seeing & Believing: The Influence of Television* (UK: Routledge, 1990).

22. Lesley Henderson, *Incest in Brookside: Audience Responses to the Jordache Story* (UK: Channel 4 Television, 1996).

23. Tamar Liebes and Elihu Katz, *The Export of Meaning: Cross-Readings of Dallas* (US: Oxford University Press, 1990; UK: Polity Press, 1993).

24. Simon Cottle, 'Television news and citizenship: packaging the public sphere' in *No News is Bad News: Radio, Television and the Public* (UK: Pearson Educational, 2001), edited by Michael Bromley. Cottle's *UK News Access* project examined, as he explains in Note 7 of his chapter, 'Patterns and forms of TV and press news access and forms' focusing on two weeks, Monday to Friday beginning on 23 January 1995 and 5 June of the same year. Formats 1–10 are presented in chart form on page 74 of *No News is Bad News*.

25. Cultural citizenship. Simon Cottle argues that the media have a responsibility to contribute to the development and maintenance of cultural citizenship, of public sphere 'rights' by opting for forms of presentation which prove to be accessible and participant. He refers to the four citizenship rights posed by Graham Murdock in 'Rights and representations: public discourse and cultural citizenship' published in *Interpreting Television: Current Research Perspectives* (UK: Routledge, 1999), edited by W.D. Rowland and B. Watkins. These are: rights to *information*; rights to *experience* whereby the public have access to 'the greatest possible diversity of representations of personal and social experience'; rights to *knowledge*, indicating access to 'frameworks of interpretation'; and rights to *participation*, encouraging the public, as individuals or groups, 'to speak about their own lives and aspirations in their own voice, and to picture the things that matter to them in ways they have chosen'.

26. Dorothy Hobson, *'Crossroads': The Drama of a Soap Opera* (UK: Methuen, 1982).

27. Ann Gray, *Video Playtime: The Gendering of a Leisure Technology* (UK/US: Routledge, 1992).

28. Cynthia Cockburn, *Machinery of Dominance: Women, Men and Technical Know-How* (UK: Pluto Press, 1985).

29. Roger Silverstone, 'Television and everyday life: towards an anthropology of the television audience' in Marjorie Ferguson (ed.), *Public Communication: The New Imperatives* (UK: Sage, 1990).

30. Silverstone and Eric Hirsch (eds), *Consuming Technologies: Media and Information in Domestic Spaces* (UK/US: Routledge, 1992).

31. Tim Miller, 'The data-base revolution', *Columbia Journalism Review*, September/October 1988.

32. Tom Koch, *Journalism for the 21st Century: Online Information, Electronic Databases and the News* (UK: Adamantine Press, 1991).

33. Steve Jones (ed.), *Doing Internet Research: Critical Issues and Methods for Examining the Net* (US/UK: Sage, 1999).
34. Jennifer Stromer Galley's 1998 research was conducted in conjunction with a larger study by the Annenburg Public Policy Centre and the Annenburg School of Communication at the University of Pennsyvania, and funded by the Pew Charitable Trust.
35. Mizuko Ito, 'Personal, portable, pedestrian: lessons from Japanese phone use', japanfocus.org posting of a paper given by Ito at the Mobile Communication and Social Change Conference in Seoul, Korea, 18–19 October 2004. Ito is a cultural anthropologist of technology use, working with the Annenberg Centre for Communication at the University of South Carolina and Keio University, Tokyo.
36. Mizuko Ito, Daisuke Okabo and Misa Matsuda, *Personal, Portable, Pedestrian: Mobile Phones in Japanese Life* (US: MIT Press, 2005, new edition, 2006).
37. Richard MacManus' findings on patterns of Net traffic were reported by Nicholas Carr in his weekly column for *Technology/Guardian*. In 'The Net is being carved up into information plantations' (17 May 2007), Carr worries that

> On the Internet, the big get bigger... The Internet was supposed to be an open, democratic medium, an information bazaar putting individuals on the same footing as big companies. In the end, though, the Internet seems to be following the same pattern that has always characterized popular media. A few huge outlets come to dominate readership and viewership and smaller, more specialized ones are consigned to the periphery.

Carr concludes that '[a]ll the signs point to a continuing concentration of traffic within the fences of the new information plantations'.
38. The *4 Cs* (cross-cultural consumer categorization). This mode of segmenting consumers was prevalent in the ad business in Britain in the 1980s. *Mainstreamers* were much the largest category, gauged as 40% of the market. *Aspirers* were the young and upwardly mobile section of the consuming population. *Succeeders* had already arrived socially and economically while the smallest group, *Reformers*, were nevertheless, because of their education and commitment to the quality of life, the most articulate in expressing their needs and wielding influence.
39. Arnold Mitchell, *The Nine American Lifestyles* (US: Macmillan, 1983).
40. Hakuhodo Institute of Life and Living, 'Hitonami: keeping up with the Satos' (Japan: PHP Research Institute, 1982). The tribal theme has proved a favourite with researchers for the commercial sector. A report by Alex McKie in the UK for Barclays Bank, and published in 1999, identified six tribal clusters – New Hippies, Neo-Calvinists, Global Villagers, Post-Punk Outlaws, Barbie Babes and Ken Clones and Nomadic

Networkers. McKie writes, 'Whereas tribes over the past 40 years have tended to be groups of people who dressed alike, danced alike and thought alike, be they mods, punk rockers or Teddy boys – now people want flexibility to be lots of different people at the same time'. Market analysts, Datamonitor, scrutinizing the online purchasing patterns of 12,000 people in France, Germany, Spain, Sweden and the UK, classified five 'breeds' of netshopper – the rhino, the puma, the gazelle, the gorilla and the jackal. The puma, for example, is very young, generally single with a high income, a predator who wants delivery yesterday and has no problems with using new technology, while the rhino as purchaser via the Net is slow, conservative and liable to panic into the bush. This process of segmentation has been the subject of criticism and sometimes derision. Professor Laurie Taylor in his *Guardian* column, Off-cuts (4 August 1999), referring to the Barclays Six Tribe classification, says that, 'Many of the definitions are so trivial and superficial that one suspects they were not so much based on research as dreamed up one night in a warm bath'.

41. Anthony Giddens, *Modernity and Self-Identity: Self and Society in the Late Modern Age* (UK/US: Polity Press, 1991).
42. John Eldridge (ed.), *Getting the Message: News, Truth and Power* (UK: Routledge, 1994).
43. Larry Gross, 'Out of the mainstream: sexual minorities and the mass media' in Ellen Seiter, Hans Borchers, Gabriele Kreutzner and Eva-Maria Warth (eds), *Remote Control: Television, Audiences and Cultural Power* (UK/US: Routledge, 1991).
44. Rita Grosvenor and Arnold Kemp, 'Spain's Falling Soldier really did die that day', *Observer*, 1 September 1996.

21st Century Perspectives

11

AIMS

> ➤ To revisit some of the dominant issues, namely the convergence of media ownership on a global scale running in parallel with the convergence of communication technology.
> ➤ To view the current position concerning regulation of ownership, in particular the pressure of the private sector on government policies concerning public service broadcasting.
> ➤ Bearing in mind the power of transnational corporations to reach a worldwide audience in a myriad communicative ways, to address some of the cultural concerns expressed by critics; and to link up pessimistic forecasts with the ongoing belief expressed by many scholars in the resistive or active audience, specifically in terms of networking opportunities and the phenomenon of citizen journalism.
> ➤ To confirm the need for study of the local as well as the global, but with a disengagement from ethnocentric perspectives.
> ➤ In the light of an increasingly mediated, and currently fractured, world to briefly consider the responsibilities of media to the global citizen.

In the Introduction I referred to the story by Machado de Assis in which a canary defines the world – as he perceives it. What the canary knows 'for a fact' is his own personal experience – life in a cage hanging from a nail and the shop which surrounds it. Beyond that, 'everything is illusion and deception'. Outside of the canary's world, in the zone of human beings and mass communication in what has varyingly been termed the *mediasphere* or *mediapolis*, there are events, discourses and perceptions.

Each one is a player in a game called Reality. The event, it might for a moment be argued, is the closest to the real: it happens. Or does it? Perhaps it is only real for the brief time it takes for humans to perceive it; and once they perceive it, the denotational swiftly becomes inscribed in the connotational: discourse is at work.

Culture, cultural cultivation, enculturalization form the language of discourses which, in this context, seek to define what is occurring in society, what forces are at work for good or ill; whether these forces – such as that exercised by the great corporations – benefit the world. Debates over cultural influence tend to be high on indignation and sometimes short on fact; but when were facts sufficient to dampen perceptions born of experience, values, beliefs and – yes – vision?

Many commentators *envision* communication as power; and where communication works on a global scale, such commentators perceive power working to the same scale culturally, politically and economically. The opening phase of this chapter focuses on a kind of power game played out between competing agendas – that of the state (the policy agenda), that of the corporations and that of the media (increasingly part of corporate portfolios to the point where critics are fearful that it has become the MediaCorp agenda). It has also, of course, become the world's 'reality agenda' in the sense that, outside our own personal experience, mass communication is the *definer* of the real, the *imager* of what is 'true'.

Target of all the agendas are the public – voters (the policy interest), consumers (the corporate interest) and audience (everybody's interest). Yet we are more than any of these. We are citizens. In part thanks to the global performance of the media and the availability of network communication, we are more and more 'of the world', aware of its interconnectivity and our interdependence.

As never before we are aware of others across time and space; more knowledgeable about them yet often uneasy about how we should relate to them. Media communication can assuage fears or provoke them, emphasize our common humanity or exploit what divides us. Thus the media's global responsibility is awesome. In turn, it is the people's duty in whatever way they can to hold the media to their obligations, to demand accuracy and truthfulness; to espouse diversity and plurality, to celebrate both commonality and difference.

Power: pacts, profits, patriotism

Throughout this book we have seen that communication – of the appropriate sort, in the right place and at the right time – is power; and this power is political, economic and cultural. Who commands the means of communication has the capacity to wield power, locally, nationally and, increasingly, globally. As we have seen, the media (and their masters, the owners and controllers) have the power to set agendas; to dominate public discourses, to define reality through representation.

The costumes and the sets of media drama have altered substantially from the days when, during the middle of the 19th century, the marriage of publication and advertising, blessed by new technologies, gave birth to mass communication; turning media into potentially the biggest profit-spinning business and eventually creating the Age of Information.

Yet certain key factors have remained constant: the need for an audience to consume media; the need to generate income and investment; the pressure to adopt new technologies; the nature of media as a public as well as a private enterprise. Arising from these are the conflicting ambitions of the chief players – those in authority such as governments, those who control the means of production and communication and those, within media or looking in upon it, who serve as public advocates: journalists, educationalists, media researchers and analysts, pressure groups; in short, watchdogs, the eyes and ears of public interest.

New wine, old bottles?

Current conflicts of interest are not all that different from what they have been in the past. Governments, even in democracies with legislation guaranteeing open access to information and freedom of expression, have an inherent tendency towards secrecy. Where the kind of censorship exercised by authoritarian regimes is not possible, governments subject to the ballot-box resort to propaganda, what today we term *spin-doctoring*; the goal of which is the *manufacture of consent*.

Information is not banned, it is massaged, until those 'nuisances', the media, start asking awkward questions and putting those in authority 'on the spot'. Critics, however – those watchdogs of public interest scrutinizing the media scene – fear that not enough questions are asked; or enough questions of the right kind: are the media censoring themselves? Are they favouring entertainment over the pursuit of (usually uncomfortable) truths? Are they set on a course of dumbing-down, and thus under-estimating the intelligence of the people? In whose interests are the media functioning?

Questions such as these have been posed and analyzed exhaustively. The Frankfurt School of analysts in the 1930s and through to the 1960s dwelt broodingly on the harmful effects of mass media, their power to manipulate, to corrupt. In the same tradition, more recent commentators grieve over the retreat from quality and the inequalities of provision.

Herbert Schiller, in *Information Inequality: The Deepening Social Crisis in America*,[1] laments the decline of *dissent* in the media generally. Opposing voices win less and less attention; are squeezed out. He refers to a 'near-disappearance from the American scene of a national and comprehensive adversarial view'. TV, at the centre of the dominance of advertising discourses, 'falls far short of its informational–cultural potential', subverting all to the god of profit with 'endless affirmations of commercial culture'.

Nothing new there, except in one sense: the 'monster' – the Leviathan – which the Frankfurt School feared might take over the world has, in the view of many commentators, actually achieved its objective; and in doing so it has swallowed up – 'incorporated' – formerly independent countries as well. The election of George W. Bush to the presidency of America in 2000 was followed immediately by his government's abandonment of the Kyoto Agreement on the global reduction of gas emissions: could this decision have been in any way to do with the fact that the biggest oil company in the world, Esso, had also been the largest subscriber to Bush's election campaign?

Corporate Man may not own everything, may not control everything, but his influence permeates as never before every quarter of the globe, and he has achieved this position, believe the pessimists, by converting the world to the religion of consumerism. Such a scenario is dramatic, indeed bordering on the melodramatic, or 'hyperbolic' as Denis McQuail puts it in the Epilogue of *McQuail's Mass Communication Theory*.[2] This indicates his own take on mass media as being 'a dictatorial, irresistible and somewhat irrational potentate occupying a central seat of power and radiating influence to the far corners of the land, not to mention the effects on hearts and minds'.

McQuail states that the 'essential features of mass communication invite resistance and rebellion on the part of those who love independence, diversity, individuality, quality of cultural life, perhaps truth itself'. Why? Because:

> It is mass communication that has cemented the power of dictators in the twentieth century, smothered dissent and substituted propaganda for truth. It is mass communication that has displaced the culture and language and identity of many people to make room for an invasive and shallow commercialization of culture. Dictatorships aside, it is mass communication that has gained for the economic power holders of global markets a ready means of access to and some control over our private lives, aspirations and lifestyles.

These are harsh words from an author who has dedicated his life to the study of media; and he follows them up with the comment that 'if mass communication as we have known it does wither away, there will be few mourners, at least not before we know what will take its place'.

Assertions of this kind need to be seriously and constantly addressed: if both nations and peoples have shifted, or are shifting inexorably into the grip of market forces, increasingly under the thumb of corporate power-brokers, where do the *people* stand in terms of sovereignty? Except as consumers, do the people matter any more; and are mass media now in default concerning their role as watchdogs of public interest? Further, are the media sufficiently prepared to see beyond their corporate remit, to honour higher-order responsibilities such as engagement with global citizenship?

Let us recap briefly on the trends that have prompted debate about the perceived threat to sovereignty, of power vested in the people; where it is feared that the *will* of the people as expressed at the ballot-box may count for less among governments than corporate priorities.

Convergence and alliance

Millennium year saw the largest media deal in history, when the world's biggest media corporation, Time Warner, merged with AOL (America On Line). It was a particularly dramatic example of convergence in media ownership, matching the rapid technological convergence brought about by digitization. It was the culmination of extraordinary advances occurring throughout the 1990s when Time Warner and Disney, as has been noted in Chapter 8, tripled in size.

Takeovers, mergers and joint ventures – or alliances – took place at the expense of smaller rivals who were bought, absorbed or shut down. This, it can be argued, may not be such a bad thing if there is genuine competition between the giants, and if quality and diversity have a healthy chance of surviving and even prospering as a result of economies of scale. Access to more substantial resources, which bigger companies have available, should at least sustain quality if not improve it.

Critics argue that increased investment is not always, or regularly, the result of takeovers; rather the more familiar experience is of cuts and redundancies. This might suggest that it is competition that forces these cuts, and to an extent this is true; but not necessarily competition that produces quality rather than cuts; or genuine competition between equals.

A characteristic of media convergence has been what one might term 'mutual grooming', based upon shared interests. For the most part, the big guys don't duel, they embrace; yet this is as much out of insecurity as common interest.

The Time Warner–AOL coupling soon ceased to resemble a marriage made in heaven. Time Warner abandoned the AOL suffix to its title, having seen its shares plummet since the merger. AOL now operates as a division of Time Warner, along with Warner Brothers film studios, cable news channel CNN and *Time* magazine.

At the time of the demerger, Steve Case, the founder of AOL was reported as saying that 'Time Warner has proven too big, too complex, too conflicted and too slow-moving – in other words, too much like a classic conglomerate – to seize new opportunities'.[3]

Talk of media dinosaurs too big and too slow to adjust to rapidly changing circumstances is premature. Cumbrous turn around there might be, but the turn has been happening – and in the direction of network communication. As we have seen, Google acquired YouTube, while Rupert Murdoch's News Corp appropriated MySpace, which swiftly seized 16% of Net traffic (see Chapter 10, Note 37).

Early in 2007, after completing the acquisition of the Relegance Corporation, a New York-based company offering web users financial news feeds derived from more than 20,000 sources, Time Warner divested itself of 30 magazines to a Stockholm-based publisher; 300 staff were laid off. The Holy Grail is to be located in the New Jerusalem, network communication, in particular social networking: kids and teenagers especially are in Time Warner's sights (though there is evidence that the over-60s are fast-discovering the delectations of cybersurfing).

We do well to remember that whatever the web ambitions of the great corporations, they remain in control of mainstream media to a worrying extent. Their capacity to influence the content of the press, radio, TV; to largely decide what films are made, what music published, remains undiminished. Escape routes (that is, alternatives to what is on offer) close as corporate services expand.

The 'Fox effect'

One of the most serious criticisms of American media performance since 9/11 has been of the way newspapers, radio and television slavishly followed the government line on the 'war on terror'; and how sheepishly uncritical US news reporting has been of the invasion and occupation of Iraq.

In a Media Education Foundation (MEF) online article, 'Media and Iraq: war coverage analysis', Mariellen Diemand quotes the charge made by syndicated columnist Norman Solomon that the 'overwhelming bulk of news stations' served 'as amplification systems for Washington's warriors in times of crisis'.[4] Diemand believed that what deflected journalists from striving for balance and objectivity in reporting the war was the fear of being accused of lacking patriotism and giving aid and comfort to the terrorist enemy. She quotes Anthony Arnove, writer for *Z Magazine* and editor of *Iraq Under Siege: The Deadly Impact of Sanctions and War*:[5]

> The media lines up with the government on fundamental matters…because the media themselves are huge corporations that share the same economic and political interests with the tiny elite that runs the U.S. government.

Diemand writes of US war coverage as 'frighteningly one-sided: pro-war, anti-Iraq and anti-alternative voices'. There have, of course, been those who did voice criticism. Robert Sheer of the *Los Angeles Times* called US reporting of the Iraq war 'the most shameful era of American media' which has been 'sucker-punched completely by the administration'.[6]

Wars, it would seem, are good for circulation, but only if reportage avoids rocking the national boat or damaging profits. In *Weapons of Mass Destruction: The Uses of Propaganda in Bush's War on Iraq*[7] Sheldon Rampton and John Stauber write:

> Fox Network owner Rupert Murdoch brilliantly exploited the wartime political environment, in which even extreme nationalist rhetoric was accepted and popular, while liberals and critics of the White House were pressured to walk softly and carry no stick at all. In addition to Fox, Murdoch owns a worldwide network of 140 sensationalist tabloid newspapers – 40 million papers a week, dominating the newspaper markets of Britain, Australia and New Zealand – all of which adopted editorial positions in support of war with Iraq.

What Rampton and Stauber call the 'patriotism police' also patrolled American radio. They cite Clear Channel Communications, owner of more than 1200 stations, whose 'executives have not hesitated to use their power to impose ideological direction'. In the period running up to the invasion of Iraq in 2003, Clear Channel stations 'offered financial sponsorship and on-air promotion for pro-war "Rallies for America"', as well as pulling the Dixie Chicks from their playlists when Natalie Maines, the group's lead singer, confessed to fans in London that they were ashamed of coming from the same state as President Bush.

In relation to the optimistic concept of the *active audience* it would be reassuring to learn that Fox News' 'belligerent brand of hyper-patriotism' sent viewers scurrying for more balanced and more measured coverage of the war. It did not. Fox won the ratings war, and its success with audiences triggered what Rampton and Stauber term a 'ripple effect' as other broadcast networks 'tailored their coverage to compete' with Fox's burgeoning success.

Encore hegemony

The people who run politics and the people who run the media are not natural enemies, nor are they naturally the same people. Rather they are normally different constituents of the same ruling class. They may squabble one with another, and make different alliances to achieve their ends; but they share the same universe of elite domination.

Colin Sparks, in *De-Westernizing Media Studies*[8]

The retreat from regulation

During the 1990s governments in many countries, particularly in the West, pursued policies of *deregulation* of broadcasting or were willing to modify existing regulation by introducing 'light touch' supervision. This was what the corporate sector wished for and for which corporate alliances had pressured governments.

The policy agenda acknowledged, and bowed to, corporate muscle. After all, the transnational corporations (TNCs) are major investors, tax-payers and, most important, employers with the capacity to take their business elsewhere; hence the almost universal reluctance of governments to support workers in their clashes with management over pay and working conditions. Not giving offence to Big Brother Business has long been a vital commandment of governments of whatever political hue.

Corporations resist any form of regulation that limits their freedom to trade and generate profits. Media regulations contribute to a general pattern of checks and balances within the remit of governments to uphold and protect the rights of the electorate – as citizens, workers and consumers. A vital check upon the tendency towards corporate monopoly is a government's power to restrict by law media takeovers in order to preserve diversity and plurality. Such a defence of the public interest is usually to be found in party election manifestos. All too often, once parties are in government, the ideal meets the real and pragmatism is likely to prevail over principle.

As Brian McNair points out in *News and Journalism in the UK,*[9] 'There *are* some constraints on media ownership [in Britain] but as the Thatcher government showed in its dealings with Rupert Murdoch in the 1980s, these can be waived if it is politically convenient to do so'.

'Now here's the deal...'

Four corporations control 90% of the British press: should such corporations be permitted to buy into broadcasting, therefore extending cross-media ownership; should one corporation own both a city's newspapers and its radio station? Only regulation stands in the way of the same corporations controlling radio and TV in the way they control the press.

Need a government worry if it stands to gain by looking the other way when media entrepreneurs snap up their rivals? After all, didn't the incoming New Labour government of 1997 owe something to the support of Rupert Murdoch and the decision of the *Sun* and *News of the World* to abandon the Tories and pitch for Labour (SUN BACKS BLAIR)? McNair explains that 'Labour made Murdoch's realignment easier by signalling that they would provide him with a sympathetic business environment should they win the election'.

While the Government White Paper of 2000, *A New Future for Communications*[10] proposed to guarantee the future of public service broadcasting, at least in the short term, the intention to loosen regulation concerning cross-media ownership prompted protests from groups such as the National Union of Journalists (NUJ) and the Campaign for Press and Broadcasting Freedom (CPBF) who feared the tightening hand of media monopoly.

The CPBF's response document[11] saw the proposed legislation as betraying 'a one-sided preference for promoting an expansion of market based communications networks', favouring 'competition and markets as central policy tools ... incompatible with the provision of high quality accountable media'.

The Communications Act (UK) of 2003 differed little from the proposals in the White Paper. Essentially deregulation was its guiding principle and what regulation the Act confirmed was to be 'light-touch'. Gillian Doyle in a *Sociology Review* article, 'Changes in media ownership' (February 2004), declared that the Act allowed 'unprecedented opportunities for major commercial radio and television broadcasters to expand their share in the UK media market'. Britain became an open stall for foreign companies to bid for what they fancied.

The Office of Communications (Ofcom), created alongside the Act to serve as a 'super-regulator', was empowered to 'further the interests of citizens and consumers by promoting competition and protecting consumers from harmful or offensive material'. Since its inception Ofcom has sponsored useful media research, but its goals are seen to be problematic, if not contradictory. Patricia Holland, in 'Commodity or public asset?', an article for the UK Campaign for Press and Broadcasting Freedom's newsletter, *Free Press* (March–April 2007) writes:

> Ofcom ... has two faces. One which is relatively benign ... [This] looks kindly on concepts such as public service broadcasting; the other sees communication as a business opportunity. Away with namby-bamby ideas like 'public' and 'service'. 'Value' means monetary value, and market forces rule.

Students of media would do well to monitor the activities of Ofcom in its attempt to speak for, and serve, two masters (see Note 12 on the Digital Dividend).

Here was the News

A particular fear expressed by media watchers in relation to corporate advances in media control is what is happening to news broadcasting, especially investigative reporting. The issue is not about 'dumbing down', what Jean Seaton in *Carnage and the Media: The Making and Breaking of News About Violence*[13] terms 'a crude and unilluminating category'. Important news, she says, 'does not require a posh accent and a dinner jacket'. However, in her view, 'mainstream broadcast news is wilting under the pressure of the market and losing intelligence, style, authority and audience'.

Media companies, believes Seaton, are forced 'to value profit exclusively over reach and content'. She draws our attention to America 'where the process has gone much further [than in Britain]' and she finds 'the prospects chilling':

There, the television network news services, once the world's greatest news machines, have been killed off through 'deregulation'. As a result Americans consume less news from any screen (including their computers) than they did twenty years ago, and even more disturbingly, news values have narrowed. Breaking news dominates everywhere. Much American news now involves chasing the local fire engine, followed by 'bombs around the world'.[14]

If such concerns as those expressed by Jean Seaton and others accurately describe a 'descent' from public service on the part of media nationally and globally, our attention needs to be re-focused on the very purposes of media in the modern world; a task to which we will return later in this final chapter.

Audience: deconvergence

Debate over who rules the airways, and who rules the rulers continues and will continue apace, but attention must not be deflected from the people all these regulations or deregulations are intended to please or to satisfy – the audience for media; essentially the consuming public. A prevailing trend has been towards audience *fragmentation*. Denis McQuail in *Audience Analysis*[15] traces the evolution of audience through the four models shown in Figure 11.1.

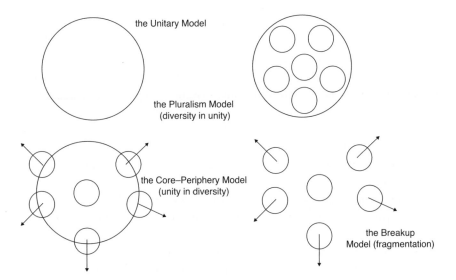

Figure 11.1 Four stages of audience fragmentation
Models from McQuail, with acknowledgement to Jan van Cullenberg.

In the period when, in the UK, the BBC was the monopoly provider of broadcasting, the *unitary* model prevailed, 'implying a single audience that is more or less coextensive with the general public'. When commercial TV was introduced and a degree of channel diversity, the unitary gave way to the *pluralism* model characterized, as McQuail puts it, by 'a pattern of limited internal diversification'.

The *core–periphery* model 'is one in which the multiplication of channels makes possible additional and competing alternatives outside this framework'. The b*reak-up* model 'represents extensive fragmentation and the disintegration of the central core'. Core–periphery largely describes the current scene in Britain and most of Europe, Australia, India and New Zealand, but with digitization and the consequent multiplication of channels and programmes, further dramatic fragmentation seems likely and unavoidable.

Bearing in mind the dramatic growth in network communication and the provision of information and entertainment independent of traditional media, the days of vast audiences sharing the same experiences of information, education and entertainment, of a kind of communal togetherness, would seem to be coming to an end.

McQuail says that in the fourth model 'there is only sporadically shared audience experiences'. There has been widespread uneasiness expressed about the consequences of broadcasting being overtaken by 'narrowcasting', by 'niche programming', with the possibility of each television viewer creating, from a giddy range of possibilities, his or her own schedules. 'The core–periphery stage,' believes McQuail, 'has arrived (although not yet everywhere),' but it has not yet led 'to a significant growth of new and exclusive minority audiences.'

It is a cautious but still credible opinion, that for 'most people, most of the time, the "core" still dominates their television use behaviour'. People are slower to change their socio-cultural habits than the imperatives of technology would suggest. McQuail acknowledges 'the near-universal appeal of mainstream content' which happens to coincide with 'the advantages to media organizations of continuing with mass provision'. He is of the view that '[m]edia change is not enough on its own to disrupt established patterns of shared culture'.

The question frequently asked in relation to the concept of 'shared culture', of what McQuail in *McQuail's Mass Communication Theory*[2] terms 'the collective character of "audiencehood"', is how far media will continue to serve such *communities* of media experience. In a world in which systems of communication have become rapidly globalized, what price the individuality of culture – the 'domestic' experience?

Will media producers, with world markets in mind, increasingly opt for programmes and programming with a universal appeal; will sameness prevail over difference; will traditional preferences and tastes be subsumed by the necessities of global consumerism?

Nothing to beat home cookin'?

According to research published by the UK Office of Communication (Ofcom) in 2007, audiences are more localite in their tastes than cosmopolite. Those living in the north west favour *Coronation Street*, while those in the south, opt more for *Eastenders*. In turn the Scots follow *Taggart* or *Rebus*. The findings arise from researches conducted between 2002 and 2006 into terrestrial TV viewing habits.

Ofcom's first public service broadcasting annual report produced the following figures showing how locally-based drama commands bigger audiences: *Doc Martin* (ITV1), South West, +39%; *Taggart* (ITV1), Scotland, +37%; *Shameless* (Channel 4) and *Coronation Street* (ITV1), North West, each +30%; *Emmerdale* (ITV1) and *Heartbeat*, Yorkshire, +17% and +10% respectively; and *Eastenders* (BBC1), London, +8%.

Net exodus?

Top of the list of questions concerning audience is how far, and how fast, it is tipping away from traditional mass media towards network services and entertainment. Newspaper circulation in both the USA and the UK is in rapid decline; broadcasting figures fluctuate dramatically and worries for the future of mass communication as we have known it are all too understandable when MySpace, YouTube, Bebo or Facebook report hits by the million.

Presented with such challenges, many media employers have rushed to cut costs by sacking staff, while those remaining in work have to labour harder. The inevitable result, sooner or later, is falling standards; the danger, a vicious spiral of decline.

What is for sure is that we are on shifting ground; perception rules as powerfully as the facts. We remember the displacement of radio by television; we take comfort from the fact that radio, in the UK once driven to the margins of audience use, has rallied, concentrated on its strengths and again become competitive. Also, we note that the mass media only temporarily regarded cyberspace as a zone of exclusion.

For the most part, they have adapted to it and become accommodated by it. Yet the overall impression is that traditional media are having to run faster in order to stand still.

The media environment: global warnings

Some of the most readable literature on the cultural impact of mass communication has concerned *threat*: the media environment is in danger of pollution. Our lifestyles, our customs, our values, our relationships, our perceptions of reality are – some commentators believe with fervour and complain often with eloquence – subject to influences which, on a bad day, amount to brainwashing. Like smoking, goes the claim, the media can seriously endanger our health.

We eat a burger and fries: we are in danger of becoming *McDonaldized*; we take a trip to Disney World or Disneyland and we risk becoming *Disneyized*. Indeed culture generally, it would seem, has been *consumerized*, subjected to the manipulative powers of the great corporations in their pursuit of profit and a viable future.

Whether the theories are proved or not is less important than the extent to which the theorizing has made people think. George Ritzer in *The McDonaldization of Society* (later followed up by *The McDonaldization Thesis*), see Note16, describes a process 'by which the principles of the fast food restaurants are coming to dominate more and more sectors of American society as well as of the rest of the world'.

Ritzer states that he is not offering a critique of the fast food business; but sees in McDonald's a paradigm of a 'wide-ranging process' which can be identified through contemporary society – in 'education, work, health care, travel, leisure, dieting, politics, the family, and virtually every other aspect of society'. The paradigm works from four principles of action on which the business practices of McDonald's have been built. These are:

- Efficiency
- Calculability
- Predictability
- Control

The service offered by McDonald's is efficient. Customers are served quickly; they eat quickly; they leave quickly. Service and cost are eminently calculable ('Quantity has become the equivalent of quality'); and what is provided, from Seattle to Sydney is predictable ('There is great comfort in knowing that McDonald's offers no surprises').

Control is about the disciplines of both production and consumption. Essentially, what McDonald's represents is a *rational* system. So far, so good; but Ritzer expresses concern that 'rational systems inevitably spawn irrationalities'.

While any convincing proof will be difficult to come by, discussion of the wider manifestation of the four McDonald's principles will give pause for thought. School league tables, for instance – are they not in a way seeking to rationalize the process of education through exercising criteria of efficiency, calculability, predictability and control? Of course these criteria were not invented by McDonald's. Indeed they may be said to have formed the basis of the industrial revolution and been manifested in mass production from the era of the Model T Ford to the present day.

Have our tastes and eating habits, as a result of the marketing genius of McDonald's, become, as it were, *burgerized?* Has the public become content with what Douglas Kellner in *Resisting McDonaldization*,[17] edited by Barry Smart, calls 'the paradigm of mass homogeneity, sameness' and 'standardization which erases individuality, specificity and difference'?

It might be conceded that Ritzer and Kellner have a case; at the same time one would have to point out the remarkable public interest stimulated in recent years as a result of TV cooks, male as well as female, young as well as middle-aged, who have introduced healthy food and original dishes to a generation that is perfectly willing to sample a McDonald's one night and Thai, Indian, Vietnamese or Hungarian the next.

Et tu, Disney?

What is not in question is the attempt by multinational companies to influence; to promote their business with a view to maximizing profit. Academics rather than the public spot possible, and sometimes hidden, dangers. Occasionally the worriers about enculturalization, about the potential for a generation of people to be brainwashed, are (with some justification) accused of elitism: what they are worrying about, as they adopt the role of prophets of doom, is largely *other people*.

In this scenario, McDonald's is not 'corrupting' *our* taste buds (because we don't eat at McDonald's) but the taste buds (not to mention the state of mind) of *them*, people out there; not the least, a young generation of *other* who, if McDonaldization (and Disneyization) are not resisted, will end up in thrall to them.

So what, then, constitutes Disneyization, another bogeyman or demon identified by some critics? Like McDonaldization, it has to be seen as an offspring of the daddy of the family, *consumerization*. Indeed it could be said that the principles of performance of Disney align with those of McDonald's and for that matter any highly successful corporation: efficiency, calculability, predictability and control.

Specifically critics see in Disney, particularly the corporation's theme parks, an *ordering* of history and culture – a manipulation of knowledge itself – which is less to do with true records and more to do with entertainment; and if entertainment is to reach the largest number of consumers and to send them home happy, then a degree of sanitization, of re-writing history within a favourable ideological framework, is okay.

It comes as no surprise to find that authors fearful of the world being McDonaldized link the process to that of being 'Disneyized'. In Chapter 7 of *Resisting McDonaldization*, 'Theme parks and McDonaldization', Alan Bryman writes, 'In its rendering of the past or of the present, Disney occludes [shuts out] poverty, wars, racism, discrimination against ethnic minorities or women, except in very brief optimistic renderings'.

If Disney can be accused of 'modifying' the past there are critics who see it as attempting to 'adjust' the future. Alexander Wilson in 'The betrayal of the future: Walt Disney's EPCOT Center', in *Disney Discourse: Producing the Magic Kingdom*,[18] edited by Eric Smoodin, writes of Disney's 'eccentric and worrisome vision of the future'. Wilson says that publicity for EPCOT (The Experimental Prototype Community of the Future), opened in 1982, 'makes it seem as though a brighter future were just a matter of "creative thinking" and "futuristic technologies". The widespread sense of impending ecological or military catastrophe that people have today is thoroughly absent'.

Wilson takes us on a critical tour of EPCOT, seeing in its manifestations of 'Spaceship Earth' a paradigm value system for the modern age. A sub-head summarizes his argument: 'Corporate patriotism: history as PR [Public Relations]'. What we are envisaging is both the American Adventure and the American Dream, the one the name of the pavilion 'that sits at the head of the lake in World Showcase', the other its symbolic meaning. Of the first, Wilson writes:

> It provides a spectacular history of the heroic American nation, sponsored by Coca-Cola and American Express. The building's design is the bastardized Georgian usually associated with A & P shopping plazas and Southern cafeteria chains. This style is often employed

in vernacular architecture to connote 'history'... The American Adventure attempts to mobilize us with its sweeping pop collage of historical bric-a-brac... what we have is a simulacrum [image, semblance] of history, a middlebrow impersonation of an epic story that never took place.

For Wilson, genuine history is betrayed in the interests of the consumerist ideology:

EPCOT discards the history of genuinely utopian initiatives of the American people in favour of an ideology of growth and development... it is a future of hierarchy, continued industrialization, enforced scarcity, and a ravished planet. A future of emancipation, on the other hand, can only be reclaimed by a society willing to debate its own survival. Walt Disney's EPCOT Center stands squarely in the way of that debate and condemns us to a recurrent and eternal present.

As God needs the Devil, consumerism needs its critics

If Andrew Wilson seems a trifle ungrateful for the splendours of Disney he is only one of a line of society-watchers dismayed by the turn of events, and reading in to these events signs of conspiracy. Over the centuries in Christian countries the Devil was seen to lead us into sin through the distraction of pleasure. Today, some commentators fear, Old Nick seeks to lure us from the straight and narrow through the pleasures of consumption.

In *The Consumer Society: Myths and Structures*,[19] Jean Baudrillard sees an age-old conflict re-enacted: 'Just as medieval society was balanced on God *and* the Devil, ours is balanced between consumption *and* its denunciation.' He argues:

Like every great myth worth its salt, the myth of 'Consumption' has its discourse and its anti-discourse. In other words, the elated discourse on affluence is everywhere shadowed by a morose, moralizing, 'critical' counter-discourse on the ravages of consumer society and the tragic end to which it inevitably dooms society as a whole.

Ironically, not only is the counter-discourse 'to be found in intellectualist discourse, which is always ready to distance itself by its scorn for "simple-minded values" and "material satisfactions", but it is now present within "mass culture" itself: advertising increasingly parodies itself, integrating counter-advertising into its promotional technique'. It seems that you can't win: while the critics do their worst, the target of their critique turns the attack into yet another consumerist device:

> *Paris-Soir, Paris-Match*, the radio, the TV, and ministerial speeches all contain as an obligatory refrain the lament on this 'consumer society', where values, ideals and ideologies are giving way to the pleasures of everyday life.

Baudrillard states that this 'endlessly repeated indictment is part of the game: it is the critical mirage, the anti-fable which rounds off the fable – the discourse of consumption and its critical undermining'. Perhaps the only answer is not to play the game – and then what? For Baudrillard, what constitutes the power of the myth of consumption requires the two parts to be working together – the affirmation and its 'critical undermining'.

By protesting, it would seem, we merely become part of the myth. Critics may purport to create a genuine distance between themselves and consumption, but for Baudrillard their position 'establishes no *real* distance'. According to him, 'No heresy is possible in a state of affluence'.

De-Westernizing media studies

This heading is the title of a book edited by James Curran and Myung-Jin Park[20] which makes the case that the study of media should strive to extricate itself from ethnocentric perspectives, essentially Western in orientation and hue, and seek – as Curran says in his 'Introduction: beyond globalization theory' – to broaden 'media theory and understanding in a way that takes account of the experience of countries outside the Anglo-American orbit'.

In preparing *De-Westernizing Media Studies* the editors 'adopted ... the device of setting a global exam paper, and inviting leading media academics around the world to sit it'. Four questions were asked:

1. How do the media relate to the power structure of society?
2. What influences the media, and where does control over the media lie?
3. How have the media influenced society?
4. What effect has media globalization and new media had on the media system and society?

Curran speaks warningly of an 'aerial perspective that simplifies', meaning that overviews – global overviews – fail to detect the nitty-gritty differences identifiable through the study of the specific; the *national*, in fact. He provides a number of reasons why 'nations are still critically important', arguing that 'their continuing significance tends to be underplayed by globalization theory'. Curran believes that:

> ... perhaps the key point to emphasize is that media systems are shaped not merely by national regulatory regimes and national audience preferences, but by a complex ensemble of social relations that have taken shape in national contexts. It is precisely the historically grounded density of these relationships that tends to be excluded from simplified global accounts, in which theorists survey the universe while never straying far from the international airport.

By balancing global with national perspectives, by being *glocal* in our approach to study, we reduce the danger of sweeping generalizations. This point is emphasized by Annabelle Sreberny in her contribution to *De-Westernizing Media Studies*. Discussing TV in the Middle East, she refers to the 'dynamics of the "inside"'. There has been a temptation among critics to focus on outside pressures on media and audience response to the neglect of internal dynamics.

Serious analytic enterprise, Sreberny believes, would need to 'examine the conjunction and effects of global processes within specific, localized settings, exploring the dynamics of external forces combined with internal processes'. As my own students have affirmed in preparing their international media profiles, diversity of the nature of societies is as likely to be reflected in media provision and performance as conformity to encroaching global norms.

True, the forces for change – of new technology, of cultural artefacts crossing national boundaries, of marketization of public communications – are similar, often the same; but responses to them within national contexts vary. Anticipating specialist chapters in *De-Westernizing Media Studies*, ranging from China to Egypt, from Mexico to Zimbabwe, from Russia to Israel, Curran sees patterns of divergence of effect.

Is the market, for instance, an agency of increased independence from state control, helping media to disengage themselves, at least in part from serving as the ideological state apparatus of power? Might the workings of the market offer opportunities for the media to loosen their leash as guard dogs of the power elite? Well, contributors to *De-Westernizing Media Studies* suggest this is the case in Mexico, China and Taiwan.

In Chapter 7, 'Media, political power, and democratization in Mexico', Daniel C. Hallin commends the 'kind of comparative enterprise' represented by *De-Westernizing Media Studies* which forces us 'to think in more subtle ways about the variety of relationships which can exist among the state, commercial media, civil society, the profession of journalism, and other key elements of the system of public communication'. In referring to Mexico, Hallin continues:

> It is clear, in particular, that the assumption that market forces inevitably push toward depoliticization and narrowed spectrum of debate is too simple. Under certain historical conditions market forces may undermine existing structures of power, providing incentives for the media to respond to an activated civil society.

Such is the view from Mexico, yet, Curran says in his Introduction, 'in one country after another, the opposite argument is advanced, with the market emerging as a mechanism that fuses the circuits of freedom and critical disclosure'; and this is because 'in many countries, the owners of private media are part of the system of power, and use their authority to muzzle criticism of the state'.

The jury, it would seem, is still out on the issue of the extent of corporate appropriation of once-indigenous cultures through a predominantly Westernizing media-led culture. If we are to avoid sweeping assertions driven by hunch-theories we must recognize – and scrutinize – local differences, for only then will we be able to judge the nature of resistance and the ability of audiences to *domesticate* – convert to their own uses – media communication, whatever its source. Curran brings his Introduction to a close with the following statement:

> If there is one thing that emerges above all else from this book, it is that the nation – its history, cultural tradition, economic development, national configuration of power, and state policies – is still very important in shaping the media's global system. Rumours of the nation's death, to adapt Mark Twain, are much exaggerated.

Practitioners and public: resistance through coalition

At the beginning of this chapter Herbert Schiller[1] was quoted as lamenting the decline in media dissent. Practitioners, he implies, are cowed by the pressures and constraints of corporate ownership, and there is plenty of evidence indicating how strong these pressures are, and how extensively they permeate and influence the mediasphere.

There is also heartening evidence of media practitioners challenging dominant alliances – policy and corporate – by rival coalitions, between themselves as practitioners and pressure groups in the community. Aidan White, General Secretary of the International Federation of Journalists, in his online article 'Media monopolies versus editorial independence: signs of hope in Korea',[21] writes that 'a new collective struggle is emerging as abstract anxiety about professional standards under increasing media concentration gives way to more immediate confrontation between journalists and their employers'. He goes on:

> There are examples of this struggle across the world. In Canada, the standards in broadcasting policy are the subject of heated dispute between media staff and regulators; in Germany, Europe's largest journalists' union has launched a national campaign to combat 'dumbing down'; in Italy, journalists are launching a long-overdue campaign to clip the wings of media magnate Prime Minister Silvio Berlusconi [voted out of office in the Italian elections of 2006]; and in Korea, journalists and civic groups are taking on powerful newspapers in a nationwide campaign for journalistic freedom.

White concedes that this is, 'by any reckoning, an unequal struggle' but suggests that successful resistance in one part of the globe can ignite successful resistance on a broader front. He commends the example of a coalition of journalists and civil society groups in South Korea 'engaged in a high profile dispute over media policy with government, and powerful newspaper companies' and believes that the 'battle for control of the newsroom in South Korea is one that strikes at the heart of corporate interests everywhere'; offering a 'model of professional solidarity and a much-needed strategic lifeline to beleaguered newsgatherers elsewhere'.

It would seem that old truths die hard: communication may be power, and rest substantially in the hands of those who own the *means* of communication; but power also lies in *collective action*. White concludes his article by saying:

> Corporate power in media is not impervious, but it will take unity among media professionals, strong coalitions with the public at large, and political backbone to bring about change that will put quality journalism back on the news agenda, everywhere.

'We are all journalists now'

The prospect of powerful coalitions being able to bring about better journalism remains an aspiration. Yet a certainty is that journalism itself, the reporting of and commenting on the news, has with the advent of network communication undergone significant change. As we have seen, access to information for the journalist is swift, the sources seemingly limitless and there is the crucial bonus of interactivity.

Yet reporting and commenting are no longer the privileges of the professional journalist. As the sub-head to this section affirms, we can all be journalists; first, because we have access to the same sources as the professional; second, we have the means of delivering our texts and a likelihood that at least a few members of the cybercommunity will key in to our communications.

What has come to be termed *citizen journalism* is proving a development that challenges exclusivity. In the news firmament, traditional media pundits face competition from a galaxy of bloggers, alternative news and comment websites. According to American guru blogger Matt Drudge:[22]

> We have entered an era vibrating with the din of small voices. Every citizen can become a reporter, can take on the powers that be ... time was only newsrooms had access to the full pictures of the news events, but now every citizen does. We get to see the kind of cuts that are made for all kinds of reasons; endless layers of editors with endless agendas changing bits and pieces, so by the time your newspaper hit your welcome mat, it had no meaning. Now, with a modem, anyone can follow the world and report on the world – no middle man, no big brother.

Before we join the Drudge Report website in celebrating the demise of big brother we need to acknowledge that one model of mediation is being swapped for another. The Matt Drudge website, based in Hollywood, has proved itself a fervent enemy of the Democratic party of the USA. Its revelations concerning President Clinton's relationship with Monica Lewinsky were something of a landmark in citizen journalism, venturing where traditional media were hesitant to tread, while at the same time emulating tabloid practices of sensationalism and no small degree of malice.

The blog may promise difference, but it guarantees neither accuracy nor truthfulness. Equally, it promotes connectivity, challenges and is challenged; and sometimes has a feed, storywise or in terms of on-the-spot images of news events that have the traditional media queuing up to use. In any case, professional journalists, abiding by the principles of thorough research, balanced reporting and analysis are already forging hybrid careers, as at home on the Net as on paper or on air.

Critical though he is of many claims for journalism in cyberspace, Jim Hall, in *Online Journalism: A Critical Primer*,[23] concedes:

> The emergence of new, or revived, journalistic forms on the web seems to offer some hope for a kind of participatory democracy in a depoliticized era. By returning a voice to the public, journalism gives it the possibility of rethinking itself and untangling itself from the commodity.

The global responsibilities of media communication

The Greek *polis*, or city, in which was located the *agora*, or open space for debate and decision-making, was mentioned in Chapter 4, Media in Society: Purpose and Performance, and encapsulated in the term *mediapolis*. This describes both the tangible and intangible elements of community in its relationship to media purpose and performance.

The media have *become* the agora; and they share the polis with the people, yet on a grander scale than ever existed in Athens or the other Greek states; for the mediapolis is the world, both of *us* and of *other*. It is all-embracing and in principle *inclusive*.

The mediapolis is also to be viewed, as Roger Silverstone puts it in *Media and Morality: On the Rise of the Mediapolis*,[24] as 'a site for the construction of a moral order … commensurate with the scope and scale of global interdependence'. The theme is that of *one world*; indeed our *only* world. The author is under no illusion about the kind of mediapolis we currently inhabit:

> There is of course no integrity within the contemporary mediapolis. The public space which it constitutes is fractured by cultural difference and the absence of communication, as much as it is by the homogenization of global television and genuine, if only momentary, collective attention to global events, crises and catastrophes.

The mediapolis is 'manifestly … embryonic and imperfect; and even in its potential can never be imagined as fully realizable. But,' argues Silverstone, 'it has to be seen as a necessary starting point for the creation of a more effective global civil space'. It is 'both a reality and an ambition'.

This argument is given strong support by Kai Hafez in *The Myth of Media Globalization*.[25] Hafez seriously questions the current existence of a globalized media, that is, one that crosses national boundaries and is a force for good, generating 'connectivity and system change'. As the book's title suggests, we are back in the realm of myth. The current myth of globalization, says Hafez in his Introduction 'mixes fact with exaggerated projections ... [and] fuses truth and falsehood':

> The question at stake today is nothing less than whether we have a functioning 'world communication system', allowing an undistorted view of the world, or whether we will have one in the future and under what circumstances.

What is largely myth is also incipient truth and, in the author's view, deserves to be worked on, 'because the world probably needs positive myths of this kind'. In his 'Conclusion: globalization – a necessary myth?' Hafez says:

> Casting light on the myth of 'globalization' as it affects cross-border communication does not mean exposing it as pure fiction. Nor does it mean denying the significance of myths generally. The ceaseless alternation between the formation and transformation is one of the key dynamics in the creation of culture.

Kai Hafez and Roger Silverstone are at one in believing that the mediapolis is still a vision, one that is vulnerable, liable to regress behind protective national boundaries; such regression occurring not the least because of the (often xenophobic) way in which the media report the world; representing it, as Hafez puts it, as 'chaotic and crisis-ridden'.

Hospitality as a guiding principle

The kind of mediapolis Silverstone envisages is essentially a challenge 'to the inequities of representation and the persistence of exclusion' currently characteristic of the exercise of media power, 'both by capital and by the state, and within the ideological and prejudicial frames of unreflexive reporting and storytelling'.

Bearing in mind what Roger Silverstone considers the most important determinant of 'our moral worth and our status as human beings', that is, 'our relationship to the other, to the stranger', it follows that the mediapolis must highlight above its portals a declaration of hospitality.

This Silverstone considers 'an obligation to welcome the stranger'. Hospitality is a 'right not just to freedom of speech [granted to Other],' but 'an obligation to listen and hear'. In this sense hospitality 'is intimately linked with issues of justice and with truthfulness ... ' It follows that the obligation to listen and hear require the creation of 'space for effective communication'.

The French philospher Jacques Derrida also sees in hospitality a prime, indeed primal, virtue. In *On Cosmopolitanism and Forgiveness*,[26] and quoted by Silverstone in his chapter on hospitality and justice, Derrida writes of hospitality as 'culture itself and not simply one ethic amongst others'.

Publics also have their responsibilities

If the ideals mentioned here apply to the practitioners of media, we as audience, the reading, listening, watching and networking public, also have obligations. Silverstone states:

> A responsible and accountable media culture ... depends on a critical and literate citizenry (as well as a critical and literate, that is reflexive, profession), a citizenry above all, which is critical with respect to, and literate in the ways of, mass mediation and media representation.

This brings us back to the crucial role that the study of media plays in contemporary society. Of course media literacy is not to be confined to students; it is a responsibility of the citizen of the mediapolis. Both among producers and consumers media literacy 'needs to be recognized as increasingly necessary'. At the core of media literacy, argues Silverstone,

> ... should be a moral agenda, always debated, never fixed, but permanently inscribed in public discourse and private practice, a moral discourse which recognizes our ultimate responsibility for the other person in a world of great conflict, tragedy, intolerance and indifference, and which critically engages with our media's incapacity (as well as its occasional capacity) to engage with the reality of that difference, responsibly and humanely. For it is in our understanding of the world, and our willingness and capability to act in it, that our humanity or inhumanity is defined.

Summary

Surveyed in this chapter are issues high on the agendas of media analysts. Chiefly they concern the links between governments and corporations and the shift in many Western countries from public control of the media to private control. It has been seen that the power agenda and the corporate agenda have, for ideological and practical reasons, recognized in *deregulation* mutual benefits. Critics have expressed concern that the rush to privatization and globalization potentially damages the quality and diversity of media.

The culture of consumerism disseminated by the media worldwide is classified by writers such as George Ritzer as McDonaldization, while other critics have seen in Disney's harnessing of history to profit-making entertainment risks of over-simplification that obstruct the kind of understanding necessary to learn the lessons of history. Mention is made of Baudrillard's rather fatalistic belief that there is no escape from the myth of consumerism, criticism of it merely helping to reinforce rather than subvert it.

Reference is made to the deconvergence of audience though there is evidence that people are slow to abandon traditional media content, a situation that does not necessarily displease the major providers of programmes. The chapter then focuses on the recommendation by James Curran and Myung-Ji Park[20] that the study of media needs to be 'de-Westernized', shifted from the tendency to view the world and its media practices from an ethnocentric position. At the same time we are warned against an over-reliance on global perspectives, the danger being that we underestimate the diversity of national cultural patterns and processes.

The challenge to traditional media practices resulting from opportunities made possible by the Internet for citizen journalism is touched upon. Finally, the issue (and myth) of globalized communication is discussed in relation to the notion of the mediapolis and Roger Silverstone's belief that the media ought to be, and can be, 'a site for the construction of a moral order'.

KEY TERMS

convergence   manufacture of consent   cross-media ownership
deconvergence   unitary/pluralism   core–periphery/
break-up models (of audience fragmentation)   narrowcasting
niche programming   McDonaldized/McDonaldization   Disneyized
efficiency, calculability, predictability, control   ethnocentric
glocal   marketization   culture of consumption   de-Westernization
citizen journalism   myth of globalization   mediapolis   hospitality
media literacy   moral agenda

Suggested activities

1. Discussion

   (a) 'Myths are alive, well and prospering in the 21st century'. How far might it be said that the globalization of communication is a myth?

   (b) How far do you consider your education has been, and is, governed by efficiency, calculability, predictability and control?

   (c) Baudrillard considers that in the modern world consumerism is inescapable. Do you agree?

   (d) Bearing in mind the advances of citizen journalism, do we really need professionals any more?

   (e) If, as Roger Silverstone argues, *hospitality to other* is a key principle of conduct in the mediapolis, how might society be persuaded of its importance?

   (f) Why do you consider media literacy has generally been undervalued?

2. Draw up a set of guiding principles on the media's global obligations and responsibities and mail these to newspaper editors, TV and radio executives inviting their comments. If you are fortunate enough to get responses write these up in an article and post it on the Net.

3. Compile a listing of corporate ownership of media worldwide. It would be useful to create a diagram of ownership which illustrates the *connections* the major corporations have with each other; include the connections media corps have with companies whose products complement rather than compete with media (for example, burgers, ice-cream etc 'synergizing' with movies and TV).

4. Prepare a 5-minute blog on the work of Ofcom: is it furthering the interests of citizens or merely promoting competition? Is it succeeding in doing both? How does its work compare with regulatory bodies in the USA or Europe?

5. Lead and record a buzz group discussion on (a) Audience, where is it at, where is it going? and (b) Does audience get the media service it deserves?

6. Essay practice: Examine the plus, minus and interesting aspects of Citizen Journalism.

Now read on

George Ritzer followed up work quoted here with *Explorations in the Sociology of Consumption: Fast Food, Credit Cards and Casinos* (US: Sage, 2001), a useful reminder of how consumerism not only attempts to shape our identities and lifestyles but penetrates our once-secret worlds; it is also apposite for those in the UK uneasy about the onrush of casino culture. See also *Consumer Culture: History, Theory and Politics* (US/UK: Sage, 2007) by Roberta Sassatelli.

Readable and still relevant are Robert Goldman and Stephen Papson's *Nike Culture: The Sign of the Swoosh* and *Barbie Culture* by Mary F. Rogers, both from Sage and published in 1998. Sage too seems to have been thinking along the lines recommended by James Curran, with four publications issued in 2000 – *Television Across Europe: A Comparative Introduction*, edited by Jan Wieten, Graham Murdock and Peter Dahlgren, *Satellites Over South East Asia: Broadcasting, Culture and the Public Interest* by David Page and William Crawley, *Television in Contemporary Asia*, edited by David French and Michael Richards and Kirk Johnson's *Television and Social Change in India*.

There are excellent contributions to *The New Media Reader* (UK: Open University Press, 2006), edited by Robert Hassan and Julian Thomas, and in another Open University publication, *Media Audiences* edited by Marie Gillespie and published in 2005. Also from the OU, try *Understanding Media: Inside Celebrity* (2005), edited by Jessica Evans and David Hesmondhalgh.

The market is filling up with tomes focusing on the Internet; recommended from the University of Columbia Press, published in the USA and UK, is *Virtual Publics: Policy and Community in an Electronic Age* (2005), edited by Beth E. Kolko. On the theme of journalistic responsibility, Tony Harcup's *The Ethical Journalist* (US/UK: Sage, 2006) is recommended alongside Roger Silverstone's *Media and Morality* (see Note 24) quoted in this chapter.

Finally, time to check whether your library has ordered multiple copies of *McQuail's Reader in Mass Communication Theory* (UK: Sage, 2002), edited by Denis McQuail and featuring contributions by some of the world's top media scholars, from Pertti Alasuutari and Ien Ang through James Carey, Peter Dahlgren, Edward Herman, Todd Gitlin, Stuart Hall and Elihu Katz to Janice Radway, Haye Tuckman, Judith Williamson and Liesbet van Zoonen.

Notes

1. Herbert Schiller, *Information Inequality: The Deepening Social Crisis in America* (UK/US: Routledge, 1996).
2. *McQuail's Mass Communication Theory* (UK: Sage, 5th edition, 2005).
3. Steve Case, founder of America On Line (AOL), reported in BBC News online, 'Case calls for Time Warner split', 10 December 2005.
4. Norman Solomon, quoted by Mariellen Diemand in 'Media and Iraq: war coverage analysis', a posting on Media Education Foundation (MEF), 17 April 2003. Solomon's original article appeared in *Media Beat*.
5. Anthony Arnove (ed.), *Iraq Under Siege: The Deadly Impact of Sanctions and War* (UK: Pluto Press, 2nd edition, 2003)
6. Robert Sheer speaking at a 3-day Media and War Conference at the University of California (Berkeley) School of Journalism, 2004.
7. Sheldon Rampton and John Stauber, *Weapons of Mass Deception: The Uses of Propaganda in Bush's War on Iraq* (UK: Constable and Robinson, 2003).
8. Colin Sparks, 'Media theory after the fall of European communism: why the old models from east and west won't do any more', Chapter 3 in *De-Westernizing Media Studies* (UK/US Routledge, 2000), edited by James Curran and Myung-Jin Park.
9. Brian McNair, *News and Journalism in the UK* (UK: Routledge, 3rd edition, 1999).
10. UK: Labour government White Paper 'A New Future for Communications' CM5010 (DTI/CMS, HMSO, December 2000).
11. Campaign for Press and Broadcasting Freedom: The Response of the Campaign for Press and Broadcasting Freedom to the White Paper 'A New Future for Communications' (February 2001).
12. Patricia Holland's article focuses on what has been termed the Digital Dividend. With the switch from analogue to digital broadcasting, high-frequency wavelengths will be freed up, offering, in Holland's words, 'the potential to expand many different types of communication, including broadcasting'. This is an immensely precious 'dividend' and a one-off. At the time of writing, the plan is to put the spectrum space up for auction: the highest bidder takes all. Holland says, 'Once space on the spectrum has been sold, its owners can do what they like with it. They can leave it empty, develop some new, hitherto unthought-of use, or trade it to make money out of it. They have no obligation to provide any sort of service that will benefit the public'.
13. Jean Seaton, *Carnage and the Media: The Making and Breaking of News About Violence* (UK: Allen Lane, 2005).
14. Breaking news: in Jean Seaton's words, 'attention grabbing top stories that are often visually dramatic'; to be differentiated from 'explanatory news' and from the rarest form of all – facing extinction if market forces have their way – 'deep background' investigatory news 'that tracks

issues to the root'. Seaton argues, 'In a world of globalised corporate power, full scale detailed investigation is essential to provide the public with the truth about what is going on'.

15. Denis McQuail, *Audience Analysis* (UK: Sage, 1997).

16. George Ritzer, *The McDonaldization of Society* (US: Pine Forge Press, 1992, 2nd edition, Sage, US/UK, 2006). Ritzer's ideas are subjected to critical review in *Resisting McDonaldization* (UK: Sage, 1999) edited by Barry Smart.

17. Douglas Kellner in *Resisting McDonaldization*. See Note 16.

18. Alexander Wilson, 'The betrayal of the future: Walt Disney's EPCOT Center', Chapter 8 in *Disney Discourse: Producing the Magic Kingdom* (US/UK: Routledge, 1994), edited by Eric Smoodin.

19. Jean Baudrillard, *The Consumer Society: Myths and Structures*. Originally published as *La Société de Consommation* by Editions Denoel, 1970; English translation, Sage, 1998. The introduction to the Sage edition is written by George Ritzer, hinting that networks of interest as typified by the TNCs (transnational corporations) are not unheard of in the academic world. Ritzer points out that for Baudrillard the affluent society itself is a myth; for all societies combine, as Baudrillard puts it, 'structural excess' with 'structural penury'. Growth may well produce wealth but it also produces poverty; in fact one is a function of the other. While praising Baudrillard Ritzer hesitates to confirm the 'grand narrative' sweep of his ideas and consequently his judgements about contemporary society. Ritzer says that Baudrillard, while being 'uniformly positive about primitive society … fails to see anything wrong with it'; at the same time 'he fails to see anything positive about, or right with, modern (or postmodern) consumer society. He is unremittingly critical of that society'. Ritzer argues that 'An even slightly more balanced portrait of *both* primitive and modern societies would have enhanced Baudrillard's analysis'.

20. *De-Westernizing Media Studies* (UK/US: Routledge, 2000), edited by James Curran and Myung-Jin Park. Annabelle Sreberny contributes Chapter 5, 'Television, gender and democratization in the Middle East' to this excellent reader.

21. Aidan White, 'Media monopolies versus editorial independence: signs of hope in Korea', online article, 4 February 2002, openDemocracy website (www.openDemocracy.net).

22. A Hollywood-based website, The Drudge Report, was initiated in 1994 by Matt Drudge. The site broke the Clinton–Lewinsky scandal and has been varyingly described as a 'threat to democracy' and an 'idiot with a modem'. Drudge Report postings are claimed to be 'to the left' of the average American citizen. Drudge's address to the US National Press Club is quoted by Jim Hall in his *Online Journalism: A Critical Primer* (UK: Pluto Press, 2001).

23. Jim Hall, see Note 22.

24. Roger Silverstone, *Media and Morality: On the Rise of the Mediapolis* (UK/ US: Polity Press, 2007).

25. Kai Hafez, *The Myth of Media Globalization* (UK/US: Polity Press, 2007), translated by Alex Skinner. As far as cross-border communication is concerned, Hafez is a sceptical believer. He responds coolly, for example, to claims that the Internet is the answer to global media aspirations. In fact a sub-title in his chapter on the Internet is 'The Net as Tower of Babel'. He writes an interesting chapter on media and immigration, stating, 'What is certain is that neither the quality of media content nor attitudes towards foreigners have noticeably changed or become more sophisticated in the era of globalization'.

26. Jacques Derrida, *On Cosmopolitanism and Forgiveness* (UK/US: Routledge, 2002), translated by Mark Dooley and Michael Hughes.

Concluding Remarks

In the study of media communication there can be few conclusions and no Conclusion, because essentially our voyage takes us to the frontiers of meaning; and wherever meaning is confronted, there is doubt and debate, discourse and counter-discourse. The 'truth' about cyberspace, the 'power' of media and the capacity of audiences to resist or reject that power; the 'inevitability' of technological change, the 'victory' of capitalism over communism, of the private over the public, of individualism over community, the progress of media globalization, are ongoing issues, not certainties or inexorable trends.

While sharpening and practising our critical faculties as observers of media we need to remember to smile as well as to frown, to recognize in much media performance, and in countless media artefacts, artistry and delight, the capacity of media to stimulate, enlighten, reveal; to make us wonder, to make us laugh and to create in us both a relish for our own individuality and a sense of community.

We can be sure that those in control of, or with influence over, media communication systems will take pains (and sometimes cause pain) in order to stay in control. They will use communication for that purpose, which makes it all the more important that we recognize communication as a force for change; that we understand the strategies which are employed to defend privilege, assert inequality, deny freedoms, censor truth.

If, as James Carey has said in *Communication as Culture: Essays on Media and Society* (UK/US: Routledge, 1992), communication and culture are interchangeable, then we might argue that communication and democracy are equally so: the one creates, supports, furthers and protects the other. We blur the connection at our peril.

At the same time, most dramatically since 9/11, the notions of freedom and democracy, of equality between peoples, nations, races and (not the least) between the sexes have been challenged and tested; in some cases and some places, almost to breaking point. Uncertainties escalate; what George Gerbner (see Glossary) termed a 'mean world syndrome' (generated by media coverage of violence, real and fictional) is a flame fanned by headlines and images. The 'way things have been' seems to be everywhere questioned, often threatened; identity, whether it is that of the individual, the group, or the nation seems to be in turmoil if not crisis.

The media are not the cause of conflict, disillusion and pessimism about the human condition; yet they are contributors. At their worst, they either favour rubbing our noses in the darker side of life, or choose to tempt us with the baubles of consumerist entertainment into ignoring it, or pretending it does not exist. As Roger Silverstone suggests, the media have a vital responsibility to participate in possible solutions, just as a media-literate public must in turn demand the highest standards in an increasingly mediated world.

Technology has improved rather more quickly than human behaviour. Sometimes we forget that it does not have a life of its own, that so far at least it remains the servant of human masters. We are struck by its apparent neutrality; sometimes in awe of its seeming indifference to whether it is used for good or ill, to the benefit of humankind or to its detriment.

A responsibility lies with people-generated media to constantly remind us who are the robots; whose interests are furthered by 'progress'; in short, to chart the path of all-embracing citizenship through minefields of vested interests, whether these be consumerist, nationalist, globalist, colonialist, populist or propagandist; to serve as watchdog of public rights, of the individual and the community in the context of often conflicting cultural, political, territorial, ideological and religious imperatives.

Such scenarios make the study of media communication an essential feature of healthy democracy – challenged as well as challenging, sometimes painful, the complex lurking behind the obvious; replete with questions but short on assertive answers. By its nature it courts controversy, prompts scepticism; by its value – its potentially subversive value – it stirs in some quarters disapproval. It is above all, *relevant* because it examines and upholds the view that communication is the key to human activity, and probably to human survival.

Appendix 1
A Brief ABC of Perceived Media Effects

Agenda-setting effect
The media rank events in a hierarchy of importance; encouraging people not so much in what to think but what to think about.

Alienation effect
Notion that the mass character of media creates in audiences feelings of isolation; disengagement from membership of the community and therefore a sense of alienation, or estrangement, from society's values.

Amplification effect
By giving intensive cover to certain stories and issues, their importance is amplified in importance.

Boomerang effect
When media coverage backfires and achieves contrary responses or reactions from the public than those desired by the media.

Catharsis effect
The word *catharsis* comes from the Greek, meaning 'purification' or 'purgation'. Today it is defined as emotional release. We watch a play, film or TV drama and its humour, tragedy or violence triggers release of our emotions. Some commentators believe that watching screen violence has a cathartic effect. It releases tensions which in some circumstances might be expressed through real violence. In other words, fictionalized violence may head-off real violent behaviour.

Copy-cat effect
What people experience through the media may stimulate copy-cat behaviour; acts of individual violence, for example, or street rioting.

Desensitizing effect
Over-exposure to violence or suffering might make us 'hardened' to what we see; blasé even. This has been related to what has been termed 'compassion fatigue'.

Displacement effect
This happens between media, for example the arrival of television, while not eclipsing radio certainly displaced it, shifting it towards the margins of audience use in comparison with its former dominant position.

Distraction effect
Usually relates to the ways in which the media often distract public attention from important issues by concentrating on other, usually more entertaining, stories.

Enlargement effect
Capacity to expand people's knowledge and system of beliefs.

Hastening effect
When media coverage of events hastens the development of those events and responses to them, usually on the part of those in authority. Media publicity on health hazards may hasten government legislation.

Inoculation effect
Flu jabs inject a mild dose of the flu virus into the bloodstream thereby serving to built up resistance to contagion; the same goes for the media 'bug'.

Mainstreaming effect
Part of cultivation theory most closely associated with American researcher George Gerbner; the nature of media coverage tends to create a convergence of political attitudes towards a mainstream position, but one that drifts rightwards. Coverage *blurs*, *blends* otherwise divergent groups and then *bends* the mainstream 'in the direction of the medium's interests in profit, populist politics and power'.

Narcoticizing dysfunction effect
The media has the effect of drugging people, leading to mass apathy and general passivity.

No previous knowledge effect
Where audience is uninformed about matters it is more likely to believe what the media tell them.

Reciprocal effect
Coverage affects and changes the nature of what is covered. A game such as darts, traditionally a bar-room game to accompany the pint, has through TV coverage become a spectator sport; and particularly suited to television. Equally, a party political conference, traditionally an occasion for chewing the political fat and permitting ordinary party members to get things off their chests is, once covered by TV, turned into a political spectacle where image triumphs over substance.

Reinforcement effect
Opinions, attitudes, beliefs, prejudices are deemed more likely to be reinforced than changed by media coverage.

Spill-over effect
When people outside the intended target audience are affected by media coverage and comment.

Third person effect
Perception of effects on 'others'; thus fears about the effects of the portrayal of violence relate for example to children or teenagers rather than those actually doing the perceiving (see Appendix 2).

Trivializing effect
Charge made against television that it trivializes most of the matters it deals with out of a need to retain audience attention.

Appendix 2
Screen Violence as Influence and Commodity: An Ongoing Debate

Among researchers, commentators, community leaders and the public at large, violence on screen, in the movies or on television, is seen as an issue of importance. Once again, opinions divide between the Strong Effects school (or cultivationist position) and those with a belief in the Active Audience, that is, viewing audiences as resistant to influence and quite capable of differentiating between fiction and fact.

The cultivationist argument is a simple one, and it would be rash to dismiss it without due consideration. It asserts that the more we see of violence, the more we might become insensitive to it, and thus eventually immune. Either way, it might confirm our view that out there is a dangerous and hostile world.

It has been estimated that in the United States the average American child, by the age of 18, will have witnessed 18,000 simulated murders on television. Following the screening of Michael Cimino's *The Deer Hunter* (1978), with its notorious Russian roulette scene, 35 young men in the USA committed suicide in like manner.

The anecdotal evidence could fill many pages. Carrying more weight, however, are the many studies into the effects of violence that do indicate a link between images and realities. In a contribution 'Colours of violence' to *Index on Censorship*[1] Anne Nelson writes:

> The debate is not about dramas or documentaries which hinge on a killing; nor on the violence of war reports. Public concern focuses on the gratuitous violence of cinema and TV that makes dialogue subordinate to the shocking visual image and saturates the audience with its morbid repetition: the kind of movie violence that propels young men to stand up in their seats, jab their fists in the air and shout 'Aw-right!'

Nelson refers to a July 1993 issue of the American magazine *Mother Jones* which estimates that there had been over 80 separate research studies, all of them affirming the causal link between television violence and actual violence.

However, in a letter published in a subsequent issue of *Index* (September/October 1994), the acting executive director of Feminists for Free Expression, Catherine Sieman, writes a riposte to the position taken up by Nelson:

> [she] perpetuates the myth that the connection between television violence and real-life violence has been established, while citing little actual evidence. The hypothesis that images of violence cause violence in real life is not supported by history.

Sieman argues that one of the most violent periods in American history was between 1929 and 1932, 'when there was no television and most people lacked regular access even to the movies'. Violence in the 19th century, says Sieman, referring in support of her point of view to the position taken up by the American National Research Council, was higher than now.

She also states that in industrialized countries with high TV-viewing figures the actual violence rates are lower than many developing nations that have 'low television viewing and very high rates of violence':

> The American Psychological Association (1993) and the National Research Council (1993) conclude that violence is caused by parental abuse, rejection and neglect, accompanied by factors such as poverty and the belief that educational or job opportunities are closed because of racial or ethnic discrimination.

Sieman is insisting that before we decide one way or another about the connection between mediated and lived violence we should hesitate before loading the blame for the perceived increase in violence in our communities upon the media. Cultivation may appear to be happening but proof that audiences are actually 'cultivated' by media rather than by circumstances unrelated to media must be more substantial, and more convincing if it is to carry weight. What is more, there is always the fear that concentrating on 'media-bred violence' will deflect attention from other sources of violence – inequality, deprivation, racial hatred and alienation.

Perhaps the most extensive and long-running research into the effects of television violence on audience has been conducted by George Gerbner and his team at the Annenberg School of Communication.

The assassination of President John Kennedy followed by that of his brother Robert and then of the Reverend Dr Martin Luther King led to the establishment in the United States in 1968 of the National Commission on the Causes and Prevention of Violence.

The Mass Media Task Force commissioned Gerbner to provide an analysis of violence on television. *Cultural Indicators*, the title of the research project, was to produce massive and significant data. Yet it seems that the more this research enterprise revealed, the less attention, in official and media circles, was paid to it.

In a chapter entitled 'Violence and terror in and by the media' published in *Media, Crisis and Democracy: Mass Communication and the Disruption of the Social Order*,[2] Gerbner writes:

> Humankind may have had more bloodthirsty eras but none as filled with images of violence as the present. We are awash in a tide of violent representations such as the world has never seen. There is no escape from the massive infusion of colourful mayhem into the homes and cultural life of ever-larger areas of the world.

Anne Nelson[1] believes that the American networks continue with screen violence because they believe it is popular:

> The networks' audience share has plummeted over the past few years as a result of the massive inroads of cable, satellite and videotape. As commercial network audiences have dropped, so have their standards. In the attempt to recapture a bored, channel-hopping audience that they themselves have disaffected, the networks become ever more shrill, crude and action-orientated.

Yet Gerbner and his colleagues argue in 'The demonstration of power: violence profile number 10'[3] that 'there is no general correlation between violence and the ratings of comparable programmes aired at the same time'. In other words, violence is not essential for programme profit, so why does it persist, why go on 'drenching nearly every home in the rapidly expanding "free world" with graphic scenes of expertly choreographed brutality'?

Violence: good for business?

Perceptions, however, often over-ride and over-rule facts. If violence is perceived to be an essential ingredient of popular programming, whether of fiction or 'tabloidized' news, then it will continue to be exploited as a *commodity*, and to the detriment of serious attempts to address all issues, including that of violence. Nelson fears that the use of violence on screen pre-empts quality programming:

> Hard news, international news, investigative journalism and analytical coverage of economic and social issues are endangered species, supplanted [in the USA] by sensational sex and murder stories, 'disease of the week' scare stories and visually-striking but meaningless footage of disasters. The current catchphrase of the US newsroom is: 'If it bleeds, it leads'.

She warns of complacence beyond American shores where public service regulation has traditionally resisted the excesses she describes in American film media. As deregulation and privatization increase globally, public service broadcasters 'who have set standards of quality and suitability for the rest of the industry, will be forced to compete for audiences in new ways'. If these concern cutting production costs, offering instant gratification to the largest possible audiences, then 'new ways' are also 'old ways':

> Violence [argues Nelson] lends itself to cheap, point-and-shoot productions to fill the caverns of airtime created by the new channels. Violence is visually commanding; as our viewer of the near future spins the 500-channel dial, violent images will register more quickly than talking heads.

Affirmation of power

Behind the portrayal of violence is the principle, long enshrined in the Western film among other genres, that without violence (the power of the gun) there can be no *order*. Violence, cultivation theory argues, serves as a metaphor for control. There is legitimate violence and there is the violence that must be condemned. By demonstrating disorder (weapons in the wrong hands) the media (by showing weapons in the 'right' hands) confirm the rules of order.

If the portrayal of violence is deemed to be not altogether bad for business, it also has its 'up-side' in a political sense. In 'Violence and terror in and by the media'[2] Gerbner says:

A market place is an arena of control by power. Left to itself it tends towards monopoly, or total power. Violence is a demonstration of power. Images of violence project hierarchies of power – gender, racial, sexual, class and national power – that the mass-cultural market place cultivates through its control of dramatic imagery rather than consumer choice or commercial need alone.

Violence stories threaten consensus, disturb consonance. Violence – so long as it is legitimately wielded – is the power that restores states of dissonance to states of consonance; re-establishes equilibrium. Things 'will turn out all right if we are on the right side (or look as if we were)'. Gerbner believes that, 'Crime may not pay in the world of dramatic fiction, but violence always does – for the winner'. He claims:

> ... the power to define violence and project its lessons, including stigmatization, demonization and the selective labelling of terror and terrorists, is the chief cultural requirement for social control. The ability and protected right to mass-produce and discharge it into the common symbolic environment may be a decisive (if unacknowledged) concentration of power-culture in domestic and global policy making.

Media violence is, therefore, 'a political scenario' working on several levels. As a symbolic exercise it is a demonstration of power, of who has it, who uses it, and who loses it.

'Few countries,' writes Gerbner, 'are willing or able to invest in a cultural policy that does not surrender the socialization of their children and the future of their language, culture and society to "Market forces"'. Such a failure, in Gerbner's view, is more likely to 'contribute to the resurgence of chauvinism, clericalism and to neo-fascism than to open, diverse and humane democratic cultures around the world'.

'This,' Gerbner is convinced, 'is not an isolated problem that can be addressed by focusing on media violence alone. It is an integral part of a market-dominated system of global cultural commercialism that permeates the mainstream of the common symbolic environment.'

The problem is pressing and it is unlikely, in Gerbner's view, to be resisted by individuals or families staking out their own agendas in the face of the flood of images of violence: 'Only a new international environmental movement, a cultural environmental movement dedicated to democratic media reform, can do justice to the challenge of violence in and by the media.'

UNESCO global media violence study

Conducted between 1996 and 1997, and involving over 5000 12-year-olds from 23 countries, the study issued a 60-item questionnaire seeking to track the importance of TV in the lives of young people, in particular to explore the impact of screen violence on perceptions and behaviour. Striking similarities were found between children in contrasting cultures, geographical and economic contexts.

Confirmation was found of *interactivity* between media and real-life violence; and in many of the children's responses an overlap, blurring between the fictional and the real. Director of the research programme, Jo Groebel of the University of Utrecht, noted the number of children who believed that violence was 'more systematically rewarded than more conciliatory ways of coping with one's life. It is often presented as gratuitous, thrilling, and interpreted as a good problem-solver in a variety of situations' (see Note 4 for extended comment on competing viewpoints concerning the media–violence connection).

The case for television violence

One of a number of media analysts who have challenged the Gerbner findings and the cultivationist position generally, is Jib Fowles, and the above sub-head is the title of his book published by Sage in the USA in 1999. Fowles argues that, contrary to the opinion that screen violence has the potential to breed real violence, it is more likely to inhibit or reduce it. 'Television violence,' states Fowles, 'is good for people' and 'the assault on television violence [by its critics] is absolutely unwarranted.' His argument starts from the premise that humans have an in-built violent impulse. Violence is ever present and it needs, in one way or another, to be managed:

> In isolation, television violence may seem reproachable and occupy the foreground with a menacing intensity, but with a longer perspective it can seem comparatively like an improvement – a purer distillation of the age-old processes for containing and redirecting violence.

Fowles reminds us that 'television violence is symbolic only... Nobody actually suffers for our pleasure'. It is 'simply the most routinized working out of innate aggressiveness and fear'. The often feverish debate over screen violence Jib Fowles classifies as a variant of *moral panic* which he sees as being characterized by the 'extreme righteousness of the condemners as they lash out at conjured or magnified transgressions'; their response always being 'out of proportion to whatever instigates it'.

Judgement suspended, decision deferred

It would seem that the debate about the effects of mediated violence on audiences, upon public attitudes and responses, will run and run. For the student of media, the *nature* of screen violence might prove a more significant avenue of investigation than its effects.

What kinds of violence are we talking about, and occurring in what contexts? Violence is overt – up front – and covert. It can be stylized, or its realism can shock: why one, why the other? Like the audience for media, screen violence is diverse, its constituency complex. We need to seek more precise classification of modes of violence, recognizing that sometimes *verbal* violence in a domestic situation can prove to be more disturbing than physical violence in other scenarios; and we need to differentiate between fictional violence and that which we see in the news and in documentaries.

Equally we need to explore the motives for censoring violence on the part of those who make the decisions to excise: why cut this example yet allow to pass through the gate other examples? Who is perceived to be 'protected' by the censorship of violence? Is there public consensus about such censorship or does that censorship provoke an interest in that which is censored which might not have been there originally?

In considering screen violence are we not also focusing on crime? Richard Osborn in an article 'Crime, media, violence' published in *Free Press* (publication of the Campaign for Press and Broadcasting Freedom), March–April, 1996 talks of crime being 'a seriously nasty business', which means that it has news value. He writes, 'Crime and television are the two great cultural definers of our present era and when they are combined they are a lethal force'. Crime, believes Osborn, has become 'the staple diet of television' for it is 'incredibly exciting, threatening, horrifying, fascinating and repellent all at once'. In consequence, it 'makes bloody good television'.

Crime and justice

Screen violence is rarely portrayed outside of a framework of justice; and the study of audience consumption and enjoyment of programmes containing violence needs to take this constantly into account. In a *Journal of Communication* article (June 2002), 'Moral judgement and crime drama: an integrated theory of enjoyment', Arthur R. Raney and Jennings Bryant state:

> Presentations of criminal activity contain much more than mere acts of aggression and hostility. Every act of intentional violence, whether intended to provoke or retaliate, can be subjected to rigorous moral reasoning with regard to justice.

Representations of violence 'make a statement about what is fair and appropriate retribution; they convey a sense of justice to the audience'. We see here an example of narrative sequencing as illustrated in Chapter 6: an event causes disequilibrium; the narrative works towards the restoration of equilibrium. So in crime narratives, disequilibrium is brought about by an injustice.

Equilibrium is restored by the righting of an injustice, hence the integral nature of the violence. What Raney and Bryant term 'moral judgement' on the part of audience concerns a cognitive process in which, as well as the meting out of justice in a crime story, the characters themselves are judged.

Responses will vary according to people's attitudes and dispositions towards the exercise of justice but the pattern, or what the authors call the *justice sequence*, operates in the same way: there is the *instigational act* (the crime) and the *retributional action* (the punishment). Part of the cognitive pleasure derived from watching crime on screen is evaluating this sequence: does the punishment fit the crime?

Our responses as audience work both affectively, for example in our sympathy with victims, and cognitively through assessing the justice of the actions we see:

> The viewer (on some level of consciousness) compares his or her notion of proper justice to the one presented in the drama through the justice sequence. Therefore, the process of ascribing enjoyment to a crime drama is dependent upon the relative degree of correspondence between the viewer's sense of justice and the statement about justice made in the drama.

Raney and Bryant are of the opinion that insufficient research attention has been paid to 'the role moral judgements actually play in the entertainment experience'.

Classifying crime

For the student of media setting out to place violence into manageable, and thus analyzable, categories, a useful start might be made by looking at the research work of Jessica Allen, Sonia Livingstone and Robert Reiner in an article published in the *European Journal of Communication*, March 1998. Entitled, 'True lies: changing images of crime in British postwar cinema', the article reports on a survey conducted by the authors of 1461 crime-related films released between 1943 and 1991.

Their findings illustrate the value of research, and of caution in judging the 'dire' effects of media. Allen, Livingstone and Reiner write that 'contrary to general beliefs about increased crime content in the media...our data shows a constant rate of representation, at least in the cinema over the past 50 years'.

The authors pose different classifications of crime and recognize an 'increasingly graphic representation of violence', emphatically insisting however that the analysis of crime and violence needs to take socio-cultural contexts into account. They refer to the 'collapse of moral certainties in society' as well as the dominance of Hollywood, the moderation of censorship and the demographic nature of cinema audiences, in large part made up of young people.

It all depends...

Humans are capable of violence without being prompted by what they see at the cinema or on the TV screen. There are those who will watch screen violence because it gives them pleasure, and some commentators believe that this serves as an emotional, a cathartic, release (see Appendix 1 for Cathartic effect). In other words, it takes the latent violence out of them, at least for a time.

Others believe that the representation of violence prompts imitation, or at the very least representation of violence makes people insensitive to it, more tolerant of it, in real life. The evidence for this is sparse. What is more worrying is when the media actually set out to provoke response, and it does not have to be pictures on the screen. Propaganda, in the 'right' circumstances, works. People are persuaded, and sometimes they are persuaded to go out and do violent things; yet rarely do such things occur in a genuinely pluralistic society.

When there is one voice, and only one, screaming for action or revenge, when counter-arguments to violence are muted or non-existent, and when leadership seems to approve of such action, then violent behaviour can be media-induced or at least media-affirmed so that violence becomes an acceptable norm.

Even in the case of the Rwanda massacres a degree of caution has to be observed in blaming the media for what occurred. It could be argued that what caused the slaughter was as much *antecedent* factors as media incitement. The Hutu/Tutsi situation had a long history, so the memory of past conflicts, oppressions, killings was as much a stimulus to violence as the rantings of Radio Hate. In other words, the violence was waiting to happen: all that was required to inflame the already-simmering conflict was a lead, a *trigger*, an authoritative justification.

What also has to be pointed out is media's potential to rein in violence, whether it is police violence against protesting crowds or individuals, or mob violence. The presence of TV cameras can both provoke response and inhibit it. In turn, TV images of violence can alert the world to what is happening, invoking sympathy and calls for remedial action. On the other hand, of course, the relentless screening of violence, of genocide, for example, may result in the public's reservoirs of compassion being drained by too much mediated exposure to suffering.

Can journalism kill?

This was the headline of an article written by Julian Lee for the UK *Times* (27 October 2000), reporting the trial of three journalists accused of inciting the slaughter of thousands of Rwandans. Lee writes of the trial before a United Nations court sitting at Arusha in Tanzania, 'It is the first time since Julius Streicher, the editor of the Nazi propaganda newspaper, *Der Sturmer*, stood before the Nuremburg judges that a journalist has stood for trial on charges of genocide...The linchpin for the prosection's case is the alleged catalogue of inflammatory broadcasts that appeared in the months leading up to the slaughter'.

The radio station in question was RTLM, Radio Television Libre de Mille Collines, nicknamed Radio Hate. The station was the voice of the majority Hutu, and the target of hate were the minority Tutsi. In April 1994, RTLM, barely a year into its existence, was urging Hutu militia groups to 'go to work', taunting the Tutsi with comments such as 'the graves are not yet full'. Regular praise for RTLM was published in the newspaper *Kangura* owned and run by one of the journalists on trial.

Pleading guilty to the charge of incitement to commit genocide, broadcaster Georges Ruggai was sentenced to imprisonment for 12 years.

In *Compassion Fatigue: How the Media Sell Disease, Famine, War and Death*,[5] Susan D. Moeller suggests that screen violence can be a 'turn-off'. She differentiates between the effects on the public of famine images and those of genocide: 'In the case of Rwanda ... the famine images touched people. The genocide pictures did not.' Moeller writes:

> In a world that moves steadily from massacres to genocide, from images of chaos, destruction, death and madness, from the gassing of the Kurds to the death camps of the Serbs to the streets and fields of slaughter of Rwandans, the public resorts to compassion fatigue as a defence mechanism against the knowledge of horror.

However, the solution to compassion fatigue, Moeller believes, 'is not for the media to respond with entertainment journalism, sensationalist journalism, formulaic journalism':

> The solution is to invest in the coverage of international affairs and to give talented reporters and camera people, editors and the producers the freedom to define their own stories – bad, good, evil and inspiring, horrific and joyous.

Such a view pulls together many of the strands of *Media Communication*; in particular it reminds us of the public sphere function of properly operating media which is a key focus for study and a guiding principle to all those with ambitions to pursue careers in the communications industry.

Dismissing screen violence as being of no significance remains a complacent option. David Trend in *The Myth of Media Violence: A Critical Introduction*[6] acknowledges a number of perspectives concerning 'bad effects', noting the tendency towards hysteria. He argues that media violence is too good for business ever to be seriously curtailed; that we enjoy it, demand it:

> Media violence enlivens stories and is a part of stories that need telling. Excitement comes from the anticipation and experience of vicarious violence. It's like salt on food. Everybody likes it even though it's not good for you.

Just the same, Trend has his concerns, echoing George Gerbner; indeed he refers to Gerbner's idea of the 'mean world syndrome'. In his chapter, 'We are afraid: media violence and society', Trend writes:

Media violence may not provoke people to become aggressive or commit crimes, but it does something more damaging. Media violence convinces people that they live in a violent world and that violence is required to make the world safer. The anxieties and attitudes that result from these beliefs about the world have profound consequences in the way people live their lives and the way society is organized.

We are back with the power of perception: what *seems* to be, according to mediated reality, becomes, often convincingly, what *is*. In the narrative of Westerns, nobody talks things out; they shoot it out; and it is interesting to conjecture whether fictional narratives (particularly of the Hollywood variety) have penetrated the psyche of those involved in conflict-resolution in the real world, for example politicians, presidents, prime ministers and the military.

The invasion of Iraq in 2003 was arguably an assertion that bang-bang scores over talk-talk; that successful engagement favours combat over compromise, shock and awe over pause and persuade. Unlike the gung-ho movie, however, the real life drama permits no neat closure. Chaos is more likely to follow than order, by which time those that instigated or led the cavalry charge have died, resigned or retired to write their memoirs.

David Trend concludes his final section, 'Responding to media violence', by stressing a key theme of the study of media, the need for active and critical readings of texts and performance in context:

> A violent scene on television will mean different things to each individual, depending on the age, race, religion, ethnicity, personal experiences, attitudes, and background of the viewer. Critical viewing reveals when violence is unneeded, wrong, or out of place. More restriction on what is available on TV or the internet won't help the situation very much. But more discussions and more consumer choices will. By discussing the various ways we understand, dislike, enjoy, and use media violence, we move the conversation forward.

Notes

1. Anne Nelson, 'Colours of violence' in *Index on Censorship*, May/June 1994. Catherine Sieman's retort is published in 'Letters: V for viewing' in the September/October 1994 edition of *Index*.

2. George Gerbner, 'Violence and terror in and by the media' in Marc Raboy and Bernard Dagenais (eds), *Media, Crisis and Democracy: Mass Communication and the Disruption of Social Order* (UK: Sage, 1992).

3. George Gerbner *et al.*, 'The demonstration of power: violence profile no. 10' in *Journal of Communication*, 29 (1979).

4. Jo Groebel, 'Media and violence', article posted on the PPU (Peace Pledge Union) website, summarizing the findings of the UNESCO study. This set out to chart the relationship between media violence and aggressive behaviour in young children, to scrutinize culture differences in response to media violence in 23 countries, several of them, like Angola, Croatia and Tajikistan, where real violence was a constant and dramatic experience in children's lives. Such has been the concern in the USA about the connection between screen violence and aggression in young people that a Senate committee, in 1999, was set up to gather findings and make recommendations. Under the chairmanship of Senator Orrin G. Hatch, the Senate Committee on the Judiciary published a report, *Children, Violence and the Media: A Report for Parents and Policy Makers*. The committee had no doubts, citing media violence as the main cause of the growth in child violence; its target was not only violence on screen but in music, computer games and the Internet. The Committee report quotes former US senator Paul Simon who asserted that, 'Thirty seconds of a soap bar commercial sells soap. Twenty-five minutes worth of glorification of violence sells violence'. The Report concludes, 'The effect of media violence on our children is no longer open to debate'.

However, though academic sceptics concerning the media–violence connection seem to be in a minority, their caution deserves serious attention. In his address to the annual convention of the American Psychological Association, in Boston (21 August 1999), Stuart Fischoff issued a broadside against what he termed a 'church of psychological political correctness and unfettered airwave pillorying'. His talk, entitled 'Psychology's Quixotic quest for the media–violence connection' refers to research designs 'which totally undercut the validity' of their declared findings. His opinion was that:

> After 50 years and over 1,000 studies (a conservative estimate), there is, I submit, not a single research study which is even remotely predictive of the Columbine massacre or similar high school shootings in the last few years … as for making the explicit connection between on-screen mayhem by the bodies of Stallone and Schwarzenegger, the minds of Oliver Stone and Wes Craven, and real-life singular, serial or mass murder, scientific psychology, albeit noble and earnest in its tireless efforts, has simply not delivered the goods. It asserts the causal nexus but doesn't actually demonstrate it.

Fischoff states,

> I should point out that it is not that I believe that media violence DOESN'T produce violent behaviour in viewers...I am merely asserting that the connection between the two has not been empirically established.

He argues the importance of considering most behaviour as 'multi-determined' and believes that peer group influence among young people is a more likely stumulant to violence than examples on screen. Violent and aggressive youths, he says, 'are attracted to violent and aggressive entertainment media'. Fischoff argues that 'the fact that rapists and murderers prefer to watch films compatible with their appetites is no indication of a causal connection, any more than the fact that golfers like to watch golf games proves that watching golf games cultivated their interest in golf'.

5. Susan D. Moeller, *Compassion Fatigue: How the Media Sell Disease, Famine, War and Death* (US/UK: Routledge, 1999).

6. David Trend, *The Myth of Media Violence: A Critical Introduction* (UK/US/Australia: Blackwell Publishing, 2007). Trend discusses a wide range of aspects of screen, computer game and network violence, including the issue of children and screen violence. For example, 'It is important,' he says, 'for children to know that human history has a violent past... Global commerce and colonialization often utilized violent means to accomplish their goals'. However, 'Just because people have had a violent history doesn't mean it must have a violent future. Knowing, representing, and teaching about violence and peace can help us make a better world'.

Bibliography

This listing of useful and readable texts is divided up under a range of handy topics arranged in alphabetic order, with the exception of books of a general, overarching nature, such as dictionaries, textbooks and readers. These are listed first. Some titles appear in more than one category.

General
Advertising/PR and media
Audience for media
Broadcasting
Censorship, spin, information manipulation
Corporations, media and globalization
Discourse/language
Gender and media
History of media
Information Age
Internet communication
Journalism
News
Politics, government and media
Press
Researching the media
Technology and media
Television formats
Theory of media
Violence and the media
War and the media

General

Boyd-Barrett, Oliver, Chris Newbold and Hilde van den Buulck (eds), *The Media Communications Book* (UK: Arnold, 2001).

Carey, James W., *Communication as Culture: Essays on Media and Society* (US: Unwin Hyman, 1989; UK: Routledge, 1992).

Curran, James and David Morley, *Media and Cultural Theory* (UK/US: Routledge, 2006).

Curran, James and Myung-Jin Park (eds), *De-Westernizing Media Studies* (UK/US: Routledge, 2000).

Downing, John, Ali Mohammadi and Annabelle Sreberny-Mohammadi, *Questioning the Media: A Critical Introduction* (US/UK/India: Sage, 1990 and subsequent editions).

Durham, Meenakshi Gigi and Douglas M. Kellner, *Media and Cultural Studies: Keyworks* (UK/US: Blackwell, 2001).

Fiske, John, *Introduction to Communication Studies* (UK/US: Methuen, 1982 and subsequent editions).

Hassan, Robert and Julian Thomas (eds), *The New Media Reader* (UK: Open University Press, 2006).

Hebdige, Dick, *Subculture: The Meaning of Style* (UK: Methuen, 1979).

Livingstone, Sonia and Leah A. Lievrouw (eds), *Handbook of New Media* (UK/US: Sage, Updated Student Edition, 2006).

McLuhan, Marshall, *Understanding the Media: The Extension of Man* (UK: Routledge edition, 1994).

McQuail, Denis, *Communication* (UK/US: Longman, 1975).

McQuail, Denis, *McQuail's Reader in Mass Communication Theory* (UK: Routledge, 2005).

Watson, James and Anne Hill, *The Dictionary of Media and Communication Studies* (UK/US: Hodder Arnold, 7th edition, 2006).

Silverstone, Roger, *Why Study the Media?* (US/UK: Sage, 1999).

Silverstone, Roger, *Media and Morality: On the Rise of the Mediapolis* (UK/US, Polity Press, 2007).

Advertising/PR and media

Baudrillard, Jean, *The Consumer Society: Myths and Structures* (US/UK: Sage, 1998).

Dinan, William and David Miller (eds), *Thinker, Faker, Spinner, Spy: Corporate PR and the Assault on Democracy* (UK: Pluto Press in association with Spinwatch, 2007).

Dyer, Gillian, *Advertising as Communication* (UK/US: Methuen, 1982).

McAllister, Matthew, *The Commercialization of American Culture: New Advertising, Control and Democracy* (US/UK: Sage, 1996).

Myers, Kathy, *Under-Stains: The Sense and Seduction of Advertising* (UK: Comedia, 1986).

Packard, Vance, *The Hidden Persuaders: An Introduction to the Techniques of Mass-Persuasion through the Unconscious* (UK: Penguin Special, 1960).

Ritzer, George, *The McDonalidization of Society* (US/UK: Pine Forge Press/Sage, 1995).

Ritzer, George, *The McDonalidization Thesis* (US/UK: Sage, 1998).

Turner, E.S. *The Shocking History of Advertising* UK: Penguin paperback, 1965).

Audience for media

Alasuutari, Pertii (ed.), *Rethinking the Media Audience: The New Agenda* (UK: Sage, 1999).

Ang, Ien, *Desperately Seeking the Audience* (UK: Routledge, 1991).

Bailey, Steve, *Media Audiences and Identity* (UK: Palgrave Macmillan, 2005).

Coudry, Nick, Sonia Livingstone and Tim Markham, *Media Consumption and Public Engagement* (UK: Palgrave Macmillan, 2007).

Fiske, John, *Reading the Popular* (US: Unwin Hyman, 1989).

Gillespie, Marie (ed.), *Media Audiences* (UK: Open University Press, 2005).

McQuail, Denis, *Audience Analysis* (UK/US: Sage, 1997).

Moeller, Susan D., *Compassion Fatigue: How the Media Sell Disease, Famine, War and Death* (UK/US: Routledge, 1999).

Nightingale, Virginia and Karen Ross (eds), *Critical Readings: Media and Audiences* (UK: Open University Press, 2003).

Ruddock, Andy, *Understanding Media Audiences: Theory and Method* (UK/US: Sage, 2003) and *Investigating Audiences* (Sage: 2007).

Tulloch, John, *Watching the TV Audience: Cultural Theories and Methods* (UK: Arnold, 2000).

Broadcasting

Crisell, Andrew, *Understanding Radio* (UK/US: Methuen, 1986).

Crisell, Andrew, *An Introductory History of British Broadcasting* (UK: Routledge, 2002).

Curran, James and Jean Seaton, *Power Without Responsibility: The Press and Broadcasting in Britain* (UK/US: Routledge, 6th edition, 2003).

Kilborn, Richard, *Staging the Real: TV Programming in the Age of Big Brother* (UK: University of Manchester Press, 2004).

Censorship, spin, information manipulation

Cohen, Stanley and Jock Young (eds), *The Manufacture of News* (UK: Constable, 1973).

Herman, Edward and Noam Chomsky, *Manufacturing Consent: The Political Economy of the Mass Media* (UK: Pantheon, 1988).

Ingram, Martin and Greg Harkin, *Stakeknife: Britain's Secret Agents in Ireland* (Ireland: O'Brien Press, 2004).

Jones, Nicholas, *Trading Information, Leaks, Lies and Tip-offs* (UK: Methuen, 2006).

Miller, Emma, *Viewing the World: How Western Television and Globalisation Distort Representations of the Developed World* (UK: Wordpower, 2006).

Pilger, John, *Hidden Agendas* (UK: Vintage, 1998).

Rampton, Sheldon and John Stauber, *Weapons of Mass Deception: The Uses of Propaganda in Bush's War on Iraq* (UK: Robinson, 2003).

Corporations, media and globalization

Alleyne, Mark D., *News Revolution: Political and Economic Decisions about Global Information* (UK: Macmillan – now Palgrave Macmillan, 1997).

De Jong, Wilma, Martin Shaw and Neil Stammers, *Global Activism, Global Media* (UK: Pluto Press, 2005).

Flew, Terry, *Understanding Global Media* (UK: Palgrave Macmillan, 2007).

Gerbner, George, Hamid Mowlana and Herbert I. Schiller (eds), *Invisible Crises: What Conglomerate Control of Media Means for America and the World* (US/UK: Westview Press, 1996).

Ginsborg, Paul, *Silvio Berlusconi: Television, Power and Patrimony* (UK: Verso, 2004).

Hafez, Kai, *The Myth of Media Globalization* (UK/US: Polity Press, 2007), translated by Alex Skinner.

Hirst, Paul and Grahame Thompson, *Globalization in Question* (UK/US: Polity Press, 1999).

Machin, David and Theo van Leeuwen, *Global Media Discourses* (UK/US: Routledge, 2007).

McNair, Brian, *Cultural Chaos: Journalism, News and Power in a Globalised World* ((UK/US: Routledge, 2005).

Ramaswami, Harindranath, *Perspectives on Global Cultures* (UK/US: Open University Press, 2006).

Rantanen, Terni, *The Media and Globalization* (UK/US: Sage, 2005).

Ritzer, George, *The Globalization of Nothing* (US: Pine Forge Press, 2003).

Schiller, Herbert I., *Culture Inc. The Corporate Takeover of Public Expression* (US: Oxford University Press, 1989).

Stevenson, Nick, *The Transformation of the Media: Globalisation, Morality and Ethics* (UK: Longman, 1999).

Thussu, Daya Kishan, *International Communication: Continuity and Change* (UK: Hodder Arnold, 2nd edition, 2006).

Wolff, Michael *Autumn of the Moguls* (US: Flamingo, 2004).

Discourse/language

Bell, Allan, *The Language of News Media* (UK: Blackwell, 1997).

Brown, Mary Ellen, *Soap Opera and Women's Talk: The Pleasure of Resistance* (US/UK: Sage, 1994).

Conboy, Martin, *the Language of the News* (UK/US: Routledge, 2007).

Fowler, Roger, *Language and the News: Discourse and Ideology in the Press* (UK: Routledge, 1991).

Machin, David and Theo van Leeuwen, *Global Media Discourses* (UK/US: Routledge, 2007).

Matheson, Donald, *Media Discourses* (UK/US: Open University Press, 2005).

McDonnell, Diane, *Theories of Discourse* (UK: Blackwood, 1986).

van Dijk, Teun A., *Discourse Studies: A Multidisciplinary Introduction*, Volume 1 entitled *Discourse as Structure and Process*; Volume 2, *Discourse as Social Interaction* (UK/US: Sage, 1996).

Wilkinson, Sue and Celia Kitzinger, *Feminism and Discourse: Psychological Perspectives* (UK: Sage, 1995).

Gender and media

Chambers, Deborah, Linda Steiner and Carole Fleming, *Women and Journalism* (UK/US/Canada: Routledge, 2004).

Creed, Pamela and Judith Cramer (eds), *Women in Mass Communication* (US/ UK: 3rd edition, 2006).

Dines, Gail and Jean M. Humez, *Gender, Race and Class in Media: A Text Reader* (US/UK: Sage, 2nd edition 2003).

Gallagher, Margaret, *Gender Setting: New Agendas for Media Monitoring and Advocacy* (UK/US: Zed Books, 2001).

Gauntlett, David, *Media, Gender and Identity: An Introduction* (UK/US: Routledge, 2002).

Gray, Ann, *Video Playtime: The Gendering of Leisure Technology* (UK/US: Sage, 1992).

Inness, Sherie A., *Tough Girls: Women Warriors and Wonder Women in Popular Culture* (US: University of Pennsylvania Press, 1998).

Joseph, Ammu and Kalpana Sharma, *Whose News? The Media and Women's Issues* (US/UK: Sage, 2nd edition, 2006).

Meyers, Marian, *News Coverage of Violence Against Women* (US/UK: Sage, 1997).

Ross, Karen and Carolyn M. Bylerly (eds), *Women and Media: International Perspectives* (UK: Blackwell, 2004).

Sakr, Naomi (ed.), *Women and Media in the Middle East: Power Through Self-Expression* ((UK/US: Tauris, 2nd edition 2004).

Tusan, Michelle Elizabeth, *Women Making News: Gender and Journalism in Modern Britain* (US: University of Illinois Press, 2005).

Globalization   See Corporations, media and globalization

History of media

Black, Jeremy, *The English Press 1621–1861* (UK: Sutton, 2001).

Curran, James and Jean Seaton, *Power Without Responsibility: The Press and Broadcasting in Britain* (UK/US: Routledge, 6th edition, 2003).

Harrison, Stanley, *Poor Men's Guardians: A Survey of the Struggles for a Democratic Newspaper Press, 1763–1973* (UK: Lawrence & Wishart, 1974).

Keane, John, *Tom Paine: A Political Life* (UK: Bloomsbury, 1995).

Koss, Stephen, *The Rise and Fall of the Political Press in Britain* (UK:Hamish Hamilton, 1982; Fontana paperback, 1990).

McArthur, Colin, *Television and History* (UK: British Film Institute monograph, 1978).

Raymond, Joad (ed.), *Making the News: An Anthology of the Newsbooks of Revolutionary England, 1641-1660* (UK: Windrush Press, 1993).

Standage, Tom, *The Victorian Internet: The Remarkable Story of the Telegraph and the Nineteenth Century's Online Pioneers* (UK: Weidenfeld & Nicolson, 1998).

Steed, Henry Wickham, *The Press* (UK: Penguin, 1938).

Turner, E.S., *The Shocking History of Advertising* (UK: Penguin paperback, 1965).

Weiner, Joel H., *The War of the Unstamped: The Movement to Repeal the British Newspaper Tax, 1830–1836* (US/UK: Cornell University Press,1969).

Williams, Kevin, *Get Me a Murder a Day! A History of Mass Communication in Britain* (UK: Arnold, 1997).

Williams, Raymond, *The Long Revolution* (UK: Chatto & Windus, 1961; Pelican paperback, 1965).

Wilson, Ben, *The Laughter of Triumph: William Hone and the Fight for the Free Press* (UK: Faber & Faber, 2005).

Winston, Brian, *Messages: Free Expression: Media and the West from Gutenberg to Google* (UK/US: Routledge, 2005).

Information age

Chun, Wendy Hui Kyong and Thomas Kennan (eds), *New Media/Old Media: A History and Theory Reader* (UK/US: Routledge, 2006).

Mayrowitz, Joshua, *No Sense of Place: The Impact of Electronic Media on Social Behaviour* (US: Oxford University Press, 1979).

Schiller, Dan, *Digital Capitalism: Networking the Global Market System* (US: MIT Press, 1999).

Standage, Tom, *The Victorian Internet: The Remarkable Story of the Telegraph and the Nineteenth Century's Online Pioneers* (UK: Weidenfeld & Nicolson, 1998).

van Dijk, Teun, *The Deepening Divide: Inequality in the Information Age* (US/UK: Sage, 2005).

Wiener, Norbert, *Cybernetics: Or Control and Communication in the Animal and the Machine* (US: Wiley, 1949).

Winston, Brian, *Freedom, Media and the West from Gutenberg to Google* (UK/US: Routledge, 2005).

Internet communication

Allan, Stuart, *Online News: Journalism and the Internet* (UK/US: Open University Press, 2006).

Dahlberg, Lincoln and Eugenia Siapera, *Radical Democracy and the Internet* (UK: Palgrave Macmillan, 2007),

Dewdney, Andrew and Peter Ride, *The New Media Handbook* (UK/US: Routledge, 2006).

Gauntlett, David and Ross Horsley, *Web Studies* (UK: Arnold, 3rd edition, 2004).

Graham, Gordon, *The Internet: A Philosophical Inquiry* (UK/US: Routledge, 1999).

Hall, Jim, *Online Journalism: A Critical Primer* (UK: Pluto Press, 2001).

Hertz, J.C., *Surfing the Internet* (US: Abacus, 1995).

Levy, Peter, *Collective Intelligence: Mankind's Emerging World in Cyberspace* (US: Perseus, 1997).

Negroponte, Nicholas, *Being Digital* (UK: Hodder & Stoughton, 1995).

Slouka, Mark, *War of the Worlds: Cyberspace and the High-tech Assaults on Reality* (US: Basic Books, 1995).

Whittaker, Jason, *The Cyberspace Handbook* (UK/US: Routledge, 2004).

Wood, Aylish, *Digital Encounters: Agency and Affect* (UK/US: Routledge, 2007).

Journalism

Allan, Stuart and Barbie Zelizer (eds), *Reporting War: Journalism in Wartime* (US/UK: Routledge, 2004).

Chambers, Deborah, Linda Steiner and Carole Fleming, *Women and Journalism* (UK/US/Canada: Routledge, 2004).

Curran, James and Jean Seaton, *Power Without Responsibility: The Press and Broadcasting in Britain* (UK/US: Routledge, 6th edition, 2003).

Dahlgren, Peter and Colin Sparks (eds), *Journalism and Popular Culture* (US/UK: Sage, 1992).

De Jong, Wilma, Martin Shaw and Neil Stammers, *Global Activism, Global Media* (UK: Pluto Press, 2005).

Hall, Jim, *Online Journalism: A Critical Primer* (UK: Pluto Press, 2001).

Harcup, Tony, *Journalism: Principles and Practice* (UK: Sage, 2003).

Harcup, Tony, *The Ethical Journalist* (UK: Sage, 2006).

McNair, Brian, *Cultural Chaos: Journalism, News and Power in a Globalised World* (UK/US: Routledge, 2005).

Politkovskaya, Anna, *A Russian Diary* (UK/US: Harvill Secker, 2007).

Randall, David, *The Great Reporters from William Howard Russell (1820–1907) to Mayere Berger (1898–1959)* (UK: Pluto Press, 2005).

Randall, David, *The Universal Journalist* (UK: Pluto Press, 3rd edition, 2007).

Starkey, Guy, *Balance and Bias in Journalism: Representation, Regulation and Democracy* (UK/US: Palgrave Macmillan, 2007).

Tusan, Michelle Elizabeth, *Women Making News: Gender and Journalism in Modern Britain* (US: University of Illinois Press, 2005).

News

Allan, Stuart, *Online News: Journalism and the Internet* (UK/US: Open University Press, 2006).

Alleyne, Mark D., *News Revolution: Political and Economic Decisions about Global Information* (UK: Macmillan – now Palgrave Macmillan, 1997).

Bromley, Michael (ed.), *No News is Bad News: Radio, Television and the Public* (UK: Longman, 2001).

Cohen, Stanley and Jock Young (eds), *The Manufacture of News* (UK: Constable, 1973).

Curran, James and Jean Seaton, *Power Without Responsibility: The Press and Broadcasting in Britain* (UK/US: Routledge, 6th edition, 2003).

Dearing, James W. and Everett M. Rogers, *Agenda-Setting* (US: Sage, 1996).

Harrison, Jackie, *News* (UK/US: Routledge, 2006).

Knightley, Phillip, *The First Casualty: The War Correspondent as Hero and Myth-Maker From the Crimea to Kosovo* (UK: Prion Books paperback, revised edition, 2000).

McCoombs, Maxwell, *Setting the Agenda: The Mass Media and Public Opinion* (UK/US: Polity Press, 2004).

Moeller, Susan D., *Compassion Fatigue: How the Media Sell Disease, Famine, War and Death* (UK/US: Routledge, 1999).

Pintak, Lawrence, *Reflections in a Bloodshot Lens: America, Islam and the War of Ideas* (UK: Pluto Press, 2006).

Poole, Elizabeth and John E. Richardson (eds), *Muslims and the News Media* (UK: Tauris, 2006).

Schudson, Michael, *The Power of the News* (US: Harvard University Press, 1995).

Seaton, Jean, *Carnage and the Media: The Making and Breaking of News About Violence* (UK: Allen Lane, 2005).

Watson, James, 'Representing realities: an overview of news framing', *Keio Communication Review*, 29 (2007) (Japan).

Politics, government and media

Curran, James, *Media and Power* (UK: Routledge, 2002).

Garnham, Nicholas, *Capitalism and Communication: Global Culture and the Economics of Information* (UK: Sage, 1990).

Gramsci, Antonio, *Selections from the Prison Notebooks* (UK: Lawrence & Wishart, 1971).

Hackett, Robert A. and William K. Carroll, *Politics and Democracy, Remaking Media: The Struggle to Democratise Public Communication* (UK/US: Routledge, 2006).

Herman, Edward and Noam Chomsky, *Manufacturing Consent: The Political Economy of the Mass Media* (UK: Pantheon, 1988).

Kuhn, Raymond, *Politics and the Media in Britain* (UK: Palgrave Macmillan, 2006).

Lewis, Justin, Sanna Inthorn and Karin Wahl-Jorgensen, *Citizens or Consumers: What the Media Tell Us About Political Participation* (UK/US: Open University Press, 2005).

Nichols, John and Robert W. Chesney, *Tragedy and Farce: How the American Media Sell Wars, Spin Elections, and Destroy Democracy* (US/UK: The New Press, 2005).

Raboy, Marc and Bernard Dagenais (eds), *Media Crisis and Democracy: Mass Communication and the Disruption of Order* (US/UK: Sage, 1992).

Press

Curran, James and Jean Seaton, *Power Without Responsibility: The Press and Broadcasting in Britain* (UK/US: Routledge, 6th edition, 2003).

Friel, Howard and Richard Falk, *The Record of the Paper: How the* New York Times *Misreports US Foreign Policy* (US/UK: Verso, 2004).

McCoombs, Maxwell, *Setting the Agenda: The Mass Media and Public Opinion* (UK: Polity Press, 2004.

McLuhan, Marshall, *The Gutenburg Galaxy: The Making of Typographical Man* (Canada: University of Toronto Press, 1962).

Researching the media

Bertrand, Ira and Peter Hughes, *Media Research Methods: Audiences, Institutions, Texts* (UK: Palgrave Macmillan, 2005).

Davies, Marie Messenger and Nick Mosdell, *Practical Research Methods for Media and Cultural Studies: Making People Count* (UK: University of Edinburgh Press, 2006).

Jones, Steve (ed.), *Doing Internet Research: Critical Issues and Methods for Examining the Net* (US/UK: Sage, 1999).

O Dochartaigh, Niall, *Internet Research Skills* (US/UK: Sage, 2nd edition 2007).

Philo, Greg and Mike Berry, *Bad News from Israel* (UK: Glasgow University Media Group, 2004).

Television

Allrath, Gaby and Marion Gymnich (eds), *Narrative Strategies in Television Series* (UK: Palgrave Macmillan, 2005).

Ang, Ien, *Watching* Dallas: *Soap Opera and the Melodramatic Imagination* (UK: Methuen, 1985; Routledge, 1991).

Bignell, Jonathan, *Big Brother: Reality TV in the Twenty-First Century* (UK: Palgrave Macmillan, 2005).

Burton, Graeme, *Talking Television: An Introduction to the Study of Television* (UK/US: Arnold, 2000).

Crisell, Andrew, *A Study of Modern Television: Thinking Inside the Box* (UK: Palgrave Macmillan, 2006).

Kilborn, Richard, *Staging the Real: Factual TV Programming in the Age of Big Brother* (UK: University of Manchester Press, 2003).

Holmes, Su and Deborah Jermyn (eds), *Understanding Reality Television* (UK/US: Routledge, 2004).

Langer, John, *Tabloid Television, Popular Journalism and the 'Other News'* (UK/US: Routledge, 1998).

Newcombe, Horace (ed.), *Television: The Critical View* (US: University of Oxford Press, 1994).

Philo, Greg, *Seeing and Believing: The Influence of Television* (UK: Routledge, 1990).

Postman, Neil, *Amusing Ourselves to Death* (UK: Methuen, 1986).

Straubhaar, Joseph, *World Television: From Global to Local* (US/UK: Sage, 2007).

Thornham, Sue, *Television Drama: Theories and Identities* (UK: Palgrave Macmillan, 2006).

Williams, Raymond, *Television: Technology and Cultural Form* (UK: Fontana, 1974).

Theory of media

Barthes, Roland, *Mythologies* (UK: Granada Publishing paperback, 1973 and subsequent editions).

Berger, Arthur Asa (ed.), *Making Sense of Media: Key Texts in Media and Cultural Studies* (UK: Blackwell, 2005).

Curran, James and David Morley, *Media and Cultural Theory* (UK: Routledge, 2005).

Dance, Frank and C. Larson, *The Functions of Human Communication: A Theoretical Approach* (US: Holt, Reinhart & Winston, 1976).

Dearing, James W. and Everett M. Rogers, *Agenda-Setting* (US: Sage, 1996).

Habermas, Jurgen, *The Structural Transformation of the Public Sphere* (UK/US: Polity Press, 1989).

Hartley, John, *The Politics of Pictures: The Creation of the Public in the Age of Popular Media* (UK: Routledge, 1992).

Louw, Eric, *The Media and Cultural Production* (UK/US: Sage, 2001).

Matheson, Donald, *Media Discourses* (UK/US: Open University Press, 2005).

Mattelart, Armand and Michele Mattelart, *Theories of Communication* (US/UK/India: Sage, 1998).

McCoombs, Maxwell, *Setting the Agenda: The Mass Media and Public Opinion* (UK: Polity Press, 2004.

Moores, Shaun, *Media/Theory* (UK: Routledge, 2005).

Potter, James W., *Media Literacy* (US/UK: Sage, 3rd edition, 2005).

Stevenson, Nick, *Understanding Media Cultures: Social Theory and Mass Communication* (UK: Sage, 1995).

Thompson, John B., *The Media and Modernity: A Social Theory of the Media* (UK/US: Polity, 1995).

Williams, Kevin, *Understanding Media Theory* (UK: Arnold, 2003).

Violence and the media

Barker, Martin and Julian Petley (eds), *Ill Effects: The Media/Violence Debate* (UK/US: Routledge, 1997).

Boyle, Karen, *Media and Violence: Gendering the Debates* (US/UK: Sage, 2004).

Freedman, Jonathan L., *Media Violence and its Effects on Aggression: Assessing the Scientific Evidence* (Canada: University of Toronto Press, 2002).

Jewkes, Yvonne, *Media and Crime* (US/UK: Sage, 2004).

Kirsh, Steven J., *Children, Adolescents, and Media Violence: A Critical Look at the Research* (US/UK: Sage, 2006).

Potter, James W., *On Media Violence* (US/UK: Sage, 1999).

Signorielli, Nancy, *Violence in the Media: A Reference Handbook* (US: Santa Barbara ABC-CLIO, 2005).

Trend, David, *The Myth of Media Violence: A Critical Introduction* (UK/US: Blackwell Publishing, 2007).

War and the media

Allan, Stuart and Barbie Zelizer (eds), *Reporting War: Journalism in Wartime* (UK/US: Routledge, 2004).

Bowen, Jeremy, *War Stories* (UK/US: Simon & Schuster, 2006).

Harris, Robert, *Gotcha! The Media, The Government and the Falklands Crisis* (UK: Faber & Faber, 1983).

Knightley, Phillip, *The First Casualty: the War Correspondent as Hero and Myth-Maker From the Crimea to Kosovo* (UK: Prion Books paperback, revised edition, 2000).

Miller, David (ed.), *Tell me No Lies: Propaganda and Media Distortion in the Attack on Iraq* (UK: Pluto Press, 2004).

Moeller, Susan D., *Compassion Fatigue: How the Media Sell Disease, Famine, War and Death* (UK/US: Routledge, 1999).

Nichols, John and Robert W. McChesney, *Tragedy and Farce: How the American Media Sell Wars, Spin Elections and Destroy Democracy* (UK/US: The New Press, 2005).

Omaar, Rageh, *Revolution Day* (UK: Viking, 2004).

Pintak, Lawrence, *Reflections in a Bloodshot Lens: America, Islam and the War on Ideas* (UK: Pluto Press, 2006).

Rampton, Sheldon and John Stauber, *Weapons of Mass Deception: The Uses of Propaganda in Bush's War on Iraq* (UK: Robinson, 2003).

Spencer, Graham, *The Media and Peace: From Vietnam to the 'War on Terror'* (UK: Palgrave Macmillan, 2005).

Sylvester, Judith and Suzanne Huffman (eds), *Reporting from the Front: The Media and the Military* (US/UK: Rowman & Littlefield, 2005).

Thussu, Daya and Des Freedman (eds), *War and the Media: Reporting Conflict 24/7* (US/UK: Sage, 2003).

Glossary

Aberrant decoding Wrong or mistaken but only in the sense that it does not accord with the preferred reading of the encoder (see Chapter 2).

Absence In news, for example, that which is excluded, off the agenda, gatekept. That which is absent may still be significant, and significant *because* of its absence.

Active audience Rather than merely accepting what it is told, the active audience is capable of thinking for itself, making its own intepretations, appropriating for its own purposes media messages (see Chapter 3).

Affective See Cognitive/Affective.

Agenda A list of items – news stories – placed in order of importance in relation to news values (see Chapter 5).

Agora An open space where matters concerning the community are discussed. The Greek agora was the true 'market place' where ideas were exchanged and decisions made concerning the affairs of state (see also Polis).

Amplitude Size; a core news value according to Galtung and Ruge, yet depending on other values such as proximity (see Chapter 5).

Analogue See Digital/analogue.

Anchorage A newspaper photograph is 'anchored' by its caption. Anchorage is a customary way of ensuring a preferred reading of the text. The voice-over in a narrative – feature film or documentary – serves a similar purpose.

Appropriation Taking over, making use of; for example corporations, through sponsorship, appropriating culture to further corporate interests.

Attributes Characteristics of persons, peoples, races or situations which the media focus on and tend to re-use, to the point of stereotyping.

Attribution Information is attributed to sources, some – such as people in authority – carrying more weight than others. If the attribution of information links to an elite source that information is more likely to be considered newsworthy.

Authoritarian press theory Operates in totalitarian regimes where the media are servants of authority, and its voice (see Chapter 4).

Blog, blogging, blogosphere   Web-logging by thousands of pundits has become one of the fastest-growing communicative activities; online bloggers often have a 'readership' of thousands, being a regular source of information and comment for traditional media.

Bricolage   Term referring to style, generally in self-presentation; the elements of that style being gleaned from other styles and modes of expression; bits and pieces from disparate origins assembled, often in defiance of convention.

Broadband   Electronic facility bringing network data and exchange into the home or office at high speed.

Channel   The physical/technical means by which a message is transmitted. In interpersonal communication the channel may be the body and the voice. The channel in television comprises the TV set, wires etc. The word channel has however been used more generally to refer to operational structures (e.g. Channel Four).

Closed texts   See Open/Closed texts.

Citizen journalism   With the advent of network communication ordinary people are often in a position to report the news, in particular aided by the mobile phone and its picture-taking capacity (see Chapter 11).

Citizenship entitlements   Another term for human rights – the right, for example, to be told the truth, without bias.

Closure   Refers to the closing-down of meaning; to communication which is closed rather than open ended. In interpersonal terms also refers to the 'closing down' of an interaction.

Code   A set of rules by which signs are meaningfully assembled. There are arbitrary or fixed codes such as Morse Code and varyingly arbitrary codes such as those of presentation and behaviour; and more open codes such as aesthetic codes. Messages are encoded and decoded (see Chapter 2).

Cognitive/Affective   Aspects of thought, understanding, working-out, problem-solving are cognitive in nature; aspects of feeling, sensitivity – the emotional side of our personalities – are affective.

Cognitive dissonance   A feeling of unease, of discomfort arising from our expectations failing to be met; or where there is discrepancy between principle and behaviour. Relates to congruity, that is, information or a situation which fits in to patterns of expectation. Where this does not occur, dissonance is experienced, and a possible response is one of avoidance or rejection.

Coin of exchange Cultural experiences – like last night's episode of a popular soap – become topics of conversation, in the family or in the workplace, and represent a valuable ingredient of social interaction.

Commanders of order An alternative term for the power elite or the Establishment.

Commercial *laissez-faire* model of effects Poses a counter-argument to 'strong effects' theory; maintaining that media are produced for commercial reasons and that profit alone is the motive for media production, not ideology.

Commonality Describes those things a community holds in common; their shared culture, values, attitudes etc.

Connotation The level of analysis in which meaning is encountered and addressed.

Connotative See Denotive/Connotative.

Consensus/Dissensus Where the majority agree/disagree. The media claim to know when there is public consensus, though actual proof is difficult if not impossible to come by. However, publishing or broadcasting that there is consensus may help create or reinforce it.

Consonance Where expectations are met; where what happens or how a person behaves falls in with our expectations, leaving us with a sense of cognitive satisfaction.

Consumerization Where the dominant socio-cultural emphasis is on consuming to the point where this rules over other, non-monetary values.

Context The situation – cultural, social, historical, economic, political and environmental – in which acts of communication take place.

Convergence Coming together, a meeting in the centre. In terms of computer technology many formerly separate modes of information converged into central hardware. Convergence also refers to media ownership which converges into the hands of fewer and fewer owners.

Co-orientation Occurs where a person is orientated both to another person and to an issue, the one proving an influence upon the other. For example, if two people like each other and agree on an issue (or another person) then they can be considered to be in a state of co-orientation; in balance.

Core/Periphery In terms of political, cultural or economic power, and in relation to the degree to which nations are information-rich, or information-poor, they are often divided into core (important, centrally significant) nations and periphery (nations at the margins of global importance).

Corporate intrusion   Describes the way large corporations exert, through advertising or patronage, influence over culture; often intrusively in terms of using cultural artefacts to market their own image, products and services.

Counterframing   Dominant forces – the power elite – in society command agendas and 'frame' the news; such framing is based upon the ideology of those setting the frame. Those in society with alternative standpoints in turn attempt to promote their own agendas by counterframing.

Covert   See Overt/Covert.

Crisis definition   A function of media generally is defining realities; in this case media are in a position to identify – and amplify – crisis.

Cross-media ownership   Where a company or media mogul owns both newspapers and broadcasting stations in a particular service area; critics see in the trend towards convergence of ownership threats to independence and plurality.

Cross promotion   Capability of large media corporations to use their diverse services and outlets to promote new ventures; or for companies with shared interests to use each other 'for free'.

Cultivation theory   Media expose audiences to attitudes, realities, ideologies and in the process, cultivate the nature and pattern of responses (see Chapters 3 and 10).

Cultural apparatus   Those elements in society which contribute to the process of enculturalization, of cohesiveness-making – education, the family, the arts, media.

Cultural capital   Our education, knowledge of the arts or of history provides us with a form of currency on which we might capitalize socially or professionally.

Cybernetics   The scientific study of feedback systems in humans, animals and machines.

Deconstruction   Analysis as dissection; the taking-apart of elements of a text and subjecting them, and their relationship to other textual elements, to critical scrutiny.

Defamation   Any statement made about a person that is untrue and may be considered damaging to that person's reputation; in its spoken or broadcast form this is termed *slander*; in print, *libel*.

Deflection   Occurs when the media focus on some stories to the exclusion of others which might be considered of equal or more importance; what is deflected is audience attention.

Democratic-participant theory One of a number of normative theories of media; very much an ideal, and rarely to be found in the real world, in which the public has access to, involvement in and a degree of control over media communication (see Chapter 4).

Demonization The media often use scare tactics to label certain public figures or groups within society as deviant. The intended effect is to persuade the public to reject what the 'demons' stand for, their ideas, what they say or do.

Denotive/Connotative Orders of meaning or signification. Basically the denotive concerns the level of identification and description, the connotative the level of analysis and interpretation.

Dependency theory Focuses on the degree to which audiences are dependent on media for their information about the world; concerns the impact the media have on our perceptions and attitudes. How far do we look to the media for confirmation?

Deregulation The policy of reducing, or eliminating altogether, regulations concerning, in particular, public service broadcasting. Regulation, for instance, might govern the amount of imported programmes a network is permitted to show or insist that lighter entertainment is balanced by more serious programmes (see Chapters 1, 8 and 11).

Development theory A normative function of media relating to the purposes and practices of media in developing or so-termed Third World countries; recognizing the vulnerability of economic progress and the risk to that progress of 'bad news' stories (see Chapter 4).

Deviance definition The power of the media to define social or political deviance from established norms, or at least the norms the media live by; laying down markers of inclusion and exclusion. Deviant behaviour is what the media disapprove of; in this sense the media are said to 'patrol the boundaries' of acceptable/not acceptable public and private behaviour, not the least in the ways they use the language of insult – 'mobs' of protesters, for example – to condemn that behaviour.

Diachronic structure According to sequencing (e.g. A to B to C), as contrasted with synchronic structures built up through comparison. Diachronic linguistics is the study of language through history; synchronic linguistics work from a point in time, comparing and contrasting.

Diffusion The spreading of information or ideas through the social system. Diffusion studies focus on the processes by which the channels of communication, from mass media to interpersonal contact, operate and interact in broadening public awareness. In turn reception studies analyze what the public makes of diffusion processes.

Digital/Analogue Terms describing how information is processed by machine. Digital operates by numbers – 'digits', and is a binary system, making use of two digits only, 0 and 1. In contrast the analogue system works by measuring variation. T.F. Fry in *Beginners Guide to Computers* (UK: Newnes Technical Books, 2nd edition 1983) illustrates the analogue process by referring to the car speedometer: 'Here the position of a needle relative to a dial represents the speed of the car in kilometres or miles per hour but is arrived at not by computing numbers but by a continuous monitoring of shaft revolution speeds and a conversion of this through the device's physical properties, gears and cables, to give the dial reading'; in other words, by analogy. By transforming all data into numbers the digital system facilitates the convergence of sound, vision and text; its powers of reduction making possible the storage of infinite amounts of information, recallable in instants.

Discourse A mode (usually public) of communication which is socially constructed, reflecting the ideology of the user; both a vehicle of debate and explanation (see Chapter 2).

Disinformation Aspect of propaganda, tailoring information to mislead, either by selection, economizing with the truth or just plain lies.

Dissensus See Consensus/Dissensus.

Dissonance A sense of uneasiness or discomfort resulting from situations in which expectations are not fulfilled; when we find perception and reality in conflict or where behaviour runs counter to values.

Diversity May refer to diversity of media source, channels or programmes. In a pluralist society diversity is seen as a key criterion, in particular diversity in media ownership and control.

Domestication The practice of localizing media artefacts – news or fiction – from across national or cultural borders; appropriating them for local consumption.

Emancipatory/Repressive use of media The first envisages a public for media which has rights of access and participation; the second closes down both the operation and consumption of media to one of top-down control; essentially restrictive; media used as agents of order (see Chapter 3).

Embedded reporting Term that gained currency during the invasion of Iraq in 2003 by American and British forces. Journalists were assigned to allied military units, partly for their own protection, but mainly as an exercise in controlling reporters and photographers in terms of where they went and what they wrote about or photographed. Perhaps inevitably, such reporting influenced (or at least threatened to influence) journalists in their relationship with personnel who socialized with them and often saved their lives. The risk was that reporting would, as a result of embeddedness, encourage self-censorship on the part of journalists.

Empowerment   Giving power to the people, individually, in groups or communities, enabling them to have influence over how decisions that concern them are arrived at. The media have a critical role in voicing the need for such empowerment – as articulated in human rights legislation and more general attitudes in society with regard, for example, to women or ethnic minorities.

Encription (or encryption)   Coding communicative signals so that access is restricted to those with the appropriate decoding device.

Encrustation   Images as they pass through time and public experience acquire fresh associations which, by a cumulative process, alter or modify their original meanings.

Entropy   That which is new, unfamiliar, strange, not part of convention, contrasting with redundancy.

Ethnocentrism   View of the world from a particular standpoint, that of one's own culture, norms and values (see Chapter 5).

Ethnographic analysis   Investigates the uses made of media by audiences in their own contextual settings, social and cultural (see Chapter 10).

Exchange   Refers to the reciprocal nature of communication, where the encoder and decoder contribute to meaning-making on an equal footing, and interactively. Network communication has furthered communicative exchange as never before (see Chapter 9).

Extracted information   That which audiences derive from their lived experience. This is matched with mediated experience and sometimes is at odds with it. Some commentators fear that mediated has come to dominate extracted experience.

Fictionworthiness   Parallels newsworthiness in that news to a degree fulfils criteria appropropriate to fictional, or story, narratives (see Chapter 6).

Field of experience   Where our life experiences overlap or have features in common meaningful communication is most likely to occur (see Wilbur Schramm's models, Chapter 2).

Folk devil   See also demonization; person or persons seen and portrayed as a threat to the community. In times of uncertainty and insecurity, folk devils are targeted as somehow the cause of 'bad times' (and subsequent 'moral panics') or capable of making them worse if people pay heed to them. They are stigmatized, subject to vilification and sometimes worse.

Fragmentation   Of audience; brought about by the diversification of modes of media consumption such as cable, video, satellite and network communication (see Chapters 3, 9 and 11).

Frames/Schemata   Our reception of media messages is conditioned by the 'mind sets', sometimes called frames or schemata, which influence our perceptions and the process of interpretation. More generally, framing refers to the range of processes, such as in the news, where reality, the 'world out there' is structured. Thus gatekeeping, agenda-setting and news values can all be described as framing devices.

Free press theory   Normative theory of media in which the basic principle is freedom from legal restriction (see Chapter 4).

Frequency   Term of varying use; frequency is a criterion for newsworthiness: events likely to fit in with the frequency of news schedules (hourly, daily) are more likely to be included than others which do not fit so easily, like stories which take a long time to unfold.

Gatekeeping   Restricting access to people or information; in news terms, a process of selecting/rejecting information for onward transmission (see Chapter 5).

Gender   Categorization, culturally defined and referring to the attitudes, perceptions, values and behaviour of males and females in relation to socio-cultural expectations.

Genre   Mode or classification in which certain characteristics of form and style are identifiable and generally constant. TV soaps or Westerns constitute genres (see Chapter 6).

Globalization   Trend towards transnational and corporate ownership of the means of communication and the production and diffusion of culture, leading – so it is feared – to the reduction of cultural diversity, the marginalization of indigenous cultures and the downsizing of state sovereignty. Globalization of media refers to cross-border communication and is linked to the advocacy of socio-cultural connectivity and equality (see Chapters 8 and 11).

Guard dog   A role media may opt to perform, or be compelled to perform, as defender of those in power – the power elite, the Establishment; in contrast with the watchdog role in which the media are the eyes, ears and voice of the public, their brief being to 'watch' those in power and ensure that they act in the public interest.

Hegemony   In society an overarching form of power/control created and sustained through popular consent. A key concept in the examination of the media's role in society.

Hermeneutic   Concerns understanding, revelation, making things clear. Barthes' hermeneutic code of narrative operates to unravel enigmas, solve mysteries (see Chapter 6).

Hierarchy Classification, social, political etc. in graded subdivisions, the most powerful, influential sectors at the top. A social hierarchy, traditionally, would constitute upper, middle and lower classes (see Chapter 1).

Hierarchy studies See Longitudinal studies.

Homo narrens Latin, for man the storytelling animal (see Chapter 6).

Hybridization The fusion of cultural forms; a process accelerated by glo-balization and the movement of peoples across geographical or cultural bor-ders, often as a result of wars, state persecution or domestic poverty.

Hypodermic needle 'theory' As the metaphor suggests, the media's mes-sage, according to this 'hunch theory', is injected into a docile and accepting audience. Also termed the mass manipulative theory.

Iconic/Indexical/Symbolic Classifications or types of sign. Iconic resem-bles, re-presents the original; the indexical sign works by association and the symbolic sign 'stands for' something else, the result of consent and general application. The alphabet is a made up of symbols whose connection with the sounds they stand for is arbitrary (see Chapter 2).

Identification Various applications: may be a stage in the process of accept-ing ideas or modes of conduct; or relate to the way audiences identify with characters, real or fictional, in books, films or broadcasting.

Ideological state apparatus (ISA) The family, education, culture and the media constitute ISAs as contrasted with the RSAs, repressive state appara-tuses such as the military, police and the law (see Chapter 1). The ISAs can be seen as instruments of hegemony.

Ideology The public dimension of values; the manifestation of the ideal through social, cultural, political and economic discourses (see Chapter 1).

Ideology of mass culture/Ideology of populism The first works within frames of disapproval, seeing popular culture as harmful, as a form of dumbing down; the second takes a much more positive, and approving stance, recog-nizing the importance of pleasure derived from popular entertainment (see Chapter 10).

Immediacy A news value characteristic of the Western media and relating to the dominance of deadlines. The more swiftly the news can be reported the more it fulfils the value of immediacy (see Chapter 5).

Impartiality Not taking sides. An ideal, challenged by some commentators as being unattainable, and by others for being undesirable.

Indexical See Iconic/Indexical/Symbolic.

Information gaps Occurring between the so-termed information-rich and information-poor within a state, or between states. Concern is expressed whether new media technologies increase, rather than decrease, information gaps between rich and poor nations.

Information model/Story model Relate to the gathering, assembly and presentation of news, the one works on the assumption that the news is essentially a mode of transmission of information, the other that news itself is a cultural artefact with narrative traditions linking it closer to fiction – of construction – than fact (see Chapter 6).

Intertextual The positioning of one text against another, spatially or temporally, deliberately or by accident can have an interactive effect in which one text plays off or plays against another, making possible new insights, new 'readings'.

Jingoism Extreme form of patriotism; usually exhibited by the media, the press in particular, in times of war and in relation to sporting events when 'We' are playing 'Them'.

Knowns/Unknowns In TV news coverage, knowns in society such as leading public figures are several times more likely to have their activities, and what they say, reported on, than unknowns such as ordinary members of the public (see Chapter 7).

Kuuki Japanese, describing a climate of opinion influential in the relationship between governments, media and public (see Chapter 5).

Labelling Relates to definitions of deviance; those defined as deviant by the media are seen to carry the 'label' of their deviance and the label continues as reinforcement of the definition (see Attributes).

Langue/Parole De Saussure identified la langue as the overall language system, while la parole is the manifestation of the system in action, in speech and writing (see Chapter 2).

Leak Occurs when information not intended for public consumption is passed on, usually to the media, by people – officials, workers – who consider the information is something the public ought to know about. Leaks generally take the form of documents, photocopied, and covertly supplied to the media. Of late, the leaking of e-mails, intended for internal consumption only, has become prevalent. Occasionally government ministers and other official bodies such as the police, contrive leaks. These may be seen as a strategic convenience: a leak prompts reaction that might provide a useful gauge of the success or otherwise of policy or action. See Spin and Whistleblower.

Lived experience See Extracted information.

Lobbying Using a range of techniques and approaches to persuade politicians/government ministers/people in authority to 'bend an ear' to the objectives of the propagandist. The lobby correspondent reports the proceedings of parliament, supposedly getting his or her stories 'in the lobby' where politicians and journalists meet. In the USA the 'Gun lobby' is the voice of armaments manufacturers who pressurize government to resist introducing legislation to control guns.

Longitudinal studies Research into media effects/influence over an extended period of time, as contrasted with hierarchy studies that measure response at a specific time.

Mainstreaming Effects of TV viewing, particularly heavy viewing, in which views from the political right and left converge into a more centrist position though the shift is, over a period, deemed to be towards the right (see Chapters 3 and 10).

Marketization Process by which all human activities are structured within the frame of consumption, of production and selling. Specifically, the transformation of what originally was conceived as public service into a private market whose prime objective is profit.

Mass manipulative theory See Hypodermic needle theory.

Mean world syndrome Theory put forward by American researcher George Gerbner (in 'Reclaiming our cultural mythology' in *Ecology and Justice*, Spring 1994 and elsewhere) that the relentless diet of violence on US TV screens nurtures in the public a view that the world is a threatening and dangerous place; that out there is a mean world; the perception, thanks to media portrayal of violence, being disproportionate to the facts.

Media imperialism Power, exported through modes of communication, from a dominant country to others, affecting social, cultural, political and economic situations in the recipient culture or country; 'conquest' by cultural means.

Mediapolis Notion of world media resembling a *polis*, the Greek term for city and what it stands for; an increasingly global phenomenon of citizens and media in a state of interdependency and mutual obligation (see Chapters 4 and 11).

Mediation Process of representing, defining and interpreting reality on the part of media and on behalf of audience; between actuality and reception is what is termed mediated experience brought to us by newspapers, radio, TV, film etc.

Message What an act of communication is *about;* that which is deliberately conveyed by the encoder to the decoder.

Metaphor Figure of speech which works by transporting qualities from one plane of reality to another, such as sporting contests being reported in the language of war. The simile *compares*, the metaphor *becomes*, hence its potential power when effectively used in media practice (see Chapter 2).

Metonym The use of a specific term to describe a generality; thus Fleet Street was generic for the British press as a whole; by drawing elements which are diverse under a single umbrella term, metonym risks being a process of oversimplification and stereotyping (see Chapter 2).

Mobilization The stirring up by the media of public interest in and subsequently support for a cause or issue (see Chapter 4). The term is also used to describe the mobile phone and its multiple uses impacting on business and social activity to the point where it is referred to as a revolution in communications, hence terms such as the *era of mobilization*, the *mobile generation* and *social networking* (see Chapters 9 and 11).

Moral economy A dimension of consumer products used in the home – such as TVs, videos and computers – where values and judgements are located; concerns choices made within the family and who makes choices in terms of the use of those products (see Chapter 10).

Moral panic Set in motion by individuals or groups in society who appear to threaten it, by their behaviour, dominant norms and values. The media are seen to be instrumental in promoting moral panics by focusing on what is construed as deviant behaviour. Threats – such as street crime, mugging, theft of mobile phones – by being intensively reported, are perceived by the public as being a greater threat than statistics would warrant. Moral panics generally are manifestations of wedom/theydom or Us and Them; 'Them' being minorities, such as asylum seekers. In recent times, stirrings of moral panic have been manifest in the reporting of Islam in terms of its perceived 'threat' to Christian values and Western traditions.

Myth In terms of media process the rendering as self-evident socio-cultural, political or economic 'truths' which careful analysis usually identifies as being justifications of the underpinnings of bourgeois, middle-class society (see Chapters 1, 8 and 11).

Narrative codes Instrumental in the creation of stories, influencing form and content and operating in relation to character, action, situation, the unfolding of mystery and story resolution (see Chapter 6).

Narrowcasting As contrasted with *broadcasting*, aiming programmes at specific, 'niche' audiences.

News management The ways and means – the strategies and tactics – of getting information on to media news agendas; its aim, to ensure 'a good press' or at least to avoid negative mediation (see Spin).

New World Information Order Proposed by United Nations Educational, Scientific and Cultural Organization (UNESCO) in order to ensure balanced and objective news reporting on a global scale. Resisted by governments and media in the West.

Noise Any impediment which gets in the way of clear communication. This can take three main forms, technical/mechanical (physical noise or discomfort; distraction), semantic (difficulty over meaning) and psychological (see Chapter 2).

Normative functions Media operate according to norms, or rules, arising from particular social and political situations. Among a number of normative theories of media are the Free Press theory and the Development theory. The term *performative* is used to describe what actually happens rather than what is supposed to happen (see Chapter 4).

Objectivity In a journalistic sense, reporting matters without taking sides or expressing opinion; free of subjective values.

Open/Closed texts Terms referring to the degree of leeway a text permits the decoder. A closed text is designed to tightly frame the reader's scope for interpretation; open texts, such as works of art, permit a plurality of responses (see Chapter 2).

Other Not 'us'; a broad term that includes those who differ from us geographically, culturally, ethnically or ideologically. Other is 'the stranger', the person or persons whose similarities to us are perceived as less important than the differences; thus 'other' is often perceived as a problem or a threat. The media are prominent in defining other. Equally, there is the tendency to define ourselves in the light of other: 'We are what we are because we are not like them' (see Wedom/Theydom).

Overt/Covert Overt is open, above-board, intentionally obvious activity; covert is indirect or hidden.

Panopticon The all-seeing one; a metaphor for control, originating with the 19th century philosopher Jeremy Bentham (1738–1832) who proposed a prison in which a central tower permitted surveillance of prisoners who would be placed in cells arranged around the tower: they would behave because they knew they were being watched. Some critics perceive electronic technology as being the modern version of the Panopticon, or as Mark Poster prefers to call it, the Superpanopticon (see Chapter 9).

Paradigm/Syntagm Syntagms are elements, or working details, within the broad categorization of a paradigm. A *genre* is paradigmatic; its syntagmic elements those features of process in which the genre is created (see Chapter 2).

Parole See Langue/Parole.

Participant observation Mode of inquiry which involves researchers obtaining their information by spending time among the subjects of research; visiting them, sometimes working alongside them or living with them: participating in their lives (see Chapter 10).

Performatives Words to describe how things are said with regard to news events, such as *announce, assert, declare, insist*, each use carrying with it an evaluative, judgemental capacity. *Say* or *said* are neutral performatives unless they are linked with other performatives which are not value-free. For example, 'Management *say* there is no extra money, but unions *demand* the money be found'; the one being presented in a good light, the other not.

Periphery See Core/Periphery.

Personalization A familiar media practice in reporting issues and events is to present them through the image of a leading player in those events. It is more convenient, if simplistic, to praise or blame an individual rather than a group; and makes livelier journalistic copy. Much war reportage takes personalized form, and often to good effect, portraying the generality of war in terms of the suffering of individuals, families or other vulnerable groups. The approach encourages identification in audiences.

Photographic negativization Portraying through media texts and images the positive norm through contrast, that is by its opposite, just as a photonegative is instrumental in producing the finished picture. It is often used by the popular press to probe sleaze and scandal, dressing up the muck-raking objective in high moral tones.

Pluralism Many faceted, a state of affairs in which many opinions are tolerated; hence the term pluralist society.

Polis Greek for city or city state; the term encapsulating the concept and principles on which the polis operates (see Mediapolis and Chapters 4 and 11).

Polysemy Many meanings.

Postmodernism Reaction to modernist views concerning the inevitability of progress; interprets contemporary life as essentially problematic, fragmentary; pulls back from grand theories explaining the nature of society and culture. Any sense of the ideal is absent from postmodernism: truth is an illusion and therefore there is little point in pursuing it.

Power elite Those persons within a culture in a position to influence, directly or indirectly, political and economic decision-making. Sometimes referred to as the Establishment. Drawn from the highest echelons of society, business, the law, the military etc.

PR Public Relations; the practice of presenting to the public a favourable image of a government, institution, or company (see Spin).

Preferred reading Preferred, that is, according to the sender or encoder of the message. Where the decoder by intent or accident 'misreads' the intended message, the result is deemed to be aberrant decoding (see Chapters 2 and 3).

Privatization The shift from public ownership of the media to private ownership and control.

Propaganda The process by which ideas are propagated; term used, in the main, to describe persuasion which is blatant, biased and manipulative.

Proximity Nearness: geographical, cultural, political or economic. Proxemics is the study of spatial relationships at the level of interpersonal communication. In terms of mass communication, proximity is seen as a news value (see Chapter 5).

PSB Public Service Broadcasting; usually the creation of governments and based upon legal charters and codes of regulation; funded either by licence fee (such as the BBC) or susbscription (the system of financing for modest versions of PSB in the United States).

Public sphere The arena, or space in which the public as citizens communicate and in theory contribute to the decision-making and running of their community; a place of debate and discourse which in real terms is a media space. Public service broadcasting is seen as the major operator in the public sphere (see Mediapolis).

Reality TV Format in which the TV eye records the day-to-day, minute-by-minute activities of humans behaving in a number of situations, *Big Brother* (UK Channel Four and many other countries) being a prime example; if anything, a misnomer, for such programmes are highly contrived – through painstaking selection of the 'candidates', the framing principle of a competitive game, the manipulation of images by the production team and the awareness of the participants that they are under constant surveillance.

Redundancy The 'slack' which is built into communicative exchanges; that which is strictly not necessary for a message to be grasped but serves to ensure that in an exchange the message, or essential parts of it, have not been lost (see Shannon and Weaver's Mathematical Model of Communication, Chapter 2).

Regulatory favours Granted by governments to corporations in return for favourable treatment by the media controlled by those corporations. These often take the form of allowing corporations to widen their media-owning portfolio at what some critics consider to be the expense of public interest (see Chapters 8 and 11).

Repressive state apparatus (RSA) See Ideological state apparatus.

Repressive use of media See Emancipatory/Repressive use of media.

Resistive responses Linked with notions of audience empowerment, responses on the part of the reader, listener or viewer which, to a degree, resist or deny the preferred reading; countering the impression of the audience as merely reactive and accepting (see Chapters 3 and 10).

Rhetoric   Persuasion by means of presentational devices; classically, defines the skills of persuasion but in modern parlance has come to mean communication that is declamatory but without substance.

Right of reply   Advocated by a number of pressure groups, this right would empower members of the public, if subjected to unfair, inaccurate or misleading media coverage to oblige the particular medium to print or broadcast the response of the injured party.

Salience   Meaningfulness; of special importance.

Schemata   See Frames/Schemata.

Segmentation   The division of audience and/or consumers into segments considered appropriate for programming or sales; traditionally based upon differences of class and income, latterly on perceived differences of lifestyle and expectations (see Chapters 3 and 10).

Self-censorship   Not communicating information or expressing opinion in order to head off the risk of censorship further up the line of communication.

Self-fulfilling prophecy   Usually results from the process of labelling. Persons or groups classified as failures or troublemakers may behave in such a way as to confirm predictions; that is, fulfil the expectations others hold of them.

Semiology/Semiotics   The study of signs and sign systems within sociocultural contexts (see Chapter 2).

Semiotic power   The use of signifiers (such as dress, appearance) as forms of self or group expression, denoting an independent, even resistive use of the products of mass consumption.

Sign   The smallest element of the communicative process, a letter of the alphabet, a single musical note, a gesture. The sign is assembled according to codes and depends for its meaning on its relation to other signs.

Signal   The initial indicator of the communication process, like establishing eye contact before speaking, or the ringing of the telephone.

Significant others   People of our acquantance or in public life whose opinion about matters is important to us; people of influence.

Sound-bite   A segment of a news bulletin, of very short duration. In a general sense communication using such segments, where the assertive prevails over the explanatory or analytical.

Source   The origins from which information on a news story arises; the majority of news tends to come from official sources (see Chapter 7).

Spin Putting a favourable 'spin' on information emanating from governments, companies, etc. often to counteract more critical media coverage. Spin and spin-doctoring have a long history but today they are big business. Spin strives to communicate preferred readings to audience by emptying content of critical perspectives.

Spiral of silence Where in the public arena the holding of opinions threatens to isolate the communicator, there will be a tendency for such opinions to enter a spiral leading to silence; in effect, self-censorship will occur.

Story model See Information model.

Storyness The characteristric of an act of communication, or communication process (like the news) which resembles a story, employing narrative forms and techniques (see Chapter 6).

Superpanopticon See Panopticon.

Surveillance Overseeing, watching, on the look-out. An important use to which audiences put the media in their capacity as watchdog and 'windows on the world'. Equally those in authority exercise surveillance, today chiefly by electronic means, over the public (see Chapter 9).

Symbolic See Iconic/Indexical/Symbolic.

Synchronic structure See Diachronic structure.

Synergy Working to mutual benefit, where for example one form of media production is supplemented, extended and enriched as well as helped along by other modes. Great corporations are as likely to 'synergize' as compete with one another if their products are complementary and mutually sustaining (see Chapters 8 and 11).

Syntagm See Paradigm/Syntagm.

Tabloidese Language of the tabloid press – succinct, dramatic, emotive, sensationalized, personalized and often even poetic. The key linguistic device of the tabloids is the pun.

Tabloidization Refers to a perceived trend among traditionally serious newspapers, in the UK referred to as the broadsheets, towards more popular content in tabloid idiom. The term is also used to describe TV news as it strives to appeal to a broad section of the viewing public.

Text In the study of communication a text is that which is produced – a photograph, a cartoon, a novel, a movie; equally a person may be described as a text in that he/she communicates by personal appearance, body language, speech and behaviour. Roland Barthes differentiates between the work, that which has been encoded, and the text, that which is decoded (see Chapter 2).

Theydom See Wedom/Theydom.

Transaction Indicates that communication is an interactive process in which the meaning of a communicative exchange is something transacted or negotiated between encoder and decoder.

Transmission The process by which a sender transmits a message to a receiver; generally seen as a one-way operation.

Triggers In agenda-setting, particular events, incidents, occurrences or personal involvement by well known people that have the effect of driving news items up the media agenda (see Chapter 5).

Unknowns See Knowns/Unknowns.

Uses and Gratifications Theory targeted on the uses audiences make of media in order to satisfy, or gratify needs (see Chapter 3).

Visions of order Refers to the perceived purpose of the mass-produced textual or pictorial image, that is to affirm on behalf of authority the nature of order and control.

Watchdog Term describes an important role played by media in society, of being the eyes, ears and voice of public interest. In the contrasting guard dog role the media are the eyes, ears and voice of those in power.

Web 2.0 Term purporting to describe a critical stage in the development of network communication, one in which interactivity comes of age. Google, with its range of new online services encapsulates the Web 2.0 phase, key descriptors of which are participation, socialization and community, all embodied in such popular networking activities as MySpace and Facebook etc. (see Chapter 9).

Wedom/Theydom An alternative way of of saying Us and Them; the process, encouraged by the mass media, of seeing the world in terms of opposites, often conflictual. We/Us are the 'home team', They/Them, the 'visitors'; those who do not belong to *our* culture, society or nation.

Whistleblower Term given to anyone – worker, member of the public – who 'blows the whistle' on what he or she considers to be information which is kept secret, but which the whistleblower believes needs to be made public. Institutions, whether they are governments, businesses, hospitals, educational establishments etc. have an inherent dislike of allowing damaging information to be transmitted to the public. The whistleblower may have identified an abuse, an injustice, a danger; may have reported such things through formal channels – and got nowhere. He or she then goes public in the public interest, even at the risk of losing promotion or his/her job altogether. At an institutional level, of course, the media are the ultimate whistleblowers; in which case we refer to them in their watchdog role (see Chapters 4 and 7).

Index

References are to the main body of the text and to the Notes which follow each chapter. These will give the page number followed by n and the number of the note. For example, New World Information Order   139n6.

A
aberrant decoding   63, 69n21, 81
aberrant news values   164–5
Aboujouade, Elias   301, 312n24
absence   85, 271, 590
Abu Ghraib   37
access to source, hierarchy of   228
action (or prioretic) code   189
active audience   *see* **audience**
Adorno, Theodore   72
advertising   57–8, 109, 113, 118, 193, 213, 217, 230, 233, 235, 269, 273, 277, 288, 290, 303, 314, 344–7, 361, 375–6
aesthetic codes   53
aesthetic dimension of media functions   136
Africa: 'mobile phones revolutionize Africa'   273
Ageh, Tony   286–7, 311n9
agency   78
agendas
    interactive agendas   152–4
    levels and attributes   156–7
agenda-setting   150–8
    research   157–8
agora   132, 260, 280, 348, 381–2
Alasuutari, Pertti   71, 103n2
Allen, Jessica, Sonia Livingstone and Robert Reiner   403
Allen, Lily   284
Allen, Robert C.   184, 206n8
alliances
    between corporations   232, 263, 363–4
    ideological   24, 155, 170, 270
Al-Qaida   240, 258
Althusser, Louis   18, 39n4
Amazon.com   295

American Center for Media and Democracy   258
American dream   374–5
amplitude   217
analogue to digital, switch from   387n12
anchorage   56
Anderson, Robin   251–2, 277n3
Ang, Ien   81–2, 93, 98–9, 104n26, 106n34, 315, 324, 333–4, 354n1, 355n14
Annenberg School of Communication   81–2, 357n34, 396–7
Appignanesi, Lisa   247n26
Appleyard, Brian   186, 206n9, 298–9, 312n21
appropriation: corporate appropriation of culture   92–4, 288
Arendt, Hannah   141n22
Arms for Iraq enquiry (Scott Report, UK, 1996)   254–5
Armstrong, Paul B.   247n28
Arnove, Anthony   365, 387n5
Arthur, Charles   290, 311b14
Atkinson, Rowan   247n26
attachment, journalism of   222
attributes   *see* levels and attributes
audience
    active/resistive   5, 81–2, 92–7, 197–8, 221, 257, 292, 303, 326, 328, 366
    agency   104n10
    as consumers/as citizens   99
    attention span/recall   82–3, 200–2
    break-up, core–periphery, pluralism and unitary models   370
    categorization, resistance to   98–100
    'citizen entitlements'   134–5
    compassion fatigue   405
    'critical distance'   82
    critical response of   329

cultivation theory 80–1
cultural citizenship 332
cultural resistance 90–2
decodings: audience
    differences 331–2
deconvergence of 369–71
dependency theory 77–8, 216
different formats, varied
    responses 331–2
discursive engagement of 332
domestication of texts by
    audience 96, 97, 126
emancipatory use of media 78–9
ethnographic perspectives on audience
    response 90–1, 98–9
fragmentation of 98, 100, 369–71
frames of reference: referential and
    critical 85
Frankfurt school of media
    analysts 100, 104n4
HICT project 369–71
Internet use by audiences 291–3
intervening variables 152
latent critique 329
lived experience, mediated
    experience 86
localite preferences 371
localites/cosmopolites 89–90
Lull's listing of audience uses of
    media 76–7
models of audience 369–70
modes of response *see* response
    modes
pleasure, recognition of 333
project of self 89–90
public responsibilities of audience for
    media 383
'receiver rights' 121
receiver's image of the
    communicator 216
resistance through appropriation 94–6
resistance through style 91–2
response modes: dominant, negotiated,
    oppositional 62
response to *Jordache Story* 330–1
retention of information 105n16
selective attention 72, 83
significant others 86–7
social environment of 220
technology of media, audience use of
    (appropriation, objectification,
    incorporation, conversion) 334–7
uses and gratifications theory 73–6
authoritarian theory of media 117

B
Ball-Rokeach, Sandra J. and Melvin
    DeFleur 77–8, 104n9
Bardoel, Jo 218, 246n7
Barney, Darin 305–6, 312n28
Barsamian, David 166, 178n18
Barthes, Roland (1915–80) 49, 55, 59–62,
    68n14, 183, 189–91, 206n7, 207n13,
    252, 277n4, 332, 436
Bass, A.Z. 148–9
Baudrillard, Jean 57, 68n17, 375–6,
    388n19
BBC xiv, 32, 34, 57–8, 59, 113, 115, 219,
    223–6, 240, 255, 260, 261, 269, 270,
    312n24, 326–30
    and ethnic under-representation 240
Beaverbrook, Lord (1879–1964) 108
Bebo 343, 371
Bell, Allan 144, 145, 163, 166, 171,
    177n2, 212, 227, 245n4
Bell, Martin 222
Bell Telephone Laboratories 43
Benedikt, Michael 287, 311n10
Bentham, Jeremy (1748–1832) 295
Berelson, B. and G.A. Steiner 161,
    178n14
Berger, Arthur Asa 180, 187, 206n1
Berlusconi, Silvio 110n257, 278n12
Berry, Colin 82
bias 318
Big Brother 104n14
binary framing 187, 194, 206–7n12
Bird, Elizabeth S. 200–1, 207n21
Birt, John 45
black cinema 241–2
blogging xv, 259, 289–90, 380–1, 421
blogosphere 78
'blog placement' 259
Blumer, Herbert 325–6, 328
Blumler, Jay 73, 267, 279n23
    and Elihu Kaltz 73, 105n5
    and Dennis McQuail and J.R.
        Brown 73, 108n6
blurred, blended, bent 80
Bormann, Ernest 182–3
boundary event/journalist event 230
Bourdieu, Pierre 19–20, 39n5
Bowen, Jeremy 160, 178n12, 223,
    246n11
Boyer, J.H. 130m 140n15
breaking news 387n14
British Broadcasting Corporation *see*
    BBC
broadcasting *see* **media**

Bromley, Michael and Hugh
Stephenson 172, 178n23
Brookings Institute (USA) 236
Brookside, Jordache Story 197–8, 330–1
Brottons, Mario 350
Browne, Christopher 261, 278n15
Bruner, Jerome 181m 206n5
Brunsden, Charlotte and David
Morley 326, 355n19
Bryman, Alan 374
Buonanno, Milly 194–5
Buonanno's criteria for
fictionworthiness 195, 207n17
Bush, George W. 240, 252, 298, 362
business practice, paradigm of 372
'bystander journalism' 222–3

C
Campaign for Press and Broadcasting
Freedom (CPBF) 367–8, 387n11,
401
Campbell, Christopher 162, 178n15
Campbell, Colin 95–6, 106n29
Capa, Robert 349–50
Carey, James W. 30–2, 36, 40n13, 390
Carnivore 296–7
Carr, Nicholas 357n37
Carroll, Jill 237
Carroll, Rory 257
Casablanca 184
Case, Steve 364, 387n3
casualization of labour (in media
industry) 69
celebrity *see* media
'celebrity, virus of' 219
censorship 119–20, 136n5, 149–50, 215,
216, 217, 220, 221, 224, 232
and the Internet 293–7, 298
Center for Online Addiction 300
Centre for Contemporary Cultural
Studies (CCCS), University of
Birmingham 62, 326
Chakrabarti, Shami 247n26
Chang, Nancy 298, 312n20
Chechen civil war: difficulties of media
access 168, 178n20
*Children, Violence and the Media: A Report
for Parents and Policy Makers*
(USA) 407n4
China and Internet surveillance 294–5
Chomsky, Noam *see* Herman, Edward
and Noam Chomsky
Citizen Kane 110, 138n1
citizen entitlement 116–17

citizen journalism xv, 218, 380–1
citizenship
cultural 350
entitlements 134–6, 421
civilizations, clash of 25, 241
clarity, brevity and colour 145
Clear Channel Communications 365–6
Cleaver, Harry 286
climate of opinion requiring
compliance 155
closed/open texts 184
closure 184, 406
Cockburn, Cynthia 335, 356n28
codes 49–56
of aesthetics 191
of narrative 189–91
cognitive/affective 64, 186, 402, 421
cognitive dissonance 83–4, 324
Cohen, Akiba and Itzhak Roeh 96,
106n30, 177n3
Cohen, Stanley and Jock Young 69n20,
145, 178n11
'coin of exchange' 337
Coleridge, Nicholas 262, 278n16
collective action of journalists 378
Collett, Peter and Roger Lamb 72–3,
103n3
commercial *laissez-faire* model of media
functions 110–12, 230, 268–9
Commission for Racial Equality (UK),
*Report on Careers in Print Media, What
People from Ethnic Minorities Think*
(2006) 239
commodity, commodification 26–7, 31,
58, 99, 135, 286
see also media
commonality 15–16, 88
compassion fatigue 405
Communications Act (UK, 2003) 368
computer games 282–3
computer technology 29–30
conglomerates 232
Connell, Robert W. 234–5, 247n22, 252,
278n6
consensus 22, 126
definition 126
consent, manufacture of 125
consonance/dissonance 83–4, 399
consonance, hypothesis of 161–2
consumerism, consumerization
of culture 94–6, 262, 362, 372–6
of history 374–5
consumerism linked with
democracy 268

consumption
  as hedonistic behaviour 95–6
  myth of 375–6
content analysis 317–9
convergence of media ownership 31, 80, 363–4, 422
convergence of research approaches 347–9
co-orientation 347
core/periphery nations 422
Corner, John 324, 355n15
corporate agendas 153, 232, 365
corporate alliances 263, 365
corporate aspirations to global control 267
corporate envelopment of public expression 264
corporate intrusion into culture 92–4
corporate patriotism 365, 374
corporate power and the media 26–8, 92–4, 262–72, 361–9
correlation 122
Cosby Show 324–5
cosmopolites/localites 89–90
Cottle, Simon 331–2, 356n24, n25
Courage in Journalism Awards 237
C+5S formula: tabloid news values 172
crime, justice and media 401–2
crime: 'staple diet of television' 401
crisis
  as news value 161
  definition by media 125
critical/referential readings of media 85
critical viewing 406
cross-border communication 389n25
cross-media ownership 266, 367
cross-promotion 288
Crossroads 333, 335
Culler, Jonathan 207n11
cultivation theory 80–1, 319, 344, 395, 396–9
cultural apparatus 18
cultural capital 19–21
cultural citizenship 356n25
Cultural Indicators (CI) project (USA) 319, 355n5, 397
cultural resistance 90–2
cultures, travelling 106n31
Curran, James 133, 267
  and Michael Gurevitch 279n22
  and Myung-Jin Park 246n10, 376–8, 388n20
Curtis, James 215
cybernetics 45

cyberspace 8, 274, 281–7
  see also **Internet**

D
Dahlberg, Andrea 336
Dahlgren, Peter 181, 206n6
Dallas 272, 314–15, 331
Davies, Gavyn 226
Dearing, James and Everett Rogers 152–3, 157–8
de Balzac, Honoré 275
de Certeau, Michel 93, 105n27, 282, 311n6
Deer Hunter, The 395
defamation 213
Deibert, Ronald J. 304–5, 312n27
democracy 36, 267, 381, 390, 391
'democratic deficits' 267
democratic-participant theory 121
demonization 125, 164, 250
denotation/connotation 2–3, 59–60, 193
Dennis, Everette 264, 279n20
dependency theory 77–8
deregulation 127, 266, 366–9, 384, 398
  see also regulation
Derrida, Jacques 383, 389n26
Dervin, Brenda 317, 354n2
de Saussure, Ferdinand (1857–1913) 49, 54, 68n7, 207n11
Destry Rides Again 190
development theory of media 120–1
deviance definition 424
de-Westernizing media studies 376–8
diachronic structure 199
'diaspora element' 170, 178n21
Diemand, Mariellen 365, 387n4
digital/analogue 424–5
Dijk, Teun van see van Dijk, Teun
discipline of the norm 295–6
discourse 58–9, 152–5, 183–5
disinformation 220, 228, 249–59, 271
Disney 261
Disneyization 261, 372, 373–5
dissent, decline of in media 362, 378
dissonance/consonance 210, 399
diversity 126–8
Dixie Chicks 366
'dodgy dossier' 226
dominant, negotiated, oppositional responses to media messages 62–4
double articulation of news 167
Downing, John, Ali Mohammadi and Annabelle Srebeny-Mohammadi 279n27

Doyle, Gillian 368
Doyle, Leonard 285–6
Drudge, Matt, Drudge Report 380, 388n22
Drummond, Phillip and Richard Paterson 324
'dumbing down' 361
Dyer, Gillian 52, 68n12
Dyke, Greg 226, 240, 268

E

Eastenders 57–8
Echelon 296–7
Eco, Umberto 11, 63, 69n21
economies of size 288
effects of media 326–31; *see* Appendix 1, A Brief ABC of Perceived Effects
efficiency, calculability, predictability, control 372–3
Eisenstein, Sergei (1898–1948) 191
Eldridge, John 246n14, 348, 358n42
emancipatory use of media 79–80
embedded reporting 149, 429
empowerment 425
encode/decode 242
enculturalization 14–15, 22, 92–4
enigma (or hermeneutic) code 189
Enloe, Cynthia 247n21
Entman, Robert 186, 206n10
Enzensburger, Hans Magnus 78, 104n11
EPCOT (The Experimental Prototype Community of the Future) 374–5
equality 132–3
Erikson, Richard V., Patricia Barnah and Janet B.L. Chan 123–4, 14n8, 194, 207n15
ethnic imbalance (in media professions) 237–42
ethnocentrism *see* **researching media**
European Convention on Human Rights and Fundamental Freedoms (ECHR) 139n4
event 48
extracted information 426

F

Facebook 283, 343, 371
Falklands War (1982) 149, 150
Farmanfarmaian, Abuoali 278n7
fast-food paradigm 372–3
Favier, Jaap 259

Federal Communications Commission (USA) 114, 261, 266, 289
feedback 46
Festinger, Leon 83–4, 105n17, n18
fictionworthiness 194–5
First Amendment of the American Constitution 128
First Amendment of the Internet 290
Fischoff, Stuart 407–8n4
Fisher, Walter 181, 206n3
Fiske, John 50, 53, 60, 68n10, n13, 91–2, 105n22, 130, 140n14, 201–2, 207n22
Five Principles of Research (Blumer) 325
flak 232, 253
flog 259
focus groups (research) 326–31
Forsetta, Diane and Daniel Price 258, 278n13
Foucault, Michel (1926–84) 295–6, 312n17
Fowles, Jib 400–1
'Fox effect' 364–6
fragmentation of audience 99, 100, 369–71
frames of reference 85, 426
framing: purposes and locations 186–7
Francis, Karl 224
Frankfurt school of theorists 67n1, 72–3, 104n4, 361, 362
Freedland, Jonathan 256, 278n11
Freedom of Information Act (UK, 2005) 129
freedom of speech 267
free press theory of media 117–18
'friendly fire' 177n5
Frum, David and Richard Perle 271n5
Fukuyama, Francis 39n9
Fuller, Mary and Henry Jenkins 311n5
functions of media *see* normative functions of media

G

Gallagher, Margaret 236, 247n23
Galtung, Johan and Mari Ruge 146, 158–66, 178n11
Gandy, Oscar Jr. 98, 106n33
Gans, Herbert 127, 140n11, 144, 171, 177n1
Garnham, Nicholas 267–8, 269, 279n24, n26
gatekeeping 146–50

gender coding   191–2
gender imbalance (in media
    professions)   232–7
genre   187–8
Gerbner, George   47–8, 68n6, 80, 319,
    344, n6, 391, 393, 396–7, 407n2, n3,
    430
    and Hamid Mowlana and Herbert I.
        Schiller   247n21, 278n7, 355n5
Ghannoushi, Soumaya   xiii, xviii-n2
Gibbons, Sheila   247n23
Gibson, William   281
Giddens, Anthony   347, 358n41
Gidley, Mick   247n28
Gilligan, Andrew   225–6, 256
Giro City   224
Gitlin, Todd   26–7, 39n11
Glasgow University Media Group   147,
    228, 246n14, 318, 330–1, 347–9,
    354n4
globalization
    convergence of media ownership   31,
        80, 363–4, 422
    core/periphery nations   422
    corporate agendas   153, 232, 365
    corporate aspirations to global
        control   267
    global civil space   381
    global–local axis   97
    global village   31
    'glocal' perspectives   376–8
    information, imbalances of   270
    information rich/information
        poor   270–2
    myth of media globalization   382
    New World Information Order   139
    world communication system   382
Goffman, Erving   55, 68n15
Golden Shield Project (China)   294
Golding, Peter, Graham Murdock and
    Philip Schlesinger   279n26
Google   340, 361
Gramsci, Antonio (1899–1937)   22, 39n8
Gray, Ann   334–5, 356n27
Gray, Vanessa   275, 279n31
Groebel, Jo   400, 407n3
Gross, Larry   348, 358n43
Grosvenor, Rita and Arnold Kemp   349,
    358n44
guard dog/watchdog   121–3, 124
Guerin, Veronica   237
Gulf War (1991)   252
Gunson, Phil   252–3, 278n10
Gutenberg, John of (c.1400–68)   18, 30

H
Hafez, Kai   382, 389n25
Hakuhodo Institute of Life and Living in
    Japan   345–6, 357n40
Hall, Jim   292–3, 311n15, 387, 388n22
Hall, Stuart   62, 159, 167, 168
    and Tony Jefferson   91, 105n23, 145
Hallin, Daniel C.   202, 207n23, 378
Hamelink, Cees   270
Hamill, Pete   218–19, 246n8
Hardy, Eamon   229, 246n15, n16
Harrison, Jackie   132, 140n17
Hearst, William Randolph
    (1863–1951)   109
Hebdige, Dick   91, 104n24
'hegemonic masculinity'   234, 252
hegemony   22–9, 34, 59, 62, 287, 293,
    366
Henderson, Lesley   197–8, 207n19,
    330–1, 356n22
Herman, Edward and Noam
    Chomsky   125, 140n9, 232, 246n19
hero mythologies   251–2
Hertz, J.C.   281, 311n2
HICT (Household Uses of Information
    and Communication Technologies)
    project   336–7
hierarchy/longitudinal research
    studies   157
hierarchy of access (to news
    sources)   228
Hindley, Myra   249
Hirsch, Eric   336
history as PR   374
history, the end of?   39n9
'hitonami consciousness'   346
Hobson, Dorothy   333, 335, 356n26
Hodge, Robert and Gunther Kress   58–9,
    68n18
Holland, Patricia   368, 387n12
Hollywood narrative mode/rhetorical
    mode   184–5, 286
homogeneity   34
homo narrens   180–1
Horkheimer, Max   72
hospitality as operational principle of the
    mediapolis   382–3
Household Uses of Information and
    Communication Technologies
    project   see HICT
Howard, Richard   189
Hoynes, William   263–4, 267, 279n18
Huntington, Samuel   25, 39n10
Hutton Report (UK, 2004)   226, 269

hypodermic needle 'theory' of mass
communication effect 428
hypothesis of consonance 161–2

I
iconic, indexical, symbolic 51–3
ID cards xv, 299
identification: consumerism with
democracy 268
identity and Internet use: issues 299–306
ideological state apparatus (ISA)/
repressive state apparatus
(RSA) 18–19, 25, 377, 488
ideology 23–26, 33, 35, 59, 61, 110, 111,
123, 135, 160, 167–70, 196, 225–6,
231, 252, 253, 266, 268, 317–18, 348,
382
of mass culture/of populism 334
immediacy as a news value 170–1
impartiality 225
information
age of 30
control by legislation 139n5
extracted 426
flow of 271
gaps 271–2
global imbalances of 270
information model/story model 181
information rich/information
poor 270–2
Innis, Harold 128, 140n13
Institute for Social Research,
Frankfurt 72
interactivity of texts 57–8
International Law Enforcement
Telecommunication Seminar
(ILETS) 297
International Federation of Journalists
(IFJ) 309
International Press Institute (IPI) 237
International Telecommunications Union
(ITU): report on growth of mobile
use in Africa 273, 279n31
International Women's Media Foundation
(IWMF) 237
Internet
addiction and 300–1
advertising on the Net 291
and traditional media 291
appropriation of 288
as agent of change 285–7
as 'explosion of narrative' 284
as Panopticon 243–6
as research tool 293–6

'assault on reality' 301–2
as 'Tower of Babel' 389n25
'blurring of fiction and reality' on the
Net 301–4
censorship and the Net 293–7
China and the Net 294–5
'culture of simulation' 302–4
cyberspace as Storyville 284
'digital soup' 338–9
dot.gones 288
enabling potential of 306–7
faking realities 302–4
First Amendment of the
Internet 289–90
digital fish 249
Golden Shield Project (China) 294
hierarchy, freedom from 287
identities on 299–306,
interactivity, specificity 337
Jenkins–Fuller dialogue 282
'kitchen table democracy' 294
marketization of 287–9
Net revolution xiv–xvi
network neutrality 288–90
'notional space' of 281
postmodernist resonances and the
Net 304–5
reality: loss of authority 302
Regulation and Investigatory Powers
Act (RIPA) UK, 2000 297, 298
rootedness versus attachment 305–6
source: issues of 339–40
spam 291
specificity of 194, 197, 337–9
surveillance and the Net 281, 293–99
tolls 288–9
virtual reality 281, 301–4
Web 2.0 283, 311n7
Wikipedia 340
intertextuality 57–8
intervening variables 158, 198
Iraq war(s), coverage by media 365–6, 406
Iran-Contra hearings 250–2
ISAs, RSAs *see* ideological/repressive
state apparatuses
Italian Story, An 257
Ito, Mizuko, and Daisuke Okabe and
Misa Matsuda 342–4
Ito, Youichi 155, 177–8n8

J
Jakobson, Roman 207n11
Jansen, Sue Curry 234–5, 247n21, 252,
278n7

Jenkins, Henry and Mary Fuller 282–3, 311n5
Jian, Mia 94
Johnson, Alan 215
jolts per minute (JPMs) 202
Jones, Steve 341, 357n33
Jordache Story 196–8
journalism *see* media

K

Keane, John xvii, xviii-n4, 133–4, 141n19, 273, 279n30
'*keitei* culture' 342–3
Kellner, Douglas 373, 288n17
Kelly, Dr David 226
Kit-Wai Mu, Eric 221, 246n10
Knightley, Phillip xvii, xviii-n5
knowledge: institutional, ethnographic 99
Koch, Tom 230–1, 246n17, n18, 339, 356n32
Koenig's steam press 30
Korea, media in 105n20
Kornblum, William, and Carolyn D. Smith 320–1, 355n8
Kress, Gunther 69n19, 154–5, 177n7
Kumar, Krishan 15, 39n1
kuuki 155, 178n8

L

label-libelling 250
Langer, John 182
language 15–17, 42–3, 56–7, 60, 62
langue, parole 54
Lasswell, Harold 47, 68n5
Lazarsfeld, Paul 86, 105n19
Leach, Edmund 51, 68n11
Le Duc, D.R. 127, 140n12
Lee, Chin-Chuan 126, 140n10, 246n10
Lee, Julian 404
levels and attributes 156–7
Lessig, Lawrence, and Robert W. McChesney 288–9, 311n12
Leviathan 134, 141n20
Lewin, Kirt 146
Lewis, Flora 170
Lewis, Justin 199–200, 207n20, 324–5, 355n16, n17
Liebes, Tamar and Elihu Katz 76, 85, 104n7, 272, 279n28, 331, 356n23
Lievrouw, Leah A. and Sonia Livingstone xv, xviii-n3
Lippman, Walter 159, 178n10

Livingstone, Sonia 336, 403
and Leah A. Lievrouw xv, xviii-n3
Lloyd, Terry 177n5
lobbying 429
localites/cosmopolites 89–90
Loose Change 253
longitudinal/hierarchy studies 157
Lull, James 97, 104n8, 106n32, 322, 355n11
Lull's listing of audience needs 76–7
Lusted, David 196

M

MacArthur, John R. 150, 177n4
MacBride Commission report for UNESCO (1978)/New World Information Order 139n6
MacManus, Richard 343, 357n37
mainstreamers, aspirers, succeeders and reformers (cross-cultural consumer categories – the 4 Cs) 344, 357n38
mainstreaming 80, 319, 355n6, 393
Ma Jian 294, 311n16
manufacture of consent 125, 361
Marcuse, Herbert 72, 104n4
Martin-Barbero, Jèsus 21
Marx, Karl (1818–83) 18
mass culture, ideology of/populism, ideology of 334
mathematical theory of communication 44–5
Mazzoleni, Gianpetro 278n12
McChesney, Robert *see* Lessig and McChesney
McCombs, Donald and Malcolm Shaw 151–2, 168
McCombs, Maxwell, and Esteban Lopez-Escobar and Juan Pablo Llamas 156–7
McCullin, Don 150
McDonaldize, McDonaldization 372–3
McKie, Alex 357n40
McLellan, Jim 286, 311n9
McLuhan, Marshall 77
McNair, Brian 100, 106n35, 236, 297n24, 367, 387n9
McNelly, J.T. 147
McQuail, Denis 71, 73, 82, 103n1, 114, 116, 122, 131, 133, 139n3, 140n16, n18, 362, 369–71, 387n2, 388n15
and Sven Windahl 152, 177n6
McQuail's five basic functions of media 122

McRobbie, Angela 317–18, 324, 354n3, 355n13
Mead, George Herbert 181, 204n4
meaning 51, 52, 54, 60, 63, 68n17, 180, 182, 183, 315, 348, 390
mean world syndrome 391
media
    accuracy and sincerity as principles of media performance 132
    alliances involving media 263, 270
    as agents of control 123
    autonomy, myth of 223–6
    boundary event/journalistic event 230
    breaking news 387–8n14
    'bystander journalism' 222–3
    casualization of labour in media professions 269
    'citizen entitlements' 134–5
    citizen journalism 380
    commercial *laissez-faire* model of media functions 110–12, 218–19
    consensus definition 126
    control features of 224
    convergence of media ownership 369–71
    corporate power and 267–72, 361–9
    crisis definition by 125
    databases: benefits to journalists 231
    deconvergence of audiences for 369–71
    'democratic deficits' 267–8
    deregulation 127, 266, 366–9, 384, 398
    deviance-defining role of 123–4
    disengagement, problems of 220–3
    displacement by trivialization 354–5
    diversity, accessibility, plurality 126–8, 267
    ethnic imbalance (in media professions) 232–7
    'Fox effect' 364–6
    gender imbalance (in media professions) 232–7
    globalization of media, myth of 382
    'hegemonic masculinity' of 234
    'hierarchies of access' to 228
    ideology of mass culture/ideology of populism 334
    Iraq war(s), coverage 365–6
    macro-myth, micro-myth 223
    mainstreaming 80, 319
    manufacture of consent 125
    market forces and employment in media 268–70
    market orientation of 267

mediapolis 136, 141n22
minorities and 348–9
mass culture, ideology of 334
mobilizing role of 124–5
news values 158–74; tabloid news values 171–4
New World Information Order 139n6
New Media Studies xv
normative theories of media 116–21
objectivity, impartiality, balance 129–31, 365
Ofcom (Office of Communication, UK) 368
one world responsibilities of media 381–2
ownership and control *see* Chapters 8 and 11
patriotism and 365
pleasure and the popular 333–4
populism, ideology of 334
professionalism, dilemmas of 221–6
propagandist model of media functions 108–10
public service model of media functions 113–16
public v. private 259–61
racism and 237–8
regulation, retreat from 366–8
regulatory favours 260
representatives of order 123
Rwanda massacre and 404
spin-doctoring 227–31, 361, 435
watchdogs/guard dogs 121–3
women and 232–7
mediation 6, 86, 89, 134, 147–8, 174, 202, 217, 249, 306, 313, 315, 380, 430
metaphor/metonym 56–7, 182, 183, 281, 307, 338, 430
Miller, Daniel 94–5, 105n28
Miller, David 228–9, 246n14
Miller, Tim 338, 356n31
mise-en-scène 190
Mitchell, Arnold 345, 357n39
'mobile phones revolutionize Africa' 273
mobilization xiv–xv, 102, 124, 430
models of mass communication
    Bass's 'double action' model (1969) 148–9
    commercial *laissez-faire* 110–12
    criteria of public service communication 130
    Enzenberger's model of repressive versus emancipatory use of media (1972) 78–9

features of hegemony   23
Galtung and Ruge's model of selective
    gatekeeping (1965)   158
Gerbner's model (1956)   47–9
Lasswell's model (1948)   47
Maletzke's model of mass
    communication (1963)   210, 214
McCombs and Shaw's agenda-setting
    model (1976)   151–2, 168
McNelly's model of news flow
    (1959)   147
McQuail's four stages of audience
    fragmentation (1997)   369–71
one-step, two-step, multi-step flow
    model of communication   87
propagandist or mass manipulative
    model   42, 108–10
research as co-orientation   347
Rogers and Dearing's model of
    agenda-setting process
    (1997)   152–3, 278n17
Schramm's model (1954)   45–6
semiological model   66
Shannon and Weaver model
    (1949)   43–5
signifier-signified   50
socio-cultural pyramid   20
tripolar model of agendas   154, 263
Westerstähl and Johansson's model
    of news factors in foreign news
    (1994)   168–9
White's gatekeeping model
    (1950)   145–7
Moeller, Susan D.   405, 408n5
montage   191
Moore, Martin   228, 246n13
Moores, Shaun   322–3, 327, 336, 355n10
moral agenda   383
'moral economy', four constituents
    of   336–7
moral panic   240–1, 401, 431
Morley, David   326, 336, 355n18, 356n20
    and Sonia Livingstone, Andrea
        Dahlberg and Eric Hirsch   336
'Mr Gate'   146
multi-accentuality (of the sign)   51
Murdoch, James   172
Murdoch, Rupert   110, 114, 172, 261, 20,
    364, 367
Murdock, Graham   356n25
MySpace   283–5, 290, 343, 364
myth   60–1, 183, 249, 262, 286
    of consumption   375–6
    of media globalization   382
of professionalism   223–6
of 'value freedom'   225
mythologies: hero mythologies   251–2

N
narrative
and popular culture   181
and visions of nationhood   183
as cohesion-making   192
as verification   181
Barthes' codes of narrative   189–91,
    251
binary framing   187
characters in   192–3
citizen stories   203
closure   184, 202
codes of   *see* Barthes' codes of
    narrative
disequilibrium/equilibrium   182
fictionworthiness   194–5
fidelity   181
frames of   184–7
gender coding   191–2
genre   187–8
Hollywood narrative mode/rhetorical
    mode   184, 406
homo narrens   181, 203
information model, story model   181
Internet narratives   203, 283–5
knowingness (on part of
    audience)   188
mimetic plain, semiosic plain   193
montage   191
needs, cognitive and affective   186
news as narrative   199–200
newsworthiness/
    fictionworthiness   196–8
primary/secondary texts   197
probability   181
Propp's classification of
    characters   192–3
proximity as fiction value   195
rhetorical fantasies   182
sequencing (according to visions of
    order)   194
soap narratives   185–6, 200–2
story level/meaning level   193
time and narrative   185
topicality   195
narrowcasting   370
Nash, Elizabeth   198
National Commission on the Causes and
    Prevention of Violence (USA)   397
Nationwide (BBC TV)   326–7

Neill, Andrew 173–4, 178nn24
Nelson, Anne 385–6, 406n1
network neutrality 288–9
networks *see* Chapter 9
neutrality, network neutrality 288–90
New Future for Communications, A, UK
  government White Paper on
  Broadcasting 367, 387n10
New Labour and the media 367
New Media Studies xv
news
  aberrant news values 164–5
  access as news value 168
  agenda-setting 150–8
  amplification of issues 152
  amplitude as news value 217
  as construct 145, 202
  as cultural reinforcement 144
  as 'olds' 144
  as ritual 144
  attribution as news value 166
  breaking news 387–8n14
  clarity, brevity and colour
    (as criteria for news
    presentation) 171
  corporate agendas and news 153–4
  crisis as news value 161
  democratization of 201
  disorder as news value 194
  'double action' process of news
    flow 149
  eliteness as news value 163–4
  embedded reporting 149–50
  ethnocentric nature of 143
  formats and audience response 331–2
  'Fox effect' 364–6
  gatekeeping 146–50
  gathering stage/processing
    stage 148–9
  'good news' stories 228–9
  immediacy as news value 170–1
  interactive agendas 152–4
  issue champions 157
  knowns/unknowns 144
  levels and attributes 156–7
  levels of value: formal, ideological 167
  'maleness' of 274–6
  manufacture of 146
  'Mr Gate' 146
  negativity of 164–5
  news values 158–65
  newsworthiness/
    fictionworthiness 191–6, 235
  proximity as news value 143

reality definition 143
ritualistic nature of 144
satellite media tours (SMTs) 259
selection, distortion, replication 165–6
soundbite treatment of news 202
source, status of 166–7
spin 227–9
surveillance 143
tabloid news values 171–4
television's news values 165
'threshold value' 159
tribal nature of 144
triggers 157
video news releases (VNRs) 258–9
violence as news value 168
new world 'dysorder' 34
New World Information Order 139n6,
  431
Nicholls, Bill 180, 206n2
Nie, Norman 300
Nightingale, Virginia and Karen
  Ross 207n21
9/11 xii, 25, 29, 34, 126, 240, 250, 252,
  253, 298, 364, 390
Nintendo 282–3
Noelle-Neumann, Elisabeth 177–8n8
noise 43–44
Nokia 116
normative/performative 95
normative functions of media 116–23
North, Oliver and the Iran-Contra
  hearings 250–3
Northcliffe, Lord (1865–1922) 109
Northern Ireland Office 228–9
Norton-Taylor, Richard 254, 278n9

O
objectivity 129–31, 211, 230, 231, 315,
  365
Ofcom (Office of Communication,
  UK) 276, 368, 371
Official Secrets Act (UK) 7, 218
Ogden, C.K. and I.A. Richards 50, 68n9
one world responsibility of media 381–3
open/closed texts 55
openDemocracy website 263
operational codes 53–54
O'Reilly, Tim 311n7
Orwell, George (1904–50) 15, 82, 104n14
Osama bin Laden 125
Osborn, Richard 401
other, relationship towards 382, 432
ownership and control *see* Chapters 8
  and 11

P

Paine, Thomas (1737–1809)   286
Panopticon/Superpanopticon   xvi,
    283–99, 432
paradigm/syntagm   54–5
parasocial interaction   74
Paris, Texas   184
participant observation   90, 319
participatory democracy, via the
    Internet   381
Patriot Act (USA, 2001)   298
'patriotism police', media as   365
Peirce, Charles (1834–1914)   49, 50, 51,
    68n8
people power   121
performatives   432
personalization by media   125, 164, 433
Peters, John Durham   42, 67n2
Philo, Greg   83, 84, 105n15, 328–30,
    356n21
photographic negativization   123, 194
Pilger, John   211, 245n3
Pilkington Committee Report on
    Broadcasting (1962)   21, 39n6
pleasure and the popular   333–4
pluralism, plurality   113, 118, 267, 292,
    307, 347
polis, mediapolis   381
Poor Man's Guardian   108
politics of pleasure   91
Porter, Henry   111, 139n2
Poster, Mark   284, 295, 300, 311n18, 432
Postman, Neil   81, 104n12
postmodernism   303–6, 433
Potter, Dennis   136
power elite   22, 39n7, 59, 62, 113, 115,
    163–4, 203, 231, 282
power forms   17–19
power value   93, 148
PR (public relations)   255–9
preferred reading   62–4, 81, 91, 229, 326,
    328, 332
presentational codes   52, 53
press barons   108–12, 113
Press TV (Iran)   247n23
primary/secondary texts   197–8
printing press   18
prior restraint   213
privatization   261, 264, 266
producer choice   269
professionalism
    dilemmas of   221–6
    myths of   223–6
project of self   89–90, 131, 209, 219

propaganda   16–17, 21, 47, 56, 72, 108,
    255, 303, 403–4
propagandist model of media
    functions   107–10
Propp, Valdimir   192–3, 207n14
public expression (corporate envelopment
    of)   264–6
public relations (PR)   255–9
public service broadcasting (PSB)   xiv,
    32–4, 135, 136, 259–61, 368
public service model of media
    functions   113–16
public sphere   5, 33, 260, 405, 434
public/private   259–61

R

Raboy, Marc and Bernard
    Dagenais   160–1, 178n12, 407n2
Racist and Religious Hatred Act (UK,
    2006)   247n26
radio   233, 371
'Radio Hate'   404
Radway, Janice   323–4, 355n12
'Rallies for America'   365
Rampton, Sheldon and John
    Stauber   365, 382n7
Raney, Arthur R. and Jennings
    Bryant   402
'reality' TV   434
redundancy   44–5
Rees, Jasper   207n12
referent   50
referential (or cultural) code   190
reflexivity   89
regulation   126, 260–1, 266, 366–8
Regulation of Investigatory Powers Act
    (RIPA), UK, 2000   297, 298
regulatory favours   266–7
researching media
    agenda-setting research   157–8
    audience use of technology   334–7
    authentication through
        research   349–50
    avoiding the judgemental in
        research   323–4
    Birmingham University Centre for
        Contemporary Culture Studies
        (CCCS)   326
    Blumer's five principles of
        research   325–6
    colour coding   335
    commercial research, academic
        research   316
    contacts   *see* insider contacts

researching media (*cont.*)
content analysis 317–19
convergence of research
approaches 347–9
crime: classifying crime in media
texts 403
Cultural Indicators project 319,
355n5, 397
Datamonitor 358n40
empowerment through research 317
ethnographic research 90–1, 98–100,
319–24, 342–4
focus groups 326–31
Glasgow University Media
Group 318, 328, 330–1, 347–8
Google 340
Hakuhodo Institute of Life and Living
in Japan 345–6, 357n40
hierarchy/longitudinal research 157–8
Houseshold Uses of Information and
Communication Technology
(HICT) project 336–7
insider contacts 323–4
Internet and research 337–44
keitei culture, exploration of 342–4
marketplace approach to 344–7,
358n40
mobiles, research into use of 342–4
network communication, research
into 341–2
non-directive/leading questions 327
objectivity 315
Ofcom (Office of Communication,
UK) 368
participant observation 90
pleasure, focus on 333–4
qualitative/quantitative 320, 322
reciprocation 320
recruitism, danger of 324
research as change agent 316–17
research as co-orientation: model 347
segmentation *see* marketplace
approach to
subjectivity, recognition of 317
technology, audience use of 334–7
VALS typology 345
resistance through style 91–2
resistive audience 81–2
response codes: dominant, negotiated,
oppositional 62–4
retention of information by
audience 105n16
Rheingold, Henry 281–2, 311n4
Ridley, Yvonne 236, 247n23

Ritzer, George 372, 388n16
critique of Baudrillard 388n19
Rogers, Everett M., and James W.
Dearing 152–3, 262
rootedness versus attachment 305–6
Ross, Karen 242, 246n27
Rowntree Trust xii

S
Saatchi & Saatchi 255–6
Safronov, Ivan 120, 215
Samizdat 119
Sarup, Madan 57, 68n16
satellite photography 271
Saussure, de, Ferdinand *see* de Saussure
Scargill, Arthur, demonization of 250
Schiller, Herbert 28, 40n12, 92–4,
105n25, 264–6, 268, 279n19, 362,
378, 387n1
Schlesinger, Philip 170–1, 178n22,
223–5, 246n12
Schramm, Wilbur 45–6, 68n4, 187
Scott Report (UK, 1996) 254–5, 278n8
Seaton, Jean 368–9, 387n13
segmentation 20, 218, 344–7, 358n40
Seiter, Ellen 348
selection, distortion, replication 165–6
self-formulation 89
self-fulfilling prophecy 85, 105n18
self-image
of communicator 210
of receiver 218–20
semantic code 189
Semetko, Holli A. and Patti M.
Valkenburg 156–7
semiology/semiotics 49–61
semiotic power 92
Shannon, Claude and Warren
Weaver 43–4, 67n2
showbusiness, age of 81
Sieman, Catherine 396, 406n1
sign 49–53
multi-accentuality of 51
types of: iconic, indexical,
symbolic 51–2
significant other(s) 54, 86–7
signification, orders of 51
signifier/signified 50
signifiers, blizzards of 65, 68n17
Silverstone, Roger 136, 141n22, 250,
253, 177n1, 306–7, 312n30, 336, 344,
356n29
and Eric Hirsch 356n30; 381–4,
389n24, 391

sit-coms   188
Slouka, Mark   301–4, 312n25
Smart, Barry   373, 388n16
Smith, Anthony   164–5, 178n16
Smith, Carolyn D. and William
    Kornblum   320, 355n8
Smoodin, Eric   374
soaps   74, 172–3, 185–6, 188, 196–8, 220,
    258, 330–1, 333–4
social responsibility theory of media   118
Solidarity (Poland)   166–7
Solomon, Norman   365, 387n4
source(s)   227–31
    online   231
sovereignty of peripheral nations, threat
    to   272
Soviet media theory   119
Spain's Falling Soldier   349–50
Sparks, Colin   214–15, 245n5, 366, 387n8
specificity   297, 337
spin-doctoring   227–31, 361, 435
spiral of silence   435
Spottiswoode, Roger   222
Sreberny, Annabelle   377, 388n20
Stanford University Institute for the
    Qualitative Study of Society   300
Steiler, Kaspar   158
'stenographers of power'   166
stereotyping   56, 84, 162, 192, 237–9, 249,
    347, 349
Stevenson, Nick   134–6, 141n21
Storey, David   104n10
storytelling   *see* **narrative**
Stromer-Galley, Jennifer   341–2, 357n34
structure/agency   *see* **audience**
Struggle, The Unfinished   258
surveillance   xvi, 32, 75, 98, 104n14, 143,
    281, 321
Swainton, John   133–4
Sykes Committee Report on Broadcasting
    (UK, 1923–4)   113, 260, 278n14
symbolic code of narrative   190–1
symbolic convergence theory   182
symbolic distancing   97
synergy   173, 263, 436
S/Z   189, 192, 207n13

T
taboidese   214
tabloidization   147, 178n9, 426
tabloid news values   171–4
Taylor, Laurie   358n40
Taylor, Mark C. and Esa Saarinen   287,
    311n11

Taylor, Philip M.   16, 39n2
technology of media
    and ideology   202
    and news narrative   22
    apparent neutrality of   391
    appropriation, objectification,
        incorporation, conversion   336–7
    as facilitator of Net narrativity   284
    'calculated ignorance' of   335
    convergence of   8, 29–32, 383
    digital/analogue   425–5
    digital dividend   387n12
    Gutenberg, John of   18, 30
    impact on present and future
        broadcasting   115
    Internet as 'uprooting' technology
    Koenig's steam press   30
    mobilization, xii   124, 430
    multimedia terminals   116
    network neutrality   288–90
    researching audience use of   334–7
    socially situated   334
    speed as principle of operation   218
    Superpanopticon: Internet as   295–6
    'technologies of power'   285
    telegraphese   32
    telegraphy   30–1
    time, space and   29–32
    video recorder (VCR), audience use
        of   334
    Web 2.0   283–4
    world communication system   382
Tehranian, Majid   34–5, 40n16
text(s)   55–9, 196
    primary/secondary   197
    texting   32
television   99, 104n14, 116, 131, 136, 146,
    149, 157, 163, 165, 173, 182, 184,
    188, 194, 195, 199, 200–2, 233, 250,
    256, 258, 300, 303, 318–9, 325, 327,
    328–34, 337, 354n4, 362, 395, 396,
    400, 401, 404
Thelma and Louise   192
Thomass, Barbara   268, 279n25
Thompson, John B.   17–18, 28–9, 39n3,
    89–90, 93–4, 97, 105n21, 209, 245n1,
    272–3, 279n29, 299, 312n22
Thompson, Mark   269
'three minute culture'   83
Tilly, Adrian   196, 207n18
Time Warner   261, 363–4
TNCs (transnational corporations)   127,
    264–70, 388n19
To Catch a Thief   192

Top People and *The Times* 218
Toynbee, Polly 173
transmission, language of 42–3
travelling cultures 106n31
Trend, David 405–6, 408n6
trigger(s) 157, 404
Tunstall, Jeremy 165, 178n17
   and Michael Palmer 266, 279n21
Typper, Martin F. 31, 40n14

U
unambiguity as news value 160–1
Under Fire 222
UNESCO
   and media 138n6
   global media violence study 400
Unfinished Struggle, The 258
'unholy alliance' between Western
   governments and multinational
   corporations 269–70
USA Patriot Act (2001) 298
uses and gratifications theory 73–6

V
valeur 49
VALS typology (Values and
   Lifestyles) 345
values: news values 158–74
van Dijk, Teun 237–40, 247n25
van Zoonen, Liesbet 233–4, 247n20,
   320, 355n7
Verstraeten, Hans 33, 40n15
video news releases (VNRs) 258–9
video recorder (VCR), audience use
   of 334
virtual reality 281, 301–4
'virus of celebrity' 219
violence on screen *see* Appendix 2,
   Screen Violence as Influence
   and Commodity: An Ongoing
   Debate 395–408
visibility 299

W
Wales, Jimmy 340
Walkerdine, Valerie 321–2, 355n9
'war on terrorism' 351, 240
watchdog/guard dog 121–3, 361
weapons of mass destruction
   (WMDs) 89, 226
Web 2.0 283, 311n7, 437
Weil, Simone 306, 312n29
Weir, Stuart, Andrew Blick and Tufyal
   Choudhury xii, xviii-n1
Westerstähl, Jorgen and Folke
   Johansson 168–9, 178n19
whistleblower 437
White, Aidan 379, 388n21
White, David 146
Wiener, Norbert 45, 68n3, 281,
   310n1
Wikipedia xv, 293, 340
Williams, Bernard 132
Wilson, Alexander 374–5, 388n18
Wind of Passion 247
Wired UK 286
Witmer, Diane F., Robert W. Colman
   and Sandra Lee Katzman 341
Witt-Barthel, Annegret 247n23
women in journalism 232–7
work/text (Barthes' differentiation) 332
world communication system 382
Wright Mills, C. 22
Wu, Timothy 289

Y
yellow press 109
Young, Kimberley 300, 312n23
YouTube 283, 284, 290, 293, 364, 371

Z
Zelizer, Barbie 216, 245n6